Food, Nutrition and Sports Performance II

D0220845

The amount, composition and timing of food intake can profoundly affect sports performance. Good nutritional practice helps athletes train hard, recover quickly and adapt more effectively with less risk of illness and injury. The right foods contribute not only to success in sport, but also to enjoyment of life.

In June 2003, 30 of the world's leading researchers in sport and exercise nutrition met at the International Olympic Committee headquarters in Lausanne, Switzerland, to discuss nutrition in sports. The aims of the conference were to review the latest developments in the world of sports nutrition, to review new developments since the previous, 1991, conference, and to draw guidelines to help athletes and coaches to optimise their performance by using nutrition to support training and maximise performance in competition.

The subjects discussed include:

- Energy balance and body composition
- The role of carbohydrates, fat, proteins and amino acids
- Macronutrient metabolism and availability
- Athletes' fluid and electrolyte requirements
- The use of dietary supplements
- Nutrition and immune function
- Nutritional strategies for training and competition

Contributors to *Food, Nutrition and Sports Performance II* represent all 5 continents and are all experts in their fields. Some are research pioneers in the sports science laboratory, others lead the way in applied nutrition, spending their daily lives working with elite athletes. This combination of scientific rigour and an applied experience has resulted in a unique perspective on current issues in sports nutrition.

R.J. Maughan is Visiting Professor at Loughborough University, UK. **L.M. Burke** is head of The Department for Sports Nutrition at the Australian Institute of Sport and holds a Visiting Chair in Sports Nutrition at the School of Health Sciences, Deakin University, Melbourne. **E.F. Coyle** directs the Human Performance Laboratory and is Professor of Kinesiology and Health Education at The University of Texas at Austin. He likewise coordinates the graduate program in Sports Sciences and Nutrition at UT.

Food, Nutrition and Sports Performance II

The International Olympic Committee
Consensus on Sports Nutrition

**Edited by R.J. Maughan, L.M. Burke
and E.F. Coyle**

LONDON AND NEW YORK

First published 2004
by Routledge
11 New Fetter Lane, London EC4P 4EE

Simultaneously published in the USA and Canada
by Routledge
29 West 35th Street, New York, NY 10001

Routledge is an imprint of the Taylor & Francis Group

© 2004 R.J. Maughan, L.M. Burke and E.F. Coyle

Typeset in Goudy by BC Typesetting Ltd, Bristol
Printed and bound in Great Britain by
MPG Books Ltd, Bodmin, Cornwall

British Library Cataloguing in Publication Data
A catalogue record for this book is available from the British Library

Library of Congress Cataloging in Publication Data
A catalog record for this book has been requested

ISBN 0–415–33906–5 (hbk)
ISBN 0–415–33907–3 (pbk)

Contents

Preface

In February 1991, the Medical Commission of the International Olympic Committee hosted the first Consensus Conference on Foods, Nutrition and Sports Performance. This meeting brought together some of the world's leading experts to review and discuss the key issues in sports nutrition, with a focus on the effects of exercise on nutritional requirements and on the effects of dietary manipulations on sports performance. At the end of the conference, an agreed consensus statement on sports nutrition was published and the scientific papers which formed the basis of the discussions were published as a supplement to the *Journal of Sports Sciences* (Volume 9, Special issue, Summer 1991) and later as a book edited by the scientific co-chairmen of the conference (Williams and Devlin, 1992).

The consensus statement was a landmark development in the relatively young field of sports nutrition. It opened with a bold and unambiguous statement: 'Diet significantly affects athletic performance'. It then went on to qualify that statement by adding detail to take account of the various activities that are encompassed within the field of sport and the varying needs of the elite performer and the recreational participant. That the scientific proceedings are still in use today as a standard text that summarizes much of what we know about sports nutrition is a testament to the efforts of the authors and to the skills of the chairmen.

Many new developments have taken place in the years since the 1991 conference, and it is inevitable that some of the information in the proceedings now looks rather dated. The establishment of the IOC Medical Commission Working Group on Sports Nutrition in 2002 provided an impetus for the subject to be revisited with another consensus conference. The delegates for this conference duly assembled at the IOC Headquarters in Lausanne on 15–18 June 2003. This conference followed the format that had worked so well in 1991. Ten authors covered a broad range of topics, and each prepared a manuscript that reviewed the new developments in their allotted area. Two discussants, also experts in the field, were assigned to each of these topics and their remit was to subject the manuscripts to close scrutiny. These manuscripts were circulated to all of the conference participants in advance of the meeting. At the conference itself, each author made a short presentation of the key issues and this was followed by an extended discussion, which was opened by the nominated discussants but to which all of the participants made a full contribution.

The key messages that emerged from the discussion process were distilled into a one-page consensus statement, and this is reproduced here. After the conference, authors had the opportunity to revise their papers in the light of the review completed by the two discussants and the comments made at the meeting. Those revised papers comprise the bulk of this issue of the journal. All participants at the conference were also invited to submit a commentary to expand upon specific issues that emerged from the discussion. Two commentaries survived the review process and are published here.

The willingness of the authors and the discussants to share their knowledge and experiences and to engage in full and frank discussion was an essential element of the meeting. We were pleased that Mr Frankie Fredericks, one of the world's most successful sprinters, was able to join us and to ensure that we never lost sight of the need to keep the athlete in mind. We were pleased, too, that Dr Alain Garnier, European Chair of the World Anti-Doping Agency, was also able to participate and to bring his knowledge and expertise to bear on some difficult questions.

Many people contributed to the success of the conference. We are pleased to acknowledge our debt to the Prince Alexandre de Merode, who had the foresight to support the 1991 conference and who was a strong supporter of the fledgling Sports Nutrition Working Group until his untimely death in 2002. His successor, Professor Arne Ljungquist, has also been a great champion and we are indebted to him for his support. Dr Patrick Schamasch, Medical Director of the IOC, has ensured that the pace has not slackened and has given both direction and support. Dr Jacques Rogge, the President of the International Olympic Committee, has also been a source of support and his recognition of the important role of nutrition in helping athletes to realize their potential has been crucial to developments within the IOC. Finally, none of this would have been possible without the assistance of The Coca-Cola Company, and we are grateful to them for their generous support.

THE IOC WORKING GROUP ON SPORTS NUTRITION

Reference

1 Williams, C. and Devlin, J.T. (1992). *Foods, Nutrition and Sports Performance*. London: E & FN Spon.

Foreword

Nutrition is particularly important for each of us to keep in shape. It is one of the key elements for an athlete's success, as it contributes greatly to accomplishing the performance for which he or she is training and avoids any deterioration in health. An appropriate diet must include the elements that are essential for, and specific to, each sport.

On 18–20 June 2003, the IOC brought together around 30 scientists, all specialists in different areas of nutrition, to establish the guiding principles of nutrition in sport. This meeting was organized by the IOC Medical Commission Nutrition and Sport Working Group.

A consensus declaration was produced following this meeting. The next stage consists of communicating these principles to the athletes and coaches. This will be carried out mainly through the IOC Athletes' Commission.

The protection of athletes' health is one of the IOC's main missions. Indeed, the IOC is convinced that an appropriate nutritional programme is one of the best alternatives to the negative influences that can affect athletes.

PATRICK SCHAMASCH
Medical Director of the International Olympic Committee

Consensus conference participants

Speakers

Professor Louise M. Burke, Australian Institute of Sport, PO Box 176, Belconnen, ACT 2616, Australia (lburke@ausport.gov.au)

Dr Edward F. Coyle, Human Performance Laboratory, Department of Kinesiology and Health Education, The University of Texas at Austin, Austin, TX 78712 USA (coyle@mail.utexas.edu)

Professor Michael Gleeson, School of Sport and Exercise Sciences, Loughborough University, Loughborough LE11 3TU, UK (m.gleeson@lboro.ac.uk)

Professor Mark Hargreaves, School of Health Sciences, Deakin University, Burwood, VIC 3125, Australia (mharg@deakin.edu.au)

Dr Anne B. Loucks, Department of Biological Sciences, Ohio University, Athens, OH 45701, USA (loucks@ohio.edu)

Professor Ron J. Maughan, School of Sport and Exercise Sciences, Loughborough University, Loughborough LE11 3TU, UK (r.j.maughan@lboro.ac.uk)

Dr Scott K. Powers, Departments of Exercise and Sport Sciences and Physiology, Center for Exercise Science, University of Florida, Gainesville, FL 32611, USA (spowers@hhp.ufl.edu)

Dr Susan M. Shirreffs, School of Sport and Exercise Sciences, Loughborough University, Loughborough LE11 3TU, UK (s.shirreffs@lboro.ac.uk)

Dr Lawrence L. Spriet, School of Human Biology, University of Guelph, Guelph, Ontario N1G 2W1, Canada (lspriet@uoguelph.ca)

Dr Kevin D. Tipton, Department of Surgery, University of Texas Medical Branch, Shriner's Hospital for Children, 815 Market Street, Galveston, TX 77550, USA (ktipton@utmb.edu)

Discussants

Dr Lawrence E. Armstrong, Human Performance Laboratory, University of Connecticut, 2095 Hillside Road, Box U-110, Storrs, CT 06269-1110, USA (lawrence.armstrong@uconn.edu)

Dr Dimitrios Chasiotis, Hellenic Sports Research Institute, Olympic Sport Center of Athens, Kifissias 37, Maroussi, 151 23 Athens, Greece (ekae96@compulink.gr)

Dr Samuel N. Cheuvront, US Army Research Institute of Environmental Medicine, 42 Kansas Street, Natick, MA 01760-5007, USA (samuel.cheuvront@na.amedd.army.mil)

Dr Karen Cunningham, Scientific and Regulatory Affairs, Coca-Cola Great Britain & Ireland, 1 Queen Caroline Street, Hammersmith, London W6 9HQ, UK (kacunningham@eur.ko.com)

Dr Jacques Décombaz, Senior Research Nutritionist, Nestle Research Centre, Nestec Ltd – POB 44, Vers-chez-les-Blanc, CH-1000, Lausanne 26, Switzerland (jacques.décombaz@rdls.nestle.com)

Dr Martin J. Gibala, Exercise Metabolism Research Group, Department of Kinesiology, IWC Room AB122, McMaster University, Hamilton, Ontario L8S 4K1, Canada (gibalam@mcmaster.ca)

Dr José Gonzalez-Alonso, Copenhagen Muscle Research Centre, Rigshospitalet, Section 7652, Blegdamsvej 9, DK 2100, Copenhagen Ø, Denmark (jga@cmrc.dk)

Professor John A. Hawley, Exercise Metabolism Group, School of Medical Sciences, Faculty of Life Sciences, RMIT University, PO Box 71, Bundoora, VIC 3083, Australia (john.hawley@rmit.edu.au)

Dr John L. Ivy, Human Performance Laboratory, Department of Kinesiology and Health Education, The University of Texas at Austin, Austin, TX 78712, USA (johnivy@mail.utexas.edu)

Dr Asker Jeukendrup, Human Performance Laboratory, School of Sport and Exercise Sciences, University of Birmingham, Edgbaston, Birmingham B15 2TT, UK (a.e.jeukendrup@bham.ac.uk)

Dr Bente Kiens, Copenhagen Muscle Research Centre, August Krogh Institute of Human Physiology, 13 Universitetsparken, DK-2100, Copenhagen Ø, Denmark (bkiens@aki.ku.dk)

Dr Doug S. King, Department of Health and Human Performance, 248 Forker Building, Iowa State University, Ames, IA 50011, USA (dsking@iastate.edu)

Mr Trevor Lea, Manchester United Football Club, Sir Matt Busby Way, Old Trafford, Manchester M16 0RA, UK (trev@diets.freeserve.co.uk)

Professor Victor Matsudo, CELAFISCS, Avenida Goias 1400, Sao gaetano du Sul, CEP 095210300 Sao Paolo, Brasil (celafiscs@celafiscs.com.br)

Professor D. Joe Millward, Centre for Nutrition and Food Safety, School of Biomedical and Life Sciences, University of Surrey, Guildford, Surrey GU2 7XH, UK (d.millward@surrey.ac.uk)

Dr David C. Nieman, Department of Health, Leisure and Exercise Science, Appalachian State University, Boone, NC 28608, USA (niemandc@appstate.edu)

Professor Clyde Williams, School of Sport and Exercise Sciences, Loughborough University, Loughborough LE11 3TU, UK (c.williams@lboro.ac.uk)

Dr Robert R. Wolfe, Department of Surgery, University of Texas Medical Branch, Shriner's Hospital for Children, 815 Market Street, Galveston, TX 77550, USA (rwolfe@utmb.edu)

Dr Zeyi Yang, Sports Nutrition Center, National Research Institute of Sports Medicine, Beijing, China (zeyiyang@public3.bta.net.cn)

IOC Delegates

Dr Patrick Schamasch, IOC Medical Director, Chateau de Vidy

Dr Alain Garnier

Mr Frankie Fredericks

Consensus Statement

The amount, composition and timing of food intake can profoundly affect sports performance. Good nutritional practice will help athletes train hard, recover quickly and adapt more effectively with less risk of illness and injury. Athletes should adopt specific nutritional strategies before and during competition to help maximize their performance. Athletes will benefit from the guidance of a qualified sports nutrition professional who can provide advice on their individual energy and nutrient needs and also help them to develop sport-specific nutritional strategies for training, competition and recovery.

A diet that provides adequate energy from the consumption of a wide range of commonly available foods can meet the carbohydrate, protein, fat and micronutrient requirements of training and competition. The right diet will help athletes achieve an optimum body size and body composition to achieve greater success in their sport. When athletes restrict their food intake, they risk nutrient deficiency that will impair both their health and their performance. Careful selection of nutrient-dense foods is especially important when energy intake is restricted to reduce body and/or fat mass. Fat is an important nutrient and the diet should contain adequate amounts of fats.

Athletes should aim to achieve carbohydrate intakes that meet the fuel requirements of their training programmes and also adequately replace their carbohydrate stores during recovery between training sessions and competition. This can be achieved when athletes eat carbohydrate-rich snacks and meals that also provide a good source of protein and other nutrients. A varied diet that meets energy needs will generally provide protein in excess of requirements. Muscle mass is maintained or increased at these protein intakes, and the timing of eating carbohydrate and protein may affect the training adaptation.

A high carbohydrate intake in the days before competition will help enhance performance, particularly when exercise lasts longer than about 60 min. Dehydration impairs performance in most events, and athletes should be well hydrated before exercise. Sufficient fluid should be consumed during exercise to limit dehydration to less than about 2% of body mass. During prolonged exercise, the fluid should provide carbohydrate. Sodium should be included when sweat losses are high, especially if exercise lasts more than about 2 h. Athletes should not drink so much that they gain weight during exercise. During recovery from exercise, rehydration should include replacement of both water and salts lost in sweat.

Athletes are cautioned against the indiscriminate use of dietary supplements. Supplements that provide essential nutrients may be of help where food intake or food choices are restricted, but this approach to achieving adequate nutrient intake is normally only a short-term option. The use of supplements does not compensate for poor food choices and an inadequate diet. Athletes contemplating the use of supplements and sports foods should consider their efficacy, their cost, the risk to health and performance, and the potential for a positive doping test.

Excessive training and competition are associated with some negative consequences. Robust immunity and reduced risk of infection can be achieved by consuming a varied diet adequate in energy and micronutrients, ensuring adequate sleep and limiting other life stress. Attention to dietary intake of calcium and iron is important in athletes at risk of deficiency but use of large amounts of some micronutrients may be harmful. Female athletes with menstrual disorders should be promptly referred to a qualified specialist physician for diagnosis and treatment.

Food can contribute not only to the enjoyment of life, but also to success in sport.

Lausanne, 18 June 2003

1 Energy balance and body composition in sports and exercise

ANNE B. LOUCKS

Many athletes, especially female athletes and participants in endurance and aesthetic sports and sports with weight classes, are chronically energy deficient. This energy deficiency impairs performance, growth and health. Reproductive disorders in female athletes are caused by low energy availability (defined as dietary energy intake minus exercise energy expenditure), perhaps specifically by low carbohydrate availability, and not by the stress of exercise. These reproductive disorders can be prevented or reversed by dietary supplementation in compensation for exercise energy expenditure without any moderation of the exercise regimen. Energy balance is not the objective of athletic training. To maximize performance, athletes strive to achieve an optimum sport-specific body size, body composition and mix of energy stores. To pursue these objectives, athletes need to manage fat, protein and carbohydrate balances separately, but it is impractical for athletes to monitor these balances directly, and appetite is not a reliable indicator of their energy and macronutrient needs. To guide their progress, athletes need to eat by discipline and to monitor specific, reliable and practical biomarkers of their objectives. Skinfolds and urinary ketones may be the best biomarkers of fat stores and carbohydrate deficiency, respectively. Research is needed to identify and validate these and other markers.

Keywords: biomarker, body composition, energy balance, exercise, reproduction, sport.

Introduction

This article updates, but does not replace, the excellent chapter on the state of knowledge about energy balance in sports in the Proceedings of the 1991 IOC Consensus Conference on Foods, Nutrition and Sports Performance (Westerterp and Saris, 1991). That chapter made four main points that warrant additional commentary in the light of experience since that conference. The first of those points was one that would appear to most people to be obvious: that total energy intake must be raised to provide the energy expended during athletic training and performance. As will be described in more detail below, many athletes, but female athletes in particular, do not do so. The second point was one that many had taken for granted: that maintenance of energy balance in athletes can be assessed by monitoring body weight, body composition and food intake. In practice, these techniques have not led to confident assessments of energy balance, again especially in female athletes. The third point was that in sports in which low body weight is advantageous for performance, many athletes, and again especially female athletes, practise weight loss techniques that place their reproductive and skeletal health as well as performance at risk. Athletes in such sports were cautioned to lose weight gradually. Recent research has identified low energy availability as the hazard in such sports, and quantified its dose-dependent effects on metabolic and reproductive function. The final point was that during training and competition in sports of high intensity and long duration, the limiting factor for performance is energy intake, especially carbohydrate intake. Recent research suggests that in such sports the limiting factor for reproductive and skeletal health is carbohydrate availability – that is, the difference between carbohydrate intake and oxidation during exercise.

Energy balance in athletes

Westerterp and Saris (1991) provided a table of data on the energy intake of athletes in different endurance, strength and team sports in units of kilojoules per kilogram of body weight per day. Recently, much more extensive observational data on the energy and carbohydrate intakes of athletes in many sports have been compiled in the same normalized units (Burke *et al.*, 2001). These data were compiled before 1971, between 1971 and 1989, and since 1990. The latter data offer insight into the dietary habits of athletes since the publication of the 1991 IOC consensus recommendations. If these data are to be believed, however, one observation is particularly noteworthy. With the notable exception of cross-country skiers, female athletes consume only about 70% as much energy and carbohydrate – normalized for body weight – as do male athletes (see Figs 1 and 2).

Many investigators have been sceptical of data from the dietary records of female athletes, because studies comparing such data to estimations or measurements of their energy expenditure have repeatedly found apparently huge negative energy balances, some exceeding $4 \text{ MJ} \cdot \text{day}^{-1}$ in athletes with stable body weights (Mulligan and Butterfield, 1990; Wilmore *et al.*, 1992; Edwards *et al.*, 1993; Beidleman *et al.*, 1995; Hill and Davies, 2002). Such large discrepancies have been interpreted as indicating that female athletes grossly under-report their dietary intake. In support of this allegation, investigators have cited certain other special sub-populations that have been found to under-report, but a meta-analysis of studies comparing dietary assessments to measurements of energy expenditure by doubly labelled water found that women do not under-report more than men (Trabulsi and Schoeller, 2001). Some investigators have questioned the methods used to measure energy intake and expenditure. Indeed, the study that found virtually identical energy intakes in female and male cross-country skiers took extraordinary pains to achieve accurate measurements of energy intake (Sjodin *et al.*, 1994). As a result of such concerns, quantitative criteria have been developed to assess whether reported energy intakes

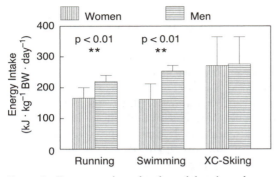

Figure 1. Energy intakes of male and female endurance athletes in running, swimming and cross-country skiing (Burke *et al.*, 2001).

in studies of various numbers of athletes over various lengths of time pass what might be called the 'laugh test' (Goldberg *et al.*, 1991).

Considering the lack of confidence in studies of energy balance in athletes, it is surprising that few have included biochemical measurements to validate energy intake and expenditure data, because under-reporting would not account for biochemical evidence of energy deficiency. In several studies characterizing reproductive disorders in female athletes, metabolic substrates and hormones have been measured, and they tell a consistent story of chronic energy and carbohydrate deficiency (Myerson *et al.*, 1991; Loucks *et al.*, 1992; Jenkins *et al.*, 1993; Laughlin and Yen, 1996, 1997; De Souza *et al.*, 2003). Female athletes display a spectrum of metabolic substrate and hormone abnormalities indicative of the mobilization of fat stores, the slowing of metabolic rate and a decline in glucose utilization, with more extreme abnormalities in amenorrhoeic athletes and less extreme abnormalities in regularly menstruating athletes. So, while some might question whether lower energy and carbohydrate intakes might be

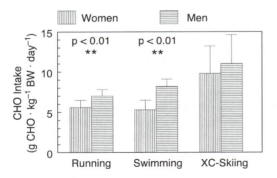

Figure 2. Carbohydrate (CHO) intakes of male and female endurance athletes in running, swimming and cross-country skiing (Burke *et al.*, 2001).

appropriate for women if their energy and carbohydrate expenditures are less than those of men, the biochemical data from these studies demonstrate that female athletes are, indeed, chronically energy deficient.

It is to be emphasized here that 'efficiency' is the wrong concept to apply to pathologic adjustments to chronic energy deficiency. Scarce metabolic fuels consumed in locomotion are unavailable for important physiological functions such as immune function, growth and maintenance functions such as tissue turnover, as well as reproductive development and function. For example, 50% of peak bone mass is deposited during adolescence, but energy deficiency reduces the rate of bone formation by suppressing growth factors and increases the rate of bone resorption by suppressing reproductive hormones. The resulting skeletal demineralization while girls should be accumulating their peak bone mass leads to some amenorrhoeic athletes having the bone densities of 60-year-old women. Osteoporosis in a 20-year-old athlete is a disaster. Osteopaenia is a disaster waiting to happen. Accordingly, the American College of Sports Medicine has published a Position Stand on the Female Athlete Triad as a syndrome requiring prompt intervention to prevent chronic under-nutrition from inducing reproductive disorders and skeletal demineralization (Otis et al., 1997).

Other consequences of hypo-oestrogenism in amenorrhoeic athletes include impaired endothelium-dependent arterial vasodilation (Hoch et al., 2003a,b), which reduces perfusion of working muscle and increases the risk of developing cardiovascular disease, and impaired skeletal muscle oxidative metabolism (Harber et al., 1998).

Part of the nutritional challenge for an athlete is that 'there is no strong biological imperative to match energy intake to activity-induced energy expenditure' (Truswell, 2001). Many studies have shown that hunger is actually suppressed briefly by a single bout of exercise ($>60\%$ $\dot{V}O_{2max}$) (Blundell and King, 1998). In the laboratory, two bouts of exercise (50 min at 70% $\dot{V}O_{2max}$) in a single day induced no increase in ad libitum food intake on that or the following 2 days (King et al., 1997). Experimentally, too, food deprivation increased hunger, but the same energy deficit produced by exercise energy expenditure did not (Hubert et al., 1998). Furthermore, large shifts in carbohydrate and fat oxidation (Stubbs et al., 1995a,b) and in glycogen stores (Snitker et al., 1997) have produced no changes in ad libitum macronutrient intake. Even a 20% increase in energy expenditure during 40 weeks of marathon training induced no increase in energy intake (Westerterp et al., 1991, 1992). Together, these findings demonstrate that the body possesses no mechanism for automatically accommodating energy intake either to the oxidation of specific metabolic fuels or to the expenditure of energy in general by working muscle.

In our laboratory, women say that they have to force themselves to eat far beyond their appetites to consume the amount of food that compensates their dietary energy intake for their exercise energy expenditure and thereby prevents the disruption of luteinizing hormone (LH) pulsatility. Other investigators have had to offer special treats to induce exercising amenorrhoeic monkeys to increase their energy intake enough to restore their menstrual cycles (Williams *et al.*, 2001). For athletes, appetite is not a reliable indicator of either energy balance or specific macronutrient requirements. Athletes must eat by discipline to maximize performance.

Reproductive disorders in athletes

Compared with the idealized ovarian and menstrual cycles described in text-books, reproductive disorders in athletes occur in progressively more severe forms from follicular suppression through luteal suppression, anovulation and oligomenorrhoea to amenorrhoea. Many studies have established that the prevalence of amenorrhoea is highest in endurance and aesthetic activities, in which it is commonly ten times higher than in the general population (Otis *et al.*, 1997). The less severe disorders of ovarian function (follicular suppression, luteal suppression and anovulation) may display no menstrual symptoms so that the affected women are entirely unaware of their condition until they undergo an endocrine work-up. Among regularly menstruating athletes, the incidence of luteal suppression and anovulation appears to be extremely high: endocrine data revealed that 78% of regularly menstruating female runners were luteally suppressed or anovulatory in at least one month out of three (De Souza *et al.*, 1998).

Amenorrhoeic athletes display low plasma glucose concentrations (Laughlin and Yen, 1996), low insulin (Laughlin and Yen, 1996), low insulin-like growth factor I (IGF)/IGF binding protein-1 (Laughlin and Yen, 1996), low leptin (Laughlin and Yen, 1997), low triiodothyronine (T3) (Myerson *et al.*, 1991; Loucks *et al.*, 1992) and low resting metabolic rates (Myerson *et al.*, 1991), as well as elevated growth hormone (Laughlin and Yen, 1996) and mildly elevated cortisol (Loucks *et al.*, 1989; DeSouza *et al.*, 1991; Laughlin and Yen, 1996). All these abnormalities are signs of chronic energy deficiency. Compared with eumenorrhoeic sedentary women, luteally suppressed eumenorrhoeic athletes also display low insulin (Laughlin and Yen, 1996), leptin (Laughlin and Yen, 1996) and T3 (De Souza *et al.*, 2003), as well as elevated growth hormone (Laughlin and Yen, 1996) and mildly elevated cortisol (Loucks *et al.*, 1989; Laughlin and Yen, 1996).

Similar metabolic and reproductive disruptions occur in men, especially those who participate in endurance sports and sports with weight classes. A prospective study of wrestlers, for example, found that body weight, fat mass and strength decreased during the wrestling season as growth hormone increased and IGF-I and testosterone decreased, with testosterone declining below the normal range (Roemmich and Sinning, 1997a,b). Figure 3a shows that the wrestlers were consuming only half of their recommended energy intake before the season began and that they did not increase their energy intake during the season. After the season, they increased their energy intake, but only to near the recommended level. Figure 3b shows that the failure to increase energy

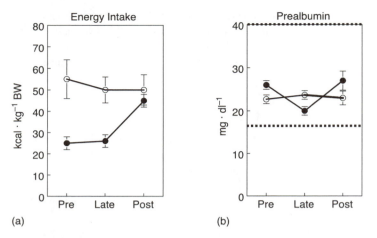

Figure 3. (a) Energy intake and (b) prealbumin concentration in male wrestlers (●) and weight-matched controls (○) before (Pre), late during (Late) and after (Post) the wrestling season. Dashed lines indicate the normal range of prealbumin (reproduced with permission from Roemmich and Sinning, 1997a).

intake during the season suppressed prealbumin. Prealbumin is a classic bio-marker of starvation.

Figure 4 shows the corresponding measurements of growth hormone, IGF-I and testosterone in these wrestlers. During the season, the male wrestlers display growth hormone resistance, with suppressed IGF-I concentrations despite elevated growth hormone, as do female athletes with menstrual disorders. Growth hormone resistance is another classic sign of energy deficiency. As in energy-deficient female athletes, the reproductive systems in these under-nourished male athletes are also suppressed, as evidenced by the decline in testosterone to below the normal range. As might be expected with reduced anabolic stimulation by testosterone and IGF-I, the wrestlers' fat-free mass, and their mid-arm and mid-thigh cross-sectional areas, all declined during the season. As a result, their arm and leg strength and power declined by an average of 13% (Roemmich and Sinning, 1997a), in conflict with the belief that weight loss conveys a competitive advantage.

We have investigated the independent effects of energy availability and exercise stress on reproductive function in exercising women (Loucks et al., 1998). All previous investigations of the 'activity–stress paradigm' had confounded the stress of exercise with its energy cost by having animals exercise longer and longer for smaller and smaller food rewards. Furthermore, despite 60 years of research on exercise stress, there was still no objective definition of exercise stress itself. As shown in Fig. 5, we defined energy availability operationally as dietary energy intake minus exercise energy expenditure, and we defined exercise stress operationally and independently as everything associated with exercise, except exercise energy expenditure. Habitually sedentary women of

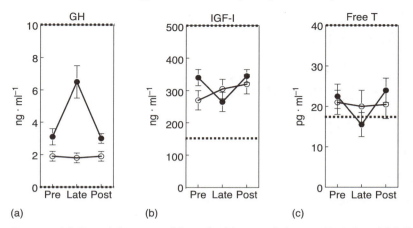

Figure 4. (a) Growth hormone, (b) insulin-like growth factor I (IGF-I) and (c) free testosterone in male wrestlers (●) and weight-matched controls (○) before (Pre), late during (Late) and after (Post) the wrestling season. Dashed lines indicate the normal ranges of growth hormone, IGF-I and free testosterone (reproduced with permission from Roemmich and Sinning, 1997b).

normal body composition were assigned to sedentary or exercising groups and were administered balanced and deprived energy availability treatments in random order under controlled conditions in the laboratory.

After 4 days, blood was sampled at 10 min intervals for 24 h for the assessment of LH pulsatility, upon which ovarian function critically depends. As

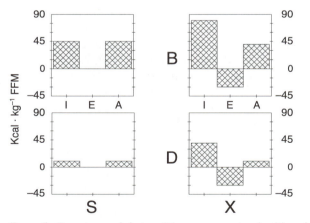

Figure 5. Experimental design. Dietary energy intake (I) and exercise energy expenditure (E) were controlled to achieve balanced (B = 45 kcal · kg^{-1} FFM · day^{-1}) and deprived (D = 10 kcal · kg^{-1} FFM · day^{-1}) energy availability (A = I − E) treatments. Deprived energy availability was achieved by dietary restriction alone in sedentary women (S) and by exercise energy expenditure alone in exercising women (X) (1 kcal = 4.18 kJ) (reproduced with permission from Loucks *et al.*, 1998).

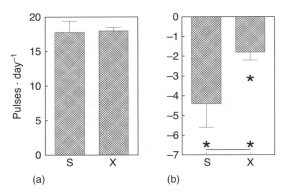

Figure 6. (a) Luteinizing hormone (LH) pulse frequency in sedentary (S) and exercising (X) women with the same energy availability. (b) Reduction in LH pulse frequency caused by low energy availability in sedentary (S) and exercising (X) women. *$P < 0.01$ (adapted from Loucks *et al.*, 1998)

shown in Fig. 6, the stress of exercise had no suppressive effect on LH pulse frequency, whereas low energy availability suppressed LH pulse frequency, regardless of whether the low energy availability was caused by dietary energy restriction alone or by exercise energy expenditure alone. (Similar results were obtained when half of the reduction in energy availability was caused by dietary energy restriction and half by exercise energy expenditure.) Low energy availability also suppressed T3, insulin, IGF-I and leptin (Hilton and Loucks, 2000), while it increased growth hormone and cortisol in a pattern very reminiscent of amenorrhoeic and luteally suppressed eumenorrhoeic athletes. Unexpectedly, the effects of low energy availability on LH pulse frequency and on the metabolic hormones in the exercising women were smaller than those in the dietarily restricted women, even though their balanced and deprived energy availabilities were exactly matched, and no-one had ever hypothesized that exercise would be protective of reproductive function. Further investigation revealed that the exercising women had a higher carbohydrate availability (defined observationally as dietary carbohydrate intake minus exercise carbohydrate oxidation), due to a glucose-sparing alteration in skeletal muscle fuel selection during energy deprivation.

Endocrine markers of energy deficiency have also been found in a prospective study of young, healthy, lean men during the US Army's 8-week course for training and selecting the elite combat unit leaders known as Rangers (Friedl *et al.*, 2000). This course is conducted in four consecutive 2-week stages in forest, mountain, desert and swamp environments. Besides environmental exposures to heat and cold, soldiers are exposed to workloads demanding sustained high energy expenditures (18 MJ · day^{-1} measured by doubly labelled water), sleep deprivation (< 4 h · day^{-1}) and chronic energy deficiency (4 MJ · day^{-1} average negative energy balance). Participants lose 13% of body weight, including 51% of fat mass and 6% of fat-free mass. Illness, infections and injuries are

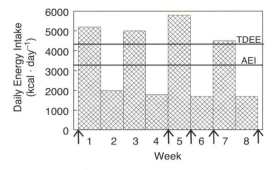

Figure 7. Energy intake and expenditure during the US Army Rangers training course. TDEE = total daily energy expenditure determined by doubly labelled water; AEI = average energy intake from controlled feeding. Arrows indicate blood sampling times (1 kcal = 4.18 kJ) (reproduced with permission from Friedl *et al.*, 2000).

commonplace. These rigours are so extreme that only 30% of participants finish the course. Figure 7 shows the schedule of alternating weeks of controlled semi-starvation and refeeding and the timing of blood sampling in relation to total daily energy expenditure and average energy intake during the course.

Figure 8 shows the effects of all these factors on metabolic and reproductive hormones. Note that effects on reproductive as well as metabolic hormones follow the feeding schedule, despite continued exercise and environmental stresses. One week of controlled refeeding during the course and one week of *ad libitum* refeeding after the 8-week course fully restored both metabolic and reproductive hormones to their initial values. Note that the restoration of reproductive function during week 5 occurred despite the continuation of the exercise and other stresses in the training programme.

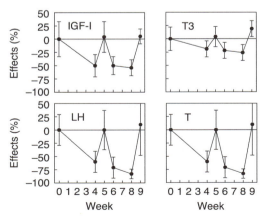

Figure 8. Effects of US Army Rangers training course on metabolic (IGF-I and T3) and reproductive (LH and testosterone (T)) hormones. Error bars indicate ± I standard error (adapted from Friedl *et al.*, 2000).

In a study of another group of candidates in a Rangers training course, strength, power and vertical jump all declined by ∼20% during the course (Nindl *et al.*, 1997), showing that sustained energy deficiency substantially impairs physical performance.

Meanwhile, experiments have shown that increasing exercise energy expenditure induces amenorrhoea in female monkeys and that dietary supplementation then restores their menstrual cycling without any moderation of their exercise regimen (Williams *et al.*, 2001). All these results show that low energy availability, not the stress of exercise – and neither dietary energy intake nor exercise energy expenditure alone – is what disrupts the reproductive system in men and women, as well as female monkeys, and that this disruption can be prevented by dietary supplementation in compensation for exercise energy expenditure without any moderation of the exercise regimen (or other stresses).

We have also investigated the dose-dependent effects of energy availability on LH pulsatility and on metabolic substrates and hormones in exercising women (Loucks and Thuma, 2003). Figure 9 shows the experimental design in which energy availability was set at 10, 20, 30 and 45 kcal·kg^{-1} FFM·day^{-1}, by having all participants perform 15 kcal·kg^{-1} FFM·day^{-1} of exercise at 70% $\dot{V}O_{2max}$ (similar to running 7 miles) while consuming 25, 35, 45 or 60 kcal·kg^{-1} FFM·day^{-1} of dietary energy (where FFM = fat-free mass). All participants were administered the balanced energy availability treatment (45 kcal·kg^{-1} FFM·day^{-1}) and one of the restricted energy availability treatments in random order.

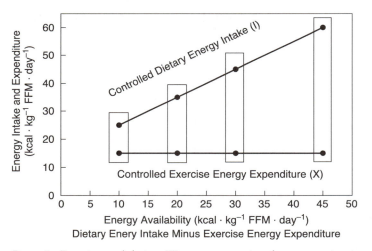

Figure 9. Experimental design. Women were assigned to contrasting energy availability treatments of 45 and 10, 45 and 20, and 45 and 30 kcal·kg^{-1} FFM·day^{-1}. All participants performed 15 kcal·kg^{-1} FFM·day^{-1} of exercise at 70% $\dot{V}O_{2max}$ under supervision while their dietary energy intake was controlled to achieve the intended energy availability treatments (1 kcal = 4.18 kJ) (reproduced with permission from Loucks and Thuma, 2003). © The Endocrine Society.

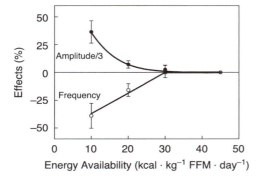

Figure 10. Incremental effects of low energy availability on LH pulse amplitude (●, top) and LH pulse frequency (○, bottom). Effects are expressed relative to values at $45 \, \text{kcal} \cdot \text{kg}^{-1} \, \text{FFM} \cdot \text{day}^{-1}$. Effects on LH pulse amplitude have been divided by three for graphical symmetry. As energy availability declines from energy balance at approximately $45 \, \text{kcal} \cdot \text{kg}^{-1} \, \text{FFM} \cdot \text{day}^{-1}$, effects begin at a threshold at approximately $30 \, \text{kcal} \cdot \text{kg}^{-1} \, \text{FFM} \cdot \text{day}^{-1}$ and become more extreme as energy availability is further reduced below $20 \, \text{kcal} \cdot \text{kg}^{-1} \, \text{FFM} \cdot \text{day}^{-1}$ ($1 \, \text{kcal} = 4.18 \, \text{kJ}$) (reproduced with permission from Loucks and Thuma, 2003). © The Endocrine Society.

Figure 10 shows the dose-dependent effects of energy availability on LH pulsatility. Luteinizing hormone pulse frequency was suppressed and amplitude increased below a threshold of energy availability between 20 and $30 \, \text{kcal} \cdot \text{kg}^{-1}$ $\text{FFM} \cdot \text{day}^{-1}$. Figure 11 shows the dose-dependent effects of energy availability on metabolic substrates and hormones. Statistical analysis showed that the dose-dependent effects on LH pulsatility were most similar to those on the metabolic substrates glucose and β-hydroxybutyrate and to the metabolic hormones cortisol and growth hormone, and contrasted with the dependencies displayed by the other metabolic hormones. These results support the hypothesis that reproductive function reflects the availability of metabolic fuels, especially glucose, which may be signalled in part by activation of the adrenal axis. They also suggest that athletes may be able to prevent menstrual disorders by maintaining energy availabilities above $30 \, \text{kcal} \cdot \text{kg}^{-1} \, \text{FFM} \cdot \text{day}^{-1}$.

Energy balance is not the objective

Athletic performance is maximized, in part, by a sport-specific (and in team sports, position-specific) optimum body size, body composition and mix of stored metabolic fuels. Sprinters have no use for fat stores, for example, whereas runners in ultra-endurance events need them for fuel, swimmers need them for buoyancy and cold-water swimmers need them for insulation. Commonly, aspiring competitive athletes do not manifest these optima for their chosen sports and much of their training aims to modify their bodies to achieve them. Considering the initial conditions of many athletes in many sports, however,

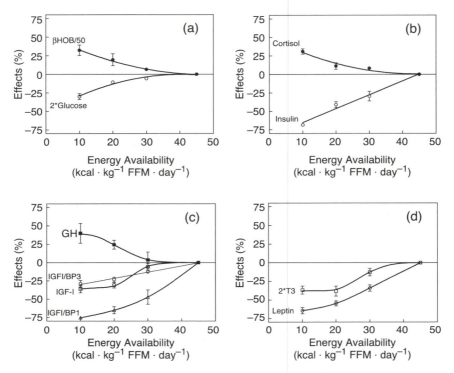

Figure 11. Incremental effects of energy availability on metabolic substrates and hormones. (a) Incremental effects on the metabolic substrates β-hydroxybutyrate (●, upper left top) and plasma glucose (○, upper left bottom). Effects are shown relative to values at 45 kcal · kg^{-1} FFM · day^{-1}. Effects on β-hydroxybutyrate have been divided by 50 and effects on plasma glucose have been doubled for graphical symmetry. Effects on β-hydroxybutyrate and glucose become progressively more extreme as energy availability decreases. (b) Incremental effects on the metabolic hormones cortisol (●, upper right top) and insulin (○, upper right bottom). Effects are shown relative to values at 45 kcal · kg^{-1} FFM · day^{-1}. Insulin declines linearly with energy availability, while effects on cortisol become progressively more extreme as energy availability decreases. (c) Incremental effects on the somatotrophic metabolic hormones growth hormone (GH) (■, lower left top) and IGF-I (□, lower left bottom) and the ratios IGF-I/IGFBP-1 (△, lower left bottom) and IGF-I/IGFBP-3 (○, lower left bottom). Effects are shown relative to values at 45 kcal · kg^{-1} FFM · day^{-1}. Effects on GH and IGF-I tend to flatten out below 20 kcal · kg^{-1} FFM · day^{-1} as growth hormone resistance becomes more extreme. Both estimates of bioactive IGF-I have declined significantly and substantially at 30 kcal · kg^{-1} FFM · day^{-1}. (d) Incremental effects on the metabolic hormones T3 (□, lower right top) and leptin (○, lower right bottom). Effects are shown relative to values at 45 kcal · kg^{-1} FFM · day^{-1}. The effect on T3 is doubled for graphical clarity. Both T3 and leptin have declined significantly and substantially at 30 kcal · kg^{-1} FFM · day^{-1}. These effects tend to flatten out below 20 kcal · kg^{-1} FFM · day^{-1} (1 kcal = 4.18 kJ) (reproduced with permission from Loucks and Thuma, 2003). © The Endocrine Society.

their aims are often to reduce fat mass while increasing fat-free mass and glycogen stores.

In athletes, body weight is not a reliable indicator of either energy or macronutrient balance. Because protein and glycogen stores are associated with much more body water than are fat stores, for example, a weight gain due to small increases in protein or glycogen energy stores can counterbalance the weight loss due to larger reductions in fat energy stores during negative energy balance. Energy balance, itself, conveys little information about an athlete's present status or progress towards multiple objectives that may be in opposite directions for different components of body composition.

For several reasons, the nutritionist's expression of the first law of thermodynamics (energy balance = energy intake − energy expenditure) and quantitative information about energy intake and expenditure (even if it is accurate) are of little practical use to athletes who aim to achieve selective changes in their body size and composition and in their stores of specific fuels. To begin, it is not feasible for athletes to measure their energy intake and expenditure accurately on a day-to-day basis as a method for managing their athletic training. Major metabolic processes activated in response to diet and exercise are out of the athlete's control and perception. Moreover, macronutrients are metabolized differently and stored separately so that the conversion of one macronutrient into another for storage does not represent important metabolic pathways (Flatt, 1988). Fats eaten above the day's nutritional requirement are nearly all stored in the body (Schutz et al., 1989), but not all fats are obesogenic (Wang et al., 2002). Seven weeks of a high saturated fat diet increased fat mass, whereas an isocaloric diet equally high in n-3 polyunsaturated fats reduced fat mass compared to an isoenergetic low fat diet. Switching mice from the diet high in saturated fats to the one high in n-3 polyunsaturated fats then reversed the increase in fat mass within 4 weeks.

Humans can ingest large amounts of carbohydrate without initiating *de novo* lipogenesis at rates greater than fat oxidation (Acheson et al., 1982). In humans, *de novo* lipogenesis from excess glucose occurs to only a negligible degree in the liver (Hellerstein et al., 1991; Aarsland et al., 1997). In adipose tissue, it occurs only during experimentally imposed sustained, extreme carbohydrate overfeeding, and then only with low efficiency (Macdonald, 1999) until glycogen storage capacity has been saturated (Acheson et al., 1988). The more efficient conversion that occurs after glycogen stores are experimentally saturated is unlikely to occur in everyday life and even less likely in athletes, especially endurance athletes, who mobilize and oxidize substantial amounts of glycogen during and after exercise each day. A transient excess dietary carbohydrate intake stimulates insulin release, which promotes glucose uptake and oxidation as well as glycogen synthesis and storage. A transient excess protein intake also stimulates its own oxidation and, like carbohydrate, is only stored short term.

In the tricarboxylic acid cycle, substantial quantities of both fats and carbohydrates are oxidized during and after exercise, but the magnitudes and proportions of each depend on the duration of the exercise performed and on the size and macronutrient content of the diet (Folch *et al.*, 2001). Considering energy expenditure both during and after exercise, glycogen balance is positive only when large carbohydrate-rich meals are consumed, but less positive, of course, on a day of exercise than on a day of rest when the increased oxidation of glycogen during and after exercise is avoided (Folch *et al.*, 2001). Fat balance, on the other hand, is negative regardless of whether carbohydrate-rich meals are large or small, and more negative on a day of exercise than on a day of rest, regardless of the exercise intensity (Folch *et al.*, 2001).

Therefore, because macronutrients are metabolized differently and stored separately, an athlete needs to manage fat, protein and carbohydrate balances separately to achieve sport-specific body size, body composition and energy store objectives. To reduce fat mass, athletes need to induce negative fat balance by minimizing the intake of saturated fats and maximizing the oxidation of fats by exercising for several hours a day. Since lean body mass may be increasing as fat mass is declining, this may not necessarily involve a reduction in energy intake, energy balance or body weight. To increase fat-free mass, athletes need to induce positive protein balance by consuming adequate amounts of complete protein, together with sufficient carbohydrate, to fuel anabolic processes and by exercising in a specific manner for promoting the development of target skeletal muscle and bone components. Athletes also need to consume plenty of carbohydrates to elevate insulin concentrations to promote the uptake of amino acids and the synthesis of protein by muscle, as well as to replenish muscle glycogen stores for future exercise, and to replenish liver glycogen stores for brain as well as muscle metabolism.

In this regard, it is essential to remember that because fatty acids do not cross the blood–brain barrier, the brain relies on glucose for energy. Furthermore, in humans, the brain is so large and so metabolically active that its daily energy requirement exceeds the entire liver glycogen storage capacity (Bursztein *et al.*, 1989). Moreover, muscle glycogen stores are not available to the brain, because glucose stored as muscle glycogen cannot be returned to the bloodstream. This is why liver glycogen stores have to be replenished every day by dietary carbohydrate. Furthermore, since skeletal muscle has access to liver glycogen stores, skeletal muscle competes directly against the brain for all available carbohydrate. In a marathon race, working muscle consumes as much glucose in 2 h as the brain requires in a week. Under conditions in which the brain is deprived of glucose, physiological mechanisms are activated to mobilize fat stores and to convert the resulting fatty acids to ketones, which are the brain's only alternative energy source. Available evidence suggests that reproductive function depends not on energy availability in general, but rather on brain glucose availability (i.e. liver glycogen stores) in particular.

Management by objectives

Separately managing fat, protein and carbohydrate balances will be even less practical than managing energy balance if athletes attempt to estimate fat, protein and carbohydrate intakes and expenditures in place of energy intake and expenditure. Nor will athletes be aided much by sophisticated markers of conditions that are not objectives, such as energy balance. Athletes need specific markers of their status and progress towards particular body size, body composition and energy store objectives. Is fat mass decreasing? Is fat-free mass increasing? Are muscle glycogen stores being adequately replenished? Are liver glycogen stores being adequately maintained?

Research is needed to validate specific, accurate and practical biomarkers for answering such questions. Ideally, a single measurement of a biomarker would provide the desired information. For many candidate markers, however, the normal range in the general population is wide compared with the effects of improper nutrition. Recall that testosterone was the only hormone outside the normal range in wrestlers (Roemmich and Sinning, 1997b). Repeated measures of metabolic hormones may be necessary to detect changes over time within an individual. Preferably, a biomarker would also be inexpensive, convenient to administer and minimally invasive. Anthropometric measurements would be preferable to a urinalysis, for example. Urinalysis, in turn, would be preferable to the assay of a blood sample, but even that would be preferable to any measurement requiring the infusion of foreign substances into the bloodstream. Ideally, a biomarker should provide instantly useful information without delays while laboratory procedures are conducted. Ideally, the measured value of a biomarker would not depend upon the compliance of the athlete. For this reason, blood glucose, insulin and other metabolic parameters strongly affected by a single meal would not be strong candidates.

Of course, an obvious biomarker specific for fat mass is skinfold thickness, which is the simplest, most direct, most immediate and least expensive technique for monitoring body fat stores, and perhaps good enough. Net lipogenesis corresponding to the accretion of fat stores due to an excessively positive carbohydrate balance can be detected by a respiratory quotient higher than 1.0, but the equipment for measuring it is expensive.

Densitometry and electrical impedance can be used to monitor fat-free mass, but the most useful biomarkers of muscle development may be measures of strength and endurance performance.

There is considerable interest in metabolic hormone concentrations in the blood as biomarkers of carbohydrate availability. Concentrations of T3 are determined by carbohydrate availability, not carbohydrate intake (Loucks and Callister, 1993). On the usual mixed diet, T3 is suppressed at a threshold of energy availability corresponding to a critical carbohydrate availability (Loucks and Heath, 1994), like LH pulsatility. Leptin, too, reflects carbohydrate availability. Synthesized in adipose tissue cells, leptin was originally thought to communicate information about fat stores (Maffei *et al.*, 1995). Later reports of leptin varying profoundly before any changes in adiposity in response to fasting (Kolaczynski *et al.*, 1996b; Weigle *et al.*, 1997), dietary restriction (Weigle *et al.*, 1997), refeeding after dietary restriction (Kolaczynski *et al.*, 1996b; Jenkins *et al.*, 1997) and overfeeding (Kolaczynski *et al.*, 1996a) led to the hypothesis that leptin signals information about dietary intake, particularly carbohydrate intake (Jenkins *et al.*, 1997). Since then, we have shown that the diurnal rhythm of leptin depends instead on the *availability* of energy and, more specifically, of carbohydrate (Hilton and Loucks, 2000). Research now indicates that leptin is regulated by the tiny flux of glucose through the hexosamine biosynthesis pathway (Wang *et al.*, 1998).

Nevertheless, single measurements of metabolic hormones do not reliably identify energy-deficient individuals, because their normal ranges across the population are wide compared with the effects of energy deficiency on them. For example, Fig. 12 shows substantially overlapping distributions of T3, IGF-I, leptin at 07.00 h and leptin averaged over 24 h in a group of regularly menstruating women after 5 days at a balanced energy availability of $45 \, \text{kcal} \cdot \text{kg}^{-1} \, \text{FFM} \cdot \text{day}^{-1}$ and again after 5 days at a severely deficient energy availability of $10 \, \text{kcal} \cdot \text{kg}^{-1} \, \text{FFM} \cdot \text{day}^{-1}$. Such repeated measures reveal the effects of energy deficiency on these hormones, but single measurements of the hormones in even such extremely energy-deficient individuals still fall within the range of energy-balanced individuals, and single measurements in energy-balanced individuals fall within the range of energy-deficient individuals.

Figure 13 shows that the same is also true for 24-h mean glucose, 24-h mean IGF-binding protein 1 (IGFBP1) and 24-h mean cortisol, although 24-h mean insulin concentration in severely energy-deficient women displays little overlap with that in energy-balanced women. Unfortunately, Fig. 14 shows that 24-h

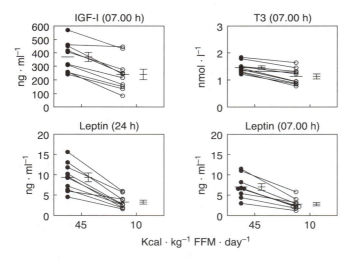

Figure 12. Concentrations for IGF-I at 07.00 h, T3 at 07.00 h, 24 h mean leptin and leptin at 07.00 h in a group of regularly menstruating women after 5 days at a balanced energy availability of $45 \, \text{kcal} \cdot \text{kg}^{-1} \, \text{FFM} \cdot \text{day}^{-1}$ and after 5 days at a severely low energy availability of $10 \, \text{kcal} \cdot \text{kg}^{-1} \, \text{FFM} \cdot \text{day}^{-1}$ (1 kcal = 4.18 kJ).

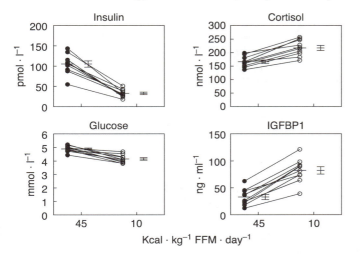

Figure 13. The 24-h mean insulin, cortisol, glucose and IGF-I binding protein-1 (IGFBP1) concentrations in a group of regularly menstruating women after 5 days at a balanced energy availability of 45 kcal·kg^{-1} FFM·day^{-1} and after 5 days at a severely low energy availability of 10 kcal·kg^{-1} FFM·day^{-1} (1 kcal = 4.18 kJ).

mean insulin fails to identify less energy-deficient women at the threshold of reproductive disorders at an energy availability of 30 kcal·kg^{-1} FFM·day^{-1}.

The most convenient indicator of sustained carbohydrate deficiency may be urinary ketones. Figure 15 shows the distributions of serum β-hydroxybutyrate and urinary aceto-acetate concentrations in the same group of women after 5 days at energy availabilities of 45 and 10 kcal·kg^{-1} FFM·day^{-1}. Both serum and urinary ketones unambiguously identify such severely energy-deficient individuals. Figure 16 shows that urinary ketones identify even less energy-deficient individuals almost equally reliably at 30 kcal·kg^{-1} FFM·day^{-1}. Urinary aceto-acetate is a better discriminator of energy deficiency than serum β-hydroxy-butyrate, because ketones are not present in the urine under energy-balanced conditions.

Ketone concentrations rise when fat stores are mobilized to substitute for deficient glycogen stores. Initially, ketones produced as a byproduct of lipolysis in the liver are taken up from the blood and metabolized by the heart, kidney and skeletal muscle so that circulating concentrations in the blood remain low. If negative carbohydrate balance continues for only a few days, however, ketone utilization by these tissues declines, blood concentrations rise making the ketones available as an alternative metabolic fuel for the brain, and the ketones begin to pass through the kidneys into the urine. Athletes can purchase 'keto-sticks' inexpensively in most pharmacies to monitor their own urinary ketones at home.

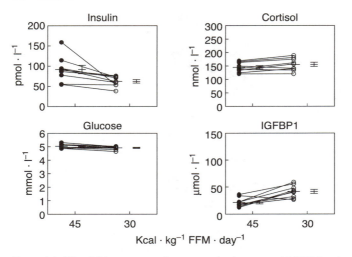

Figure 14. The 24 h mean insulin, cortisol, glucose and IGF-I binding protein-1 (IGFBP1) concentrations in a group of regularly menstruating women after 5 days at a balanced energy availability of 45 kcal·kg^{-1} FFM·day^{-1} and after 5 days at a low energy availability of 30 kcal·kg^{-1} FFM·day^{-1} (1 kcal = 4.18 kJ).

Summary

Many athletes, especially female athletes and those who participate in endurance and aesthetic sports and sports with weight classes, are chronically energy deficient. This energy deficiency impairs performance, growth and health. Reproductive disorders in female athletes are caused by low energy availability – perhaps specifically by low carbohydrate availability – and not by the stress of exercise. In athletes expending large amounts of energy in exercise training, neither an eating disorder nor dietary restriction is necessary to induce menstrual disorders. Less severe reproductive disorders may have no menstrual

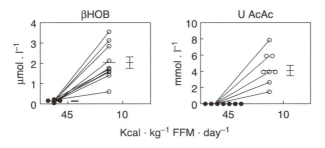

Figure 15. Serum β-hydroxybutyrate (βHOB) and urinary aceto-acetate (U AcAc) concentrations at 07.00 h in a group of regularly menstruating women after 5 days at a balanced energy availability of 45 kcal·kg^{-1} FFM·day^{-1} and after 5 days at a severely low energy availability of 10 kcal·kg^{-1} FFM·day^{-1} (1 kcal = 4.18 kJ).

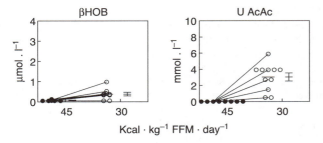

Figure 16. Serum β-hydroxybutyrate (βHOB) and urinary aceto-acetate (U AcAc) concentrations at 07.00 h in a group of regularly menstruating women after 5 days at a balanced energy availability of 45 kcal · kg⁻¹ FFM · day⁻¹ and after 5 days at a low energy availability of 30 kcal · kg⁻¹ FFM · day⁻¹ (1 kcal = 4.18 kJ).

symptoms. Reproductive disorders due to low energy availability can be prevented or reversed by dietary supplementation without any moderation of the exercise regimen. Because energy balance is not the objective of athletic training, information about energy balance is not particularly useful for guiding athletic training. To maximize performance, athletes strive to achieve an optimum sport-specific body size, body composition and mix of energy stores. To guide their progress, athletes need to monitor specific, reliable and practical biomarkers of these objectives. Research is needed to identify and validate such markers.

Acknowledgements

This research was supported in part by Grant DAMD 17-95-1-5053 from the US Army Medical Research and Material Command (Defense Women's Health & Military Medical Readiness Research Program) and in part by Grant M01 RR00034 from the General Clinical Research Branch, Division of Research Resources, National Institutes of Health. The information presented here does not necessarily reflect the position or the policy of the government, and no official endorsement should be inferred.

References

1 Aarsland, A., Chinkes, D. and Wolfe, R.R. (1997). Hepatic and whole-body fat synthesis in humans during carbohydrate overfeeding. *American Journal of Clinical Nutrition*, **65**, 1774–1782.
2 Acheson, K.J., Flatt, J.P. and Jéquier, E. (1982). Glycogen synthesis versus lipogenesis after a 500 gram carbohydrate meal in man. *Metabolism*, **31**, 1234–1240.
3 Acheson, K.J., Schutz, Y., Bessard, T., Anantharaman, K., Flatt, J.P. and Jéquier, E. (1988). Glycogen storage capacity and *de novo* lipogenesis during massive carbohydrate overfeeding in man. *American Journal of Clinical Nutrition*, **48**, 240–247.

4 Beidleman, B.A., Puhl, J.L. and De Souza, M.J. (1995). Energy balance in female distance runners. *American Journal of Clinical Nutrition*, **61**, 303–311.

5 Blundell, J.E. and King, N.A. (1998). Effects of exercise on appetite control: loose coupling between energy expenditure and energy intake. *International Journal of Obesity and Related Metabolic Disorders*, **22**, S22–S29.

6 Burke, L.M., Cox, G.R., Cummings, N.K. and Desbrow, B. (2001). Guidelines for daily carbohydrate intake: do athletes achieve them? *Sports Medicine*, **31**, 267–299.

7 Bursztein, S., Elwyn, D.H., Askanazi, J. and Kinney, J.M. (1989). Fuel utilization in normal, starving, and pathological states. In *Energy Metabolism, Indirect Calorimetry, and Nutrition*, pp. 119–171. Baltimore, MD: Williams & Wilkins.

8 De Souza, M.J., Maguire, M.S., Maresh, C.M., Kraemer, W.J., Rubin, K.R. and Loucks, A.B. (1991). Adrenal activation and the prolactin response to exercise in eumenorrheic and amenorrheic runners. *Journal of Applied Physiology*, **70**, 2378–2387.

9 De Souza, M.J., Miller, B.E., Loucks, A.B., Luciano, A.A., Pescatello, L.S., Campbell, C.G. and Lasley, B.L. (1998). High frequency of luteal phase deficiency and anovulation in recreational women runners: blunted elevation in follicle-stimulating hormone observed during luteal–follicular transition. *Journal of Clinical Endocrinology and Metabolism*, **83**, 4220–4232.

10 De Souza, M.J., Van Heest, J., Demers, L.M. and Lasley, B.L. (2003). Luteal phase deficiency in recreational runners: evidence for a hypometabolic state. *Journal of Clinical Endocrinology and Metabolism*, **88**, 337–346.

11 Edwards, J.E., Lindeman, A.K., Mikesky, A.E. and Stager, J.M. (1993). Energy balance in highly trained female endurance runners. *Medicine and Science in Sports and Exercise*, **25**, 1398–1404.

12 Flatt, J.P. (1988). Importance of nutrient balance in body weight regulation. *Diabetes/Metabolism Reviews*, **4**, 571–581.

13 Folch, N., Péronnet, F., Massicotte, D., Duclos, M., Lavoie, C. and Hillaire-Marcel, C. (2001). Metabolic responses to small and large ^{13}C-labelled pasta meals following rest or exercise in man. *British Journal of Nutrition*, **85**, 671–680.

14 Friedl, K.E., Moore, R.J., Hoyt, R.W., Marchitelli, L.J., Martinez-Lopez, L.E. and Askew, E.W. (2000). Endocrine markers of semistarvation in healthy lean men in a multistressor environment. *Journal of Applied Physiology*, **88**, 1820–1830.

15 Goldberg, G.R., Black, A.E., Jebb, S.A., Cole, T.J., Murgatroyd, P.R., Coward, W.A. and Prentice, A.M. (1991). Critical evaluation of energy intake data using fundamental principles of energy physiology: 1. Derivation of cut-off limits to identify under-recording. *European Journal of Clinical Nutrition*, **45**, 569–581.

16 Harber, V.J., Petersen, S.R. and Chilibeck, P.D. (1998). Thyroid hormone concentrations and muscle metabolism in amenorrheic and eumenorrheic athletes. *Canadian Journal of Applied Physiology*, **23**, 293–306.

17 Hellerstein, M.K., Christiansen, M., Kaempfer, S., Kletke, C., Wu, K., Reid, J.S., Mulligan, K., Hellerstein, N.S. and Shackleton, C.H. (1991). Measurement of *de novo* hepatic lipogenesis in humans using stable isotopes. *Journal of Clinical Investigation*, **87**, 1841–1852.

18 Hill, R.J. and Davies, P.S.W. (2002). Energy intake and energy expenditure in elite lightweight female rowers. *Medicine and Science in Sports and Exercise*, **34**, 1823–1829.

19 Hilton, L.K. and Loucks, A.B. (2000). Low energy availability, not exercise stress, suppresses the diurnal rhythm of leptin in healthy young women. *American Journal of Physiology: Endocrinology and Metabolism*, **278**, E43–E49.

20 Hoch, A.Z., Jurva, J., Staton, M., Vetter, C., Young, C. and Gutterman, D. (2003a). Is endothelial dysfunction that is associated with athletic amenorrhea reversible? *Medicine and Science in Sports and Exercise*, **35**, S12.

21 Hoch, A.Z., Dempsey, R.L., Carrera, G.F., Wilson, C.R., Chen, E.H., Barnabei, V.M., Sandford, P.R., Ryan, T.A. and Gutterman, D.D. (2003b). Is there an association between athletic amenorrhea and endothelial cell dysfunction? *Medicine and Science in Sports and Exercise*, **35**, 377–383.

22 Hubert, P., King, N.A. and Blundell, J.E. (1998). Uncoupling the effects of energy expenditure and energy intake: appetite response to short-term energy deficit induced by meal omission and physical activity. *Appetite*, **31**, 9–19.

23 Jenkins, A.B., Markovic, T.P., Fleury, A. and Campbell, L.V. (1997). Carbohydrate intake and short-term regulation of leptin in humans. *Diabetologia*, **40**, 348–351.

24 Jenkins, P.J., Ibanez-Santos, X., Holly, J., Cotterill, A., Perry, L., Wolman, R., Harries, M. and Grossman, A. (1993). IGFBP-1: a metabolic signal associated with exercise-induced amenorrhea. *Neuroendocrinology*, **57**, 600–604.

25 King, N.A., Lluch, A., Stubbs, R.J. and Blundell, J.E. (1997). High dose exercise does not increase hunger or energy intake in free living males. *European Journal of Clinical Nutrition*, **51**, 478–483.

26 Kolaczynski, J.W., Ohannesian, J., Considine, R.V., Marco, C.C. and Caro, J.F. (1996a). Response of leptin to short-term and prolonged overfeeding in humans. *Journal of Clinical Endocrinology and Metabolism*, **81**, 4162–4165.

27 Kolaczynski, J.W., Considine, R.V., Ohannesian, J., Marco, C., Opentanova, I., Nyce, M.R., Myint, M. and Caro, J.F. (1996b). Responses of leptin to short-term fasting and refeeding in humans: a link with ketogenesis but not ketones themselves. *Diabetes*, **45**, 1511–1515.

28 Laughlin, G.A. and Yen, S.S.C. (1996). Nutritional and endocrine-metabolic aberrations in amenorrheic athletes. *Journal of Clinical Endocrinology and Metabolism*, **81**, 4301–4309.

29 Laughlin, G.A. and Yen, S.S.C. (1997). Hypoleptinemia in women athletes: absence of a diurnal rhythm with amenorrhea. *Journal of Clinical Endocrinology and Metabolism*, **82**, 318–321.

30 Loucks, A.B. and Callister, R. (1993). Induction and prevention of low-T3 syndrome in exercising women. *American Journal of Physiology: Regulatory, Integrative, and Comparative Physiology*, **264**, R924–R930.

31 Loucks, A.B. and Heath, E.M. (1994). Induction of low-T3 syndrome in exercising women occurs at a threshold of energy availability. *American Journal of Physiology: Regulatory, Integrative, and Comparative Physiology*, **266**, R817–R823.

32 Loucks, A.B. and Thuma, J.R. (2003). Luteinizing hormone pulsatility is disrupted at a threshold of energy availability in regularly menstruating women. *Journal of Clinical Endocrinology and Metabolism*, **88**, 297–311.

33 Loucks, A.B., Mortola, J.F., Girton, L. and Yen, S.S.C. (1989). Alterations in the hypothalamic–pituitary–ovarian and the hypothalamic–pituitary–adrenal axes in athletic women. *Journal of Clinical Endocrinology and Metabolism*, **68**, 402–411.

34 Loucks, A.B., Laughlin, G.A., Mortola, J.F., Girton, L., Nelson, J.C. and Yen, S.S.C. (1992). Hypothalamic–pituitary–thyroidal function in eumenorrheic and amenorrheic athletes. *Journal of Clinical Endocrinology and Metabolism*, **75**, 514–518.

35   Loucks, A.B., Verdun, M. and Heath, E.M. (1998). Low energy availability, not stress of exercise, alters LH pulsatility in exercising women. *Journal of Applied Physiology*, **84**, 37–46.

36   Macdonald, I.A. (1999). Carbohydrate as a nutrient in adults: range of acceptable intakes. *European Journal of Clinical Nutrition*, **53**, S101–S106.

37   Maffei, M.J., Halaas, J., Ravussin, E., Pratley, R.E., Lee, G.H., Zhang, Y., Fei, H., Kim, S., Lallone, R. and Ranganathan, S. (1995). Leptin levels in human and rodent: measurement of plasma leptin and ob RNA in obese and weight-reduced subjects. *Nature Medicine*, **1**, 1155–1161.

38   Mulligan, K. and Butterfield, G.E. (1990). Discrepancies between energy intake and expenditure in physically active women. *British Journal of Nutrition*, **64**, 23–36.

39   Myerson, M., Gutin, B., Warren, M.P., May, M.T., Contento, I., Lee, M., Pi-Sunyer, F.X., Pierson, R.N., Jr. and Brooks-Gunn, J. (1991). Resting metabolic rate and energy balance in amenorrheic and eumenorrheic runners. *Medicine and Science in Sports and Exercise*, **23**, 15–22.

40   Nindl, B.C., Friedl, K.E., Frykman, P.N., Marchitelli, L.J., Shippee, R.L. and Patton, J.F. (1997). Physical performance and metabolic recovery among lean, healthy men following a prolonged energy deficit. *International Journal of Sports Medicine*, **18**, 317–324.

41   Otis, C.L., Drinkwater, B., Johnson, M., Loucks, A.B. and Wilmore, J.H. (1997). American College of Sports Medicine position stand: The Female Athlete Triad. *Medicine and Science in Sports and Exercise*, **29**, i–ix.

42   Roemmich, J.N. and Sinning, W.E. (1997a). Weight loss and wrestling training: effects on nutrition, growth, maturation, body composition, and strength. *Journal of Applied Physiology*, **82**, 1751–1759.

43   Roemmich, J.N. and Sinning, W.E. (1997b). Weight loss and wrestling training: effects on growth-related hormones. *Journal of Applied Physiology*, **82**, 1760–1764.

44   Schutz, Y., Flatt, J.P. and Jéquier, E. (1989). Failure of dietary fat intake to promote fat oxidation: a factor favoring the development of obesity. *American Journal of Clinical Nutrition*, **50**, 307–314.

45   Sjodin, A.M., Andersson, A.B., Hogberg, J.M. and Westerterp, K.R. (1994). Energy balance in cross-country skiers: a study using doubly labeled water. *Medicine and Science in Sports and Exercise*, **26**, 720–724.

46   Snitker, S., Larson, D.E., Tataranni, P.A. and Ravussin, E. (1997). Ad libitum food intake in humans after manipulation of glycogen stores. *American Journal of Clinical Nutrition*, **65**, 941–946.

47   Stubbs, R.J., Harbron, C.G., Murgatroyd, P.R. and Prentice, A.M. (1995a). Covert manipulation of dietary fat and energy density: effect on substrate flux and food intake in men eating *ad libitum*. *American Journal of Clinical Nutrition*, **62**, 316–329.

48   Stubbs, R.J., Ritz, P., Coward, W.A. and Prentice, A.M. (1995b). Covert manipulation of the ratio of dietary fat to carbohydrate and energy density: effect on food intake and energy balance in free-living men eating *ad libitum*. *American Journal of Clinical Nutrition*, **62**, 330–337.

49   Trabulsi, J. and Schoeller, D.A. (2001). Evaluation of dietary assessment against doubly labeled water, a biomarker of habitual energy intake. *American Journal of Physiology: Endocrinology and Metabolism*, **281**, E891–E899.

50   Truswell, A.S. (2001). Energy balance, food and exercise. *World Review of Nutrition and Dietetics*, **90**, 13–25.

51 Wang, J., Liu, R., Hawkins, M., Barzilai, N. and Rossetti, L. (1998). A nutrient-sensing pathway regulates leptin gene expression in muscle and fat. *Nature*, **393**, 684–688.

52 Wang, H., Storlien, L.H. and Huang, X.F. (2002). Effects of dietary fat types on body fatness, leptin, and ARC leptin receptor, NPY, and AgRP mRNA expression. *American Journal of Physiology: Endocrinology and Metabolism*, **282**, E1352–E1359.

53 Weigle, D.S., Duell, P.B., Connor, W.E., Steiner, R.A., Soules, M.R. and Keujper, J.L. (1997). Effect of fasting, refeeding, and dietary fat restriction on plasma leptin levels. *Journal of Clinical Endocrinology and Metabolism*, **82**, 561–565.

54 Westerterp, K.R. and Saris, W.H.M. (1991). Limits of energy turnover in relation to physical performance, achievement of energy balance on a daily basis. *Journal of Sports Sciences*, **9**(special issue), 1–15.

55 Westerterp, K.R., Verboeket-Van de Venne, W.P.H.G., Meijer, G.A.L. and ten Hoor, F. (1991). Self-reported energy intake as a measure for energy intake: a validation against doubly labeled water. In *Obesity in Europe 91* (edited by G. Ailhaud, B. Guy-Grand, M. Lafontan and D. Ricquier), pp. 17–22. London: John Libbey.

56 Westerterp, K.R., Meijer, G.A.L., Janssem, E.M.E., Saris, W.H.M. and ten Hoor, F. (1992). Long term effect of physical activity on energy balance and body composition. *British Journal of Nutrition*, **68**, 21–30.

57 Williams, N.I., Helmreich, D.L., Parfitt, D.B., Caston-Balderrama, A.L. and Cameron, J.L. (2001). Evidence for a causal role of low energy availability in the induction of menstrual cycle disturbances during strenuous exercise training. *Journal of Clinical Endocrinology and Metabolism*, **86**, 5184–5193.

58 Wilmore, J.H., Wambsgans, K.C., Brenner, M., Broeder, C.E., Paijmans, I., Volpe, J.A. and Wilmore, K.M. (1992). Is there energy conservation in amenorrheic compared with eumenorrheic distance runners? *Journal of Applied Physiology*, **72**, 15–22.

2 Carbohydrates and fat for training and recovery

LOUISE M. BURKE, BENTE KIENS and
JOHN L. IVY

An important goal of the athlete's everyday diet is to provide the muscle with substrates to fuel the training programme that will achieve optimal adaptation for performance enhancements. In reviewing the scientific literature on post-exercise glycogen storage since 1991, the following guidelines for the training diet are proposed. Athletes should aim to achieve carbohydrate intakes to meet the fuel requirements of their training programme and to optimize restoration of muscle glycogen stores between workouts. General recommendations can be provided, preferably in terms of grams of carbohydrate per kilogram of the athlete's body mass, but should be fine-tuned with individual consideration of total energy needs, specific training needs and feedback from training performance. It is valuable to choose nutrient-rich carbohydrate foods and to add other foods to recovery meals and snacks to provide a good source of protein and other nutrients. These nutrients may assist in other recovery processes and, in the case of protein, may promote additional glycogen recovery when carbohydrate intake is suboptimal or when frequent snacking is not possible. When the period between exercise sessions is < 8 h, the athlete should begin carbohydrate intake as soon as practical after the first workout to maximize the effective recovery time between sessions. There may be some advantages in meeting carbohydrate intake targets as a series of snacks during the early recovery phase, but during longer recovery periods (24 h) the athlete should organize the pattern and timing of carbohydrate-rich meals and snacks according to what is practical and comfortable for their individual situation. Carbohydrate-rich foods with a moderate to high glycaemic index provide a readily available source of carbohydrate for muscle glycogen synthesis, and should be the major carbohydrate choices in recovery meals. Although there is new interest in the recovery of intramuscular triglyceride stores between training sessions, there is no evidence that diets which are high in fat and restricted in carbohydrate enhance training.

Keywords: carbohydrate, energy intake, glycaemic index, glycogen, performance.

Introduction

An important goal of the athlete's everyday diet is to provide the muscle with substrates to fuel the training programme that will achieve optimal adaptation and performance enhancements. Body fat and carbohydrate stores provide the major sources of exercise fuel; whereas fat sources (plasma free fatty acids derived from adipose tissue and intramuscular triglycerides) are relatively plentiful, carbohydrate sources (plasma glucose derived from the liver or dietary carbohydrate intake, and muscle glycogen stores) are limited (for a review, see Coyle, 1995). In fact, the availability of carbohydrate as a substrate for the muscle and central nervous system becomes a limiting factor in the performance of prolonged sessions (>90 min) of submaximal or intermittent high-intensity exercise, and plays a permissive role in the performance of brief high-intensity work. As a result, sports nutrition guidelines have focused on strategies to enhance body carbohydrate availability. Such practices include intake of carbohydrate before and during a workout to provide fuel for that session, as well as intake of carbohydrate after the session and over the day in general to promote refuelling and recovery (for a review, see Hargreaves, 1999).

Although other reviews in this issue will discuss strategies for promoting carbohydrate availability before (Hargreaves *et al.*, 2004) and during exercise (Coyle, 2004) in relation to the enhancement of competition performance, these practices should also be integrated into the athlete's training diet. The focus of this article, however, is successful refuelling from day to day, to recover between the daily sessions or multiple workouts undertaken in the athlete's training programme. Strategies to achieve these goals will be particularly important for the serious athlete whose fuel requirements for everyday training are likely to challenge or exceed normal body carbohydrate stores. Key issues related to carbohydrate intake for training and recovery raised in the 1991 position stand on nutrition for sport (Devlin and Williams, 1991) are summarized in Table 1. The aim of this article is to review areas in which these guidelines have been changed or updated.

Update on post-exercise glycogen recovery

The application of the biopsy technique to the study of exercise metabolism in the 1960s allowed sports scientists to measure directly the glycogen content of isolated muscle samples, and thus determine the factors that enhance or impair storage of this important fuel. Since 1991, techniques involving nuclear magnetic resonance spectroscopy have also become available to provide a non-invasive estimate of muscle glycogen content (Roden and Shulman, 1999), and have increased the practical opportunities to study such factors.

A new dimension to the literature on glycogen synthesis and utilization is the discussion of the presence of two glycogen pools within muscle, proglycogen and macroglycogen (Adamo and Graham, 1998). Initially, these were thought to be separate and metabolically distinct compounds (Shearer and Graham, 2002), but the current understanding is that they probably represent the extremes of a spectrum of glycogen molecules of different size. Studies have isolated a primer for glycogen synthesis, the protein glycogenin, which acts both as the core of the glycogen molecule and the enzyme stimulating self-glycosylation (Alonso *et al.*, 1995). The initial accumulation of glucose units to glycogenin forms proglycogen, which is of relatively smaller size. Proglycogen storage is most prominent during the first phase of recovery and is sensitive to the provision of dietary carbohydrate (Adamo *et al.*, 1998). During the second phase

Table 1. Summary of 1991 guidelines for carbohydrate needs for training and recovery (Devlin and Williams, 1991)

Stated guidelines

- In the optimum diet for most sports, carbohydrate is likely to contribute about 60–70% of total energy intake.
- After each bout of exercise, the diet should contain sufficient carbohydrate to replenish the glycogen stores and to maximize subsequent performance. The requirement for sugar and starches, in both solid and liquid forms, will vary, depending on the timing and nature of the physical activity.
- Carbohydrate intake after exhaustive exercise should average 50 g per 2 h of mostly moderate and high glycaemic carbohydrate foods. The aim should be to ingest a total of about 600 g in 24 h.

Additional or underpinning information (Coyle, 1991)

- After exhaustive exercise, muscle glycogen synthesis needs of ~ 100 mmol $\cdot$ kg^{-1} occur at an average rate of ~ 5 mmol $\cdot$ kg$^{-1} \cdot$ h^{-1}, requiring ~ 20 h for recovery (normalization) of glycogen stores.
- The intake of carbohydrate in the first 2 h after exercise allows a somewhat faster rate of glycogen synthesis (i.e. 7–8 mmol $\cdot$ kg$^{-1} \cdot$ h^{-1}) than normal. The athlete should ingest sufficient carbohydrate as soon after exercise as is practical, the most important reason being to start recovery as soon as possible and maximize the time for glycogen synthesis.
- Glycogen synthesis over the day is similar whether carbohydrate is consumed as large meals or as a series of smaller snacks.
- There is no difference in glycogen synthesis when liquid or solid forms of carbohydrate are consumed; however, practical issues may dictate the choices of athletes.
- Carbohydrate-rich foods with a moderate to high glycaemic index provide a readily available source of carbohydrate for muscle glycogen synthesis. Carbohydrate-rich foods with a low glycaemic index should not make up more than a third of recovery meals.

---

of glycogen recovery, glycogen storage occurs mainly in the pool of macroglycogen: a glycogen molecule with greater amounts of glucose relative to the glycogenin core. An increase in the macroglycogen pool appears to account for glycogen supercompensation in the muscle after 2–3 days of high carbohydrate intake (Adamo *et al.*, 1998). Future studies may allow us to exploit this information, and determine new factors and strategies that enhance the metabolic availability of glycogen pools or increase storage. In the meantime, however, we will consider glycogen as a generic storage form for carbohydrate within the muscle and liver, and discuss the factors that influence restoration of glycogen following exercise depletion.

Amount of dietary carbohydrate

Typically, the most important dietary factor affecting muscle glycogen storage is the amount of carbohydrate consumed. Data from various studies that have monitored muscle glycogen storage after 24 h of recovery from glycogen-depleting exercise are summarized in Fig. 1, plotting glycogen storage against dietary carbohydrate intake. Despite differences between study methodologies such as the calibre of the athletes, the size of their active muscle mass and type of carbohydrate feedings, these data suggest that there is a direct and positive relationship between the quantity of dietary carbohydrate and post-exercise glycogen storage, at least until the muscle storage capacity or threshold has been reached. Only two studies have directly investigated this relationship by feeding different amounts of carbohydrate to trained individuals over a 24-h recovery period; the results of these studies show an increase in glycogen storage with increasing carbohydrate intake and a glycogen storage threshold at a daily carbohydrate intake of around $7–10$ $g \cdot kg^{-1}$ BM (where BM = body mass) (Costill *et al.*, 1981; Burke *et al.*, 1995).

Although these figures have evolved into the recommended carbohydrate intakes for optimal muscle glycogen recovery, it is worth noting that they are derived from studies of glycogen storage during a passive recovery period. As a result, requirements for total daily carbohydrate intake may be lower for athletes whose training programmes do not challenge daily glycogen stores, but may also be higher for some individuals or some situations. For example, athletes who undertake strenuous training or competition programmes may also need to meet the daily fuel requirements of their continued exercise in addition to post-exercise recovery. For example, well-trained cyclists undertaking 2 h of training each day were found to have higher muscle glycogen stores after a week of a daily carbohydrate intake of 12 $g \cdot kg^{-1}$ BM, than when consuming the 'recommended' carbohydrate intake of 10 $g \cdot kg^{-1}$ BM $\cdot day^{-1}$ (Coyle *et al.*, 2001).

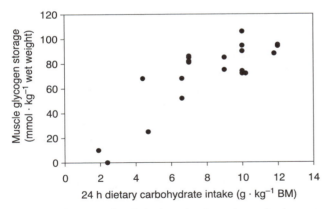

Figure 1. Amount of carbohydrate intake and muscle glycogen storage. The relationship between daily carbohydrate intake and muscle glycogen storage during 24 h of passive recovery from glycogen-depleting exercise is plotted from data taken from Burke *et al.* (1993, 1995, 1996, 2003), Costill *et al.* (1981), Kiens and Richter (1998), Parkin *et al.* (1997) and Starling *et al.* (1997). Taken together, these data suggest an increase in glycogen storage with increasing dietary carbohydrate intake, until the muscle storage threshold is reached.

Furthermore, Tour de France cyclists riding at least 6 h each day have been reported to consume carbohydrate intakes of 12–13 g·kg^{-1} BM·day^{-1} (Saris et al., 1989). Increased carbohydrate intake may also be useful in the case of muscle damage (e.g. after eccentric exercise), which typically impairs the rate of post-exercise glycogen resynthesis. Costill and co-workers (1990) reported that low rates of glycogen restoration in damaged muscles might be partially over-come by increased amounts of carbohydrate intake during the first 24 h of recovery.

The 1991 guidelines for carbohydrate intake during the first 4–6 h of recovery (viz. ~1 g·kg^{-1} BM every 2 h) are based on studies that failed to find differ-ences in post-exercise glycogen storage following carbohydrate intakes of 0.7 and 1.4 g·kg^{-1} BM (Blom et al., 1987), or between 1.5 and 3.0 g·kg^{-1} BM (Ivy et al., 1988b), fed at intervals of 2 h. However, more recent investigations of feeding during the first 4 h of recovery (Doyle et al., 1993; Piehl Aulin et al., 2000; van Hall et al., 2000) have achieved glycogen synthesis rates of up to 10–11 mmol·kg^{-1} ww·h^{-1} (where ww = wet weight), or about 30% higher than values previously reported in the literature. Features of these recent studies include larger carbohydrate intakes (e.g. 1.0–1.8 g·kg^{-1} BM·h^{-1}) and repeated small feedings (e.g. intake every 15–60 min) rather than single or several large meals. Unfortunately, because these studies did not make a direct comparison between glycogen storage and different amounts of carbo-hydrate and different feeding schedules, it is difficult to draw final conclusions about optimal carbohydrate intake in the early recovery phase. Nevertheless, the results of other studies (van Loon et al., 2000; Jentjens et al., 2001) suggest that the threshold for early glycogen recovery (0–4 h) is reached by a carbo-hydrate feeding schedule that provides 1.2 g·kg^{-1} BM·h^{-1}, based on the failure to increase muscle glycogen storage when extra energy (protein) was consumed.

Timing of carbohydrate intake

The highest rates of muscle glycogen storage occur during the first hour after exercise (Ivy et al., 1988a), due to activation of glycogen synthase by glycogen depletion (Wojtaszewski et al., 2001), and exercise-induced increases in insulin sensitivity (Richter et al., 1988) and permeability of the muscle cell membrane to glucose. Carbohydrate feeding immediately after exercise appears to take advantage of these effects, as shown by higher rates of glycogen storage (7.7 mmol·kg^{-1} ww·h^{-1}) during the first 2 h of recovery, slowing thereafter to the more typical rates of storage (4.3 mmol·kg^{-1} ww·h^{-1}) (Ivy et al., 1988a). The most important finding of this study, however, is that failure to consume carbohydrate in the immediate phase of post-exercise recovery leads to very low rates of glycogen restoration until feeding occurs (Ivy et al., 1988a). Therefore, early intake of carbohydrate after strenuous exercise is valu-able because it provides an immediate source of substrate to the muscle cell to start effective recovery, as well as taking advantage of a period of moderately enhanced glycogen synthesis. Although early feeding may be important when there is only 4–8 h between exercise sessions (Ivy *et al.*, 1988a), it may have less impact over a longer recovery period. For example, Parkin and co-workers (1997) found no difference in glycogen storage after 8 and 24 h of recovery whether carbohydrate-rich eating was begun immediately after exercise or delayed for 2 h (see Fig. 2). Overall it would appear that when the interval between exercise sessions is short, the athlete should maximize the effective recovery time by beginning carbohydrate intake as soon as possible. However, when longer recovery periods are available, athletes can choose their preferred meal schedule as long as total carbohydrate intake goals are achieved. It is not always practical to consume substantial meals or snacks immediately after the finish of a strenuous workout.

Whether carbohydrate is best consumed in large meals or as a series of snacks has also been studied. Studies examining 24-h recovery have found that restoration of muscle glycogen is the same whether a given amount of carbohydrate is fed as two or seven meals (Costill *et al.*, 1981), or as four large meals or 16 one-hourly snacks (Burke *et al.*, 1996). In the latter study, similar muscle glycogen storage was achieved despite marked differences in blood glucose and insulin profiles over 24 h (Burke *et al.*, 1996). In contrast, very high rates of glycogen

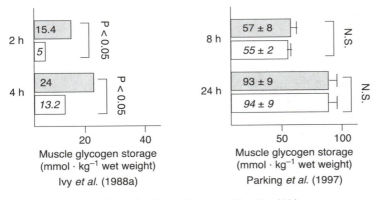

Figure 2. Timing of carbohydrate intake and glycogen storage. Delaying intake of carbohydrate until 2 h after the finish of a prolonged exercise session has a significant effect on short recovery periods (up to 6–8 h). Since effective refuelling does not occur until substantial amounts of carbohydrate are consumed, recovery after 4 h is impaired with delayed feeding compared with intake of the same amount of carbohydrate immediately after exercise and during recovery (Ivy *et al.*, 1988a). When recovery periods are long enough (8–24 h), immediate intake of carbohydrate provides no further enhancement of glycogen storage as long as total carbohydrate intake is adequate (Parkin *et al.*, 1997).

synthesis during the first 4–6 h of recovery have been reported when large amounts of carbohydrate were fed at 15–30 min intervals (Doyle *et al.*, 1993; van Hall *et al.*, 2000; van Loon *et al.*, 2000; Jentjens *et al.*, 2001), and attributed to the higher sustained insulin and glucose profiles achieved by such a feeding protocol. However, as previously noted, these outcomes were compared with other literature values of post-exercise glycogen restoration rather than directly tested against a control amount of carbohydrate fed in less frequent meals. One way to reconcile these apparently conflicting results is to propose that the effects of enhanced insulin and glucose concentrations on glycogen storage are most important during the first hours of recovery or when total carbohydrate intake is below the threshold of maximal glycogen storage. However, during longer periods of recovery or when total carbohydrate intake is above this threshold, manipulations of plasma substrates and hormones within physiological ranges do not add further benefit.

In summary, it would appear that meeting total carbohydrate requirements is more important than the pattern of intake, at least for long-term recovery, and the athlete is advised to choose a food schedule that is practical and comfortable. A more frequent intake of smaller snacks may be useful in overcoming the gastric discomfort often associated with eating large amounts of bulky high-carbohydrate foods, but may also provide direct benefits to glycogen storage during the early recovery phase.

Type of carbohydrate intake

Since glycogen storage is influenced both by insulin and a rapid supply of glucose substrate, it is logical that carbohydrate sources with a moderate to high glycaemic index (GI) would enhance post-exercise refuelling. This hypothesis has been confirmed in the case of single nutrient feedings of mono- and disaccharides; intake of glucose and sucrose after prolonged exercise both produce higher rates of muscle glycogen recovery than the low GI sugar, fructose (Blom *et al.*, 1987). Unfortunately, early investigations of real foods (Costill *et al.*, 1981; Roberts *et al.*, 1988) used the structural classification of 'simple' and 'complex or starchy' carbohydrates to construct recovery diets; the conflicting results of these studies are probably due to the failure to achieve a real or consistent difference in the glycaemic index of the diets. The first fully reported comparison of foods based on published GI values found greater glycogen storage during 24 h of post-exercise recovery with a carbohydrate-rich diet based on high GI foods compared with an identical amount of carbohydrate eaten in the form of low GI foods (Burke *et al.*, 1993). However, the magnitude of increase in glycogen storage (~30%) was substantially greater than the difference in 24-h blood glucose and insulin profiles; the meal consumed immediately after exercise produced a large glycaemic and insulinaemic response, independent of the glycaemic index of the carbohydrate consumed, which overshadowed the differences in response to the rest of the diet. Other studies have confirmed an exaggerated glycaemic response to carbohydrate consumed immediately after exercise compared with the same feeding consumed at rest; this occurs as a result of greater gut glucose output and greater hepatic glucose escape (Rose *et al.*, 2001). Increased muscle glucose uptake also occurs under these conditions, favouring glycogen storage. In summary, although it would appear that high GI carbohydrate foods achieve better post-exercise glycogen storage, this cannot be totally explained in terms of an enhanced glucose and insulin response.

An additional mechanism to explain less efficient glycogen storage with low GI carbohydrate-rich foods is that a considerable amount of the carbohydrate in these foods may be malabsorbed (Wolever *et al.*, 1986; Jenkins *et al.*, 1987). Indeed, Joszi and co-workers (1996) theorized that the poor digestibility of a high amylose starch mixture (low GI) was responsible for lower muscle glycogen storage observed during 13 h of post-exercise recovery compared with intake of glucose, maltodextrins and a high amylopectin starch (all high GI). They observed that indigestible carbohydrate forms provide a poor substrate for muscle glycogen resynthesis and overestimate the available carbohydrate consumed by individuals (Joszi *et al.*, 1996). This issue requires further study in relation to real foods. Nevertheless, a study of chronic exposure to a lower GI diet in recreationally active people found a decline in muscle glycogen storage over 30 days compared both with pre-trial values and values at the end of a high GI trial (Kiens and Richter, 1996). Thus, it would appear prudent to allow low GI foods to play only a minor role in post-exercise recovery meals; this is generally the case in Western eating patterns.

Effect of gender

Most studies of glycogen storage have been conducted with males, based on the assumption that the results will also apply to female athletes. There is some evidence that the menstrual status of female athletes affects glycogen storage, with greater storage of glycogen occurring during the luteal phase rather than the follicular phase (Nicklas *et al.*, 1989; Hackney *et al.*, 1994). Several studies of carbohydrate loading (i.e. prolonged glycogen storage) have provided direct or indirect evidence that female athletes are less responsive than their male counterparts (Tarnopolsky *et al.*, 1995; Walker *et al.*, 2000). However, the criticism of at least one study is that a methodology that simply requires individuals to increase carbohydrate intake as a proportion of 'usual' (self-reported) energy intake will result in a considerably smaller increase in carbohydrate intake, both in absolute amounts and relative to body mass, for females who are restrained eaters (Tarnopolsky *et al.*, 1995). A further study by this group of workers found that female athletes needed to increase both carbohydrate *and* energy intake before a significant increase in glycogen storage was achieved (Tarnopolsky *et al.*, 2001). Regarding the acute recovery period, female athletes in the mid-follicular phase of their menstrual cycle have produced identical rates of glycogen storage to male athletes after intakes of matched amounts (per kilogram of body mass) of carbohydrate or a carbohydrate–protein drink (Tarnopolsky *et al.*, 1997).

Effect of energy intake and co-ingestion of other nutrients

It would appear that the relationship between carbohydrate intake and glycogen storage is underpinned by consideration of total energy intake (Tarnopolsky *et al.*, 2001). The simplest way to consider this relationship is that dietary intake must provide for the body's immediate fuel requirements as well as storage opportunities. It is likely that during energy restriction, greater proportions of available carbohydrate substrates (e.g. dietary carbohydrate) are oxidized to meet immediate energy needs, whereas carbohydrate consumed during a period of energy balance or surplus may be available for storage within the muscle and liver. But it is also possible that the co-ingestion of other macronutrients, either present in carbohydrate-rich foods or consumed at the same meal, may have additional effects on muscle glycogen storage, independently of their effect on increasing total energy intake. While this hypothesis has not been tested systematically, factors that might directly or indirectly affect glycogen storage include the provision of gluconeogenic substrates, as well as effects on digestion, insulin secretion or the satiety of meals. The co-ingestion of protein with carbohydrate meals has received most attention in terms of glycogen recovery and has provided a source of some debate, with some studies reporting both an increase in glycogen storage when protein is added to a carbohydrate feeding (Zawadzki *et al.*, 1992; van Loon *et al.*, 2000; Ivy *et al.*, 2002) and others finding no effect (Tarnopolsky *et al.*, 1997; Roy and Tarnopolsky, 1998; Carrithers *et al.*, 2000; van Hall *et al.*, 2000).

Many of the conflicting results among studies, however, can probably be explained by differences in experimental design, including the frequency of supplementation, and the amounts of carbohydrate and protein provided. For example, in studies demonstrating that the addition of protein to a carbohydrate supplement will enhance muscle glycogen storage, feeding intervals of 2 h were used (Zawadzki *et al.*, 1992; Ivy *et al.*, 2002). Those studies that did not demonstrate a benefit of protein used feeding intervals of 15–30 min (Tarnopolsky *et al.*, 1997; Carrithers *et al.*, 2000; van Hall *et al.*, 2000; Jentjens *et al.*, 2001) and generally fed a high total amount of carbohydrate (van Hall *et al.*, 2000; Jentjens *et al.*, 2001), though in some studies a low amount of protein (Tarnopolsky *et al.*, 1997; Carrithers *et al.*, 2000). Regardless of the differences in experimental design, most evidence suggests that feeding a high amount of carbohydrate at frequent intervals negates the benefits of added protein. However, the evidence is compelling that the co-ingestion of protein with carbohydrate will increase the efficiency of muscle glycogen storage when the amount of carbohydrate ingested is below the threshold for maximal glycogen synthesis or when feeding intervals are more than 1 h apart (Zawadzki *et al.*,

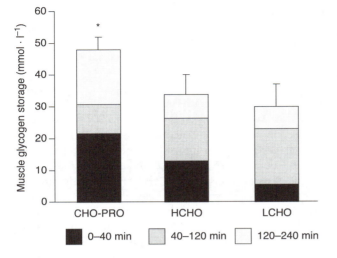

Figure 3. Muscle glycogen storage following co-ingestion of carbohydrate and protein. Muscle glycogen storage at 0–40, 40–120 and 120–240 min of recovery from an exhaustive cycling exercise. Treatments were carbohydrate–protein (CHO-PRO), isocaloric carbohydrate (HCHO) and isocarbohydrate (LCHO) supplements provided immediately after exercise and after 2 h of exercise. *Significantly different than HCHO and LCHO (Ivy *et al.*, 2002).

1992; Ivy *et al.*, 2002; van Loon *et al.*, 2000). The effectiveness of protein to enhance muscle glycogen storage appears limited to the first hour after supplementation (Ivy *et al.*, 2002). As illustrated in Fig. 3, glycogen storage during the first 40 min of recovery after exercise was twice as fast after a carbohydrate–protein feeding than after an isoenergetic carbohydrate feeding, and four times faster than after a carbohydrate feeding of the same carbohydrate concentration. This trend also continued following the second feeding 2 h into recovery. These results have important implications for sports that have very short recovery periods during competition, such as soccer and ice hockey.

It is still uncertain whether the enhanced rates of glycogen storage due to co-ingestion of protein and carbohydrate may be achieved via the increased insulin response from protein *per se*, or as a result of the increase in energy intake. Thus it is prudent to conclude at this time that the presence of other macronutrients with carbohydrate feedings does not substantially alter muscle glycogen synthesis when total carbohydrate intake is at the level for the glycogen storage threshold. However, when the athlete's energy intake or food availability does not allow them to consume such amounts of carbohydrate, the presence of protein in post-exercise meals and snacks may enhance overall glycogen recovery. In fact, intake of protein in recovery meals is recommended to enhance net protein balance, tissue repair and adaptations involving synthesis of new proteins (see Tipton and Wolfe, 2004). The consumption of excessively large amounts of protein and fat in an athlete's diet, however, is discouraged because it may displace carbohydrate foods within the athlete's energy requirements and gastric comfort, thereby indirectly interfering with glycogen storage by preventing adequate carbohydrate intake.

Alcohol is another nutrient of interest in terms of glycogen recovery, since there is evidence that some athletes, particularly in team sports, consume alcohol in large amounts in the post-exercise period (Burke *et al.*, 2003). Rat studies have shown that intragastric administration of alcohol interferes with glycogen storage during 30 min of recovery from high-intensity exercise in oxidative but not non-oxidative fibres (Peters *et al.*, 1996). Separate studies of 8 h and 24 h of recovery in well-trained cyclists who consumed alcohol immediately after an exercise bout showed that muscle glycogen storage was impaired during both periods when alcohol was used for isoenergetic displacement of carbohydrate intake from the recovery diet (Burke *et al.*, 1996). Evidence for a direct effect of elevated blood alcohol concentrations on muscle glycogen synthesis was unclear, but it appeared that if an immediate impairment of glycogen synthesis existed, it might be compensated by adequate carbohydrate intake and a longer recovery period (Burke *et al.*, 1996). It is likely that the most important effects of alcohol intake on glycogen resynthesis are indirect – by interfering with the athlete's ability, or interest, to achieve the recommended amounts of carbohydrate required for optimal glycogen restoration. Athletes are therefore encouraged to follow the guidelines for sensible use of alcohol in sport (Burke and Maughan, 2000), in conjunction with the well-supported recommendations for recovery eating.

Update on guidelines for carbohydrate needs for daily training

Previously developed dietary guidelines for athletes have been unanimous in their recommendation of high carbohydrate intakes in the everyday or training diet, based on the perceived benefits of promoting optimal recovery of muscle glycogen stores between training sessions (Devlin and Williams, 1991; Ekblom and Williams, 1994; Maughan and Horton, 1995; ACSM *et al.*, 2000). An update on nutritional strategies to achieve this goal is summarized in Table 2, but before this can be accepted as a key principle of the proposed new guidelines of the International Olympic Committee, it is important to recognize that the advice has been criticized on two separate accounts. The first criticism is the apparent failure of athletes to achieve such carbohydrate-rich diets in training (Noakes, 1997), with the rationale that if it were advantageous to training adaptations and performance, we would expect athletes to follow the practice. A review of the dietary surveys of serious athletes published since the announcement of the 1991 sports nutrition guidelines found that the mean values for the reported daily carbohydrate intake of athletes was about 50–55% of total energy intake (Burke *et al.*, 2001) compared with the 60–70% of energy intake

Table 2. Revised guidelines for the intake of CHO in the everyday or training diets of athletes

---

Recommendations for

- Athletes should aim to achieve carbohydrate intakes to meet the fuel requirements of their training programme and to optimize restoration of muscle glycogen stores between workouts. General recommendations can be provided, but should be fine-tuned with individual consideration of total energy needs, specific training needs and feedback from training performance:
  - ○ Immediate recovery after exercise (0–4 h): 1.0–1.2 $g \cdot kg^{-1} \cdot h^{-1}$ consumed at frequent intervals
  - ○ Daily recovery: moderate duration/low-intensity training: 5–7 $g \cdot kg^{-1} \cdot day^{-1}$
  - ○ Daily recovery: moderate to heavy endurance training: 7–12 $g \cdot kg^{-1} \cdot day^{-1}$
  - ○ Daily recovery: extreme exercise programme (4–6 h + per day): 10–12 + $g \cdot kg^{-1} \cdot day^{-1}$
- It is valuable to choose nutrient-rich carbohydrate foods and to add other foods to recovery meals and snacks to provide a good source of protein and other nutrients. These nutrients may assist in other recovery processes and, in the case of protein, may promote additional glycogen recovery when carbohydrate intake is suboptimal or when frequent snacking is not possible.
- When the period between exercise sessions is < 8 h, the athlete should begin carbohydrate intake as soon as practical after the first workout to maximize the effective recovery time between sessions. There may be some advantages in meeting carbohydrate intake targets as a series of snacks during the early recovery phase.
- During longer recovery periods (24 h), the athlete should organize the pattern and timing of carbohydrate-rich meals and snacks according to what is practical and comfortable for their individual situation. There is no difference in glycogen synthesis when liquid or solid forms of carbohydrate are consumed.
- Carbohydrate-rich foods with a moderate to high glycaemic index provide a readily available source of carbohydrate for muscle glycogen synthesis, and should be the major carbohydrate choices in recovery meals.
- Adequate energy intake is important for optimal glycogen recovery; the restrained eating practices of some athletes, particularly females, make it difficult to meet carbohydrate intake targets and to optimize glycogen storage from this intake.

Recommendations against

- Guidelines for carbohydrate (or other macronutrients) should not be provided in terms of percentage contributions to total dietary energy intake. Such recommendations are neither user-friendly nor strongly related to the muscle's absolute needs for fuel.
- The athlete should not consume excessive amounts of alcohol during the recovery period, since it is likely to interfere with their ability or interest to follow guidelines for post-exercise eating. The athlete should follow sensible drinking practices at all times, but especially in the period after exercise.

---

suggested in the guidelines (Devlin and Williams, 1991). However, the apparent mismatch between sports nutrition guidelines and the real-life dietary patterns of athletes can largely be explained as a result of confusion arising from the terminology used to make these recommendations (Burke *et al.*, 2001).

The 1991 summary guidelines for carbohydrate intake for athletes (Devlin and Williams, 1991) follow the traditional terminology used in population dietary guidelines, where recommendations for the intake of macronutrients are expressed as the proportion of dietary energy that they should typically contribute. However, population guidelines for carbohydrate result from taking a number of issues into account for a generic group of people (e.g. meeting requirements for protein, achieving benefits from reducing fat intake) rather than trying to meet specific muscle fuel needs for a specialized subgroup or, more particularly, for an individual. The athlete's fuel needs are better estimated from more direct information, such as the carbohydrate intake required to optimize glycogen recovery, or the carbohydrate expenditure of the training programme. Such estimates of carbohydrate needs should be provided relative to the body mass of the athlete to roughly account for the size of the muscle mass that must be fuelled. General guidelines derived from such information are suggested in Table 2, but should also be considered as 'ball-park' ranges that can be fine-tuned for the individual athlete with more specific knowledge of their actual training programme, past and present response to training and their total energy budget. The dietary surveys of athletes published over the past decade show mean values of reported daily carbohydrate intake to be 7.6 and 5.8 g·kg^{-1} BM for male endurance and non-endurance athletes, respectively, and 5.7 and 4.6 g·kg^{-1} BM for female endurance and non-endurance athletes, respectively (Burke *et al.*, 2001). These values suggest the daily carbohydrate intakes of the typical male athlete fall within the suggested ranges for fuel needs (Table 2), especially if the usual feature of under-reporting on dietary records is taken into account. Of course, these mean estimates do not guarantee that all athletic groups or specific athletes meet these recommended intakes or, indeed, meet their actual fuel requirements; such determinations can only be made on an individual basis. However, female athletes are at higher risk of carbohydrate intakes below these ranges, largely as a result of lower energy intakes.

The use of energy ratio terminology to recommend or assess the carbohydrate intake of athletes should be actively discouraged. Examination of dietary survey data from endurance-trained athletes (1970–2001) provides clear evidence that carbohydrate intake expressed as a percentage of dietary energy and intakes expressed as grams relative to body mass are not interchangeable concepts (see Fig. 4). Among groups of male athletes, there is evidence of a loose but positive correlation between reported intakes of carbohydrate (grams per kilogram) and the energy contributed by carbohydrate in the diet. In other words, male athletes who change their eating patterns to increase the energy contribution of carbohydrate in their diets are likely to increase their carbohydrate intake

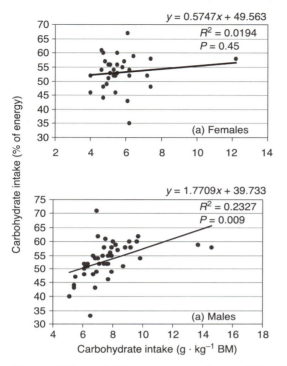

$$y = 0.5747x + 49.563$$
$$R^2 = 0.0194$$
$$P = 0.45$$

(a) Females

$$y = 1.7709x + 39.733$$
$$R^2 = 0.2327$$
$$P = 0.009$$

(a) Males

Carbohydrate intake (% of energy)

Carbohydrate intake (g · kg^{-1} BM)

Figure 4. Relationship between reported mean daily carbohydrate intake, represented as g · kg^{-1} BM and percent of energy, from dietary surveys of groups of serious endurance athletes (taken from Burke *et al.*, 2001). Each data point represents the mean value reported for a separate group of athletes.

per kilogram of body mass; however, targeting a particular carbohydrate:energy ratio will not guarantee that specific fuel needs based on grams per kilogram of body mass are achieved. In contrast, there is no correlation between the carbohydrate:energy ratio in the diets reported by female endurance athletes and their total carbohydrate intake (grams per kilogram of body mass), due to the confounding issue of restricted energy intake in some individuals or groups.

Do high carbohydrate diets really enhance training adaptations?

The second, and more important, criticism of the recommendation for high carbohydrate intakes lies with the failure of longitudinal studies to show clear and consistent benefits to training adaptations and performance compared with moderate carbohydrate diets (see Table 3). Although there is clear evidence of superior recovery of muscle glycogen with a higher carbohydrate intake, a minority of the available studies show enhancement of training

Table 3. Longitudinal studies comparing high carbohydrate (CHO) intakes (HCHO) and moderate carbohydrate intakes (MCHO) on training adaptation and performance of athletes undertaking intensive training

Study	Athletes	Duration of study (days)	CHO intake (g · kg^{-1} · day^{-1})	Effect on muscle glycogen	Performance protocol	Performance advantage with HCHO
Costill et al. (1988)	Well-trained swimmers (12 M)	10 days; participants self-selected into two dietary groups (8 HCHO and 4 MCHO)	8.2 vs 5.3	Declined in MCHO; maintained in HCHO	Training; doubling of usual 1.5 h · day^{-1} training programme Performance battery: power (swim bench); 2 × 25 yards freestyle swim with 2–3 min recovery interval; $\dot{V}O_{2max}$ in pool; swimming efficiency at submaximal pace	No for final performance. No difference in 25 yards swim, swim power or $\dot{V}O_{2max}$ from pre-trial or between groups. However, stroke efficiency reduced in MCHO Yes for training performance. MCHO group reported 'chronic fatigue' during training programme
Lamb et al. (1990)	Well-trained swimmers (14 M)	9 days; crossover design	12.1 vs 6.5	Not available	2 × daily training sessions. Intervals over a variety of distances +1500 m and 3000 m timed for afternoon sessions during last 5 days	No. No difference in mean swimming times over range of distances between diets
Kirwan et al. (1988)	Well-trained runners (10 M)	5 days: crossover design	8.0 vs 3.9	Declined in both groups but greater reduction in MCHO	Training increased by 150% for 5 days. Economy tested on treadmill at two speeds on days 4 and 6 Overnight fasted	Yes. Reduction in running economy with MCHO
Sherman et al. (1993)	Trained runners (2 × 9 M)	7 days; parallel group design	10 vs 5	Declined in MCHO; maintained in HCHO	2 × time to exhaustion on a treadmill at 80% $\dot{V}O_{2max}$ with 5 min recovery period. Trials undertaken at end of day after 1 h training	No. No difference in endurance between groups during either run. Sum time = 613 ± 36 s and 560 ± 106 s for MCHO and HCHO respectively (not significant)

Study	Subjects	Duration; design		Muscle glycogen	Protocol	Conclusion
Achten et al. (2003)	Well-trained runners (7 M)	4 days + 7 days intensified training; crossover design	8.5 vs 5.4	Decrease in muscle glycogen utilization during training sessions at 58 and 77% $\dot{V}O_{2max}$ during MCHO trial compared with HCHO	Pre-load + 8-km treadmill time-trial on days 1, 5, 8 and 11; 16-km road time-trial on days 6, 7, 9 and 10 *Overnight fasted*	**Yes.** Intensified training led to deterioration of 8-km time-trial performance by 61 s in HCHO and 155 s in MCHO, and deterioration in 16-km time-trial performance in MCHO only. HCHO reduces symptoms of over-reaching during intensified training compared with MCHO, but does not prevent it entirely
Simonsen et al. (1991)	Collegiate rowers (12 M, 10 F)	28 days; parallel group design	10 vs 5	MCHO allowed maintenance of muscle glycogen stores, while HCHO allowed an increase in stores	3 × 2500-m rowing ergometer time-trial with 8 min recovery interval undertaken on days 1, 3 and 5 of each week. *Trials undertaken at evening workout*	**Yes.** Power output maintained during ergometer rowing time-trial over the course of MCHO, leading to overall improvement of 1.6% at end of 4 weeks. Improvement in power output in HCHO over same time-frame = 10.7%
Sherman et al. (1993)	Trained cyclists (2 × 9 M)	7 days; parallel group design	10 vs 5	Declined in MCHO; maintained in HCHO	2 × time to exhaustion on cycle ergometer at 80% $\dot{V}O_{2max}$ with 5 min recovery period. *Trials undertaken at end of day after 1 h training*	**No.** No difference between groups on endurance during either bout. Sum time = 550 ± 85 s and 613 ± 45 s for MCHO and HCHO respectively (not significant)
Vogt et al. (2003)	Well-trained duathletes (11 M)	35 days; crossover design	6.9 vs 3.6	Maintained on both diets	$\dot{V}O_{2max}$, cycling time-trial undertaken after progressive submaximal pre-load; outdoor 21-km run (all undertaken on separate days). *Trials undertaken post-meal (composition of meal varied with dietary treatment)*	**No.** No difference in aerobic capacity, cycling time-trial power or half-marathon run time between diets (e.g. 21-km run = 80 min 12 s ± 86 s and 80 min 24 s ± 82 s for HCHO and MCHO)

Abbreviations: M = male; F = female.

outcomes (Simonsen *et al.*, 1991; Achten *et al.*, 2003). The most recent of these studies creates considerable interest with its finding that a higher carbohydrate intake was able to reduce, but not entirely prevent, the 'over-reaching' syndrome that can occur when a period of intensified training is undertaken (Achten *et al.*, 2003). However, it is curious that benefits from high carbohydrate eating have not been a universal outcome from training studies. Several methodological issues are important, including the overlap between what is considered a 'moderate' and 'high' carbohydrate in various studies. Other important issues are whether sufficient time was allowed for differences in the training responses of athletes to lead to significant differences in the study performance outcome, and whether the protocol used to measure performance was sufficiently reliable to detect small but real improvements that would be of significance to a competitive athlete (Hopkins *et al.*, 1999).

One possible conclusion from the available studies of chronic dietary patterns and exercise performance is that athletes can adapt to the lower muscle glycogen stores resulting from moderate carbohydrate intakes such that it does not impair training or competition outcomes. However, no study has shown that moderate carbohydrate intakes promote superior training adaptations and performance compared with higher carbohydrate diets. Clearly, further research needs to be undertaken, using specialized and rigorous protocols, to examine further the issue of chronic carbohydrate intake in heavily training athletes. Since such studies require painstaking control over a long period, it is not surprising that there are few in the literature. In the meantime, although the lack of clear literature support is curious, the evidence from studies of acute carbohydrate intake and exercise performance remains our best estimate of the chronic carbohydrate needs of athletes.

Fat as a muscle substrate

Since the adipose fat stores in the body are relatively large even in the leanest athlete, the replacement of the fat oxidized during an exercise session has not been thought to limit performance. The 1991 consensus statement did not make any special recommendations in relation to dietary fat and recovery. Since that time, however, and in spite of methodological problems of undertaking measurements of this substrate (Watt *et al.*, 2002), there has been an increased interest in the utilization of intramuscular triacylglycerol (IMTG) stores during exercise and their replacement during recovery. There is now consensus that IMTGs provide a potentially important energy source for the contracting muscle (Watt *et al.*, 2002), and emerging evidence that the consumption of a high carbohydrate/low fat diet in the recovery period after prolonged exercise may fail to provide for efficient recovery of this substrate (Decombaz *et al.*, 2001; van Loon *et al.*, 2003). Furthermore, one of the studies reviewed in the previous section identified that a moderate carbohydrate diet allowed a two-fold increase in IMTG stores compared with a high carbohydrate diet (Vogt *et al.*, 2003). The importance of the replenishment of IMTG for the performance of exercise is presently unknown, but is discussed in greater detail in the context of training adaptations by Spriet and Gibala (2004). The present review will conclude with a brief exploration of the possibility that chronic adaptation to high fat diets during the training phase may confer an advantage to performance by decreasing the muscle's reliance on its limited glycogen stores as an exercise fuel.

Effect of high fat/low carbohydrate diets on training adaptations and performance

The effect of consuming a high fat/low carbohydrate diet for 1–3 days, while continuing to exercise, is to lower resting muscle and liver glycogen stores, resulting in reduced exercise capacity and endurance (Bergstrom *et al.*, 1967; Starling *et al.*, 1997; Pitsiladis and Maughan, 1999). This impairment in performance is likely to result from a combination of the premature depletion of (lowered) muscle glycogen stores and the absence of any worthwhile increase in the capacity for fat utilization during exercise to compensate for the reduction in available carbohydrate fuel. In contrast, there is evidence that a longer period (>7 days) of adherence to a high fat/low carbohydrate diet causes metabolic adaptations that substantially enhance fat oxidation during exercise and, to a large extent, compensate for the reduced carbohydrate availability. In fact, many 'popular' diet books claim that 'fat loading' strategies enhance performance capabilities of endurance and ultra-endurance athletes by making them better able to 'tap into body fat stores' (Sears, 1995).

Studies in which trained individuals have been exposed to a high fat diet (>60–65% of dietary energy [E]) for 5–28 days show markedly higher rates of fat oxidation and reduced rates of muscle glycogen use during submaximal exercise compared with consumption of an isoenergetic high carbohydrate diet, despite the already enhanced capacity for fat oxidation expected in the trained individual (Phinney *et al.*, 1983; Lambert *et al.*, 1994; Goedecke *et al.*, 1999). However, examination of the performance outcomes from these studies shows either a lack of a performance benefit (see Table 4) or methodological/design flaws that require a conservative and cautious interpretation of the results (for a review, see Burke and Hawley, 2002). For example, while the study of Phinney *et al.* (1983), in which five well-trained cyclists were tested before and after 4 weeks of adaptation to a high fat (85% E)/low carbohydrate (<20 g · day^{-1}) diet, is frequently cited in support of performance enhancement after fat-loading, the participants actually achieved *similar* endurance times under both experimental conditions. Furthermore, the group results were skewed by an abnormally large improvement in the performance of one cyclist: the remaining four cyclists showed little change or, indeed, an impairment of exercise capacity after the high fat treatment.

Table 4. Longitudinal studies comparing long-term adaptation to high fat/low carbohydrate (HFAT) intakes and moderate to high carbohydrate (CHO) intakes on endurance performance in well-trained individuals

Study	Athletes	Fat adaptation protocol	Performance protocol	Performance advantage with HFAT
Phinney et al. (1983)	Well-trained cyclists (5 M); crossover design with order effect (control diet first)	28 days; CHO (57% carbohydrate), then 28 days HFAT (fat = 85% E, carbohydrate = <20 g·day^{-1})	Cycling time to fatigue at 80% $\dot{V}O_{2max}$ Overnight-fasted + no carbohydrate intake during exercise	No. No difference in time to fatigue between trials (151 vs 147 min for HFAT vs CHO). However, group data skewed by performance of one participant who increased time to fatigue by 156% on the fat trial
O'Keefe et al. (1989)	Moderately trained cyclists (7 F); crossover design	7 days; HFAT (fat = 59% E, carbohydrate = 1.2 g·kg^{-1} BM); CHO (carbohydrate = 6.4 g·kg^{-1} BM)	Cycling time to fatigue at 80% $\dot{V}O_{2max}$ 3–4 h post-meal, no carbohydrate intake during exercise	No. In fact, performance deterioration with HFAT. Time to fatigue reduced by 47% on HFAT trial
Lambert et al. (1994)	Well-trained cyclists (5 M); crossover design	14 days; HFAT (fat = 67% E, carbohydrate = 17% E*); CHO (carbohydrate = 74% E*)	Cycling time to fatigue at 60% $\dot{V}O_{2max}$ (preceded by Wingate test and time to fatigue at 90% $\dot{V}O_{2max}$)Overnight-fasted + no carbohydrate intake during exercise	Yes. Time to fatigue increased by 87% on HFAT trial. No significant differences in performance between trials on preceding high-intensity cycle tests
Goedecke et al. (1999)	Well-trained cyclists (2 × 8 M); parallel group design	15 days; HFAT (fat = 69% E, carbohydrate = 2.2 g·kg^{-1} BM); CHO (carbohydrate = 5.5 g·kg^{-1} BM)	150 min cycling at 70% $\dot{V}O_{2max}$ + ~60-min time-trial (time to complete 40 km) MCT intake 1.5 h pre-event (~14 g); MCT (0.3 g·kg^{-1}·h^{-1}) and carbohydrate (0.8 g·kg^{-1}·h^{-1}) during exercise Performance measured at 0, 5, 10 and 15 days	No. Time-trial performance improved over time in both groups as a result of training protocol. Significant improvements seen in both groups by day 10, but no difference in mean improvement between groups
Rowlands and Hopkins (2002)	Well-trained cyclists (7 M); crossover design	14 days; HFAT (fat = 66% E, carbohydrate =~2.4 g·kg^{-1} BM); HCHO (carbohydrate =~8.6 g·kg^{-1} BM, 70% carbohydrate)	5-h cycling protocol, including 15-min time-trial + incremental test + 100-km time-trial HFAT = high fat pre-event meal; HCHO = high carbohydrate pre-event meal; both 0.8 g·kg^{-1}·h^{-1} carbohydrate during ride	Yes: Submaximal intensity exercise No: Higher intensity exercise Relative to baseline testing: HCHO showed small non-significant decreases in both 15-min time-trial and 100-km time-trial. HFAT showed larger but non-significant decrease in 15-min time-trial but small non-significant improvement in 100-km time-trial

Abbreviations: M = male: F = female; $\dot{V}O_{2max}$ = maximal oxygen uptake. *g·kg^{-1} BM intakes unavailable.

An important finding of Goedecke *et al.* (1999), who showed that matched groups showed similar training effects after 2 weeks of a high fat diet or an iso-energetic high carbohydrate diet, was that the adaptations to the high fat diet (65% of dietary energy) were achieved in as little as 5 days. If fat adaptation can be demonstrated as an effective strategy for performance enhancement for athletes, by itself or as part of a 'dietary periodization' protocol that subsequently replaces muscle glycogen stores (Burke and Hawley, 2002), then brief exposure is more practical and better tolerated by most individuals than more prolonged periods of intervention. Therefore, it is best considered as a pre-competition strategy (see Hargreaves *et al.*, 2004) rather than a long-term training practice. Indeed, studies in which previously sedentary individuals undertook training while following a high fat or high carbohydrate diet indicate that prolonged exposure of more than 4 weeks to a high fat diet causes an impairment of training adaptations and subsequent performance (Helge *et al.*, 1996, 1998).

Summary and future directions for research

There is clear evidence that adequate carbohydrate intake is important for the restoration of muscle glycogen stores, and that other dietary strategies related to the timing of intake, type of carbohydrate source or addition of other nutrients may either directly enhance the rate of glycogen recovery or improve the practical achievement of carbohydrate intake targets. Education strategies that focus on post-exercise glycogen restoration can be made clearer to athletes by providing recommendations for carbohydrate intake in terms of grams per kilogram of body mass rather than percentage of dietary energy intake. The role of specific strategies to recover muscle fat stores utilized during exercise is unclear at this time. It is difficult to demonstrate the translation of chronic strategies of daily recovery of muscle glycogen stores through high carbohydrate intakes into superior training adaptations and performance using conventional intervention studies. However, the results of acute studies clearly show that enhanced carbohydrate availability is of benefit to endurance capacity and performance. This serves as a reasonable basis to continue to advise athletes to consume adequate carbohydrate to meet the daily fuel needs of their training programmes, or at least to optimize their intake of carbohydrate within eating patterns that meet their energy needs and other aspects of healthy nutrition. Guidelines based on our present knowledge are summarized in Table 2. Major areas for future research include:

1 For situations where adequate carbohydrate can be consumed:
   - At what intake of carbohydrate is the threshold for glycogen storage reached over the first 4 h of post-exercise recovery?
   - Is there an advantage during the first 4 h of recovery to consuming carbohydrate in the form of frequent snacks rather than a single bolus or large meals?

- Are low GI carbohydrate foods less suitable for post-exercise recovery, particularly when available carbohydrate is taken into account? What is the mechanism involved? To what extent can they be included in recovery meals?

2 For situations where energy restriction causes suboptimal carbohydrate intake:
- Is there any difference in glycogen storage from a suboptimal intake of carbohydrate in terms of manipulating:
  - ○ Frequency of intake?
  - ○ High versus low GI carbohydrate to manipulate insulin response to meals?
  - ○ Addition of other nutrients (particularly protein)?

References

1 Achten, J., Halson, S., Mosely, L., Rayson, M.P., Casey, A. and Jeukendrup, A.E. (2003). Effect of diet on symptoms of overreaching in runners during a period of intensified training. *Medicine and Science in Sports and Exercise*, **35**(suppl.), S211.

2 Adamo, K.B. and Graham, T.E. (1998). Comparison of traditional measurements with macroglycogen and proglycogen analysis of muscle glycogen. *Journal of Applied Physiology*, **84**, 908–913.

3 Adamo, K.B., Tarnopolsky, M.A. and Graham, T.E. (1998). Dietary carbohydrate and postexercise synthesis of proglycogen and macroglycogen in human skeletal muscle. *American Journal of Physiology: Endocrinology and Metabolism*, **275**, E229–E234.

4 Alonso, M.D., Lomako, J., Lomako, W.M. and Whelan, W.J. (1995). A new look at the biogenesis of glycogen. *FASEB Journal*, **9**, 1126–1137.

5 American College of Sports Medicine, American Dietetic Association and Dietitians of Canada (2000). Nutrition and athletic performance. *Medicine and Science in Sports and Exercise*, **32**, 2130–2145.

6 Bergstrom, J., Hermansen, L., Hultman, E. and Saltin, B. (1967). Diet, muscle glycogen and physical performance. *Acta Physiologica Scandinavica*, **71**, 140–150.

7 Blom, P.C.S., Hostmark, A.T., Vaage, O., Vardel, K.R. and Maehlum, S. (1987). Effect of different post-exercise sugar diets on the rate of muscle glycogen synthesis. *Medicine and Science in Sports and Exercise*, **19**, 491–496.

8 Burke, L.M. and Hawley, J.A. (2002). Effects of short-term fat adaptation on metabolism and performance of prolonged exercise. *Medicine and Science in Sports and Exercise*, **34**, 1492–1498.

9 Burke, L.M. and Maughan, R.J. (2000). Alcohol in sport. In *Nutrition in Sport* (edited by R.J. Maughan), pp. 405–414. Oxford: Blackwell Science.

10 Burke, L.M., Collier, G.R. and Hargreaves, M. (1993). Muscle glycogen storage after prolonged exercise: the effect of the glycemic index of carbohydrate feedings. *Journal of Applied Physiology*, **75**, 1019–1023.

11 Burke, L.M., Collier, G.R., Beasley, S.K., Davis, P.G., Fricker, P.A., Heeley, P., Walder, K. and Hargreaves, M. (1995). Effect of coingestion of fat and protein with carbohydrate feedings on muscle glycogen storage. *Journal of Applied Physiology*, **78**, 2187–2192.

12 Burke, L.M., Collier, G.R., Davis, P.G., Fricker, P.A., Sanigorski, A.J. and Hargreaves, M. (1996). Muscle glycogen storage after prolonged exercise: effect of the frequency of carbohydrate feedings. *American Journal of Clinical Nutrition*, **64**, 115–119.

13 Burke, L.M., Cox, G.R., Cummings, N.K. and Desbrow, B. (2001). Guidelines for daily carbohydrate intake: do athletes achieve them? *Sports Medicine*, **31**, 267–299.

14 Burke, L.M., Collier, G.R., Broad, E.M., Davis, P.G., Martin, D.T., Sanigorski, A.J. and Hargreaves, M. (2003). The effect of alcohol intake on muscle glycogen storage following prolonged exercise. *Journal of Applied Physiology*, **95**, 983–990.

15 Carrithers, J.A., Williamson, D.L., Gallagher, P.M., Godard, M.P., Schulze, K.E. and Trappe, S.W. (2000). Effects of postexercise carbohydrate–protein feedings on muscle glycogen restoration. *Journal of Applied Physiology*, **88**, 1976–1982.

16 Costill, D.L., Sherman, W.M., Fink, W.J., Maresh, C., Witten, M. and Miller, J.M. (1981). The role of dietary carbohydrates in muscle glycogen resynthesis after strenuous running. *American Journal of Clinical Nutrition*, **34**, 1831–1836.

17 Costill, D.L., Flynn, M.G., Kirwan, J.P., Houmard, J.A., Mitchell, J.B., Thomas, R.T. and Park, S.H. (1988). Effects of repeated days of intensified training on muscle glycogen and swimming performance. *Medicine and Science in Sports and Exercise*, **20**, 249–254.

18 Costill, D.L., Pascoe, D.D., Fink, W.J., Robergs, R.A., Barr, S.I. and Pearson, D. (1990). Impaired muscle glycogen resynthesis after eccentric exercise. *Journal of Applied Physiology*, **69**, 46–50.

19 Coyle, E.F. (1991). Timing and method of increased carbohydrate intake to cope with heavy training, competition and recovery. *Journal of Sports Sciences*, **9**(suppl.), 29–52.

20 Coyle, E.F. (1995). Substrate utilization during exercise in active people. *American Journal of Clinical Nutrition*, **61** (suppl.), 968S–979S.

21 Coyle, E.F. (2004). Fluid and fuel intake during exercise. *Journal of Sports Sciences*, **22**, 39–55.

22 Coyle, E.F., Jeukendrup, A.E., Oseto, M.C., Hodgkinson, B.J. and Zderic, T.W. (2001). Low-fat diet alters intramuscular substrates and reduces lipolysis and fat oxidation during exercise. *American Journal of Physiology: Endocrinology and Metabolism*, **280**, E391–E398.

23 Decombaz, J., Schmitt, B., Ith, M., Decarli, B., Diem, P., Kreis, R., Hoppeler, H. and Boesch, C. (2001). Post-exercise fat intake repletes intramyocellular lipids but no faster in trained than in sedentary subjects. *American Journal of Physiology*, **281**, R760–R769.

24 Devlin, J.T. and Williams, C. (eds) (1991). Final consensus statement: foods, nutrition and sports performance. *Journal of Sports Sciences*, **9**(suppl.), iii.

25 Doyle, J.A., Sherman, W.M. and Strauss, R.L. (1993). Effects of eccentric and concentric exercise on muscle glycogen replenishment. *Journal of Applied Physiology*, **74**, 1848–1855.

26 Ekblom, B. and Williams, C. (eds) (1994). Final consensus statement: foods, nutrition and soccer performance. *Journal of Sports Science*, **12**(suppl.), S3.

27 Goedecke, J.H., Christie, C., Wilson, G., Dennis, S.C., Noakes, T.D., Hopkins, W.G. and Lambert, E.V. (1999). Metabolic adaptations to a high-fat diet in endurance cyclists. *Metabolism*, **48**, 1509–1517.

28 Hackney, A.C., McCracken-Compton, M.A. and Ainsworth, B. (1994). Substrate responses to submaximal exercise in the midfollicular and midluteal phases of the menstrual cycle. *International Journal of Sport Nutrition*, **4**, 299–308.

29 Hargreaves, M. (1999). Metabolic responses to carbohydrate ingestion: effects on exercise performance. In *Perspectives in Exercise Science and Sports Medicine* (edited by D.R. Lamb and R. Murray), pp. 93–124. Carmel, IN: Cooper.

30 Hargreaves, M., Hawley, J.A. and Jeukendrup, A.E. (2004). Pre-exercise carbohydrate and fat ingestion: effects on metabolism and performance. *Journal of Sports Sciences*, **22**, 31–38.

31 Helge, J.W., Richter, E.A. and Kiens, B. (1996). Interaction of training and diet on metabolism and endurance during exercise in man. *Journal of Physiology*, **492**, 293–306.

32 Helge, J.W., Wulff, B. and Kiens, B. (1998). Impact of a fat-rich diet on endurance in man: role of the dietary period. *Medicine and Science in Sports and Exercise*, **30**, 456–461.

33 Hopkins, W.G., Hawley, J.A. and Burke, L.M. (1999). Design and analysis of research on sport performance enhancement. *Medicine and Science in Sports and Exercise*, **31**, 472–485.

34 Ivy, J.L., Katz, A.L., Cutler, C.L., Sherman, W.M. and Coyle, E.F. (1988a). Muscle glycogen synthesis after exercise: effect of time of carbohydrate ingestion. *Journal of Applied Physiology*, **64**, 1480–1485.

35 Ivy, J.L., Lee, M.C., Brozinick, J.T. and Reed, M.J. (1988b). Muscle glycogen storage after different amounts of carbohydrate ingestion. *Journal of Applied Physiology*, **65**, 2018–2023.

36 Ivy, J.L., Goforth, H.W., Damon, B.D., McCauley, T.R., Parsons, E.C. and Price, T.B. (2002). Early post-exercise muscle glycogen recovery is enhanced with a carbohydrate–protein supplement. *Journal of Applied Physiology*, **93**, 1337–1344.

37 Jenkins, D.J.A., Cuff, D., Wolever, T.M.S., Knowland, D., Thompson, L., Cohen, Z. and Prokipchuk, E. (1987). Digestibility of carbohydrate foods in an ileostomate: relationship to dietary fibre, *in vitro* digestibility, and glycemic responses. *American Journal of Gastroenterology*, **82**, 709–717.

38 Jentjens, R.L., van Loon, L.J.C., Mann, C.H., Wagenmakers, A.J.M. and Jeukendrup, A.E. (2001). Addition of protein and amino acids to carbohydrates does not enhance postexercise muscle glycogen synthesis. *Journal of Applied Physiology*, **91**, 839–846.

39 Jozsi, A.C., Trappe, T.A., Starling, R.D., Goodpaster, B., Trappe, S.W., Fink, W.J. and Costill, D.L. (1996). The influence of starch structure on glycogen resynthesis and subsequent cycling performance. *International Journal of Sports Medicine*, **17**, 373–378.

40 Kiens, B. and Richter, E.A. (1996). Types of carbohydrate in an ordinary diet affect insulin action and muscle substrates in humans. *American Journal of Clinical Nutrition*, **63**, 47–53.

41 Kiens, B. and Richter, E.A. (1998). Utilization of skeletal muscle triacylglycerol during postexercise recovery in humans. *American Journal of Physiology: Endocrinology and Metabolism*, **275**, E332–E337.

42 Kirwan, J.P., Costill, D.L., Mitchell, J.B., Houmard, J.A., Flynn, M.G., Fink, W.J. and Beltz, J.D. (1988). Carbohydrate balance in competitive runners during successive days of intense training. *Journal of Applied Physiology*, **65**, 2601–2606.

43 Lamb, D.R., Rinehardt, K.F., Bartels, R.L., Sherman, W.M. and Snook, J.T. (1990). Dietary carbohydrate and intensity of interval swim training. *American Journal of Clinical Nutrition*, **52**, 1058–1063.

44 Lambert, E.V., Speechly, D.P., Dennis, S.C. and Noakes, T.D. (1994). Enhanced endurance in trained cyclists during moderate intensity exercise following 2 weeks adaptation to a high fat diet. *European Journal of Applied Physiology*, **69**, 287–293.

45 Maughan, R.J. and Horton, E.S. (eds) (1995). Final consensus statement: current issues in nutrition in athletics. *Journal of Sports Sciences*, **13**(suppl.), S1.

46 Nicklas, B.J., Hackney, A.C. and Sharp, R.L. (1989). The menstrual cycle and exercise: performance, muscle glycogen, and substrate responses. *International Journal of Sports Medicine*, **10**, 264–269.

47 Noakes, T.D. (1997). Challenging beliefs: *ex Africa semper aliquid novi*. *Medicine and Science in Sports and Exercise*, **29**, 571–590.

48 O'Keefe, K.A., Keith, R.E., Wilson, G.D. and Blessing, D.L. (1989). Dietary carbohydrate intake and endurance exercise performance of trained female cyclists. *Nutrition Research*, **9**, 819–830.

49 Parkin, J.A.M., Carey, M.F., Martin, I.K., Stojanovska, L. and Febbraio, M.A. (1997). Muscle glycogen storage following prolonged exercise: effect of timing of ingestion of high glycemic index food. *Medicine and Science in Sports and Exercise*, **29**, 220–224.

50 Peters, T.J., Nikolovski, S., Raja, G.K., Palmer, N. and Fournier, P.A. (1996). Ethanol acutely impairs glycogen repletion in skeletal muscle following high intensity short duration exercise in the rat. *Addiction Biology*, **1**, 289–295.

51 Phinney, S.D., Bistrian, B.R., Evans, W.J., Gervino, E. and Blackburn, G.L. (1983). The human metabolic response to chronic ketosis without caloric restriction: preservation of submaximal exercise capacity with reduced carbohydrate oxidation. *Metabolism*, **32**, 769–776.

52 Piehl Aulin, K., Soderlund, K. and Hultman, E. (2000). Muscle glycogen resynthesis rate in humans after supplementation of drinks containing carbohydrates with low and high molecular masses. *European Journal of Applied Physiology*, **81**, 346–351.

53 Pitsiladis, Y.P. and Maughan, R.J. (1999). The effects of exercise and diet manipulation on the capacity to perform prolonged exercise in the heat and in the cold in trained humans. *Journal of Physiology*, **517**, 919–930.

54 Richter, E.A., Mikines, K.J., Galbo, H. and Kiens, B. (1989). Effects of exercise on insulin action in human skeletal muscle. *Journal of Applied Physiology*, **66**, 876–885.

55 Roberts, K.M., Noble, E.G., Hayden, D.B. and Taylor, A.W. (1988). Simple and complex carbohydrate-rich diets and muscle glycogen content of marathon runners. *European Journal of Applied Physiology*, **57**, 70–74.

56 Roden, M. and Shulman, G.I. (1999). Applications of NMR spectroscopy to study muscle glycogen metabolism in man. *Annual Review of Medicine*, **50**, 277–290.

57 Rose, A.J., Howlett, K., King, D.S. and Hargreaves, M. (2001). Effect of prior exercise on glucose metabolism in trained men. *American Journal of Physiology: Endocrinology and Metabolism*, **281**, E766–E771.

58 Rowlands, D.S. and Hopkins, W.G. (2002). Effects of high-fat and high-carbohydrate diets on metabolism and performance in cycling. *Metabolism*, **51**, 678–690.

59 Roy, B.D. and Tarnopolsky, M.A. (1998). Influence of differing macronutrient intakes on muscle glycogen resynthesis after resistance exercise. *Journal of Applied Physiology*, **84**, 890–896.

60 Saris, W.H.M., Van Erp-Baart, M.A., Brouns, F., Westerterp, K.R. and ten Hoor, F. (1989). Study on food intake and energy expenditure during extreme sustained exercise: the Tour de France. *International Journal of Sports Medicine*, **10**(suppl. 1), S26–S31.

61 Sears, B. (1995). *The Zone Diet: A Dietary Road Map*. New York: Regan Books.

62 Shearer, J. and Graham, T.E. (2002). New perspectives on the storage and organization of muscle glycogen. *Canadian Journal of Applied Physiology*, **27**, 179–203.

63 Sherman, W.M., Doyle, J.A., Lamb, D.R. and Strauss, R.H. (1993). Dietary carbohydrate, muscle glycogen, and exercise performance during 7 d of training. *American Journal of Clinical Nutrition*, **57**, 27–31.

64 Simonsen, J.C., Sherman, W.M., Lamb, D.R., Dernbach, A.R., Doyle, J.A. and Strauss, R. (1991). Dietary carbohydrate, muscle glycogen, and power output during rowing training. *Journal of Applied Physiology*, **70**, 1500–1505.

65 Spriet, L.L. and Gibala, M.J. (2004). Nutritional strategies to influence adaptations to training. *Journal of Sports Sciences*, **22**, 127–141.

66 Starling, R.D., Trappe, T.A., Parcell, A.C., Kerr, C.G., Fink, W.J. and Costill, D.L. (1997). Effects of diet on muscle triglyceride and endurance performance. *Journal of Applied Physiology*, **82**, 1185–1189.

67 Tarnopolsky, M.A., Atkinson, S.A., Phillips, S.M. and MacDougall, J.D. (1995). Carbohydrate loading and metabolism during exercise in men and women. *Journal of Applied Physiology*, **78**, 1360–1368.

68 Tarnopolsky, M.A., Bosman, M., MacDonald, J.R., Vandeputte, D., Martin, J. and Roy, B.D. (1997). Postexercise protein–carbohydrate and carbohydrate supplements increase muscle glycogen in men and women. *Journal of Applied Physiology*, **83**, 1877–1883.

69 Tarnopolsky, M.A., Zawada, C., Richmond, L.B., Carter, S., Shearer, J., Graham, T. and Phillips, S.M. (2001). Gender differences in carbohydrate loading are related to energy intake. *Journal of Applied Physiology*, **91**, 225–230.

70 Tipton, K.D. and Wolfe, R.R. (2004). Protein and amino acids. *Journal of Sports Sciences*, **22**, 65–79.

71 Van Hall, G., Shirreffs, S.M. and Calbert, J.A.L. (2000). Muscle glycogen resynthesis during recovery from cycle exercise: no effect of additional protein ingestion. *Journal of Applied Physiology*, **88**, 1631–1636.

72 Van Loon, L.J.C., Saris, W.H.M., Kruijshoop, M. and Wagenmakers, A.J.M. (2000). Maximizing postexercise muscle glycogen synthesis: carbohydrate supplementation and the application of amino acid or protein hydrolysate mixtures. *American Journal of Clinical Nutrition*, **72**, 106–111.

73 Van Loon, L.J., Schrauwen-Hinderling, V.B., Koopman, R., Wagenmakers, A.J., Hesselink, M.K., Schaart, G., Kooi, M.E. and Saris, W.H. (2003). Influence of prolonged cycling and recovery diet on intramuscular triglyceride content in trained males. *American Journal of Physiology: Endocrinology and Metabolism*, **285**, E804–E811.

74 Vogt, M., Puntschart, A., Howald, H., Mueller, B., Mannhart, C., Gfeller-Tuescher, L., Mullis, P. and Hoppeler, H. (2003). Effects of dietary fat on muscle substrates, metabolism, and performance in athletes. *Medicine and Science in Sports and Exercise*, **35**, 952–960.

75 Watt, M.J., Heigenhauser, G.J.F. and Spriet, L.L. (2002). Intramuscular triacylglycerol utilization in human skeletal muscle during exercise: is there a controversy? *Journal of Applied Physiology*, **93**, 1185–1195.

76 Wojtaszewski, J.P.F., Nielson, P., Kiens, B. and Richter, E.A. (2001). Regulation of glycogen synthase kinase-3 in human skeletal muscle: effects of food intake and bicycle exercise. *Diabetes*, **50**, 265–269.
77 Wolever, T.M.S., Cohen, Z., Thompson, L.U., Thorne, M.J., Jenkins, M.J.A., Propikchuk, E.J. and Jenkins, D.J.A. (1986). Ideal loss of available carbohydrate in man: comparison of a breath hydrogen method with direct measurement using a human ileostomy model. *American Journal of Gastroenterology*, **81**, 115–122.
78 Zawadzki, K.M., Yaspelkis, B.B. and Ivy, J.L. (1992). Carbohydrate–protein complex increases the rate of muscle glycogen storage after exercise. *Journal of Applied Physiology*, **72**, 1854–1859.

3 Pre-exercise carbohydrate and fat ingestion: effects on metabolism and performance

MARK HARGREAVES, JOHN A. HAWLEY and
ASKER JEUKENDRUP

A key goal of pre-exercise nutritional strategies is to maximize carbohydrate stores, thereby minimizing the ergolytic effects of carbohydrate depletion. Increased dietary carbohydrate intake in the days before competition increases muscle glycogen levels and enhances exercise performance in endurance events lasting 90 min or more. Ingestion of carbohydrate 3–4 h before exercise increases liver and muscle glycogen and enhances subsequent endurance exercise performance. The effects of carbohydrate ingestion on blood glucose and free fatty acid concentrations and carbohydrate oxidation during exercise persist for at least 6 h. Although an increase in plasma insulin following carbohydrate ingestion in the hour before exercise inhibits lipolysis and liver glucose output, and can lead to transient hypoglycaemia during subsequent exercise in susceptible individuals, there is no convincing evidence that this is always associated with impaired exercise performance. However, individual experience should inform individual practice. Interventions to increase fat availability before exercise have been shown to reduce carbohydrate utilization during exercise, but do not appear to have ergogenic benefits.

Keywords: fatigue, free fatty acids, glucose uptake, insulin, muscle glycogen.

Introduction

The importance of carbohydrate for exercise performance has been recognized since the classic respiratory exchange studies of Christensen and Hansen in the late 1930s and the biopsy studies of Bergstrom and colleagues (Bergstrom *et al.*, 1967), who measured muscle glycogen during various dietary and exercise interventions. Since then, considerable attention has focused on nutritional strategies to maximize endogenous carbohydrate stores (liver and muscle glycogen), thereby minimizing the potential ergolytic effects of carbohydrate depletion (Coyle *et al.*, 1986). In this review, attention will focus on dietary carbohydrate during training in the days (1–7) leading up to competition and on carbohydrate and fat ingestion in the hours immediately before exercise and their effects on exercise metabolism and performance.

Carbohydrate loading in the days before exercise

In the classic carbohydrate loading study of Bergstrom et al. (1967), the inges-tion of a high carbohydrate diet, following a period of relative carbohydrate deprivation, resulted in a marked increase (supercompensation) in muscle glycogen (to as high as 200 mmol $\cdot$ kg^{-1} wet mass) and enhanced subsequent endurance exercise performance. More recently, a less extreme diet–exercise regimen was found to be equally effective in elevating pre-exercise muscle glycogen to these levels (Sherman et al., 1981), but had no effect on subsequent 21-km running performance lasting $\sim$80 min. Trained athletes were shown to increase their muscle glycogen to 180 mmol $\cdot$ kg^{-1} wet mass in as little as one day by ingesting 10 g carbohydrate $\cdot$ kg^{-1} BM (where BM = body mass) and remaining inactive (Bussau et al., 2002). Muscle glycogen did not increase further during another 2 days of rest and high carbohydrate intake. There is also evidence that well-trained athletes can maintain, or even increase, their muscle glycogen stores to 170–180 mmol $\cdot$ kg^{-1} wet mass in less than 24 h while training ($\sim$67% $\dot{V}O_{2peak}$) 2 h per day and consuming 10–12.5 g carbo-hydrate $\cdot$ kg^{-1} BM $\cdot$ day^{-1} (Coyle et al., 2001). It has even been suggested that trained athletes can greatly increase their muscle glycogen stores in less than 24 h by performing only 3 min of supramaximal exercise and then consuming a high carbohydrate diet (Fairchild et al., 2002). This protocol potentially repre-sents an improvement over previous regimens that have been tested extensively under laboratory and/or field conditions and further study is warranted. The mechanisms that allow trained individuals to rapidly increase muscle glycogen stores remain to be elucidated, but are likely to be related to their higher GLUT-4 concentrations and glycogen synthase activities (Hickner et al., 1997).

Despite a greater reliance on muscle glycogen when pre-exercise concentra-tions are elevated (Gollnick et al., 1972; Bosch et al., 1993; Hargreaves et al., 1995), increased dietary carbohydrate in the 1–7 days before exercise is gener-ally associated with enhanced performance when exercise duration exceeds about 90 min (Galbo et al., 1979; Brewer et al., 1988; Fallowfield and Williams, 1993; Rauch et al., 1995; Hawley et al., 1997b; Pitsiladis and Maughan, 1999; Walker et al., 2000), probably due to a delay in the point at which muscle glyco-gen availability is limiting for optimal exercise performance. The largest effects are observed during exercise trials to exhaustion (often referred to as endurance 'capacity') and, while still apparent, they are smaller in magnitude during tests of endurance 'performance' that are not open-ended such as total work output in a given time or time taken to complete a certain distance or amount of work (Jeukendrup et al., 1996). During prolonged, strenuous exercise, rates of carbohydrate oxidation can be as high as 3–4 g $\cdot$ min^{-1}, derived primarily from muscle glycogen (Angus et al., 2002). Assuming an active muscle mass of $\sim$10 kg during cycling, one could argue that endurance athletes should ensure their pre-event muscle glycogen concentrations are at least in the range of 150–200 mmol $\cdot$ kg^{-1} wet mass, even when carbohydrate is to be supplemented during exercise. Interestingly, carbohydrate loading has also been associated with increased exercise performance in the heat (Pitsiladis and Maughan, 1999), a condition where carbohydrate availability is not usually thought to limit exercise performance. Carbohydrate loading does not appear to further increase exercise performance when carbohydrate availability is maintained high with a pre-exercise carbohydrate meal and carbohydrate ingestion during exercise (Burke *et al.*, 2000b). Furthermore, while two studies have observed no additional benefit of carbohydrate ingestion during exercise in carbohydrate-loaded individuals (Flynn *et al.*, 1987; Widrick *et al.*, 1993), one study has observed potentiation (Kang *et al.*, 1995). A key factor may be the extent to which blood glucose concentrations are maintained during exercise in the carbohydrate-loaded state without carbohydrate ingestion. In shorter, more intense exercise bouts lasting about 60–90 min, the benefits of glycogen loading are not apparent (Sherman *et al.*, 1981; Madsen *et al.*, 1990; Hawley *et al.*, 1997a,b), possibly due to muscle glycogen availability not being a limiting factor in the non-carbohydrate-loaded trial in this type of exercise.

During single bouts of high-intensity exercise, the effects of carbohydrate loading are somewhat equivocal. Some studies have observed enhanced performance with elevated muscle glycogen concentrations after increased dietary carbohydrate intake (Maughan and Poole, 1981; Maughan *et al.*, 1997), while others have observed no benefit of elevated pre-exercise muscle glycogen (Vandenberghe *et al.*, 1995; Hargreaves *et al.*, 1997). In studies by Maughan and colleagues, the differences in performance were most obvious at the extremes of diet and may have been due as much to deleterious acid–base disturbances following consumption of a high fat–protein diet as to increased muscle glycogen availability following the high carbohydrate diet (Maughan *et al.*, 1997). With repeated bouts of high-intensity exercise, increased muscle glycogen availability is associated with enhanced intermittent exercise performance (Balsom *et al.*, 1999). Furthermore, increasing dietary carbohydrate intake from $\sim$300 to $\sim$600 g $\cdot$ day^{-1} in the 2 days before exercise improved long-term, intermittent exercise performance (Bangsbo *et al.*, 1992), while ingestion of 10 g carbohydrate $\cdot$ kg^{-1} BM improved intermittent running capacity during 22 h of recovery when compared with an isoenergetic diet without additional carbohydrate (Nicholas *et al.*, 1997).

It has been suggested that females may have a reduced ability to increase muscle glycogen during a period of dietary carbohydrate loading (Tarnopolsky *et al.*, 1995), although this observation may have been due to a lower energy intake in the female participants (Tarnopolsky *et al.*, 2001). Other studies have not observed reduced muscle glycogen storage in female athletes (Walker *et al.*, 2000; James *et al.*, 2001). Thus, with adequate energy and carbohydrate intake, female athletes benefit from carbohydrate loading as much as male athletes.

Carbohydrate ingestion 3–4 h before exercise

Ingestion of a carbohydrate-rich meal (containing about 140–330 g carbohydrate) 3–4 h before exercise has been shown to increase muscle glycogen

(Coyle *et al.*, 1985) and enhance exercise performance (Sherman *et al.*, 1989; Wright *et al.*, 1991; Schabort *et al.*, 1999). An increase in pre-exercise muscle glycogen is one explanation for the enhanced performance. Alternatively, because liver glycogen concentrations are substantially reduced after an overnight fast, ingestion of carbohydrate may increase these reserves and contribute, together with any ongoing absorption of the ingested carbohydrate, to the maintenance of blood glucose concentrations and improved performance during subsequent exercise (Casey *et al.*, 2000). In contrast, other studies have observed no benefit to exercise performance of a high carbohydrate meal 4 h before exercise (Okano *et al.*, 1996; Whitley *et al.*, 1998).

Despite plasma glucose and insulin concentrations returning to basal levels, ingestion of carbohydrate in the hours before exercise often results in a transient fall in glucose with the onset of exercise, increased carbohydrate oxidation and a blunting of free fatty acid (FFA) mobilization (Coyle *et al.*, 1985; Sherman *et al.*, 1989). These metabolic perturbations can persist for up to 6 h after carbohydrate ingestion (Montain *et al.*, 1991), but are not detrimental to exercise performance, with an increased carbohydrate availability apparently compensating for the greater carbohydrate utilization. No differences in exercise performance have been observed after ingestion of meals that produced marked differences in plasma glucose and insulin concentrations (Wee *et al.*, 1999). The effects of a high carbohydrate meal 3–4 h before exercise on subsequent performance may be equivalent to those observed with carbohydrate ingestion during exercise (Chryssanthopoulos *et al.*, 1994), although this is not always the case (Wright *et al.*, 1991) and there may be some important metabolic differences. The combination of a pre-exercise carbohydrate meal and carbohydrate ingestion during exercise may further enhance exercise performance (Wright *et al.*, 1991; Chryssanthopoulos and Williams, 1997). From a practical perspective, if access to carbohydrate during exercise is limited or non-existent, ingestion of 200–300 g carbohydrate 3–4 h before exercise may be an effective strategy for enhancing carbohydrate availability during the subsequent exercise period. Furthermore, ingestion of carbohydrate may be effective in enhancing subsequent exercise performance when the recovery period is relatively short ($\sim$4 h; Fallowfield *et al.*, 1995).

Carbohydrate ingestion 30–60 min before exercise

The ingestion of carbohydrate in the hour before exercise results in a large increase in plasma glucose and insulin concentrations. With the onset of exercise, however, there is a rapid fall in blood glucose concentration as a consequence of the combined stimulatory effects of hyperinsulinaemia and contractile activity on muscle glucose uptake and inhibition of the exercise-induced rise in liver glucose output (Marmy-Conus *et al.*, 1996; Febbraio *et al.*, 2000a,b), despite ongoing absorption of the ingested carbohydrate. An enhanced uptake and oxidation of blood glucose by skeletal muscle may account for the increased carbohydrate oxidation often observed after pre-exercise carbohydrate ingestion

(Costill *et al.*, 1977; Febbraio and Stewart, 1996; Coyle *et al.*, 1997; Horowitz *et al.*, 1997). In addition, an increase in muscle glycogenolysis has been reported by some researchers (Costill *et al.*, 1977; Hargreaves *et al.*, 1985; Febbraio *et al.*, 2000b), although others have not observed such an effect (Levine *et al.*, 1983; Fielding *et al.*, 1987; Hargreaves *et al.*, 1987; Febbraio and Stewart, 1996). The increase in plasma FFA concentrations with exercise is attenuated following pre-exercise carbohydrate ingestion, as a consequence of insulin-mediated inhibition of lipolysis (Horowitz *et al.*, 1997). Fat oxidation is reduced because of the lower plasma FFA availability, but also as a result of inhibition of lipid oxidation within muscle (Coyle *et al.*, 1997), since restoration of plasma FFA availability does not completely return fat oxidation to values seen during exercise in the fasted state (Horowitz *et al.*, 1997). Co-ingestion of medium-chain triglyceride with carbohydrate, as a strategy to increase plasma FFA, has no effect on muscle glycogen use during subsequent exercise (Horowitz *et al.*, 2000). Since these metabolic effects of pre-exercise carbohydrate ingestion are a consequence of hyperglycaemia and hyperinsulinaemia, there has been interest in strategies that minimize the changes in plasma glucose and insulin before exercise. These have included the ingestion of fructose (Levine *et al.*, 1983; Hargreaves *et al.*, 1985, 1987) or carbohydrate types other than glucose with differing glycaemic indices (Thomas *et al.*, 1991; Febbraio and Stewart, 1996; Kirwan *et al.*, 1998, 2001a,b; Sparks *et al.*, 1998; DeMarco *et al.*, 1999; Febbraio *et al.*, 2000b; Jentjens and Jeukendrup, 2003), varying the carbohydrate load (Seifert *et al.*, 1994; Jentjens *et al.*, 2003) and ingestion schedule (Short *et al.*, 1997; Moseley *et al.*, 2003), the addition of fat (Horowitz and Coyle, 1993), or the inclusion of warm-up exercise in the pre-exercise period (Brouns *et al.*, 1989). In general, while these various interventions modify the metabolic response to exercise, there appears to be no great advantage for exercise performance in blunting the pre-exercise glycaemic and insulinaemic responses.

The glycaemic responses during exercise preceded by carbohydrate ingestion are determined by several factors. These include the combined stimulatory effects of insulin and contractile activity on muscle glucose uptake, the balance of inhibitory and stimulatory effects of insulin and catecholamines, respectively, on liver glucose output, and the magnitude of ongoing intestinal absorption of glucose from the ingested carbohydrate (Kuipers *et al.*, 1999). The occurrence of rebound hypoglycaemia in susceptible individuals does not appear to be related to insulin sensitivity (Jentjens and Jeukendrup, 2002) or to the exercise intensity (Achten and Jeukendrup, 2003). Thus, the aetiology of rebound hypoglycaemia remains unknown and susceptibility to this condition must be determined by personal experience. Since the inhibition of lipolysis and fat oxidation occurs with only small increases in plasma insulin – for example, after fructose (low glycaemic index) ingestion – it could be argued that if pre-exercise carbohydrate ingestion is the only mechanism by which an athlete can increase carbohydrate availability during exercise, they would be well advised to ingest a reasonable amount of carbohydrate (perhaps as much as 100 g), without undue gastrointestinal distress, so as to compensate for the suppressed fat oxidation and to provide a pool of glucose that becomes available for use during the later stages of exercise.

The metabolic alterations associated with ingestion of carbohydrate in the 30–60 min before exercise have the potential to influence exercise performance. It has been postulated that the increase in muscle glycogenolysis observed previously (Costill *et al.*, 1977) would result in an earlier onset of fatigue during exercise, as was suggested in a subsequent study (Foster *et al.*, 1979). In contrast, every study since has shown either unchanged (Hargreaves *et al.*, 1987; Febbraio and Stewart, 1996; Sparks *et al.*, 1998; Febbraio *et al.*, 2000b; Jentjens and Jeukendrup, 2003; Jentjens *et al.*, 2003; Moseley *et al.*, 2003) or enhanced (Gleeson *et al.*, 1986; Sherman *et al.*, 1991; Thomas *et al.*, 1991; Kirwan *et al.*, 1998) endurance exercise performance after the ingestion of carbohydrate in the hour before exercise. Thus, notwithstanding the well-documented metabolic effects of pre-exercise carbohydrate ingestion, and the possible negative consequences of hypoglycaemia in susceptible individuals, on balance there appears to be little evidence to support the practice of avoiding carbohydrate ingestion in the hour before exercise, provided sufficient carbohydrate is ingested. Having said that, individual practice must be determined on the basis of individual experience with various pre-exercise carbohydrate ingestion protocols. Finally, when carbohydrate is ingested during prolonged exercise, the glycaemic index of pre-exercise carbohydrate feedings has no effect on performance (Burke *et al.*, 1998); indeed, carbohydrate ingestion during exercise may be a more effective strategy for enhancing exercise performance (Febbraio *et al.*, 2000a) if this is the only option available to an athlete.

Increased fat availability before exercise

Another potential strategy to enhance endurance exercise performance is to increase fat availability acutely, with a view to reducing carbohydrate utilization during exercise, thereby delaying the onset of carbohydrate depletion and fatigue. Increased dietary fat intake over a 24-h period increased muscle triglyceride stores, but reduced cycling time-trial performance, compared with a high carbohydrate diet (Starling *et al.*, 1997). A longer period of 'fat adaptation' (5 days + 1 day carbohydrate intake to normalize muscle glycogen) resulted in marked carbohydrate sparing during exercise bouts lasting 2–4 h, but subsequent exercise performance was not altered (Burke *et al.*, 2000a; Carey *et al.*, 2001). Furthermore, although trained athletes were able to perform intense interval training sessions on such a dietary regimen, they were associated with increased ratings of perceived exertion (Stepto *et al.*, 2002). Ingestion of high fat meals and infusion of Intralipid, both in combination with heparin administration, are effective in raising plasma FFA concentrations and have been associated with reduced muscle glycogen utilization (Costill *et al.*, 1977; Vukovich *et al.*, 1993) and carbohydrate oxidation (Hawley *et al.*, 2000). One study has observed increased endurance with elevated plasma FFA before exercise

(Pitsiladis *et al.*, 1999), while others have not seen any benefit (Okano *et al.*, 1996, 1998; Whitley *et al.*, 1998; Hawley *et al.*, 2000). Thus, it would appear that while such a strategy can have a marked effect on exercise metabolism (i.e. reduced carbohydrate utilization), there is no beneficial effect on exercise performance.

Summary

Increasing dietary carbohydrate intake to $\sim$10 g $\cdot$ kg^{-1} BM in the days leading up to athletic competition increases muscle glycogen stores and is associated with enhanced endurance exercise capacity and performance in events lasting more than 90 min. While the performance of a single high-intensity effort does not appear to be improved by carbohydrate loading, intermittent high-intensity performance may be enhanced. Female and male athletes benefit equally from carbohydrate loading, provided energy and carbohydrate intake are adequate. Ingestion of a carbohydrate-rich (about 200–300 g carbohydrate) meal after an overnight fast and 2–4 h before exercise can replenish endogenous carbohydrate reserves and is associated with improved performance. On balance, the literature indicates that ingestion of carbohydrate in the hour before exercise does not impair exercise performance. However, there may be individuals who are susceptible to hypoglycaemia and its negative consequences. There are no clear indicators of susceptibility to rebound hypoglycaemia during exercise and this should be assessed by individual experience. Increasing fat availability before exercise reduces carbohydrate utilization during subsequent exercise, but does not alter exercise performance.

References

1 Achten, J. and Jeukendrup, A.E. (2003). Effects of pre-exercise ingestion of carbohydrate on glycaemic and insulinaemic responses during subsequent exercise at differing intensities. *European Journal of Applied Physiology*, **88**, 466–471.

2 Angus, D.J., Febbraio, M.A. and Hargreaves, M. (2002). Plasma glucose kinetics during prolonged exercise in trained humans when fed carbohydrate. *American Journal of Physiology*, **283**, E573–E577.

3 Balsom, P.D., Gaitanos, G.C., Söderlund, K. and Ekblom, B. (1999). High-intensity exercise and muscle glycogen availability in humans. *Acta Physiologica Scandinavica*, **165**, 337–345.

4 Bangsbo, J., Nørragaard, L. and Thorsøe, F. (1992). The effect of carbohydrate diet on intermittent exercise performance. *International Journal of Sports Medicine*, **13**, 152–157.

5 Bergstrom, J., Hermansen, L., Hultman, E. and Saltin, B. (1967). Diet, muscle glycogen and physical performance. *Acta Physiologica Scandinavica*, **71**, 140–150.

6 Bosch, A.N., Dennis, S.C. and Noakes, T.D. (1993). Influence of carbohydrate loading on fuel substrate turnover and oxidation during prolonged exercise. *Journal of Applied Physiology*, **74**, 1921–1927.

7 Brewer, J., Williams, C. and Patton, A. (1988). The influence of high carbohydrate diets on endurance running performance. *European Journal of Applied Physiology*, 57, 698–706.

8 Brouns, F., Rehrer, N.J., Saris, W.H.M., Beckers, E., Menheere, P. and ten Hoor, F. (1989). Effect of carbohydrate intake during warming-up on the regulation of blood glucose during exercise. *International Journal of Sports Medicine*, 10, S68–S75.

9 Burke, L.M., Claassen, A., Hawley, J.A. and Noakes, T.D. (1998). Carbohydrate intake during prolonged cycling minimizes effect of glycemic index of preexercise meal. *Journal of Applied Physiology*, 85, 2220–2226.

10 Burke, L.M., Angus, D.J., Cox, G.R., Cummings, N.K., Febbraio, M.A., Gawthorn, K., Hawley, J.A., Minehan, M., Martin, D.T. and Hargreaves, M. (2000a). Effect of fat adaptation and carbohydrate restoration on metabolism and performance during prolonged cycling. *Journal of Applied Physiology*, 89, 2413–2421.

11 Burke, L.M., Hawley, J.A., Schabort, E.J., St. Clair Gibson, A., Mujika, I. and Noakes, T.D. (2000b). Carbohydrate loading failed to improve 100-km cycling performance in a placebo-controlled trial. *Journal of Applied Physiology*, 88, 1284–1290.

12 Bussau, V.A., Fairchild, T.J., Rao, A., Steele, P. and Fournier, P.A. (2002). Carbohydrate loading in human muscle: an improved 1 day protocol. *European Journal of Applied Physiology*, 87, 290–295.

13 Carey, A.L., Staudacher, H.M., Cummings, N.K., Stepto, N.K., Nikolopoulos, V., Burke, L.M. and Hawley, J.A. (2001). Effects of fat adaptation and carbohydrate restoration on prolonged endurance exercise. *Journal of Applied Physiology*, 91, 115–122.

14 Casey, A., Mann, R., Banister, K., Fox, J., Morris, P.G., MacDonald, I.A. and Greenhaff, P.L. (2000). Effect of carbohydrate ingestion on glycogen resynthesis in human liver and skeletal muscle, measured by ^{13}C MRS. *American Journal of Physiology*, 278, E65–E75.

15 Chryssanthopoulos, C. and Williams, C. (1997). Pre-exercise carbohydrate meal and endurance capacity when carbohydrates are ingested during exercise. *International Journal of Sports Medicine*, 18, 543–548.

16 Chryssanthopoulos, C., Williams, C., Wilson, W., Asher, L. and Hearne, L. (1994). Comparison between carbohydrate feedings before and during exercise on running performance during a 30-km treadmill time trial. *International Journal of Sport Nutrition*, 4, 374–386.

17 Costill, D.L., Coyle, E., Dalsky, G., Evans, W., Fink, W. and Hoopes, D. (1977). Effects of elevated plasma FFA and insulin on muscle glycogen usage during exercise. *Journal of Applied Physiology*, 43, 695–699.

18 Coyle, E.F., Coggan, A.R., Hemmert, M.K., Lowe, R.C. and Walters, T.J. (1985). Substrate usage during prolonged exercise following a preexercise meal. *Journal of Applied Physiology*, 59, 429–433.

19 Coyle, E.F., Coggan, A.R., Hemmert, M.K. and Ivy, J.L. (1986). Muscle glycogen utilization during prolonged strenuous exercise when fed carbohydrate. *Journal of Applied Physiology*, 61, 165–172.

20 Coyle, E.F., Jeukendrup, A.E., Wagenmakers, A.J.M. and Saris, W.H.M. (1997). Fatty acid oxidation is directly regulated by carbohydrate metabolism during exercise. *American Journal of Physiology*, 273, E268–E275.

21 Coyle, E.F., Jeukendrup, A.E., Oseto, M.C., Hodgkinson, B.J. and Ivy, J.L. (2001). Low-fat diet alters intramuscular substrates and reduces lipolysis and fat oxidation during exercise. *American Journal of Physiology*, 280, E391–E398.

22 DeMarco, H.M., Sucher, K.P., Cisar, C.J. and Butterfield, G.E. (1999). Pre-exercise carbohydrate meals: application of glycemic index. *Medicine and Science in Sports and Exercise*, **31**, 164–170.

23 Fairchild, T.J., Fletcher, S., Steele, P., Goodman, C., Dawson, B. and Fournier, P.A. (2002). Rapid carbohydrate loading after a short bout of near maximal-intensity exercise. *Medicine and Science in Sports and Exercise*, **34**, 980–986.

24 Fallowfield, J.L. and Williams, C. (1993). Carbohydrate intake and recovery from prolonged exercise. *International Journal of Sport Nutrition*, **3**, 150–164.

25 Fallowfield, J.L., Williams, C. and Singh, R. (1995). The influence of ingesting a carbohydrate-electrolyte beverage during 4 hours of recovery on subsequent endurance capacity. *International Journal of Sport Nutrition*, **5**, 285–299.

26 Febbraio, M.A. and Stewart, K.L. (1996). CHO feeding before prolonged exercise: effect of glycemic index on muscle glycogenolysis and exercise performance. *Journal of Applied Physiology*, **81**, 1115–1120.

27 Febbraio, M.A., Chiu, A., Angus, D.J., Arkinstall, M.J. and Hawley, J.A. (2000a). Effects of carbohydrate ingestion before and during exercise on glucose kinetics and performance. *Journal of Applied Physiology*, **89**, 2220–2226.

28 Febbraio, M.A., Keenan, J., Angus, D.J., Campbell, S.E. and Garnham, A.P. (2000b). Preexercise carbohydrate ingestion, glucose kinetics, and muscle glycogen use: effect of the glycemic index. *Journal of Applied Physiology*, **89**, 1845–1851.

29 Fielding, R.A., Costill, D.L., Fink, W.J., King, D.S., Kovaleski, J.E. and Kirwan, J.P. (1987). Effects of pre-exercise carbohydrate feedings on muscle glycogen use during exercise in well-trained runners. *European Journal of Applied Physiology*, **56**, 225–229.

30 Flynn, M.G., Costill, D.L., Hawley, J.A., Fink, W.J., Neufer, P.D., Fielding, R.A. and Sleeper, M.G. (1987). Influence of selected carbohydrate drinks on cycling performance and glycogen use. *Medicine and Science in Sports and Exercise*, **19**, 37–40.

31 Foster, C., Costill, D.L. and Fink, W.J. (1979). Effects of pre-exercise feedings on endurance performance. *Medicine and Science in Sports*, **11**, 1–5.

32 Galbo, H., Holst, J.J. and Christensen, N.J. (1979). The effect of different diets and of insulin on the hormonal response to prolonged exercise. *Acta Physiologica Scandinavica*, **107**, 19–32.

33 Gleeson, M., Maughan, R.J. and Greenhaff, P.L. (1986). Comparison of the effects of preexercise feeding of glucose, glycerol and placebo on endurance performance and fuel homeostasis in man. *European Journal of Applied Physiology*, **55**, 645–653.

34 Gollnick, P.D., Piehl, K., Saubert, C.W., Armstrong, R.B. and Saltin, B. (1972). Diet, exercise, and glycogen changes in human muscle fibres. *Journal of Applied Physiology*, **33**, 421–425.

35 Hargreaves, M., Costill, D.L., Katz, A. and Fink, W.J. (1985). Effect of fructose ingestion on muscle glycogen usage during exercise. *Medicine and Science in Sports and Exercise*, **17**, 360–363.

36 Hargreaves, M., Costill, D.L., Fink, W.J., King, D.S. and Fielding, R.A. (1987). Effect of pre-exercise carbohydrate feedings on endurance cycling performance. *Medicine and Science in Sports and Exercise*, **19**, 33–36.

37 Hargreaves, M., McConell, G.M. and Proietto, J. (1995). Influence of muscle glycogen on glycogenolysis and glucose uptake during exercise. *Journal of Applied Physiology*, **78**, 288–292.

38 Hargreaves, M., Finn, J.P., Withers, R.T., Halbert, J.A., Scroop, G.C., Mackay, M., Snow, R.J. and Carey, M.F. (1997). Effect of muscle glycogen availability on maximal exercise performance. *European Journal of Applied Physiology*, **75**, 188–192.

39 Hawley, J.A., Palmer, G.S. and Noakes, T.D. (1997). Effects of 3 days of carbohydrate supplementation on muscle glycogen content and utilisation during a 1-h cycling performance. *European Journal of Applied Physiology*, **75**, 407–412.

40 Hawley, J.A., Schabort, E.J., Noakes, T.D. and Dennis, S.C. (1997). Carbohydrate-loading and exercise performance: an update. *Sports Medicine*, **24**, 73–81.

41 Hawley, J.A., Burke, L.M., Angus, D.J., Fallon, K.E., Martin, D.T. and Febbraio, M.A. (2000). Effect of altering substrate availability on metabolism and performance during intense exercise. *British Journal of Nutrition*, **84**, 829–838.

42 Hickner, R.C., Fisher, J.S., Hansen, P.A., Racette, S.B., Mier, C.M., Turner, M.J. and Holloszy, J.O. (1997). Muscle glycogen accumulation after endurance exercise in trained and untrained individuals. *Journal of Applied Physiology*, **83**, 897–903.

43 Horowitz, J.F. and Coyle, E.F. (1993). Metabolic responses to preexercise meals containing various carbohydrates and fat. *American Journal of Clinical Nutrition*, **58**, 235–241.

44 Horowitz, J.F., Mora-Rodríguez, R., Byerley, L.O. and Coyle, E.F. (1997). Lipolytic suppression following carbohydrate ingestion limits fat oxidation. *American Journal of Physiology*, **273**, E768–E775.

45 Horowitz, J.F., Mora-Rodríguez, R., Byerley, L.O. and Coyle, E.F. (2000). Preexercise medium-chain triglyceride ingestion does not alter muscle glycogen use during exercise. *Journal of Applied Physiology*, **88**, 219–225.

46 James, A.P., Lorraine, M., Cullen, D., Goodman, C., Dawson, B., Palmer, T.N. and Fournier, P.A. (2001). Muscle glycogen supercompensation: absence of a gender-related difference. *European Journal of Applied Physiology*, **85**, 533–538.

47 Jentjens, R.L.P.G. and Jeukendrup, A.E. (2002). Prevalance of hypoglycemia following pre-exercise carbohydrate ingestion is not accompanied by higher insulin sensitivity. *International Journal of Sport Nutrition and Exercise Metabolism*, **12**, 444–459.

48 Jentjens, R.L.P.G. and Jeukendrup, A.E. (2003). Effects of pre-exercise ingestion of trehalose, galactose and glucose on subsequent metabolism and cycling performance. *European Journal of Applied Physiology*, **88**, 459–465.

49 Jentjens, R.L.P.G., Cale, C., Gutch, C. and Jeukendrup, A.E. (2003). Effects of pre-exercise ingestion of differing amounts of carbohydrate on subsequent metabolism and cycling performance. *European Journal of Applied Physiology*, **88**, 444–452.

50 Jeukendrup, A.E., Saris, W.H.M., Brouns, F. and Kester, A.D.M. (1996). A new validated endurance performance test. *Medicine and Science in Sports and Exercise*, **28**, 266–270.

51 Kang, J., Robertson, R.J., Denys, B.G., DaSilva, S.G., Visich, P., Siminski, R.R., Utter, A.C., Goss, F.L. and Metz, K.F. (1995). Effect of carbohydrate ingestion subsequent to carbohydrate supercompensation on endurance performance. *International Journal of Sport Nutrition*, **5**, 329–343.

52 Kirwan, J.P., O'Gorman, D. and Evans, W.J. (1998). A moderate glycemic meal before endurance exercise can enhance performance. *Journal of Applied Physiology*, **84**, 53–59.

53 Kirwan, J.P., Cyr-Campbell, D., Campbell, W.W., Scheiber, J. and Evans, W.J. (2001a). Effects of moderate and high glycemic index meals on metabolism and exercise performance. *Metabolism*, **50**, 849–855.

54 Kirwan, J.P., O'Gorman, D., Cyr-Campbell, D., Campbell, W.W., Yarasheski, K.E. and Evans, W.J. (2001b). Effects of a moderate glycemic meal on exercise duration and substrate utilization. *Medicine and Science in Sports and Exercise*, **33**, 1517–1523.

55 Kuipers, H., Fransen, E.J. and Keizer, H.A. (1999). Pre-exercise ingestion of carbohydrate and transient hypoglycemia during exercise. *International Journal of Sports Medicine*, **20**, 227–231.

56 Levine, L., Evans, W.J., Cadarette, B.S., Fisher, E.C. and Bullen, B.A. (1983). Fructose and glucose ingestion and muscle glycogen use during submaximal exercise. *Journal of Applied Physiology*, **55**, 1767–1771.

57 Madsen, K., Pedersen, P.K., Rose, P. and Richter, E.A. (1990). Carbohydrate supercompensation and muscle glycogen utilization during exhaustive running in highly trained athletes. *European Journal of Applied Physiology*, **61**, 467–472.

58 Marmy Conus, N., Fabris, S., Proietto, J. and Hargreaves, M. (1996). Pre-exercise glucose ingestion and glucose kinetics during exercise. *Journal of Applied Physiology*, **81**, 853–857.

59 Maughan, R.J. and Poole, D.C. (1981). The effects of a glycogen-loading regimen on the capacity to perform anaerobic exercise. *European Journal of Applied Physiology*, **46**, 211–219.

60 Maughan, R.J., Greenhaff, P.L., Leiper, J.B., Ball, D., Lambert, C.P. and Gleeson, M. (1997). Diet composition and the performance of high-intensity exercise. *Journal of Sports Sciences*, **15**, 265–275.

61 Montain, S.J., Hopper, M.K., Coggan, A.R. and Coyle, E.F. (1991). Exercise metabolism at different time intervals after a meal. *Journal of Applied Physiology*, **70**, 882–888.

62 Moseley, L., Lancaster, G.I. and Jeukendrup, A.E. (2003). Effects of timing of preexercise ingestion of carbohydrate on subsequent metabolism and cycling performance. *European Journal of Applied Physiology*, **88**, 453–458.

63 Nicholas, C.W., Green, P.A., Hawkins, R.D. and Williams, C. (1997). Carbohydrate intake and recovery of intermittent running capacity. *International Journal of Sport Nutrition*, **7**, 251–260.

64 Okano, G., Sato, Y., Takumi, Y. and Sugawara, M. (1996). Effect of 4 h preexercise high carbohydrate and high fat meal ingestion on endurance performance and metabolism. *International Journal of Sports Medicine*, **17**, 530–534.

65 Okano, G., Sato, Y. and Murata, Y. (1998). Effect of elevated blood FFA levels on endurance performance after a single fat meal ingestion. *Medicine and Science in Sports and Exercise*, **30**, 763–768.

66 Pitsiladis, Y.P. and Maughan, R.J. (1999). The effects of exercise and diet manipulation on the capacity to perform prolonged exercise in the heat and in the cold in trained humans. *Journal of Physiology*, **517**, 919–930.

67 Pitsiladis, Y.P., Smith, I. and Maughan, R.J. (1999). Increased fat availability enhances the capacity of trained individuals to perform prolonged exercise. *Medicine and Science in Sports and Exercise*, **31**, 1570–1579.

68 Rauch, L.H.G., Rodger, I., Wilson, G.R., Belonje, J.D., Dennis, S.C., Noakes, T.D. and Hawley, J.A. (1995). The effects of carbohydrate loading on muscle glycogen content and cycling performance. *International Journal of Sport Nutrition*, **5**, 25–36.

69 Schabort, E.J., Bosch, A.N., Weltan, S.M. and Noakes, T.D. (1999). The effect of a pre-exercise meal on time to fatigue during prolonged cycling exercise. *Medicine and Science in Sports and Exercise*, **31**, 464–471.

70 Seifert, J.G., Paul, G.L., Eddy, D.E. and Murray, R. (1994). Glycemic and insuline-mic response to preexercise carbohydrate feedings. *International Journal of Sport Nutrition*, **4**, 46–53.

71 Sherman, W.M., Costill, D.L., Fink, W.J. and Miller, J.M. (1981). Effect of exercise-diet manipulation on muscle glycogen and its subsequent utilization during performance. *International Journal of Sports Medicine*, **2**, 114–118.

72 Sherman, W.M., Brodowicz, G., Wright, D.A., Allen, W.K., Simonsen, J. and Dernbach, A. (1989). Effects of 4 h preexercise carbohydrate feedings on cycling performance. *Medicine and Science in Sports and Exercise*, **21**, 598–604.

73 Sherman, W.M., Peden, M.C. and Wright, D.A. (1991). Carbohydrate feedings 1 h before exercise improve cycling performance. *American Journal of Clinical Nutrition*, **54**, 866–870.

74 Short, K.R., Sheffield-Moore, M. and Costill, D.L. (1997). Glycemic and insuline-mic responses to multiple preexercise carbohydrate feedings. *International Journal of Sport Nutrition*, **7**, 128–137.

75 Sparks, M.J., Selig, S.E. and Febbraio, M.A. (1998). Pre-exercise carbohydrate ingestion: effect of the glycemic index on endurance exercise performance. *Medicine and Science in Sports and Exercise*, **30**, 844–849.

76 Starling, R.D., Trappe, T.A., Parcell, A.C., Kerr, C.G., Fink, W.J. and Costill, D.L. (1997). Effects of diet on muscle triglyceride and endurance performance. *Journal of Applied Physiology*, **82**, 1185–1189.

77 Stepto, N.K., Carey, A.L., Staudacher, H.M., Cummings, N.K., Burke, L.M. and Hawley, J.A. (2002). Effect of short-term fat adaptation on high-intensity training. *Medicine and Science in Sports and Exercise*, **34**, 449–455.

78 Tarnopolsky, M.A., Atkinson, S.A., Phillips, S.M. and MacDougall, J.D. (1995). Carbohydrate loading and metabolism during exercise in men and women. *Journal of Applied Physiology*, **78**, 1360–1368.

79 Tarnopolsky, M.A., Zawada, C., Richmond, L.B., Carter, S., Shearer, J., Graham, T. and Phillips, S.M. (2001). Gender differences in carbohydrate loading are related to energy intake. *Journal of Applied Physiology*, **91**, 225–230.

80 Thomas, D.E., Brotherhood, J.R. and Brand, J.C. (1991). Carbohydrate feeding before exercise: effect of glycemic index. *International Journal of Sports Medicine*, **12**, 180–186.

81 Vandenberghe, K., Hespel, P., Vanden Eynde, B., Lysens, R. and Richter, E.A. (1995). No effect of glycogen level on glycogen metabolism during high intensity exercise. *Medicine and Science in Sports and Exercise*, **27**, 1278–1283.

82 Vukovich, M.D., Costill, D.L., Hickey, M.S., Trappe, S.W., Cole, K.J. and Fink, W.J. (1993). Effect of fat emulsion infusion and fat feeding on muscle glycogen utilisation during cycle exercise. *Journal of Applied Physiology*, **75**, 1513–1518.

83 Walker, J.L., Heigenhauser, G.J., Hultman, E. and Spriet, L.L. (2000). Dietary carbohydrate, muscle glycogen content, and endurance performance in well-trained women. *Journal of Applied Physiology*, **88**, 2151–2158.

84 Wee, S.-L., Williams, C., Gray, S. and Horabin, J. (1999). Influence of high and low glycemic index meals on endurance running capacity. *Medicine and Science in Sports and Exercise*, **31**, 393–399.

85 Whitley, H.A., Humphreys, S.M., Campbell, I.T., Keegan, M.A., Jayanetti, T.D., Sperry, D.A., MacLaren, D.P., Reilly, T. and Frayn, K.N. (1998). Metabolic and performance responses during endurance exercise after high-fat and high-carbohydrate meals. *Journal of Applied Physiology*, **85**, 418–424.

86 Widrick, J.J., Costill, D.L., Fink, W.J., Hickey, M.S., McConell, G.K. and Tanaka, H. (1993). Carbohydrate feedings and exercise performance: effect of initial muscle glycogen concentration. *Journal of Applied Physiology*, **74**, 2998–3005.
87 Wright, D.A., Sherman, W.M. and Dernbach, A. (1991). Carbohydrate feedings before, during, or in combination improve cycling endurance performance. *Journal of Applied Physiology*, **71**, 1082–1088.

4 Fluid and fuel intake during exercise

EDWARD F. COYLE

The amounts of water, carbohydrate and salt that athletes are advised to ingest during exercise are based upon their effectiveness in attenuating both fatigue as well as illness due to hyperthermia, dehydration or hyperhydration. When possible, fluid should be ingested at rates that most closely match sweating rate. When that is not possible or practical or sufficiently ergogenic, some athletes might tolerate body water losses amounting to 2% of body weight without significant risk to physical well-being or performance when the environment is cold (e.g. 5–10°C) or temperate (e.g. 21–22°C). However, when exercising in a hot environment (>30°C), dehydration by 2% of body weight impairs absolute power production and predisposes individuals to heat injury. Fluid should not be ingested at rates in excess of sweating rate and thus body water and weight should not increase during exercise. Fatigue can be reduced by adding carbohydrate to the fluids consumed so that 30–60 g of rapidly absorbed carbohydrate are ingested throughout each hour of an athletic event. Furthermore, sodium should be included in fluids consumed during exercise lasting longer than 2 h or by individuals during any event that stimulates heavy sodium loss (more than 3–4 g of sodium). Athletes do not benefit by ingesting glycerol, amino acids or alleged precursors of neurotransmitter. Ingestion of other substances during exercise, with the possible exception of caffeine, is discouraged. Athletes will benefit the most by tailoring their individual needs for water, carbohydrate and salt to the specific challenges of their sport, especially considering the environment's impact on sweating and heat stress.

Keywords: carbohydrate, dehydration, fatigue, gastrointestinal function, hyperthermia, sodium.

Introduction

When athletes exercise during training or while competing, it is clear that they sometimes benefit by ingesting various mixtures of water, carbohydrate and electrolytes (Convertino *et al.*, 1996; Casa, 2000). The benefits can be expressed through improved performance and/or reduced physiological stress, on an athlete's cardiovascular, central nervous and muscular systems. Although ample scientific evidence exists to support the general theory for encouraging athletes to consume water, carbohydrate and electrolytes during exercise, the practical recommendations for optimally applying these general theories is not simple. This is due to the quite varied nature of the physical stresses encountered during training and competition for a wide range of sports, as well as the unique rules of each sport regarding the allowance for fluid and fuel intake during competition. Furthermore, variations in the physical intensity, duration and environment, as well as individual characteristics of a given athlete, might alter their optimal rate of water, carbohydrate and salt intake as well as the rate of gastrointestinal absorption and feelings of fullness. This task of developing consensus for general recommendations becomes less daunting when approached systematically through logical interpretation of the vast literature that has grown exponentially in the past two decades. It is also important to incorporate the experience of athletes recorded in carefully controlled 'field' studies or case reports, as this serves as a reality check regarding the conditions in which theories and laboratory findings can be applied directly to the overall welfare of athletes.

The aim of this article is to develop practical recommendations for fluid and fuel intake during exercise based upon interpretation of the scientific literature, with heavy reliance upon controlled laboratory studies as well as careful study of athletes in the field during training and competition. The focus of this review will be on identifying the conditions during which fluid and fuel intake positively or adversely affects either athletic performance or the physical well-being (i.e. acute and chronic health) of the individual athlete. Discussion of the physiological mechanisms mediating the performance effects will be limited to that which helps elucidate the practical application or refine the recommendation for fluid and fuel intake during exercise. Several excellent scientific review articles have already detailed the physiological mechanisms mediating reduced physiological strain during exercise by ingesting fluids, carbohydrate and electrolytes (Galloway and Maughan, 1998; Sawka and Coyle, 1999; Sawka and Montain, 2000; Cheuvront and Haymes, 2001; Cheuvront, 2001; Sawka *et al.*, 2001). The last 40 years have seen dramatic shifts in both scientific thinking and popular practice regarding water, carbohydrate and salt intake during exercise. Here, I develop practical guidelines for the exercising athlete, based on modern science, recognizing lessons from past application and the limitations of our present understanding.

Water or fluid intake

A person's physiological drive for fluid intake during exercise is perceived through 'thirst mechanisms' and it has long been known that when given *ad libitum* access to fluid, and thus drink voluntarily, that these mechanisms compel people to drink at a rate that replaces approximately one-half of their fluid losses and at best two-thirds (Pitts and Consolazio, 1944; Hubbard *et al.*, 1984). The concept that thirst during exercise does not drive people to take in fluid at the rate of fluid loss is termed 'voluntary dehydration'. In the 1960s, athletes were generally advised 'to drink only a little water during exercise' and to 'ignore their thirst' and to thus replace a small percentage of lost fluid. Furthermore, the scientific literature in the 1960s was interpreted to suggest that dehydration by less than 3–4% of body weight caused insignificant hyperthermia or impairment of physiological function and performance, although it was recognized that dehydration by more than 4% is dangerous to health (Wyndham and Strydom, 1969). This belief that dehydration by 3–4% was tolerable prevailed despite evidence to the contrary from carefully conducted studies around the time of the Second World War that had clearly shown that dehydration by less than 3–4% during prolonged marching in the heat impaired performance and caused exhaustion and collapse (Pitts and Consolazio, 1944; Adolph, 1947; Ladell, 1955; Coyle and Montain, 1992a,b). The athletic community of this era appears to have remained unaware or unconvinced that the demands of marching were not unlike athletic endurance events, except, of course, for the speed and practical aspects of drinking while running compared with walking.

It was not until the 1970s that athletes were generally advised to ingest something more than just 'a little water' during exercise. In 1975, the American College of Sports Medicine (ACSM) published its first position stand entitled 'Prevention of heat injury during distance running'. In 1985, the ACSM published another position stand that advised runners to drink 100–200 ml of fluid after every 2–3 km. This recommendation acknowledged the large variation in ideal rate of fluid replacement among runners, with faster runners needing more and slower runners less fluid intake per hour. However, these broad recommendations did not provide sufficiently practical guidelines for drinking relative to thirst or sweating rate. At the extremes, this recommendation could be interpreted to suggest that it is permissible for slow runners ($10 \text{ km} \cdot \text{h}^{-1}$) to drink only $330 \text{ ml} \cdot \text{h}^{-1}$, whereas the fastest runners should drink as much $2000 \text{ ml} \cdot \text{h}^{-1}$. The latter is a rate of fluid intake that is unrealistically high for most fast runners. However, this 1985 recommendation has theoretical merit in that it accurately set the limits for rates of sweating in slow and fast runners (330–$2000 \text{ ml} \cdot \text{h}^{-1}$). However, the ideal application of these broad guidelines would require the athlete to devise the schedule that meets not only their assumed need for fluid based on sweating rate, but also the rate of fluid replacement that is practical for them individually. It is unrealistic to expect that brief guidelines, which are naturally general, can be practised by all athletes in all sports under all conditions.

In its most recent position stand (Convertino *et al.*, 1996), the ACSM recommended that: 'During exercise, athletes should start drinking early and at regular intervals in an attempt to consume fluids at a rate sufficient to replace all the water lost through sweating (body weight loss), or consume the maximal amount that can be tolerated'. This document further stated that 'individuals should be encouraged to consume the maximal amount of fluids during exercise that can be tolerated without gastrointestinal discomfort up to a rate equal to that lost from sweating'.

In an attempt to bring attention to the potential for developing hyponatraemia from drinking excessively large volumes of fluid during marathon running, Tim Noakes has been critical of the 1996 guidelines from ACSM (Noakes, 2003). Noakes quotes the 1996 guidelines for his statement that 'athletes are now advised to replace all the water lost through sweating (that is, loss of body weight), or consume the maximal amount that can be tolerated, or drink 600–1200 ml per hour'. It is perplexing to the author of the current review how Dr. Noakes could interpret the 1996 guidelines from ACSM (Convertino et al., 1996) to suggest multiple recommendations, including the notion that athletes drink more fluid than is lost during exercise and therefore gain body weight. In an attempt to minimize current misinterpretation, misrepresentation or confusion, and in agreement with common sense, athletes who begin exercise in the euhydrated state should not be advised to drink fluids at a rate causing them to gain both body weight and body water during prolonged exercise. Ingested fluid that is stored in the stomach may temporarily cause people to gain body weight above euhydrated levels, yet obviously the fluid volume of the intracellular and extracellular compartments will not increase until the ingested fluid moves into the intestines for absorption and distribution throughout the body. Nevertheless, it is important to point out that unrestricted drinking that causes initially euhydrated people to gain large amounts of body weight and body water should be discouraged. Methods to safeguard against significant body weight gains during exercise can range from simple recommendations to reducing access to fluids and finally to mandatory periodic weighing during an event. In 2000, the National Athletic Trainers Association published a position statement concluding that 'Fluid replacement should approximate sweat and urine losses and at least maintain hydration at less than 2% body weight reduction' (Casa, 2000).

With regard to water intake during exercise, the above paragraph summarizes the evolution of scientific consensus as well as the challenges in developing practical guidelines that give consideration to both health and athletic performance. As discussed below, it is our general premise that athletes be encouraged to drink fluids at a rate that matches sweating rate. However, those general guidelines must consider circumstances in which it is not practical to drink at such high rates. In some sports like running, the reductions in body weight due to dehydration have been theorized, yet not proven, to have less of a negative effect on performance because of assumed concomitant reductions in energy expenditure from dehydration-induced reductions in body weight. However, these unproven theories must be tempered with the known negative effect of dehydration on health and performance. Furthermore, discussion should address the extent to which dehydration can be tolerated without heat illness depending upon variations in environment, individual state of 'fitness' and acclimation, as well as rates of heat production and heat dissipation. It would appear that the practical challenge is to better identify the specific athletic and environmental conditions in which exercising athletes should be advised to match fluid intake with sweating rate. On the other hand, during exercise in cool environments, some athletes might 'tolerate' a certain amount of dehydration, as discussed below. There presently seems to be general consensus in the literature that dehydration should not exceed 2% of body weight loss during most athletic events (Casa, 2000; Noakes and Martin, 2002). Therefore, from a practical perspective, the challenge now seems to be to identify sports, individuals and environments when 1% or 2% dehydration is 'tolerable', with little risk for heat illness and some potential performance benefits.

Practical recommendations for fluid intake during exercise

This practical challenge of identifying conditions of 'tolerable dehydration' must first recognize that dehydration reduces heat dissipation by reducing skin blood flow during exercise, usually resulting in an increased body core temperature (Coyle and Montain, 1992a,b; Gonzalez-Alonso et al., 1995). Furthermore, dehydration induces cardiovascular strain during exercise, best evidenced by a reduction in stroke volume. Using this reduced stroke volume as a reflection of cardiovascular strain during exercise, Gonzalez-Alonso (1998) has reported that dehydration without hyperthermia reduces stroke volume by 7–8% and that hyperthermia without dehydration also reduces stroke volume by 7–8%. However, the combination of dehydration and hyperthermia elicits synergistic effects in reducing stroke volume by more than 20%.

From a practical perspective, most athletes who experience significant dehydration will concomitantly experience a significant increase in core body temperature above that experienced during similar exercise conditions when euhydrated (Montain and Coyle, 1992; Gonzalez-Alonso et al., 1995, 1997; Gonzalez-Alonso, 1998). Readers should bear in mind that competitive athletes exercising at high intensity in sports such as running, cycling and soccer have high rates of heat production that require dissipation to the environment to prevent progressive heat storage and elevation of core temperature to above 39°C. Given the rates of heat production averaging 800–1200 W in many athletic conditions, it is rare that dehydration would not cause hyperthermia. Hyperthermia was prevented with dehydration by 4% of body weight when exercising when the environmental temperature was lowered to 5°C and convective cooling was further increased by exposing the bare skin of the participants to wetting and high wind speeds (Gonzalez-Alonso, 1998). This is in line with the idea that some marathon runners competing in environmental temperatures as low as 7–18°C who become dehydrated by 3–5% of body weight can still experience core temperatures of 39.0–41.7°C (Pugh et al., 1967; Maron et al., 1977; Maughan, 1984, 1985). Of course, there will be a wide range of core temperatures during exercise in a cold environment in runners with similar dehydration, based on how fast they are running towards the end of the race (Noakes et al., 1991a). However, the important point is that some athletes, often the fastest finishers, who experience significant dehydration, display core temperatures close to 40°C when running in cool environments of 7–18°C (Maron et al., 1977; Maughan, 1984, 1985). This agrees with the observation of Gonzalez-Alonso et al. (1998) that prevention of hyperthermia in athletes dehydrated by 4% of body weight is achieved only when very high rates of convective cooling are achieved through a cold environmental temperature (5°C) and high wind speed. Given that athletic events are seldom contested in such conditions, it is logical to suggest that dehydration will most commonly elicit hyperthermia in athletes competing intensely. From this basis, the question of how much dehydration is acceptable must be answered relative to how much hyperthermia is acceptable, recognizing potential individual variability in the extent to which dehydration elicits negative effects such as hyperthermia.

Recent studies have found fatigue to occur in heat-acclimated runners when core temperature reaches approximately 40°C and dehydration is not great (Gonzalez-Alonso *et al.*, 1999b; Nielsen *et al.*, 2001; Nielsen and Nybo, 2003). However, given that hyperthermia and dehydration are synergistic to fatigue, it must be recognized that dehydrated people are less tolerant of hyperthermia and they usually collapse or fatigue at core temperatures in the range of 38.5–39.5°C (Montain and Coyle, 1992; Sawka and Coyle, 1999; Cheuvront, 2001; Cheuvront and Haymes, 2001; Sawka *et al.*, 2001).

Effects of dehydration on cardiovascular strain, hyperthermia and muscle metabolism

Dehydration appears to have a robust effect on cardiovascular strain as evidenced by the observation that for every 1% of body weight loss due to dehydration, heart rate increases by 5–8 beats$\cdot$min^{-1} and cardiac output declines significantly, while core temperature also increases by 0.2–0.3°C (Brown, 1947; Coyle and Montain, 1992a,b; Sawka and Coyle, 1999; Cheuvront, 2001; Cheuvront and Haymes, 2001; Sawka *et al.*, 2001). As discussed below, dehydration during exercise reduces endurance performance through a number of interrelated mechanisms involving increased cardiovascular strain due to hyperthermia and reduced blood volume, as well as direct effects of hyperthermia on muscle metabolism and neurological function (Gonzalez-Alonso *et al.*, 1995, 1997, 1998, 1999a,b, 2000; Gonzalez-Alonso, 1998; Gonzalez-Alonso and Calbet, 2003). Dehydration and hyperthermia have profound effects on reducing stroke volume and muscle blood flow, thus limiting oxygen delivery to exercising skeletal muscle. Hargreaves *et al.* (1996) observed that dehydration increases muscle glycogen use during continuous exercise, possibly as a result of increased core temperature, reduced oxygen delivery and/or increased catecholamines.

Effects of dehydration on endurance performance

As discussed by Cheuvront *et al.* (2003), studies examining endurance performance in temperate environments (20–21°C) during exercise lasting less than 90 min have reported that dehydration by 1–2% of body weight has a statistically insignificant effect on performance (Robinson *et al.*, 1995; McConell *et al.*, 1999; Bachle *et al.*, 2001). However, dehydration by 2% of body weight, which generally occurs during exercise lasting more than 90 min, does appear to significantly impair endurance performance in environments of 20–21°C (Cheuvront *et al.*, 2003). Therefore, it would appear that athletes participating in endurance events lasting less than 90 min in temperate environments can generally tolerate dehydration by 1–2% of body weight without any significant impact upon performance. However, exercise lasting more than 90 min and with more than 2% dehydration appears to impair performance in temperate environments of 20–21°C (Fallowfield *et al.*, 1996; McConell *et al.*, 1997; Cheuvront *et al.*, 2003).

In hot environments (31–32°C), sweating rate is higher and thus 60 min of intense exercise typically elicits dehydration by approximately 2% of body weight. Exercise performance over approximately 60 min in a hot environment has been observed to be impaired by both Below *et al.* (1995) and Walsh *et al.* (1994) with dehydration amounting to 2% and 1.8%, respectively. Therefore, dehydration by 2% of body weight during exercise in a hot environment (31–32°C) clearly impairs endurance performance, but when exercise is performed in a temperate environment (20–21°C), dehydration by 2% appears to have a lesser and insignificant effect on endurance performance. Collectively, these findings suggest that athletes are advised to attempt to offset dehydration as much as possible when exercising intensely in a hot environment (31–32°C) for durations approaching 60 min and longer. When the environment is temperate (20–21°C), athletes may be better able to tolerate 2% dehydration without significant performance decrement or risk of significantly added hyperthermia compared with exercise with full fluid replacement. In cold environments, dehydration by more than 2% may be tolerable. Figure 1 displays the concept that progressively greater dehydration may be tolerable and without significant performance decrement in endurance-trained athletes as the environment gets progressively cooler. A similar concept was proposed by Adolph *et al.* (1948) and discussed recently by Sawka and Montain (2000).

Timing of fluid intake during exercise and practical issues regarding tolerable dehydration

Montain and Coyle (1993) demonstrated that the benefits of ingesting 1.2 litres of fluid (when sweating rate was $1.2 \, l \cdot h^{-1}$) during 140 min of exercise in the heat required 40–60 min to be realized in terms of reduced heart rate and core temperature as well as improved blood volume and plasma osmolality. This agrees with the time-course with which that volume of ingested fluid would be distributed throughout the body after gastric emptying, intestinal absorption and osmotic flow (Noakes *et al.*, 1991b; Schedl *et al.*, 1994). Given this 40–60 min time period needed to realize the benefits of drinking fluids in a hot environment while sweating heavily, it becomes clear that benefits from fluid intake during events lasting less than 40–60 min will not be realized during exercise. Obviously, ingested fluid that has not been distributed throughout the body and which remains in the gastrointestinal tract will be of no benefit in terms of reducing cardiovascular or thermal strain during exercise. In another light, offsetting body weight loss by drinking fluids does not offset cellular dehydration until at least 40 min has passed, which is the time needed for the ingested fluid to function.

Appreciation of this time-course of fluid absorption and distribution helps reconcile practical issues about whether the tolerable level of dehydration during exercise in a hot environment is 2% body weight loss or less. From a cellular perspective (independent of fluid in the gut), no amount of dehydration can be tolerated without strain on the cardiovascular and thermoregulatory systems. This is best observed after 120 min of exercise in the heat (33°C) with a fluid drinking schedule designed to minimize delay in fluid replacement to cells, by giving a large volume early in exercise followed by subsequent frequent feedings aimed at maintaining high gastric volumes and thus high emptying rate, yet a low gastric volume at the end of exercise (Montain and Coyle, 1992; Gonzalez-Alonso et al., 1995). Under these conditions, dehydration by 2.3% compared with only 1.1% of body weight elicited a significantly higher heart rate and core temperature (Montain and Coyle, 1992). Furthermore, when comparing dehydration ranging from 1 to 4% of body weight, it was clear that no amount of body weight reduction and dehydration was without negative physiological consequences after 120 min of exercise in the heat (Coyle and Montain, 1992a). This measurable and statistically significant effect of only a 1.2% body weight difference in true dehydration (i.e. 2.3 vs 1.1%) amounts to approximately 1 litre or less of body water. Functionally, however, the benefit of this additional 1 litre of fluid replacement is realized only when it has had time to be absorbed and distributed throughout the body. Under these conditions, each 1 litre of fluid ingested to offset dehydration had the benefit of reducing core temperature by 0.3°C and lowering heart rate by 8 beats $\cdot$ min^{-1} while raising cardiac output 1 l $\cdot$ min^{-1} (Montain and Coyle, 1992).

During exercise in the heat (33°C), therefore, dehydration by 1–2% of body weight will indeed increase core temperature and add significant cardiovascular strain (Montain and Coyle, 1992; Sawka and Coyle, 1999; Sawka and Montain, 2000; Sawka et al., 2001). Again, this is unlike exercise in a cold environment (Fig. 1). Yet, when exercising in the heat with a high sweat rate, it is not often possible for athletes to exercise with the large gastric volume needed to promote the high rates of gastrointestinal fluid absorption that are required to prevent cellular dehydration during exercise. For example, if an athlete finishes 90 min of exercise with no body weight loss but with 1.5 litres of fluid in the gastrointestinal tract, he or she would not be expected to display any physiological benefit of that 1.5 litres of fluid compared with a condition in which exogenous fluid is not present in the gastrointestinal tract. The only expected difference would be that he or she would weigh less (by the weight of 1.5 litres of fluid), amounting to a reduction in body weight of approximately 2%. Therefore, it would appear that the additional 1.5 litres of fluid ingestion, which prevents body weight from declining 2%, is not beneficial in terms of core temperature or cardiovascular strain. However, in this case, body weight would not be an accurate reflection of cellular hydration. Therefore, intelligent discussion of whether or not the tolerable level of dehydration is 0% or 1% or 2% of body weight loss must recognize the limitations of using whole-body weight as a

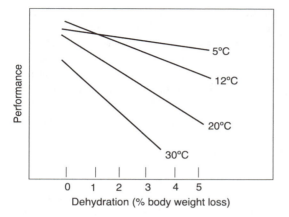

Figure 1. Theoretical effects of dehydration on endurance performance during prolonged exercise in environments that vary in temperature from 5 to 30°C (see text for discussion).

measure of dehydration when fluid remains in the gut at the time when body weight is measured.

When sweating rate exceeds $1 \, l \cdot h^{-1}$, it becomes progressively more difficult to offset cellular dehydration in many individuals because this requires exercising with a gastric volume of approximately 0.6–1.0 litre of fluid. The discomfort of that added volume and weight will not reduce physiological stress if it remains in the gut towards the end of the event and some individuals may not benefit by drinking the extra volume that ensures no body weight reduction at the end of exercise. Therefore, from a performance perspective, sometimes it may be advised to drink less than needed for full fluid replacement and finish with up to a 2% reduction in body weight provided that the drinking schedule is designed to minimize gut fluid volume towards the end of exercise. This is best achieved by drinking larger volumes early in exercise and continuing to ingest fluid throughout so that stomach volume is high with 40 min remaining and little fluid is ingested thereafter.

What do fast marathon runners experience?

In recent review articles, Cheuvront and colleagues (Cheuvront, 2001; Cheuvront and Haymes, 2001; Cheuvront *et al.*, 2003) indicate that faster marathon runners tend to experience greater dehydration at the end of the marathon with values ranging from 2 to 8% body weight loss. However, they are careful to point out that this should not be interpreted to suggest any advantage of becoming dehydrated but rather that when running faster, the difficulty encountered in drinking fluids causes a progressively greater dehydration because of an increasing mismatch between fluid loss and replacement in most runners. Furthermore, Cheuvront and colleagues (Cheuvront, 2001; Cheuvront and Haymes, 2001; Cheuvront *et al.*, 2003) point out that within the population of qualifiers for the US Olympic Trials in the marathon, that a weak relationship exists between level of dehydration and performance. The puzzling question in marathon running is how some runners perform so well despite final dehydration of 4–8% of body weight (Wyndham and Strydom, 1969; Costill, 1972) and core temperatures in excess of 40°C (Pugh *et al.*, 1967). One possibility is error in magnitude of true dehydration from the perspective that the marathon runners might have begun the race somewhat hyperhydrated at the time of pre-race body weight measurement.

Another possibility is that when running, reductions in body weight due to dehydration might lower the oxygen cost of movement. For example, if dehydration reduces body weight and the absolute oxygen cost of running by 4%, yet absolute power output is reduced by less than 4%, the power output per kilogram of body weight could theoretically be increased, although no direct data exist, to the author's knowledge, to confirm or refute this hypothesis. However, given the robust negative effect of dehydration-induced hyperthermia, this theoretical increase in performance potential (power per kilogram) can only be realized if the individual can tolerate hyperthermia when dehydrated. Bearing in mind that the combination of dehydration and hyperthermia act synergistically to impair cardiovascular function, such 'functional' dehydration is a gamble. Unfortunately, data are not available to calculate the ratio of risk of hyperthermia compared with the theoretical benefit of reduced energy expenditure as a result of reduced body weight from dehydration. Ideally, calculation of the risk–benefit ratio should be made with knowledge of the individual athlete under the specific exercise intensity and environmental conditions to identify when an individual might be best capable of surviving the clear negative effects of dehydration and hyperthermia to gain potential advantages of reduced oxygen cost.

Practical application to marathon runners

The question of optimal fluid replacement for marathon runners is not new. It has long been recognized that runners generally drink only $500 \text{ ml} \cdot \text{h}^{-1}$ of fluid and thus allow themselves to dehydrate at rates of $500\text{–}1000 \text{ ml} \cdot \text{h}^{-1}$. The performance question again boils down to whether the time lost as a result of drinking larger volumes will be compensated by the physiological benefits drinking produces and the faster running pace that might be achieved during the last half of the race. However, if the goal is safety, which means minimizing hyperthermia, there is no question that the closer that the rate of drinking can match the rate of dehydration, the better (Coyle and Montain, 1992a,b). Runners need to determine this for themselves, as there is much individual variability in the time lost when drinking larger fluid volumes both because of the methods of drinking on the run as well as the amount of gastric discomfort encountered due to a variety of individually unique factors, such as gastric emptying rate and how gastric anatomy interacts with running style and sensation of stomach fullness. This appears to be a case where one general recommendation will not be ideal for a significant number of runners, but it represents a starting point for them to begin the trial-and-error process for themselves.

Noakes and Martin (2002) recently advised that 'runners should aim to drink as needed between 400–800 ml per hour, with the higher rates for the faster, heavier runners competing in warm environmental conditions and the lower rates for the slower runners/walkers competing marathon races in cooler environmental conditions'. This is also a reasonable starting point from which individual runners should begin the trial-and-error process. It is likely that some fast runners will be able to drink more than 800 ml · h^{-1}, which may be especially beneficial in environments eliciting heavy sweating of 1000–1500 ml · h^{-1}. Therefore, individuals should attempt to drink 1000 ml · h^{-1} or more during fast training runs so that they can best learn to meet their unique needs. Obviously, higher rates of fluid replacement are most important to individuals who experience more dehydration and who are more adversely affected by dehydration-induced hyperthermia. Furthermore, because of the running time lost in obtaining and drinking more fluid, recognizing individual variability in potential discomfort from stomach fullness must be considered. From a practical perspective, it is quite inefficient for runners to drink from open cups handed to them. Athletes and race organizers should devise better practical methods by which runners can drink larger volumes without slowing or having to carry fluid containers in their hands.

Excessive fluid intake and hyponatraemia

A serious although infrequent problem is the development of hyponatraemia, especially in runners and walkers who drink excessively large volumes of low sodium fluids throughout prolonged exercise (Noakes *et al.*, 1985; Barr and Costill, 1989; Vrijens and Rehrer, 1999; Montain *et al.*, 2001; O'Brien *et al.*, 2001; Speedy *et al.*, 2001). Fast drinking in these slow-moving individuals (4–6 hour marathon times) causes them to gain significant body water over the course of the marathon distance because fluid replacement is far in excess of sweating rate. Therefore, recommendations should always convey quantitative limits. For example, a very simple recommendation that might serve as a deterrent to hyponatraemia for slow runners, while not misguiding the faster runners, is that a marathon distance requires consumption of not more than 2–4 litres of fluid. Hyponatraemia is discussed further in the section on salt intake during exercise.

Fluid intake and performance during sports and intermittent exercise

Many sports such as basketball, ice hockey, soccer and tennis are contested over prolonged periods consisting of intermittent yet high-intensity exercise. The question is whether these athletes should attempt full fluid replacement compared with their typical practice of incurring dehydration of approximately 2% or more of body weight (Bangsbo et al., 1991; Maughan, 1991; Maughan et al., 1993; Bangsbo, 1994; Maughan and Leiper, 1994). The situation is not unlike marathon running in terms of whether there is an allowable level of dehydration relative to the environment and the individual athlete and the practical realities involved in drinking large volumes of fluid. Furthermore, successful performance in these sports involves more than energy expenditure and fatigue resistance, as winning also depends on cognitive function for decision making as well as proper execution of complex skills, making assessment of sport performance quite challenging.

Williams and colleagues have developed a shuttle-running test (Loughborough Intermittent Shuttle Test) aimed at simulating the intense 'stop and go' nature of sports such as soccer (Nicholas et al., 2000). They have observed that fluid replacement prevents a reduction in soccer skill performance and mental concentration due to dehydration (McGregor et al., 1999b; Nicholas et al., 1999).

Carbohydrate intake

Background with prolonged continuous exercise

Although there was some evidence long ago that carbohydrate ingestion during exercise improved athletic performance, the discovery of the importance of muscle glycogen as a source of carbohydrate energy for athletes in the 1960s and 1970s (Bergstrom et al., 1967) appears to have obscured thinking until the 1980s regarding the potential energy contribution of ingested carbohydrate (Coyle et al., 1986; Coggan and Coyle, 1991; Hargreaves, 1996). For example, Costill and Miller (1980) emphasized the need for fluid intake during exercise but they did not recommend ingesting very much carbohydrate. This recommendation is understandable at that time, given that the physiological benefits of fluid replacement were beginning to be established, as reflected in the 1975 ACSM position stand, whereas the physiological benefits of carbohydrate ingestion for blood glucose supplementation as well as the physiological mechanisms explaining this benefit were yet to be firmly established (Hargreaves, 1996). In the 1980s, the observation that the addition of carbohydrate to water temporarily slowed gastric emptying rate was interpreted to suggest that fluid replacement solutions should not contain much carbohydrate (Coyle et al., 1978). It is now understood that the slight slowing of gastric emptying caused by solutions containing up to 8% carbohydrate is a relatively minor factor in fluid replacement rate compared with the large influence of increased fluid volume for increasing gastric emptying and fluid replacement rate (Maughan, 1991; Maughan and Noakes, 1991; Coyle and Montain, 1992a,b; Maughan et al., 1993). It was also thought, albeit mistakenly, that 'ingested glucose contributes very little to the total energy utilized during exercise' (Costill and

Miller, 1980). Therefore, the prevailing recommendation in 1980 was that 'under conditions that threaten the endurance athlete with dehydration and hyperthermia, fluid replacement solutions should contain little sugar (>25 g/L or $>2.5\%$) and electrolytes' (Costill and Miller, 1980).

In the 1980s, it was established that ingested carbohydrate and blood glucose can indeed be oxidized at rates of approximately 1 g$\cdot$min^{-1} and that this exogenous carbohydrate becomes the predominant source of carbohydrate energy late in a bout of prolonged continuous exercise (Convertino *et al.*, 1996). Therefore, carbohydrate ingestion delays fatigue during prolonged cycling and running and it also improves the power output that can be maintained (Millard-Stafford, 1992; Millard-Stafford *et al.*, 1995, 1997; Hargreaves, 1996). Therefore, as reviewed previously, it is generally recommended that endurance athletes ingest carbohydrate at a rate of 30–60 g$\cdot$h^{-1} (Convertino *et al.*, 1996; Casa, 2000). The carbohydrate can be in the form of glucose, sucrose, malto-dextrins or some high glycaemic starches. Fructose intake should be limited to amounts that do not cause gastrointestinal discomfort (Convertino *et al.*, 1996; Casa, 2000). This rate of carbohydrate ingestion can be met by drinking 600–1200 ml$\cdot$h^{-1} of solutions containing 4–8% carbohydrates (4–8 g$\cdot$100 ml^{-1}) (Rehrer *et al.*, 1993; Rehrer, 1994; Convertino *et al.*, 1996; Casa, 2000).

Performance during short-term intermittent high-intensity bouts of exercise

The benefits of carbohydrate ingestion during performance of high-intensity intermittent exercise attempted after at least 60 min of continuous moderate-intensity exercise (65–80% $\dot{V}O_{2max}$) was the focus of a study beginning in the late 1980s. Power measured over 5–15 min of high-intensity and predominantly aerobic exercise has generally been observed to be increased by ingesting carbo-hydrate (Murray *et al.*, 1987, 1989; Coggan and Coyle, 1988; Mitchell *et al.*, 1989; Sugiura and Kobayashi, 1998). In the 1996 ACSM position statement on 'Exercise and Fluid Replacement', it was concluded that 'During intense exercise lasting longer than 1 h, it is recommended that carbohydrates be ingested at a rate of 30–60 g/h to maintain oxidation of carbohydrates and delay fatigue' (Convertino *et al.*, 1996).

During the past decade, attention has focused on determining if carbohydrate intake during sporting events such as soccer and tennis improves various indices of performance. As discussed below, carbohydrate ingestion appears frequently to benefit performance, as demonstrated in tests of 'shuttle-running' ability, which simulate the stop and start nature of many sports requiring bursts of speed and some fatigue resistance (Nicholas *et al.*, 2000). The physiological mechanisms for this ergogenic effect of carbohydrate ingestion are unclear and have been theorized to involve more than simply skeletal muscle metabolism, implying a neuromuscular component. The challenge at the present time seems to be how to identify the types of physical activity and sporting scenarios for which carbohydrate ingestion is advisable, as well as identifying those circumstances in which such a recommendation is not effective or even counterproductive.

Conditions in which carbohydrate ingestion during exercise does not appear to improve performance

Performance or fatigue resistance can be governed by many physiological factors involving primarily the skeletal muscle, the cardiovascular system and the nervous system. It is to be expected that some primary causes of fatigue are not influenced by carbohydrate ingestion during exercise. For example, the negative effect of hyperthermia on performance of prolonged exercise in a hot environment (33–35°C) does not appear to be lessened by carbohydrate ingestion (Febbraio et al., 1996a; Fritzsche et al., 2000). However, during exercise in a cool environment (5°C) that is not limited by hyperthermia (Febbraio et al., 1996a), or when individuals drink fluids during exercise in a hot environment and do not become hyperthermic (Fritzsche et al., 2000), carbohydrate feedings indeed improve performance. Under conditions not eliciting hyperthermia, the factor most important for performance of prolonged and intense exercise appears to be maintaining carbohydrate availability and thus oxidation, especially from blood glucose oxidation as muscle glycogen concentration declines. This was better achieved by ingesting carbohydrate solutions of 7% than 14% (Febbraio et al., 1996a).

Another example of when carbohydrate ingestion during exercise would not be expected to improve performance is when fatigue is due to the accumulation of hydrogen ions in skeletal muscle (low muscle pH), as occurs during a single bout of intense exercise performed continuously for 20–30 min. Exercise that is not sufficiently stressful to cause fatigue, as evidenced by reduced power production, or that does not require high effort to maintain power, as reflected for example by high levels of various stress hormones, would not be expected to benefit from carbohydrate ingestion. Furthermore, carbohydrate intake is not generally recommended during events that are completed in 30–45 min or less, performed either continuously or intermittently. Although this last point has not been extensively studied to date, it is an assumption based upon the practice of athletes competing in events lasting only 30–45 min. As discussed, carbohydrate ingestion does not appear to lessen fatigue due to hyperthermia or dehydration-induced hyperthermia, even when exercise is prolonged (1–3 h) (Febbraio et al., 1996a; Fritzsche et al., 2000). Thus, there does not appear to be any benefit of adding carbohydrate to fluid replacement solution under these conditions. Therefore, people who exercise at moderate intensity for less than 1 h, and who do not experience fatigue, do not appear to benefit from carbohydrate ingestion during exercise. Yet ingesting 30–60 g carbohydrate $\cdot$ h^{-1} does not appear to present a general physiological risk to people who do not experience gastrointestinal discomfort.

Conditions in which carbohydrate ingestion improves performance through unexplained physiological mechanisms

Carbohydrate ingestion during prolonged exercise can benefit performance if fatigue is due to inadequate carbohydrate energy from blood glucose (Coggan and Coyle, 1991; Febbraio *et al.*, 1996b). This is one well-documented physiological mechanism by which the ergogenic benefit of carbohydrate ingestion during exercise can be explained. However, carbohydrate ingestion has been observed to improve performance under conditions where fatigue is not clearly due to lack of aerobic or anaerobic carbohydrate energy. For example, when the duration of continuous exercise is extended to approximately 60 min and thus the intensity is 80–90% $\dot{V}O_{2max}$, carbohydrate ingestion during exercise has been shown to improve power output by 6% during the 50–60 min period (Below *et al.*, 1995).

Other recent studies have also reported a performance benefit of carbohydrate feeding when the total duration of the performance bout is approximately 60 min or more. The total period of 60 min or more is broken up into shorter exercise durations, thereby simulating the demands of many sports (basketball, soccer, hockey) in which high-intensity exercise is interspersed with periods of recovery (Murray *et al.*, 1987, 1989; Mitchell *et al.*, 1989). Carbohydrate ingestion is ergogenic during 15-min bouts of intermittent 'shuttle running' performed several times (five times), as well as during repeated high-intensity intervals of 1 min duration (and 3 min recovery) (Nicholas *et al.*, 1995; Davis *et al.*, 1997, 1999, 2000a; McGregor *et al.*, 1999; Welsh *et al.*, 2002). Thus, the total duration of these work–rest bouts was over 60 min.

The physiological mechanisms responsible for these performance benefits of carbohydrate ingestion are not clear and have been theorized to involve the central nervous system, skeletal muscle and/or the cardiovascular system. It is likely that carbohydrate feeding influences the interactions of all three of these systems, possibly through the actions of neurotransmitters, hormones and other peptides that are already known (e.g. insulin, catecholamines, serotonin) or are emerging as important (e.g. interleukin-6), or those substances which have yet to be discovered. Regardless, sufficient evidence is accumulating to recommend carbohydrate ingestion during continuous or intermittent exercise that lasts for 60 min or more and where fatigue is due to factors other than hyperthermia.

Can carbohydrate ingestion during exercise be counterproductive?

It is recommended that carbohydrate be ingested at a rate of 30–60 g·h^{-1} during exercise, recognizing that ingesting more does not increase oxidation rate yet ingesting more can produce gastrointestinal discomfort in many people (Rehrer *et al.*, 1992; Wagenmakers *et al.*, 1993). Therefore, carbohydrate feeding can be counterproductive when ingested in amounts (>60–90 g·h^{-1}) or concentrations (>7–8%) that are too large (Febbraio *et al.*, 1996a; Galloway and

Maughan, 2000). This is a common practical mistake among athletes that could be remedied by simple education.

A separate question is whether carbohydrate ingestion at 30–60 g·h^{-1} during exercise can impair performance when compared with no carbohydrate ingestion. It could have a negative effect if it produced gastrointestinal discomfort, a factor that is likely to vary from sport to sport and from athlete to athlete. Caution should also be used when recommending carbohydrate ingestion during events lasting approximately 15–45 min that require repeated bouts of intense exercise lasting several minutes followed by several minutes of rest. These events have the potential to elicit large swings in blood glucose and insulin concentration, thus requiring feeding plans that are specific to the varied intensity and time demands of the event. Those feeding schedules might be more than those described below, yet without data or experience to make more specific recommendations, all that can be done at present, besides recognizing these limitations, is to encourage systematic trial and error.

From a practical perspective, the recommendation of ingesting 30–60 g·h^{-1} of carbohydrate during exercise should emphasize that this be accomplished by taking feedings every 10–30 min, as allowed by the event. The goal of the feeding schedule should be to create a steady flow of carbohydrate from the gut into the bloodstream. In other words, if carbohydrate feeding is begun during an event, it should be continued throughout the event in a manner that allows for a steady flow of exogenous glucose into the blood with minimal gastrointestinal discomfort. It is especially inadvisable to give a large bolus of carbohydrate (more and 30–60 g) early in an event and then discontinue carbohydrate feeding. This practice will prime the body for glucose metabolism, and reduce fat oxidation, and then deprive the body of the fuel it has been primed to metabolize.

Salt intake during exercise

Background

Sodium chloride is the major salt lost in sweat, with sodium being the electrolyte most critical to performance and health. Sodium levels within the extracellular fluid, as reflected by plasma sodium concentration, should remain within a range of 130–160 mmol·l^{-1} to keep cells, tissues and organs functioning with the proper volumes of fluid and thus optimal balance. A striking example of this imbalance is seen when a low serum sodium concentration (hyponatraemia below 130 mmol·l^{-1}) causes fluid movement into the brain, causing swelling with symptoms that can progress from feeling strange, to mental confusion, general weakness, collapse, seizure, coma and death. Because the sodium concentration in sweat is much lower than that of plasma, the primary cause of hyponatraemia is dilution of body water by drinking a large volume of low sodium-containing fluid over several hours, and it can be exacerbated by also losing large amounts of sodium in sweat (Vrijens and Rehrer, 1999; Montain *et al.*, 2001; O'Brien *et al.*, 2001; Rehrer, 2001).

Sodium lost in sweat can vary greatly among individuals, with concentrations ranging from 20 to 80 mmol·l^{-1} (Maughan, 1991; Schedl *et al.*, 1994). Heat acclimation generally reduces sodium losses by reducing sweat sodium concentration more than sweating rate is increased. However, it is becoming increasingly clear that some heat-acclimated athletes can still lose large amounts of sodium when sweating heavily for 2 h because of their individual, and probably genetic, trait of producing sweat very high in sodium. It is likely that excessive loss of sodium during exercise in these athletes might cause them to fatigue due to development of muscle weakness or cramps. Although it is difficult to study groups of these individuals due to the infrequency of 'muscle cramping', it would appear that provision of extra dietary salt before and during exercise is warranted in these athletes (Schedl *et al.*, 1994; Eichner, 1998).

Recommendations for sodium intake during prolonged exercise

In most athletes exercising and sweating for 4–5 h with a sweat sodium concentration of less than 50 mmol·l^{-1}, the total sodium lost is less than 10% of total body stores (total stores are approximately 2500 mmol or 58 g for a 70-kg person). These losses appear to be well tolerated by most people (Barr and Costill, 1989; Barr *et al.*, 1991; Barr, 1999). On the other hand, the inclusion of sodium in fluid replacement drinks has some theoretical benefits, and the addition of sodium poses little or no risk. In fact, the addition of sodium in certain concentrations and types improves taste while also stimulating the osmotically dependent dipsogenic factors (thirst) that appear to increase voluntary drinking, thus minimizing involuntary dehydration (Wilk and Bar-Or, 1996; Wemple *et al.*, 1997). Absorption of fluids that enter the intestines is more rapid when sodium is present and this has the potential to aid sugar absorption (Schedl *et al.*, 1994). However, sufficient sodium is present in ingested fluid or water by the time it reaches the intestines for absorption, even when no sodium is ingested, due to the movement of endogenous body sodium into fluid within the gastrointestinal tract. Therefore, there is not presently a well-documented need to include sodium in fluid replacement drinks ingested during exercise, at least in terms of fluid and sugar absorption into the body (Rehrer *et al.*, 1993; Hargreaves *et al.*, 1994; Vrijens and Rehrer, 1999; Rehrer, 2001). Yet, given the potential for sodium to stimulate thirst and drinking and since it is lost in sweat, the potential logical benefits outweigh the low risk. Therefore, it is recommended that sodium (20–40 mmol·l^{-1}) be included in fluids ingested during exercise, especially when it is prolonged (longer than 1 h). When exercise is performed for several hours, or when large amounts of sodium are lost in sweat, it is especially important for athletes to include sodium in fluid replacement solutions to minimize hyponatraemia. It is prudent to suggest that sodium be included in fluids consumed during exercise lasting more than 2 h or by individuals during any event that stimulates heavy sodium loss (more than 3–4 g of sodium).

Intake of other electrolytes during exercise

Compared with sodium and chloride, the concentration of other electrolytes in sweat is low. For example, the average concentrations are: potassium, 5 mmol·l^{-1} (range 3–15 mmol·l^{-1}); calcium, 1 mmol·l^{-1} (range 0.3–2.0 mmol·l^{-1}); and magnesium, 0.8 mmol·l^{-1} (range 0.2–1.5 mmol·l^{-1}) (Criswell et al., 1992; Cunningham, 1997; McCutcheon and Geor, 1998; Sawka and Montain, 2000). Presently, there are no data that make a compelling case for including these electrolytes in fluids consumed during exercise (Powers et al., 1990; Deuster and Singh, 1993; Sawka and Montain, 2000; Sejersted and Sjogaard, 2000).

Intake of other fuels during exercise

Protein

Protein ingestion during exercise has theoretical potential to serve both as a fuel for oxidation as well as acting to stimulate cellular responses that have benefits during exercise. At present, there are few data to support any specific recommendations regarding type, amount and timing of protein intake during exercise. However, as discussed by Tipton and Wolfe (2004), protein availability immediately after exercise may stimulate adaptation and, therefore, it may be practical to ingest it during exercise, although it may not be needed during exercise per se. Given that the major pathways for ingested protein to contribute energy for oxidation during prolonged exercise are through deamination and metabolism as carbohydrate and, to a lesser extent, fat, there do not appear to be any advantages of ingesting protein compared with carbohydrate during exercise.

In addition to serving as a fuel, ingested protein from normal foods has the potential to moderate the metabolic responses during exercise under some conditions. For example, as discussed by Burke et al. (2004) and Ivy and colleagues (Zawadzki et al., 1992; Ivy, 2001; Ivy et al., 2002), the addition of small amounts of protein to carbohydrate ingested after exercise augments the plasma insulin response, which has the potential to alter metabolism. However, at present there is insufficient theoretical rationale or data to recommend inclusion of protein in solutions ingested during exercise. A vast number of biologically active substances can be classified as proteins, including those in our common food supply, as well as a seemingly infinite number of herbal supplements as well as man-made substances including drugs. Maughan et al. (2004) discuss the wide range of supplements presently available.

Fat

Triglyceride stored in adipose tissue and within muscle fibres provides an important endogenous fuel for oxidation during exercise. Because it is not practical to ingest fatty acids during exercise, fat is ingested in the form of either long-chain or medium-chain triglycerides. Ingested long-chain triglycerides are absorbed in the intestines but delivered only slowly into the bloodstream through the lymphatic systems. Typically, long-chain triglycerides begin to enter the blood as chylomicron triglycerides approximately 2 h after ingestion (Evans *et al.*, 1999) and thus there is no rationale for eating fat during exercise lasting less than 2 h. The extent to which ingested long-chain triglycerides can add to total energy production and performance is not completely clear (Magazanik *et al.*, 1974; Howald and Decombaz, 1983; Blomstrand *et al.*, 1988; Burke and Read, 1989; Davis *et al.*, 1992, 1999, 2000b; Turcotte *et al.*, 1992; MacLean and Graham, 1993; Manore *et al.*, 1993; Schedl *et al.*, 1994; Biolo *et al.*, 1995, 1997; Davis, 1995a,b; Tipton and Wolfe, 1998; Gibala *et al.*, 1999; Rasmussen *et al.*, 2000; Herd *et al.*, 2001; Ivy, 2001; Tipton *et al.*, 2003).

Medium-chain triglycerides are digested rapidly and have theoretical advantages due to the relative ease with which they can pass through cell membranes and enter into oxidative pathways. However, despite extensive study, most investigators (Jeukendrup *et al.*, 1995, 1996; Angus *et al.*, 2000; Horowitz *et al.*, 2000), but not all (van Zyl *et al.*, 1996), have not found them to benefit performance. It would appear that ingestion of sufficiently large doses of medium-chain triglycerides causes gastrointestinal distress (Jeukendrup *et al.*, 1996).

Amino acid intake during exercise

Several amino acids have been theorized (Blomstrand *et al.*, 1988) to benefit performance when ingested during exercise on the basis of their unknown potential to alter skeletal muscle metabolism or positively influence central nervous system function. However, although their potential is intriguing, especially that of the branched-chain amino acids, studies have not identified a clear benefit to performance or physiological function (MacLean and Graham, 1993; Davis, 1995a,b; Davis *et al.*, 1999, 2000b; Gibala *et al.*, 1999).

Glycerol

Glycerol is a three-carbon carbohydrate that readily diffuses throughout the body. The main pathway by which glycerol can serve as a fuel is through liver gluconeogenesis and thus a method for maintaining blood glucose availability. In rats, glycerol feeding improves endurance, probably due to the rat's high gluconeogenic ability (Terblanche *et al.*, 1981). In humans, however, glycerol feeding has been found to be ineffective for improving endurance, probably because it has limited potential for maintaining gluconeogenesis (Miller *et al.*, 1983).

Because ingested glycerol distributes throughout the body water, except for the brain, it has the potential to osmotically increase body water stores and has been advocated as a method for hyperhydration before exercise (Lyons *et al.*, 1990), but does not appear generally effective for improving thermoregulation (Freund *et al.*, 1995; Latzka and Sawka, 2000). There is little reason to suspect that glycerol ingestion during exercise would be beneficial to thermoregulation through retaining more of the ingested fluid in the body, because little fluid is lost in urine during exercise, and this indeed seems to be the case (Murray *et al.*, 1991).

Caffeine

Unlike other substances that stimulate the central nervous system, caffeine appears to be a socially accepted ergogenic aid and its use is not effectively discouraged within the culture of organized sport. It has long been appreciated that caffeine improves power output, especially during the later stages of endurance performance measured under laboratory conditions (Costill *et al.*, 1978; Ivy *et al.*, 1979; Spriet, 1995). Recently, Cox *et al.* (2002) have confirmed this performance benefit during prolonged cycling when caffeine is ingested in amounts and at times that have been practised by competitive cyclists for decades (drinking a few hundred millilitres of decarbonated and caffeinated soft drinks). Specifically, a relatively small dose of caffeine (about $1.5 \text{ mg} \cdot \text{kg}^{-1}$ or approximately 100 mg), taken during the last 40 min of prolonged exercise, was found to improve time-trial performance in laboratory studies. This seems to be the most efficient method for caffeine intake during exercise and it does not appear to be less effective than taking $3-9 \text{ mg} \cdot \text{kg}^{-1}$ doses before or throughout prolonged exercise (Cox *et al.*, 2002).

Summary statements with recommendations for fluid and fuel intake during exercise

1   When possible, fluid should be ingested at rates that most closely match sweating rate. When that is not possible or practical or sufficiently ergogenic, some athletes might tolerate body water losses amounting to 2% of body weight without significant risk to physical well-being or performance when the environment is cold (5–10°C) or temperate (21–22°C). However, when exercising in a hot environment (>30°C), dehydration by 2% of body weight impairs absolute power production and predisposes individuals to heat injury. Fluid should not be ingested at rates in excess of sweating rate and thus body water and weight should not increase during exercise.

2   During exercise lasting more than 1 h and which elicits fatigue, athletes are advised to ingest 30–60 g carbohydrate $\cdot \text{h}^{-1}$, which is rapidly converted to blood glucose, because it generally improves performance. There is no clear physiological need for people to take in fluid or fuel when beginning exercise in a reasonably euhydrated state and proceeding to exercise at low

or moderate intensity for less than 1 h without experiencing undue fatigue or significant dehydration (>2% body weight loss). However, there is no apparent reason for people to avoid fluid and/or carbohydrate according to the guidelines given if this is their preference and it is well tolerated.

3 No benefit is gained by ingesting the following during exercise to justify potential discomfort or costs or potential health risks: glycerol, amino acids, alleged precursors of neurotransmitters claimed to be ergogenic.

4 Sodium should be included in fluids consumed during exercise lasting more than 2 h or by individuals during any event that stimulates heavy sodium loss (more than 3–4 g of sodium). Although the benefits of drinking fluids containing sodium are not clear during shorter-term exercise (less than 2 h) or when sweat loss of sodium is low, there does not appear to be a significant negative effect of drinking solutions containing up to 40 mmol·l^{-1} sodium. Sodium contained in pills or food is not discouraged, provided it is consumed simultaneously with sufficiently large volumes of fluid.

5 Caffeine intake during the latter stages of prolonged exercise is ergogenic when taken in amounts of 1.5 mg·kg^{-1}.

Acknowledgements

The author appreciates the advice given by Drs Clyde Williams, Jose Gonzalez-Alonso and Sam Cheuvront, as well as input from Matt Pahnke and Joel Trinity. The author is a member of the Sports Medicine Review Board of the Gatorade Sports Science Institute.

References

1 Adolph, E.F. (ed.) (1947). *Physiology of Man in the Desert*. New York: Interscience.

2 American College of Sports Medicine (1975). Position statement on the prevention of heat injury during distance running. *Medicine and Science in Sports*, vii–ix.

3 American College of Sports Medicine (1985). Position statement on the prevention of thermal injuries during distance running. *Medicine and Science in Sports and Exercise*, **17**, ix–xiv.

4 Angus, D.J., Hargreaves, M., Dancey, J. and Febbraio, M.A. (2000). Effect of carbohydrate or carbohydrate plus medium-chain triglyceride ingestion on cycling time trial performance. *Journal of Applied Physiology*, **88**, 113–119.

5 Bachle, L., Eckerson, J., Albertson, L., Ebersole, K., Goodwin, J. and Petzel, D. (2001). The effect of fluid replacement on endurance performance. *Journal of Strength and Conditioning Research*, **15**, 217–224.

6 Bangsbo, J. (1994). The physiology of soccer – with special reference to intense intermittent exercise. *Acta Physiologica Scandinavica*, suppl. **619**, 1–155.

7 Bangsbo, J., Norregaard, L. and Thorso, F. (1991). Activity profile of competition soccer. *Canadian Journal of Sport Sciences*, **16**, 110–116.

8 Barr, S. (1999). Effects of dehydration on exercise performance. *Canadian Journal of Applied Physiology*, **24**, 164–172.

9 Barr, S. and Costill, D. (1989). Water: can the endurance athlete get too much of a good thing? *Journal of the American Dietetic Association*, **89**, 1629–1632, 1635.

10 Barr, S., Costill, D. and Fink, W. (1991). Fluid replacement during prolonged exercise: effects of water, saline, or no fluid. *Medicine and Science in Sports and Exercise*, **23**, 811–817.

11 Below, P., Mora-Rodriguez, R., Gonzalez-Alonso, J. and Coyle, E. (1995). Fluid and carbohydrate ingestion independently improve performance during 1 h of intense exercise. *Medicine and Science in Sports and Exercise*, **27**, 200–210.

12 Bergstrom, J., Hermansen, L., Hultman, E. and Saltin, B. (1967). Diet, muscle glycogen and physical performance. *Acta Physiologica Scandinavica*, **71**, 140–150.

13 Biolo, G., Maggi, S.P., Williams, B.D., Tipton, K.D. and Wolfe, R.R. (1995). Increased rates of muscle protein turnover and amino acid transport after resistance exercise in humans. *American Journal of Physiology*, **268**, E514–E520.

14 Biolo, G., Tipton, K., Klein, S. and Wolfe, R. (1997). An abundant supply of amino acids enhances the metabolic effect of exercise on muscle protein. *American Journal of Physiology*, **273**, E122–E129.

15 Blomstrand, E., Celsing, F. and Newsholme, E. (1988). Changes in plasma concentrations of aromatic and branched-chain amino acids during sustained exercise in man and their possible role in fatigue. *Acta Physiologica Scandinavica*, **133**, 115–121.

16 Brown, A.H. (1947). Relative influences of heat, work, and dehydration on blood circulation. In *Physiology of Man in the Desert* (edited by E.F. Adolph), pp. 197–207. New York: Interscience.

17 Burke, L. and Read, R. (1989). Sports nutrition: approaching the nineties. *Sports Medicine*, **8**, 80–100.

18 Burke, L.M., Kiens, B. and Ivy, J.L. (2004). Carbohydrates and fat for training and recovery. *Journal of Sports Sciences*, **22**, 15–30.

19 Casa, D.J. (2000). National athletic trainer's association position statement: fluid replacement for athletes. *Journal of Athletic Training*, **35**, 212–224.

20 Cheuvront, S.S.M. (2001). Physical exercise and exhaustion from heat strain. *Journal of the Korean Society of Living Environmental Systems*, **8**, 134–145.

21 Cheuvront, S. and Haymes, E. (2001). Thermoregulation and marathon running: biological and environmental influences. *Sports Medicine*, **31**, 743–762.

22 Cheuvront, S., Carter, R. and Sawka, M.N. (2003). Fluid balance and endurance exercise performance. *Current Sports Medicine Reports*, **2**, 202–208.

23 Coggan, A.R. and Coyle, E.F. (1988). Effect of carbohydrate feedings during high-intensity exercise. *Journal of Applied Physiology*, **65**, 1703–1737.

24 Coggan, A. and Coyle, E. (1991). Carbohydrate ingestion during prolonged exercise: effects on metabolism and performance. *Exercise and Sport Science Reviews*, **19**, 1–40.

25 Convertino, V., Armstrong, L., Coyle, E., Mack, G., Sawka, M., Senay, L. and Sherman, W. (1996). American College of Sports Medicine position stand: exercise and fluid replacement. *Medicine and Science in Sports and Exercise*, **28**, i–vii.

26 Costill, D.L. (1972). Physiology of marathon running. *Journal of the American Medical Association*, **221**, 1024–1029.

27 Costill, D. and Miller, J. (1980). Nutrition for endurance sport: carbohydrate and fluid balance. *International Journal of Sports Medicine*, **1**, 2–14.

28 Costill, D., Dalsky, G. and Fink, W. (1978). Effects of caffeine ingestion on metabolism and exercise performance. *Medicine and Science in Sports*, **10**, 155–158.

29 Cox, G.R., Desbrow, B., Montgomery, P.G., Anderson, M.E., Bruce, C.R., Macrides, T.A., Martin, D.T., Moquin, A., Roberts, A., Hawley, J.A. and Burke, L.M. (2002). Effect of different protocols of caffeine intake on metabolism and endurance performance. *Journal of Applied Physiology*, **93**, 990–999.

30 Coyle, E.F. and Montain, S.J. (1992a). Benefits of fluid replacement with carbohydrate during exercise. *Medicine and Science in Sports and Exercise*, **24**, S324–S330.

31 Coyle, E.F. and Montain, S.J. (1992b). Carbohydrate and fluid ingestion during exercise: are there trade-offs? *Medicine and Science in Sports and Exercise*, **24**, 671–678.

32 Coyle, E., Costill, D., Fink, W. and Hoopes, D. (1978). Gastric emptying rates for selected athletic drinks. *Research Quarterly*, **49**, 119–124.

33 Coyle, E.F., Coggan, A.R., Hemmert, M.K. and Ivy, J.L. (1986). Muscle glycogen utilization during prolonged strenuous exercise when fed carbohydrate. *Journal of Applied Physiology*, **61**, 165–172.

34 Criswell, D., Renshler, K., Powers, S., Tulley, R., Cicale, M. and Wheeler, K. (1992). Fluid replacement beverages and maintenance of plasma volume during exercise: role of aldosterone and vasopressin. *European Journal of Applied Physiology*, **65**, 445–451.

35 Cunningham, J. (1997). Is potassium needed in sports drinks for fluid replacement during exercise? *International Journal of Sport Nutrition*, **7**, 154–159.

36 Davis, J. (1995a). Carbohydrates, branched-chain amino acids, and endurance: the central fatigue hypothesis. *International Journal of Sport Nutrition*, **5**(suppl.), S29–S38.

37 Davis, J. (1995b). Central and peripheral factors in fatigue. *Journal of Sports Sciences*, **13** (special issue), S49–S53.

38 Davis, J., Bailey, S., Woods, J., Galiano, F., Hamilton, M. and Bartoli, W. (1992). Effects of carbohydrate feedings on plasma free tryptophan and branched-chain amino acids during prolonged cycling. *European Journal of Applied Physiology*, **65**, 513–519.

39 Davis, J.M., Jackson, D.A., Broadwell, M.S., Queary, J.L. and Lambert, C.L. (1997). Carbohydrate drinks delay fatigue during intermittent, high-intensity cycling in active men and women. *International Journal of Sport Nutrition*, **7**, 261–273.

40 Davis, J., Welsh, R., De Volve, K. and Alderson, N. (1999). Effects of branched-chain amino acids and carbohydrate on fatigue during intermittent, high-intensity running. *International Journal of Sports Medicine*, **20**, 309–314.

41 Davis, J., Welsh, R. and Alerson, N. (2000a). Effects of carbohydrate and chromium ingestion during intermittent high-intensity exercise to fatigue. *International Journal of Sport Nutrition and Exercise Metabolism*, **10**, 476–485.

42 Davis, J.M., Alderson, N.L. and Welsh, R.S. (2000b). Serotonin and central nervous system fatigue: nutritional considerations. *American Journal of Clinical Nutrition*, **72**, 573S–578S.

43 Deuster, P.A. and Singh, A. (1993). Responses of plasma magnesium and other cations to fluid replacement during exercise. *Journal of the American College of Nutrition*, **12**, 286–293.

44 Eichner, E. (1998). Treatment of suspected heat illness. *International Journal of Sports Medicine*, **19**(suppl. 2), S150–S153.

45 Evans, K., Clark, M.L. and Frayn, K.N. (1999). Effects of an oral and intravenous fat load on adipose tissue and forearm lipid metabolism. *American Journal of Physiology*, **276**, E241–E248.

46 Fallowfield, J.L., Williams, C., Booth, J., Choo, B.H. and Growns, S. (1996). Effect of water ingestion on endurance capacity during prolonged running. *Journal of Sports Sciences*, **14**, 497–502.

47 Febbraio, M., Murton, P., Selig, S., Clark, S., Lambert, D., Angus, D. and Carey, M. (1996a). Effect of CHO ingestion on exercise metabolism and performance in different ambient temperatures. *Medicine and Science in Sports and Exercise*, **28**, 1380–1387.

48 Febbraio, M.A., Carey, M.F., Snow, R.J., Stathis, C.G. and Hargreaves, M. (1996b). Influence of elevated muscle temperature on metabolism during intense, dynamic exercise. *American Journal of Physiology*, **271**, R1251–R1255.

49 Freund, B.J., Montain, S.J., Young, A.J., Sawka, M.N., DeLuca, J.P., Pandolf, K.B. and Valeri, C.R. (1995). Glycerol hyperhydration: hormonal, renal, and vascular fluid responses. *Journal of Applied Physiology*, **79**, 2069–2077.

50 Fritzsche, R.G., Switzer, T.W., Hodgkinson, B.J., Lee, S.-H., Martin, J.C. and Coyle, E.F. (2000). Water and carbohydrate ingestion during prolonged exercise increase maximal neuromuscular power. *Journal of Applied Physiology*, **88**, 730–737.

51 Galloway, S. and Maughan, R. (1998). The effects of substrate and fluid provision on thermoregulatory, cardiorespiratory and metabolic responses to prolonged exercise in a cold environment in man. *Experimental Physiology*, **83**, 419–430.

52 Galloway, S. and Maughan, R. (2000). The effects of substrate and fluid provision on thermoregulatory and metabolic responses to prolonged exercise in a hot environment. *Journal of Sports Sciences*, **18**, 339–351.

53 Gibala, M.J., Lozej, M., Tarnopolsky, M.A., McLean, C. and Graham, T.E. (1999). Low glycogen and branched-chain amino acid ingestion do not impair anaplerosis during exercise in humans. *Journal of Applied Physiology*, **87**, 1662–1667.

54 Gonzalez-Alonso, J. (1998). Separate and combined influences of dehydration and hyperthermia on cardiovascular responses to exercise. *International Journal of Sports Medicine*, **19**(suppl. 2), S111–S114.

55 Gonzalez-Alonso, J. and Calbet, J.A.L. (2003). Reductions in systemic and skeletal muscle blood flow and oxygen delivery limit maximal aerobic capacity in humans. *Circulation*, **107**, 824–830.

56 Gonzalez-Alonso, J., Mora-Rodriguez, R., Below, P.R. and Coyle, E.F. (1995). Dehydration reduces cardiac output and increases systemic and cutaneous vascular resistance during exercise. *Journal of Applied Physiology*, **79**, 1487–1496.

57 Gonzalez-Alonso, J., Mora-Rodriguez, R., Below, P.R. and Coyle, E.F. (1997). Dehydration markedly impairs cardiovascular function in hyperthermic endurance athletes during exercise. *Journal of Applied Physiology*, **82**, 1229–1236.

58 Gonzalez-Alonso, J., Calbet, J.A.L. and Nielsen, B. (1998). Muscle blood flow is reduced with dehydration during prolonged exercise in humans. *Journal of Physiology*, **513**, 895–905.

59 Gonzalez-Alonso, J., Calbet, J.A. and Nielsen, B. (1999a). Metabolic and thermodynamic responses to dehydration-induced reductions in muscle blood flow in exercising humans. *Journal of Physiology*, **520**, 577–589.

60 Gonzalez-Alonso, J., Teller, C., Andersen, S.L., Jensen, F.B., Hyldig, T. and Nielsen, B. (1999b). Influence of body temperature on the development of fatigue during prolonged exercise in the heat. *Journal of Applied Physiology*, **86**, 1032–1039.

61 Gonzalez-Alonso, J., Mora-Rodriguez, R. and Coyle, E.F. (2000). Stroke volume during exercise: interaction of environment and hydration. *American Journal of Physiology*, **278**, H321–H330.

62 Hargreaves, M. (1996). Carbohydrates and exercise performance. *Nutrition Reviews*, **54**, S136–S139.

63 Hargreaves, M., Costill, D., Burke, L., McConell, G. and Febbraio, M. (1994). Influence of sodium on glucose bioavailability during exercise. *Medicine and Science in Sports and Exercise*, **26**, 365–368.

64 Hargreaves, M., Dillo, P., Angus, D. and Febbraio, M. (1996). Effect of fluid ingestion on muscle metabolism during prolonged exercise. *Journal of Applied Physiology*, **80**, 363–366.

65 Herd, S., Kiens, B., Boobis, L. and Hardman, A. (2001). Moderate exercise, postprandial lipemia, and skeletal muscle lipoprotein lipase activity. *Metabolism*, **50**, 756–762.

66 Horowitz, J.F., Mora-Rodriguez, R., Byerley, L.O. and Coyle, E.F. (2000). Pre-exercise medium-chain triglyceride ingestion does not alter muscle glycogen use during exercise. *Journal of Applied Physiology*, **88**, 219–225.

67 Howald, H. and Decombaz, J. (1983). Nutrient intake and energy regulation in physical exercise. *Experientia*, **44**(suppl.), 77–88.

68 Hubbard, R.W., Sandick, B.L., Matthew, W.T., Francesconi, R.P., Sampson, J.B., Durkot, M.J., Maller, O. and Engell, D.B. (1984). Voluntary dehydration and alliesthesia for water. *Journal of Applied Physiology*, **57**, 868–873.

69 Ivy, J. (2001). Dietary strategies to promote glycogen synthesis after exercise. *Canadian Journal of Applied Physiology*, **26**(suppl.), S236–S245.

70 Ivy, J., Costill, D., Fink, W. and Lower, R. (1979). Influence of caffeine and carbohydrate feedings on endurance performance. *Medicine and Science in Sports*, **11**, 6–11.

71 Ivy, J.L., Goforth, H.W., Jr., Damon, B.M., McCauley, T.R., Parsons, E.C. and Price, T.B. (2002). Early postexercise muscle glycogen recovery is enhanced with a carbohydrate-protein supplement. *Journal of Applied Physiology*, **93**, 1337–1344.

72 Jeukendrup, A.E., Saris, W.H., Schrauwen, P., Brouns, F. and Wagenmakers, A.J. (1995). Metabolic availability of medium-chain triglycerides coingested with carbohydrates during prolonged exercise. *Journal of Applied Physiology*, **79**, 756–762.

73 Jeukendrup, A., Saris, W., Brouns, F., Halliday, D. and Wagenmakers, J. (1996). Effects of carbohydrate (CHO) and fat supplementation on CHO metabolism during prolonged exercise. *Metabolism*, **45**, 915–921.

74 Ladell, W. (1955). The effects of water and salt intake upon the performance of men working in hot and humid environments. *Journal of Physiology*, **127**, 11–26.

75 Latzka, W. and Sawka, M. (2000). Hyperhydration and glycerol: thermoregulatory effects during exercise in hot climates. *Canadian Journal of Applied Physiology*, **25**, 536–545.

76 Lyons, T., Riedesel, M., Meuli, L. and Chick, T. (1990). Effects of glycerol-induced hyperhydration prior to exercise in the heat on sweating and core temperature. *Medicine and Science in Sports and Exercise*, **22**, 477–483.

77 MacLean, D.A. and Graham, T.E. (1993). Branched-chain amino acid supplementation augments plasma ammonia responses during exercise in humans. *Journal of Applied Physiology*, **74**, 2711–2717.

78 Magazanik, A., Shapiro, Y., Meytes, D. and Meytes, I. (1974). Enzyme blood levels and water balance during a marathon race. *Journal of Applied Physiology*, **36**, 214–217.

79 Manore, M., Thompson, J. and Russo, M. (1993). Diet and exercise strategies of a world-class bodybuilder. *International Journal of Sport Nutrition*, **3**, 76–86.

80 Maron, M.B., Wagner, J.A. and Horvath, S.M. (1977). Thermoregulatory responses during competitive marathon running. *Journal of Applied Physiology*, **42**, 909–914.

81 Maughan, R.J. (1984). Temperature regulation during marathon competition. *British Journal of Sports Medicine*, **18**, 257–260.

82 Maughan, R.J. (1985). Thermoregulation in marathon competition at low ambient temperature. *International Journal of Sports Medicine*, **6**, 15–19.

83 Maughan, R.J. (1991). Fluid and electrolyte loss and replacement in exercise. *Journal of Sports Sciences*, **9**(special issue), 117–142.

84 Maughan, R.J. and Leiper, J.B. (1994). Fluid replacement requirements in soccer. *Journal of Sports Sciences*, **12**(special issue), S29–S34.

85 Maughan, R.J. and Noakes, T.D. (1991). Fluid replacement and exercise stress: a brief review of studies on fluid replacement and some guidelines for the athlete. *Sports Medicine*, **12**, 16–31.

86 Maughan, R.J., Goodburn, R., Griffin, J., Irani, M., Kirwan, J., Leiper, J., MacLaren, D., McLatchie, G., Tsintsas, K. and Williams, C. (1993). Fluid replacement in sport and exercise – a consensus statement. *British Journal of Sports Medicine*, **27**, 34–35.

87 Maughan, R.J., King, D.S. and Lea, T. (2004). Dietary supplements. *Journal of Sports Sciences*, **22**, 95–113.

88 McConell, G., Burge, C., Skinner, S. and Hargreaves, M. (1997). Influence of ingested fluid volume on physiological responses during prolonged exercise. *Acta Physiologica Scandinavica*, **160**, 149–156.

89 McConell, G., Stephens, T. and Canny, B. (1999). Fluid ingestion does not influence intense 1-h exercise performance in a mild environment. *Medicine and Science in Sports and Exercise*, **31**, 386–392.

90 McCutcheon, L. and Geor, R. (1998). Sweating: fluid and ion losses and replacement. *Veterinary Clinics of North America Equine Practice*, **14**, 75–95.

91 McGregor, S., Nicholas, C., Lakomy, H. and Williams, C. (1999). The influence of intermittent high-intensity shuttle running and fluid ingestion on the performance of a soccer skill. *Journal of Sports Sciences*, **17**, 895–903.

92 Millard-Stafford, M. (1992). Fluid replacement during exercise in the heat: review and recommendations. *Sports Medicine*, **13**, 223–233.

93 Millard-Stafford, M., Sparling, P., Rosskopf, L., Snow, T., DiCarlo, L. and Hinson, B. (1995). Fluid intake in male and female runners during a 40-km field run in the heat. *Journal of Sports Sciences*, **13**, 257–263.

94 Millard-Stafford, M., Rosskopf, L., Snow, T. and Hinson, B. (1997). Water versus carbohydrate-electrolyte ingestion before and during a 15-km run in the heat. *International Journal of Sport Nutrition*, **7**, 26–38.

95 Miller, J., Coyle, E., Sherman, W., Hagberg, J., Costill, D., Fink, W., Terblanche, S. and Holloszy, J. (1983). Effect of glycerol feeding on endurance and metabolism

during prolonged exercise in man. *Medicine and Science in Sports and Exercise*, **15**, 237–242.

96 Mitchell, J.B., Costill, D.L., Houmard, J.A., Fink, W.J., Pascoe, D.D. and Pearson, D.R. (1989). Influence of carbohydrate dosage on exercise performance and glycogen metabolism. *Journal of Applied Physiology*, **67**, 1843–1849.

97 Montain, S.J. and Coyle, E.F. (1992). Influence of graded dehydration on hyperthermia and cardiovascular drift during exercise. *Journal of Applied Physiology*, **73**, 1340–1350.

98 Montain, S.J. and Coyle, E.F. (1993). Influence of the timing of fluid ingestion on temperature regulation during exercise. *Journal of Applied Physiology*, **75**, 688–695.

99 Montain, S., Sawka, M. and Wenger, C. (2001). Hyponatremia associated with exercise: risk factors and pathogenesis. *Exercise and Sport Science Reviews*, **29**, 113–117.

100 Murray, R., Eddy, D., Murray, T., Seifert, J., Paul, G. and Halaby, G. (1987). The effect of fluid and carbohydrate feedings during intermittent cycling exercise. *Medicine and Science in Sports and Exercise*, **19**, 597–604.

101 Murray, R., Paul, G., Seifert, J., Eddy, D. and Halaby, G. (1989). The effects of glucose, fructose, and sucrose ingestion during exercise. *Medicine and Science in Sports and Exercise*, **21**, 275–282.

102 Murray, R., Eddy, D.E., Paul, G.L., Seifert, J.G. and Halaby, G.A. (1991). Physiological responses to glycerol ingestion during exercise. *Journal of Applied Physiology*, **71**, 144–149.

103 Nicholas, C., Williams, C., Lakomy, H., Phillips, G. and Nowitz, A. (1995). Influence of ingesting a carbohydrate-electrolyte solution on endurance capacity during intermittent, high-intensity shuttle running. *Journal of Sports Sciences*, **13**, 283–290.

104 Nicholas, C., Tsintzas, K., Boobis, L. and Williams, C. (1999). Carbohydrate-electrolyte ingestion during intermittent high-intensity running. *Medicine and Science in Sports and Exercise*, **31**, 1280–1286.

105 Nicholas, C., Nuttall, F. and Williams, C. (2000). The Loughborough Intermittent Shuttle Test: a field test that simulates the activity pattern of soccer. *Journal of Sports Sciences*, **18**, 97–104.

106 Nielsen, B. and Nybo, L. (2003). Cerebral changes during exercise in the heat. *Sports Medicine*, **33**, 1–11.

107 Nielsen, B., Hyldig, T., Bidstrup, F., Gonzalez-Alonso, J. and Christoffersen, G. (2001). Brain activity and fatigue during prolonged exercise in the heat. *Pflügers Archive*, **442**, 41–48.

108 Noakes, T.D. (2003). Overconsumption of fluids by athletes. *British Medical Journal*, **327**, 113–114.

109 Noakes, T. and Martin, D. (2002). IMMDA-AIMS advisory statement on guidelines for fluid replacement during marathon running. *New Studies in Athletics*, **17**, 15–24.

110 Noakes, T., Goodwin, N., Rayner, B., Branken, T. and Taylor, R. (1985). Water intoxication: a possible complication during endurance exercise. *Medicine and Science in Sports and Exercise*, **17**, 370–375.

111 Noakes, T., Myburgh, K., du Plessis, J., Lang, L., Lambert, M., van der Riet, C. and Schall, R. (1991a). Metabolic rate, not percent dehydration, predicts rectal temperature in marathon runners. *Medicine and Science in Sports and Exercise*, **23**, 443–449.

112 Noakes, T., Rehrer, N. and Maughan, R. (1991b). The importance of volume in regulating gastric emptying. *Medicine and Science in Sports and Exercise*, **23**, 307–313.

113 O'Brien, K., Montain, S., Corr, W., Sawka, M., Knapik, J. and Craig, S. (2001). Hyponatremia associated with overhydration in U.S. Army trainees. *Military Medicine*, **166**, 405–410.

114 Pitts, G.J. and Consolazio, F.C. (1944). Work in the heat as affected by intake of water, salt and glucose. *American Journal of Physiology*, **142**, 253–259.

115 Powers, S., Lawler, J., Dodd, S., Tulley, R., Landry, G. and Wheeler, K. (1990). Fluid replacement drinks during high intensity exercise: effects on minimizing exercise-induced disturbances in homeostasis. *European Journal of Applied Physiology*, **60**, 54–60.

116 Pugh, L.G., Corbett, J.L. and Johnson, R.H. (1967). Rectal temperatures, weight losses, and sweat rates in marathon running. *Journal of Applied Physiology*, **23**, 347–352.

117 Rasmussen, B.B., Tipton, K.D., Miller, S.L., Wolf, S.E. and Wolfe, R.R. (2000). An oral essential amino acid–carbohydrate supplement enhances muscle protein anabolism after resistance exercise. *Journal of Applied Physiology*, **88**, 386–392.

118 Rehrer, N. (1994). The maintenance of fluid balance during exercise. *International Journal of Sports Medicine*, **15**, 122–125.

119 Rehrer, N. (2001). Fluid and electrolyte balance in ultra-endurance sport. *Sports Medicine*, **31**, 701–715.

120 Rehrer, N.J., Wagenmakers, A.J., Beckers, E.J., Halliday, D., Leiper, J.B., Brouns, F., Maughan, R.J., Westerterp, K. and Saris, W.H. (1992). Gastric emptying, absorption, and carbohydrate oxidation during prolonged exercise. *Journal of Applied Physiology*, **72**, 468–475.

121 Rehrer, N., Beckers, E., Brouns, F., Saris, W. and ten Hoor, F. (1993). Effects of electrolytes in carbohydrate beverages on gastric emptying and secretion. *Medicine and Science in Sports and Exercise*, **25**, 42–51.

122 Robinson, T., Hawley, J., Palmer, G., Wilson, G., Gray, D., Noakes, T. and Dennis, S. (1995). Water ingestion does not improve 1-h cycling performance in moderate ambient temperatures. *European Journal of Applied Physiology*, **71**, 153–160.

123 Sawka, M. and Coyle, E. (1999). Influence of body water and blood volume on thermoregulation and exercise performance in the heat. *Exercise and Sport Science Reviews*, **27**, 167–218.

124 Sawka, M.N. and Montain, S.J. (2000). Fluid and electrolyte supplementation for exercise heat stress. *American Journal of Clinical Nutrition*, **72**, 564S–572S.

125 Sawka, M.N., Montain, S.J. and Latzka, W.A. (2001). Hydration effects on thermoregulation and performance in the heat. *Comparative Biochemistry and Physiology A: Molecular and Integrative Physiology*, **128**, 679–690.

126 Schedl, H., Maughan, R. and Gisolfi, C. (1994). Intestinal absorption during rest and exercise: implications for formulating an oral rehydration solution (ORS). Proceedings of a roundtable discussion, 21–22 April 1993. *Medicine and Science in Sports and Exercise*, **26**, 267–280.

127 Sejersted, O.M. and Sjogaard, G. (2000). Dynamics and consequences of potassium shifts in skeletal muscle and heart during exercise. *Physiological Reviews*, **80**, 1411–1481.

128 Speedy, D., Noakes, T., Boswell, T., Thompson, J., Rehrer, N. and Boswell, D. (2001). Response to a fluid load in athletes with a history of exercise induced hyponatremia. *Medicine and Science in Sports and Exercise*, **33**, 1434–1442.

129 Spriet, L.L. (1995). Caffeine and performance. *International Journal of Sport Nutrition*, **5**(suppl.), S84–S99.

130 Sugiura, K. and Kobayashi, K. (1998). Effect of carbohydrate ingestion on sprint performance following continuous and intermittent exercise. *Medicine and Science in Sports and Exercise*, **30**, 1624–1630.

131 Terblanche, S.E., Fell, R.D., Juhlin-Dannfelt, A.C., Craig, B.W. and Holloszy, J.O. (1981). Effects of glycerol feeding before and after exhausting exercise in rats. *Journal of Applied Physiology*, **50**, 94–101.

132 Tipton, K. and Wolfe, R. (1998). Exercise-induced changes in protein metabolism. *Acta Physiologica Scandinavica*, **162**, 377–387.

133 Tipton, K.D. and Wolfe, R.R. (2004). Protein and amino acids for athletes. *Journal of Sports Sciences*, **22**, 65–79.

134 Tipton, K.D., Borsheim, E., Wolf, S.E., Sanford, A.P. and Wolfe, R.R. (2003). Acute response of net muscle protein balance reflects 24-h balance after exercise and amino acid ingestion. *American Journal of Physiology*, **284**, E76–E89.

135 Turcotte, L.P., Richter, E.A. and Kiens, B. (1992). Increased plasma FFA uptake and oxidation during prolonged exercise in trained *vs* untrained humans. *American Journal of Physiology*, **262**, E791–E799.

136 van Zyl, C.G., Lambert, E.V., Hawley, J.A., Noakes, T.D. and Dennis, S.C. (1996). Effects of medium-chain triglyceride ingestion on fuel metabolism and cycling performance. *Journal of Applied Physiology*, **80**, 2217–2225.

137 Vrijens, D.M.J. and Rehrer, N.J. (1999). Sodium-free fluid ingestion decreases plasma sodium during exercise in the heat. *Journal of Applied Physiology*, **86**, 1847–1851.

138 Wagenmakers, A.J., Brouns, F., Saris, W.H. and Halliday, D. (1993). Oxidation rates of orally ingested carbohydrates during prolonged exercise in men. *Journal of Applied Physiology*, **75**, 2774–2780.

139 Walsh, R., Noakes, T., Hawley, J. and Dennis, S. (1994). Impaired high-intensity cycling performance time at low levels of dehydration. *International Journal of Sports Medicine*, **15**, 392–398.

140 Welsh, R., Davis, J., Burke, J. and Williams, H. (2002). Carbohydrates and physical/mental performance during intermittent exercise to fatigue. *Medicine and Science in Sports and Exercise*, **34**, 723–731.

141 Wemple, R., Morocco, T. and Mack, G. (1997). Influence of sodium replacement on fluid ingestion following exercise-induced dehydration. *International Journal of Sport Nutrition*, **7**, 104–116.

142 Wilk, B. and Bar-Or, O. (1996). Effect of drink flavor and NaCl on voluntary drinking and hydration in boys exercising in the heat. *Journal of Applied Physiology*, **80**, 1112–1117.

143 Wyndham, C. and Strydom, N. (1969). The danger of an inadequate water intake during marathon running. *South African Medical Journal*, **43**, 893–896.

144 Zawadzki, K.M., Yaspelkis, B.B., III and Ivy, J.L. (1992). Carbohydrate–protein complex increases the rate of muscle glycogen storage after exercise. *Journal of Applied Physiology*, **72**, 1854–1859.

5 Fluid and electrolyte needs for preparation and recovery from training and competition

SUSAN M. SHIRREFFS, LAWRENCE E. ARMSTRONG and SAMUEL N. CHEUVRONT

For a person undertaking regular exercise, any fluid deficit that is incurred during one exercise session can potentially compromise the next exercise session if adequate fluid replacement does not occur. Fluid replacement after exercise can, therefore, frequently be thought of as hydration before the next exercise bout. The importance of ensuring euhydration before exercise and the potential benefits of temporary hyperhydration with sodium salts or glycerol solutions are also important issues. Post-exercise restoration of fluid balance after sweat-induced dehydration avoids the detrimental effects of a body water deficit on physiological function and subsequent exercise performance. For effective restoration of fluid balance, the consumption of a volume of fluid in excess of the sweat loss and replacement of electrolyte, particularly sodium, losses are essential. Intravenous fluid replacement after exercise has been investigated to a lesser extent and its role for fluid replacement in the dehydrated but otherwise well athlete remains equivocal.

Keywords: hypohydration, rehydration, water balance, electrolyte balance.

Introduction

The metabolic heat generated by exercise must be dissipated to maintain body temperature within narrow physiological limits. When ambient temperature exceeds skin temperature, heat loss can occur only by evaporation of sweat from the skin surface. Significant rates of sweat production will also occur in a cool environment if the work rate is high. Indeed, sweat rates exceeding $2 \, l \cdot h^{-1}$ can be maintained for many hours by trained and acclimated individuals exercising in warm, humid conditions. This is demonstrated by the body mass losses in marathon runners, which can range from about 1–6% (0.7–4.2 kg of body mass for a 70-kg man) at low (10°C) ambient temperatures to more than 8% (5.6 kg) in warmer conditions (Maughan and Shirreffs, 1998). With exercise in a warm environment, 30–40% of total body water may be turned over in a single day, but a deficit of even half of that amount will result in serious disability or even death (Adolph *et al.*, 1947).

When sweating takes place, the free exchange of water among body fluid compartments ensures that the water content of sweat is derived from all compartments, with the distribution being influenced by sweat rate, sweat composition and total water and electrolyte loss. Sodium is the primary cation lost in sweat, with typical concentrations of about 40–60 mmol·l^{-1}, compared with about 4–8 mmol·l^{-1} for potassium (Maughan and Shirreffs, 1998). Given the higher sodium loss and the distribution of these cations between the body water compartments, the primary water loss is likely to be from the extracellular space.

It is well documented that even small body water deficits, incurred before (Armstrong *et al.*, 1985; Sawka, 1992) or during (Cheuvront *et al.*, 2003) exercise can significantly impair aerobic exercise performance, especially in the heat (Sawka, 1992; Cheuvront *et al.*, 2003). Armstrong *et al.* (1985) studied participants in track races over 1500, 5000 and 10,000 m after reducing body mass by 2% using a diuretic. The time to complete these races was increased by 0.16, 1.31 and 2.62 min (3.4, 6.7 and 6.7%), respectively, relative to their finishing time when euhydrated.

The plasma volume decrease that accompanies dehydration may be of particular importance in influencing work capacity; blood flow to the muscles must be maintained at a high level during exercise to supply oxygen and substrates, but a high blood flow to the skin is also necessary to transfer heat to the body surface where it can be dissipated. Hypohydration is associated with higher cardiovascular strain and impaired thermoregulation and with loss of the protection conferred by acclimation (Sawka, 1992). Loss of intracellular volume may be particularly important during recovery, however, in the light of the emerging evidence of a role for cell volume in the regulation of metabolism. A reduced intracellular volume can reduce rates of glycogen and protein synthesis and a high cell volume can stimulate these processes (Lang *et al.*, 1995).

Pre-exercise hydration

For a person undertaking regular exercise, any fluid deficit that is incurred during one exercise session can potentially compromise the next exercise session if adequate fluid replacement does not occur. Fluid replacement after exercise can frequently be thought of as hydration before the next exercise bout.

However, in addition to this, the issue of pre-exercise hyperhydration has been investigated in the last decade. In a healthy individual, the kidneys excrete any excess body water; therefore, ingesting excess fluid before exercise is generally ineffective at inducing pre-exercise hyperhydration. To overcome this, ingestion of either salt or glycerol solutions has been investigated as possible means of minimizing the usual diuresis when a euhydrated individual ingests excess water. A limited amount of temporary hyperhydration occurs when drinks with high concentrations (>100 mmol·l^{-1}) of sodium are ingested (Fortney *et al.*, 1984), but there are problems of palatability with high sodium drinks and nausea and vomiting with salt tablets. Glycerol has been shown to be an effective hyperhydrating agent. Several studies have suggested that ingesting 1.0–1.5 g glycerol·kg^{-1} BM (where BM = body mass), together with a large volume of water, can significantly increase water retention and improve cycling time to fatigue (Riedesel *et al.*, 1987; Lyons *et al.*, 1990; Montner *et al.*, 1996; Hitchins *et al.*, 1999). Others (Latzka *et al.*, 1997, 1998) have observed no differences in thermoregulatory or performance parameters. In addition, there have been a number of reports of side-effects with glycerol ingestion (Latzka and Sawka, 2000) that preclude this technique as a method of pre-exercise hyperhydration. In fact, a recent review of hyperhydration and glycerol came to the conclusion that 'if euhydration is maintained during exercise-heat stress then [pre-exercise] hyperhydration appears to have no meaningful advantage' (Latzka and Sawka, 2000).

However, the practice of drinking in the hours before exercise is effective at ensuring euhydration before exercise if there is any possibility that slight hypo-hydration is present. The American College of Sports Medicine (1996) prac-tical recommendation of ingesting 400–600 ml of water 2 h before exercise to allow the kidneys time to regulate total body water volume has been used to help ensure euhydration before laboratory studies. The resulting data of urine osmolality or specific gravity and serum osmolality or hormone measures indi-cate that the practice is generally effective at achieving euhydration in such circumstances (Shirreffs *et al.*, 1996; Shirreffs and Maughan, 1998).

Post-exercise rehydration

The main factors influencing the post-exercise rehydration process are the volume and composition of the fluid consumed. The volume consumed will be influenced by many factors, including the palatability of the drink and its effects on the thirst mechanism, although with a conscious effort some people can still drink large quantities of an unpalatable drink when they are not thirsty. The ingestion of solid food, and the composition of that food, may also be important, but there are many circumstances in which solid food is avoided between exercise sessions or immediately after exercise.

Beverage composition

Sodium

Plain water is not the ideal post-exercise rehydration beverage when rapid and complete restoration of fluid balance is necessary and where all intake is in liquid form. Early studies in the area (e.g. Costill and Sparks, 1973; Nielsen *et al.*, 1986) established that the high urine flow that followed ingestion of large volumes of electrolyte-free drinks did not allow individuals to remain in positive fluid balance for more than a very short time. They also established that the plasma volume was better maintained when electrolytes were present in the fluid ingested, an effect attributed to the presence of sodium in the drinks. In none of these studies, however, could the mechanism of the action be identified, as the drinks used differed from each other in several respects, including flavouring, carbohydrate and electrolyte content.

The first studies to investigate the mechanisms of post-exercise rehydration showed that the ingestion of large volumes of plain water after exercise-induced dehydration resulted in a rapid fall in plasma osmolality and sodium concentration (Nose *et al.*, 1988a), leading to a prompt and marked diuresis caused by a rapid return to control levels of plasma renin activity and aldosterone (Nose *et al.*, 1988b). Therefore, the replacement of sweat losses with plain water will, if the volume ingested is sufficiently large, lead to haemodilution. The fall in plasma osmolality and sodium concentration that occurs reduces the drive to drink and stimulates urine output (Nose *et al.*, 1988a) and has potentially more serious consequences such as hyponatraemia.

Sodium is the major ion in the extracellular fluid, thus it is intuitive that sweat sodium losses should be replaced if plasma volume is to be restored or maintained. In a systematic investigation of the relationship between whole-body sweat sodium losses and the effectiveness of beverages with different sodium concentrations in restoring fluid balance, Shirreffs and Maughan (1998) showed that, provided that an adequate volume is consumed, euhydration is achieved when the sodium intake is greater than the sweat sodium loss, although, as discussed below, not all studies have reported similar findings (Mitchell *et al.*, 2000). However, to investigate this properly it is important that the study design allows for sufficient time for drink-induced diuresis to occur once drinking is finished. Generally a minimum of 2 h is required after drinking a bolus of fluid to allow sufficient time for any significant renal excretion of water to occur.

The addition of sodium to a rehydration beverage is therefore justified on the basis that sodium is lost in sweat and must be replaced to achieve full fluid balance restoration. It has been demonstrated that a drink's sodium concentration is more important than its osmotic content for increasing plasma volume after dehydration (Greenleaf *et al.*, 1998). Sodium also stimulates glucose absorption in the small intestine via the active co-transport of glucose and sodium, which creates an osmotic gradient that acts to promote net water absorption. This sodium can either be consumed with the drink or be secreted by the intestine. Furthermore, sodium has been recognized as an important ingredient in rehydration beverages by an inter-association task force on exertional heat illnesses (American Physiological Society, 2003) because sodium plays a role in the aetiology of exertional heat cramps, exertional heat exhaustion and exertional hyponatraemia (Armstrong and Casa, 2003).

Potassium

Potassium is the major ion in the intracellular fluid. Potassium may therefore be important in achieving rehydration by aiding the retention of water in the intracellular space. An initial study investigating this (Yawata, 1990) thermally dehydrated rats by approximately 9% of their body mass and then gave them free access to rehydration solutions consisting of isotonic sodium chloride (NaCl), isotonic potassium chloride (KCl) or tap water. While the rats drank substantially more NaCl than KCl, they urinated only slightly more after consuming the NaCl. The best rehydration was achieved with the NaCl treatment. In this study, whole-body net fluid balance was influenced by the rats' taste preferences for the beverages, in addition to the effects of the drinks on urine production. With the NaCl drink, 178% of the extracellular volume losses were restored, compared with only 50% with the KCl drink. The intracellular volume recovery did not differ significantly between groups but did tend to be higher in the KCl group. Yawata suggested that, in the extracellular space, restoring sodium concentration is more important than volume restoration but volume restoration has priority in the intracellular fluid. Also, the role of potassium in restoring intracellular volume is more modest than sodium's role in restoring extracellular volume.

This topic was subsequently investigated in men dehydrated by approximately 2% of body mass by exercise who then ingested a glucose beverage (90 mmol·l^{-1}), a sodium-containing beverage (NaCl 60 mmol·l^{-1}), a potassium-containing beverage (KCl 25 mmol·l^{-1}) or a beverage containing all three components (Maughan *et al.*, 1994). All drinks were consumed in a volume equivalent to the mass loss, but a smaller volume of urine was excreted following rehydration when each of the electrolyte-containing beverages was ingested (about 250–300 ml) compared with the electrolyte-free beverage (a mean volume of 577 ml). Therefore, there was no difference in the fraction of ingested fluid retained 6 h after finishing drinking the drinks that contained electrolytes. This may be because the beverage volume consumed was equivalent to the volume of sweat lost and, because of the ongoing urine losses, the participants were dehydrated throughout the entire study, even immediately after the drinking period. The volumes of urine excreted were close to basal values and significant further reductions in output may not have been possible when both sodium and potassium were ingested. An estimated plasma volume decrease of 4.4% was observed with dehydration over all trials, but the rate of recovery was slowest when the KCl beverage was consumed.

Potassium, therefore, may be important in enhancing rehydration by aiding intracellular rehydration, but further investigation is required to provide conclusive evidence.

Other electrolytes

The importance of including magnesium in sports drinks has been the subject of much discussion. Magnesium is lost in sweat and many believe that this causes a reduction in plasma magnesium concentrations, which has been implicated in muscle cramp. Even though there can be a decline in plasma magnesium concentration during exercise, it is most likely to be due to compartmental fluid redistribution rather than to sweat loss. There does not, therefore, appear to be any good reason for including magnesium in post-exercise rehydration and recovery sports drinks.

Sodium is the most important electrolyte in terms of recovery after exercise. Without its replacement, water retention is hampered. Potassium is also included in sports drinks in concentrations similar to those in sweat. Although there is strong evidence for the inclusion of sodium, this is not the case with potassium. There is no evidence for the inclusion of any other electrolytes.

Beverage volume

Obligatory urine losses persist after exercise, even in the dehydrated state, because of the need for elimination of metabolic waste products. Respiratory and transcutaneous losses also contribute to an ongoing loss of water from the body. The volume of fluid consumed after exercise-induced or thermal sweating must therefore be greater than the volume of sweat lost if effective rehydration is to be achieved. This contradicts earlier recommendations that after exercise athletes should match fluid intake exactly to the measured body mass loss. Shirreffs *et al.* (1996) examined the effect of drink volumes equivalent to 50, 100, 150 and 200% of the sweat loss consumed after exercise-induced dehydration equivalent to approximately 2% of body mass. To investigate the possible interaction between beverage volume and its sodium content, a relatively low sodium drink (23 mmol $\cdot$ l^{-1}) and a moderately high sodium drink (61 mmol $\cdot$ l^{-1}) were compared. Participants were unable to return to euhydration when they consumed a volume equivalent to, or less than, their sweat loss, irrespective of the drink composition. When a drink volume equal to 150% of the sweat loss was consumed, participants were slightly hypohydrated 6 h after drinking when the test drink had a low sodium concentration, and they were in a similar condition when they drank the same beverage in a volume of twice their sweat loss. With the high sodium drink, enough fluid was retained to keep the participants in a state of hyperhydration 6 h after ingesting the drink when they consumed either 150% or 200% of their sweat loss. The excess would eventually be lost by urine production or by further sweat loss if the individual resumed exercise or moved to a warm environment. Calculated plasma volume changes indicated a decrease of approximately 5.3% with dehydration. At the end of the study period, the general pattern was for the increases in plasma volume to be a direct function of the volume of fluid consumed, with the increase tending to be greater for those individuals who ingested the high sodium drink.

Although other studies have also shown the importance of drinking a larger volume of drink than the sweat volume lost (Mitchell *et al.*, 1994), an interaction between sodium intake, volume intake and whole-body rehydration has not always been reported (Mitchell *et al.*, 2000). However, it is likely that in this study the length of time participants were observed after rehydration may not have been sufficient to discern the urine production response to the treatments. Additionally, evidence has recently emerged suggesting that the rate of drinking a large rehydration bolus can have important implications for the physiological handling of the drink (Archer and Shirreffs, 2001; Kovacs *et al.*, 2002). Drinking a large volume of fluid has the potential to induce a greater decline in plasma sodium concentration and osmolality, which, in turn, have the potential to induce a greater diuresis.

Food and fluid consumption

In many cases, there may be opportunities to consume solid food between exercise bouts; this should be encouraged unless it is likely to result in gastro-intestinal disturbances. Maughan *et al.* (1996) examined the role of solid food intake in promoting rehydration from a 2.1% body mass sweat loss with consumption of either a solid meal plus flavoured water or a commercially available sports drink. The volume of fluid in the meal plus water was the same as the volume of sports drink consumed. The amount of urine produced after food and water ingestion was almost 300 ml less than that when the sports drink was consumed. Plasma volume decreased by approximately 5.4% with dehydration and was restored to the same extent with both rehydration processes. Although the quantity of water consumed with both rehydration methods was the same, the meal had a greater electrolyte content (63 mmol Na^+ and 21 mmol K^+ *vs* 43 mmol Na^+ and 7 mmol K^+) and it is most probable that the greater efficacy of the meal plus water treatment in restoring whole-body water balance was a consequence of the greater total cation content causing a smaller volume of urine to be produced. Subsequent studies have also highlighted a role for food products in post-exercise fluid balance restoration (Ray *et al.*, 1998).

Beverage palatability and voluntary fluid intake

In most scientific studies in this area, a fixed volume of fluid is consumed; in everyday circumstances, however, intake is determined by the interaction of physiological and psychological factors. When the effect of palatability and solute content of beverages in promoting rehydration after sweat loss was studied (Wemple *et al.*, 1997), participants drank 123% of the sweat volume losses with flavoured water and 163% and 133% when the solution had 25 and 50 mmol $\cdot 1^{-1}$ sodium. Three hours after starting the rehydration process, the participants had a better whole-body hydration status after drinking the sodium-containing beverages than the flavoured water. In a similar study (Maughan and Leiper, 1993), participants drank a greater volume of sports drink (2492 ml) and orange juice/lemonade mixture (2488 ml) than of either water (1750 ml) or an oral rehydration solution (1796 ml) reflecting their taste preferences. As expected, urine output was greatest with the low electrolyte drinks that were consumed in the largest volumes (the sports drink and the orange juice/lemonade mixture), and was smallest after drinking the oral rehydration solution. These studies demonstrate the importance of palatability for promoting consumption, but also confirm earlier results showing that a moderately high electrolyte content is essential if the ingested fluid is to be retained in the body. The benefits of the higher intake with the more palatable drinks were lost because of the higher urine output. Other drink characteristics, including carbonation, influence drink palatability and therefore need to be considered when a beverage is being considered for effective post-exercise rehydration (Passe *et al.*, 1997).

Intravenous rehydration

Intravenous fluid therapy has, in the last few years, been used as a rehydration method for dehydrated athletes in cases where it has not been necessary for medical treatment. The argument for its use is based upon perceived health, performance or other benefits over and above those that can be achieved with oral rehydration. In the scientific literature, comparisons have been made between oral and intravenous rehydration from very moderate dehydration on subsequent exercise performance and found no difference in exercise capacity (Nagra, 1998). Similarly, a series of papers reporting a study investigating partial rehydration (from approximately 4% to 2% dehydration) concluded that subsequent exercise performance was better when rehydration occurred irrespective of whether it was by mouth or intravenously (Casa *et al.*, 2000a,b; Maresh *et al.*, 2001). These authors reported that during the subsequent exercise, rectal temperature was lower and heart rate tended to be lower when rehydration had been achieved orally. There is, however, evidence that the sensation of thirst remains higher after partial intravenous rehydration than after partial oral rehydration (flavoured drink with 77 mmol·l^{-1} Na$^+$), which is more likely to promote subsequent drinking as required (Riebe *et al.*, 1997). In combination, these studies provide data both to support and refute intravenous rehydration, particularly when a subsequent exercise bout is to be performed.

One potentially practical use of selecting intravenous rehydration over drinking is the case in which significant dehydration (>2% body mass) is incurred over a short-time frame and with a brief rest period before subsequent exercise. For example, a trained and heat-acclimated athlete can sweat at a rate in excess of 2 l·h^{-1}. Assuming that one of two or more daily training sessions lasts 2 h and 50% of sweat losses are replaced during exercise, a 2-litre deficit occurs and 3–4 litres of fluid must be consumed (150–200% of deficit) to fully restore fluid balance (Shirreffs *et al.*, 1996) before the next workout. The challenge to rehydrate orally and then perform again could, when limited time is available, be better achieved with intravenous rehydration.

Conclusions

For a person undertaking regular exercise, any fluid deficit that is incurred during one exercise session can potentially compromise the next exercise session if adequate fluid replacement does not occur. As such, fluid replacement after exercise can frequently be thought of as hydration before the next exercise bout. However, additional specific issues in this area include ensuring euhydration before exercise and inducing a temporary hyperhydration with sodium salts or glycerol solutions.

Complete restoration of fluid balance after exercise is an important part of the recovery process, and becomes even more important in hot, humid conditions. If a second bout of exercise has to be performed after a relatively short interval, the rate of rehydration is of crucial importance. Rehydration after exercise requires not only replacement of volume losses, but also replacement of the electrolytes, primarily sodium, lost in the sweat. Daily sweat and sodium losses vary widely among individuals and depend on many factors, including the environment, diet, physical fitness and heat acclimation status. However, where sweat losses are large, the total sodium loss will generally also be high. For example, a daily loss of 10 litres of sweat at a sodium concentration of 50 mmol $\cdot$ l^{-1} (normal range of 10–80 mmol $\cdot$ l^{-1}) amounts to about 29 g of sodium chloride. A moderate excess of salt intake would appear to be beneficial as far as hydration status is concerned without any detrimental effects on health, provided that fluid intake is in excess of sweat loss and that renal function is not impaired. Any excess sodium ingested will be excreted in the urine as the kidneys restore equilibrium. Drinks intended specifically for rehydration should, therefore, probably have a higher electrolyte content than drinks formulated for consumption during exercise.

The addition of an energy source does not appear necessary for rehydration, although a small amount of carbohydrate may improve the rate of intestinal uptake of sodium and water, and will improve palatability. Where sweat losses are high, rehydration with carbohydrate solutions has implications for energy balance (e.g. 10 litres of soft drinks will provide approximately 1000 g of carbohydrate, equivalent to about 17,000 kJ or 4000 calories). The volume of beverage consumed should be greater than the volume of sweat lost to allow for the ongoing obligatory urine losses, and palatability of the beverage is a major issue when large volumes of fluid have to be consumed.

Intravenous rehydration after exercise has been investigated to a lesser extent and its role for fluid replacement in the dehydrated but otherwise well athlete remains open to discussion.

Disclaimer

The views, opinions and/or findings contained in this report are those of the authors and should not be construed as an official Department of the Army position, or decision, unless so designated by other official documentation. Approved for public release; distribution unlimited.

References

1 Adolph, E.F. and Associates (1947). *Physiology of Man in the Desert*. New York: Interscience Publishers, Inc.

2 American College of Sports Medicine (1996). Position stand on exercise and fluid replacement. *Medicine and Science in Sports and Exercise*, **28**, i–vii.

3 American Physiological Society (2003). Inter-association task force on exertional heat illnesses consensus statement (http://www.the-aps.org/news/consensus.pdf/).

4 Archer, D.T. and Shirreffs, S.M. (2001). Effect of fluid ingestion rate on post-exercise rehydration in man. *Proceedings of the Nutrition Society*, **60**(Special Issue 3A), 200A.

5 Armstrong, L.E. and Casa, D.J. (2003). Predisposing factors for exertional heat illnesses. In *Exertional Heat Illnesses* (edited by L.E. Armstrong), pp. 151–168. Champaign, IL: Human Kinetics.

6 Armstrong, L.E., Costill, D.L. and Fink, W.J. (1985). Influence of diuretic-induced dehydration on competitive running performance. *Medicine and Science in Sports and Exercise*, **17**, 456–461.

7 Casa, D.J., Maresh, C.M., Armstrong, L.E., Kavouras, S.A., Herrera, J.A., Hacker, F.T., Jr., Keith, N.R. and Elliott, T.A. (2000a). Intravenous versus oral rehydration during a brief period: responses to subsequent exercise in the heat. *Medicine and Science in Sports and Exercise*, **32**, 124–133.

8 Casa, D.J., Maresh, C.M., Armstrong, L.E., Kavouras, S.A., Herrera-Soto, J.A., Hacker, F.T., Jr., Scheett, T.P. and Stoppani, J. (2000b). Intravenous versus oral rehydration during a brief period: stress hormone responses to subsequent exhaustive exercise in the heat. *International Journal of Sport Nutrition and Exercise Metabolism*, **10**, 361–374.

9 Cheuvront, S.N., Carter, R., III and Sawka, M.N. (2003). Fluid balance and endurance exercise performance. *Current Sports Medicine Reports*, **2**, 202–208.

10 Costill, D.L. and Sparks, K.E. (1973). Rapid fluid replacement following thermal dehydration. *Journal of Applied Physiology*, **34**, 299–303.

11 Fortney, S.M., Wenger, C.B., Bove, J.R. and Nadel, E.R. (1984). Effect of hyperosmolality on control of blood flow and sweating. *Journal of Applied Physiology*, **57**, 1688–1695.

12 Greenleaf, J.E., Jackson, C.G.R., Geelen, G., Keil, L.C., Hinghofer-Szalkay, H. and Whittam, J.H. (1998). Plasma volume expansion with oral fluids in hypohydrated men at rest and during exercise. *Aviation, Space and Environmental Medicine*, **69**, 837–844.

13 Hitchins, S., Martin, D.T., Burke, L., Yates, K., Fallon, K., Hahn, A. and Dobson, G.P. (1999). Glycerol hyperhydration improves cycle time trial performance in hot humid conditions. *European Journal of Applied Physiology and Occupational Physiology*, **80**, 494–501.

14 Kovacs, E.M., Schmahl, R.M., Denden, J.M. and Brouns, F. (2002). Effect of high and low rates of fluid intake on post-exercise rehydration. *International Journal of Sport Nutrition and Exercise Metabolism*, **12**, 14–23.

15 Lang, F., Busch, G.L., Volkl, H. and Haussinger, D. (1995). Cell volume: a second messenger in regulation of cellular function. *News in Physiological Sciences*, **10**, 18–22.

16 Latzka, W.A. and Sawka, M.N. (2000). Hyperhydration and glycerol: thermoregulatory effects during exercise in hot climates. *Canadian Journal of Applied Physiology*, **25**, 536–545.

17 Latzka, W.A., Sawka, M.N., Montain, S.J., Skrinar, G.S., Fielding, R.A., Matott, R.P. and Pandolf, K.B. (1997). Hyperhydration: thermoregulatory effects during compensable exercise-heat stress. *Journal of Applied Physiology*, **83**, 860–866.

18 Latzka, W.A., Sawka, M.N., Montain, S.J., Skrinar, G.S., Fielding, R.A., Matott, R.P. and Pandolf, K.B. (1998). Hyperhydration: tolerance and cardiovascular effects during uncompensable exercise-heat stress. *Journal of Applied Physiology*, **84**, 1858–1864.

19 Lyons, T.P., Riedesel, M.L., Meuli, L.E. and Chick, T.W. (1990). Effects of glycerol-induced hyperhydration prior to exercise in the heat on sweating and core temperature. *Medicine and Science in Sports and Exercise*, **22**, 477–483.

20 Maresh, C.M., Herrera-Soto, J.A., Armstrong, L.E., Casa, D.J., Kavouras, S.A., Hacker, F.T., Jr., Elliott, T.A., Stoppani, J. and Scheett, T.P. (2001). Perceptual responses in the heat after brief intravenous versus oral rehydration. *Medicine and Science in Sports and Exercise*, **33**, 1039–1045.

21 Maughan, R.J. and Leiper, J.B. (1993). Post-exercise rehydration in man: effects of voluntary intake of four different beverages. *Medicine and Science in Sports and Exercise*, **25**(Suppl.), S2.

22 Maughan, R.J. and Shirreffs, S.M. (1998). Fluid and electrolyte loss and replacement in exercise. In *Oxford Textbook of Sports Medicine* (edited by M. Harries, C. Williams, W.D. Stanish and L.J. Micheli), 2nd edn, pp. 97–113. Oxford: Oxford University Press.

23 Maughan, R.J., Owen, J.H., Shirreffs, S.M. and Leiper, J.B. (1994). Post-exercise rehydration in man: effects of electrolyte addition to ingested fluids. *European Journal of Applied Physiology*, **69**, 209–215.

24 Maughan, R.J., Leiper, J.B. and Shirreffs, S.M. (1996). Restoration of fluid balance after exercise-induced dehydration: effects of food and fluid intake. *European Journal of Applied Physiology*, **73**, 317–325.

25 Mitchell, J.B., Grandjean, P.W., Pizza, F.X., Starling, R.D. and Holtz, R.W. (1994). The effect of volume ingested on rehydration and gastric emptying following exercise-induced dehydration. *Medicine and Science in Sports and Exercise*, **26**, 1135–1143.

26 Mitchell, J.B., Phillips, M.D., Mercer, S.P., Baylies, H.L. and Pizza, F.X. (2000). Postexercise rehydration: effect of Na^+ and volume on restoration of fluid spaces and cardiovascular function. *Journal of Applied Physiology*, **89**, 1302–1309.

27 Montner, P., Stark, D.M., Riedesel, M.L., Murata, G., Robergs, R., Timms, M. and Chick, T.W. (1996). Pre-exercise glycerol hydration improves cycling endurance time. *International Journal of Sports Medicine*, **17**, 27–33.

28 Nagra, I.S. (1998). Intravenous versus oral rehydration. *British Journal of Sports Medicine*, **32**, 265.

29 Nielsen, B., Sjogaard, G., Ugelvig, J., Knudsen, B. and Dohlmann, B. (1986). Fluid balance in exercise dehydration and rehydration with different glucose–electrolyte drinks. *European Journal of Applied Physiology*, **55**, 318–325.

30 Nose, H., Mack, G.W., Shi, X. and Nadel, E.R. (1988a). Role of osmolality and plasma volume during rehydration in humans. *Journal of Applied Physiology*, **65**, 325–331.

31 Nose, H., Mack, G.W., Shi, X.R. and Nadel, E.R. (1988b). Involvement of sodium retention hormones during rehydration in humans. *Journal of Applied Physiology*, **65**, 332–336.

32 Passe, D.H., Horn, M. and Murray, R. (1997). The effects of beverage carbonation on sensory responses and voluntary fluid intake following exercise. *International Journal of Sports Nutrition*, **7**, 286–297.

33 Ray, M.L., Bryan, M.,W., Ruden, T.M., Baier, S.M., Sharp, R.L. and King, D.S. (1998). Effect of sodium in a rehydration beverage when consumed as a fluid or meal. *Journal of Applied Physiology*, **85**, 1329–1336.

34 Riebe, D., Maresh, C.M., Armstrong, L.E., Kenefick, R.W., Castellani, J.W., Echegaray, M.E., Clark, B.A. and Camaione, D.N. (1997). Effects of oral and intra-venous rehydration on ratings of perceived exertion and thirst. *Medicine and Science in Sports and Exercise*, **29**, 117–124.

35 Riedesel, M.L., Allen, D.Y., Peake, G.T. and Al-Qattan, K. (1987). Hyperhydration with glycerol solutions. *Journal of Applied Physiology*, **63**, 2262–2268.

36 Sawka, M.N. (1992). Physiological consequences of hypohydration: exercise performance and thermoregulation. *Medicine and Science in Sports and Exercise*, **24**, 657–670.

37 Shirreffs, S.M. and Maughan, R.J. (1998). Volume repletion following exercise-induced volume depletion in man: replacement of water and sodium losses. *American Journal of Physiology*, **274**, F868–F875.

38 Shirreffs, S.M., Taylor, A.J., Leiper, J.B. and Maughan, R.J. (1996). Post-exercise rehydration in man: effects of volume consumed and drink sodium content. *Medicine and Science in Sports and Exercise*, **28**, 1260–1271.

39 Wemple, R.D., Morocco, T.S. and Mack, G.W. (1997). Influence of sodium replacement on fluid ingestion following exercise-induced dehydration. *International Journal of Sport Nutrition*, **7**, 104–116.

40 Yawata, T. (1990). Effect of potassium solution on rehydration in rats: comparison with sodium solution and water. *Japanese Journal of Physiology*, **40**, 369–381.

6 Protein and amino acids for athletes

KEVIN D. TIPTON and ROBERT R. WOLFE

The main determinants of an athlete's protein needs are their training regime and habitual nutrient intake. Most athletes ingest sufficient protein in their habitual diet. Additional protein will confer only a minimal, albeit arguably important, additional advantage. Given sufficient energy intake, lean body mass can be maintained within a wide range of protein intakes. Since there is limited evidence for harmful effects of a high protein intake and there is a metabolic rationale for the efficacy of an increase in protein, if muscle hypertrophy is the goal, a higher protein intake within the context of an athlete's overall dietary requirements may be beneficial. However, there are few convincing outcome data to indicate that the ingestion of a high amount of protein ($2–3 \mathrm{~g} \cdot \mathrm{kg}^{-1} \mathrm{BW} \cdot \mathrm{day}^{-1}$, where BW = body weight) is necessary. Current literature suggests that it may be too simplistic to rely on recommendations of a particular amount of protein per day. Acute studies suggest that for any given amount of protein, the metabolic response is dependent on other factors, including the timing of ingestion in relation to exercise and/or other nutrients, the composition of ingested amino acids and the type of protein.

Keywords: amino acids, hypertrophy, muscle, protein, strength, training.

Introduction

The importance of protein to athletes has long been recognized. From coaches of Olympians in ancient Greece to today's multi-millionaire athletes, protein has been considered a key nutritional component for athletic success. For an equally long time, the nature of that importance has been controversial. Among many athletes, especially strength and team sport athletes, protein and amino acid ingestion is considered essential to performance. Amino acid and protein supplements have become a billion dollar industry. However, information stemming from research into the efficacy of elevated protein and amino acid ingestion, as well as the requirements for top sport athletes, is still relatively sparse. There is much concerning protein nutrition for athletes that has yet to be resolved.

In 1991, Peter Lemon presented a thorough review of the state of the knowledge at that time. He reported that there was considerable controversy about the protein requirements of athletes, which, unfortunately, has yet to be resolved. Studies suggested that amino acid oxidation was increased during exercise, at least with dynamic exercise (Lemon, 1991). Thus, it was felt that habitual exercise of sufficient intensity and duration would increase dietary protein requirements. Nitrogen balance and other studies supported this contention and recommendations for protein intake were made. Strength or speed athletes were recommended to consume about 1.2–1.7 g protein·kg^{-1} BW·day^{-1} and endurance athletes about 1.2–1.4 g protein·kg^{-1} BW·day^{-1} (where BW = body weight). Whereas these recommendations exceeded the US recommended daily allowance (RDA) for protein (0.8 g protein·kg^{-1} BW·day^{-1}), they did not exceed the habitual dietary intake of most athletes, so it was felt that there was no reason to recommend that most athletes should increase the protein in their diet (Lemon, 1991). The main aim of the present review is to update the literature since 1991 and to critically examine the available information on protein nutrition for athletes.

Over the last 10–15 years, much has been published on the interaction of exercise and nutrition. Tissue metabolism, especially muscle, has received increasing attention as methods have been developed to examine the response of muscle protein metabolism to exercise and nutrition. Despite these advances, much remains to be resolved and many questions remain to be answered.

Technical difficulties clearly contribute to some of the confusion and disagreements surrounding protein requirements for active individuals. The selection of participants, their adaptation to the protein intake during a study, their training state, exercise intensity and energy balance, may all contribute to discrepant results (Butterfield, 1987; Millward, 1999). Nitrogen balance is the most common method used to estimate protein requirements. The limitations of nitrogen balance measures are well known. (Readers are referred to one of the many excellent reviews on this topic for more detailed information: Hegsted, 1976, 1978; Young, 1986; Lemon and Proctor, 1991; Tome and Bos, 2000.) However, from a practical standpoint, coaches and athletes are not usually interested in the myriad of scientific arguments for the impact of exercise on protein requirements. They simply wish to know whether a particular athlete's performance will be enhanced by consuming more, or less, protein. None of the methods that have been utilized in studies seeking to determine protein intakes for athletes has a direct relationship with athletic performance. The impact of diet on performance is what we are interested in, but it is difficult to quantify. At this time, there is no clear consensus on the importance of elevated protein for the athletic population.

Meanwhile, there is, perhaps, a more fundamental problem for determination of the protein requirements of athletes. Much of the controversy surrounding protein requirement in athletes may be due to the exact meaning of this term for this population. In our opinion, it is difficult to define protein requirement as it applies to competitive athletes. The most commonly used definition for the nutritional requirement for protein is the minimum amount ingested that will balance all nitrogen losses and thus maintain nitrogen equilibrium (Millward, 2001). Losses are considered to be the obligatory nitrogen losses (i.e. all nitrogen losses on a protein-free diet), thus representing the minimum metabolic demands for amino acid nitrogen. This definition is based on nitrogen balance studies and it, or something very similar, has typically been used in studies that examined the impact of exercise on protein requirements (Tarnopolsky *et al.*, 1988, 1992; Meredith *et al.*, 1989; Lemon *et al.*, 1997; Forslund *et al.*, 1998). Millward (2001) also suggested a more complex definition of protein requirement based on the Adaptive Demands Model, in which the metabolic demands include both obligatory and adaptive components. Thus, protein requirement is defined as the minimum protein intake that satisfies the metabolic demands and which maintains body composition. For the sedentary population, the US RDA for protein is 0.8 g protein $\cdot$ kg^{-1} BW $\cdot$ day^{-1}, but it is not clear whether athletes in training need more than this amount.

These definitions may be appropriate for normal, healthy or even clinical populations, but we feel that neither is necessarily appropriate for athletes in training. Accepted definitions of protein requirement are based on nitrogen balance measures in the laboratory and may have no relationship with athletic performance. Athletes and coaches are more interested in the optimum protein intake for athletic success, rather than the actual definition of protein requirement based on nitrogen balance. In fact, the appropriate definition of protein requirement – that is, the optimal protein intake – will vary depending on the training and competition goals of the athlete. It is important to bear in mind the goals of different athletes when discussing the importance of protein ingestion. For each individual, the impact of increased protein on whole-body and muscle nitrogen balance must be considered in terms of the different nitrogen metabolic pathways (Tome and Bos, 2000). For example, an endurance athlete would probably consider the protein necessary to maintain lean body mass and not impair performance as the protein requirement. Aside from obligatory uses, protein would be necessary for increased energy demands, protein synthesis of enzymes that are stimulated by endurance training and, perhaps, repair of muscle proteins damaged by intense training. On the other hand, a strength athlete and many team sport athletes, such as rugby or hockey players, would not consider the intake necessary for maintenance of lean body mass sufficient, but rather the protein requirement would be the amount necessary to increase muscle mass and strength or power. Additionally, not only would the definition be different for athletes in different sports, but also in individual circumstances (e.g. weight loss) in any given sport. For athletes, muscle protein is possibly the most important body protein to consider. Those athletes desiring muscle hypertrophy expect their training and diet to stimulate protein accretion. Clearly, chronic exercise training has a dramatic impact on muscle protein metabolism. Exercise training results in fundamental adaptations in the muscle. The metabolic basis for protein accretion is net muscle protein synthesis – that is, protein synthesis exceeds protein breakdown over the given period in question. The primary adaptation to resistance exercise training is muscle hypertrophy, whereas endurance training results in increased muscle oxidative capacity. The response of muscle protein metabolism to the training stimulus has a major impact on these adaptations. Very little research has examined the chronic response of muscle protein metabolism to exercise training. Phillips *et al.* (1999) demonstrated that the responses of mixed-muscle (i.e. the weighted average of all proteins in muscle) protein synthesis and breakdown to acute resistance exercise were ameliorated in resistance-trained individuals compared with untrained individuals (Fig. 1). These and more recent results (Phillips *et al.*, 2002) are consistent with the principle of general adaptation to training. That is, as a system – in this case, muscle – adapts to a stress, greater stress must be added to generate the desired adaptations. Muscle mass clearly adapts to the type and severity of training, as well as the nutritional intake of the athlete. To maintain muscle mass at greater than 'normal' (i.e. that which is genetically determined), muscle protein synthesis must be increased regularly. Over 24 h, the response of muscle to resistance exercise plus hyperaminoacidaemia is additive to the normal 24-h muscle protein balance (Tipton *et al.*, 2003) (Fig. 2). To date, there have been no studies on the impact of chronic endurance training on muscle protein metabolism. However, endurance training increases the activity and amount of mitochondrial enzymes and the size and amount of muscle mitochondria (Neufer, 1989), suggesting that muscle protein metabolism, at least for some proteins, must be influenced by endurance training.

Interestingly, both endurance and resistance exercise increase mixed-muscle protein synthesis. Clearly, muscular adaptation to endurance exercise is profoundly different from that to resistance exercise. Thus, it is difficult to accept that the response of muscle protein metabolism to an acute bout is the same for both types of training. There are several possible explanations for why the response of mixed-muscle protein synthesis to endurance and to resistance exercise is qualitatively similar. Mixed-muscle protein synthesis represents the weighted average of all the proteins in the muscle, each of which may have a unique response to a particular type of exercise. Certainly, since the major result of chronic resistance training is muscle hypertrophy, it is intuitive to expect resistance exercise to influence myofibrillar more than mitochondrial

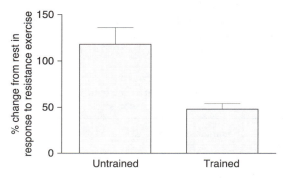

Figure 1. Change in mixed-muscle fractional synthetic rate in response to a resistance exercise bout in untrained and resistance-trained individuals (from Phillips *et al.*, 1999).

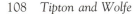

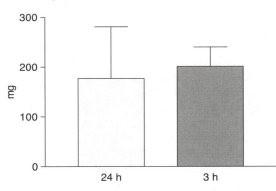

Figure 2. Difference in phenylalanine exchange (area under the curve for net muscle protein balance in mg) between rest and exercise + essential amino acid supplement (ES) over the entire 24 h and over 3 h, in both trials, corresponding to the time of amino acid ingestion and exercise in the ES trial. Thus, the response to exercise and amino acid ingestion for 3 h represents the response over the entire 24-h period (from Tipton *et al.*, 2003).

proteins; the converse would be true for endurance exercise (Table 1). In the past, methodological limitations prevented the detailed examination of the response of synthesis of different protein sub-fractions to exercise. Today, however, the techniques are available to examine muscle protein sub-fraction (Welle *et al.*, 1995; Rooyackers *et al.*, 1997; Bohe *et al.*, 2001) and even individual protein synthesis (Balagopal *et al.*, 1994; Hasten *et al.*, 2000). These methods indicate that myofibrillar protein synthesis responds to resistance exercise in a similar manner to mixed-muscle protein synthesis (Balagopal *et al.*, 1997a,b, 2001; Hasten *et al.*, 2000). Unfortunately, to date, no study has compared the response of synthesis of different types of proteins to different forms of exercise. Moreover, there is no means to directly measure degradation of different protein sub-fractions or individual proteins in humans *in vivo*. Determination of the net balance of protein sub-fractions is not possible.

There remains much controversy about the protein requirement of athletes. The following discussion will make it apparent that the results of studies appear to conflict. There is evidence to support the argument for both the efficacy of increased protein intake (i.e. intake greater than the RDA for sedentary

Table 1. Measured and proposed changes of mixed-muscle, myofibrillar and mito-chondrial protein synthesis in response to different types of exercise

	Endurance exercise	Resistance exercise	
Mixed-muscle protein synthesis	↑	↑ or ↑↑	
Myofibrillar protein synthesis	↔ or ↓	? ↑ or ↑↑	
Mitochondrial protein synthesis	↑	↔ or ↑	?

individuals) as well as for protein intakes that are similar to those of sedentary individuals. So, we will attempt to illustrate the data supporting arguments both for and against higher intakes for top sport athletes. Moreover, we hope to convey the notion that a general value for protein requirements for athletes is difficult to ascertain and determination of appropriate protein intake must take into account the demands of the individual goals and training regimen of each athlete.

Protein requirements

Since the original consensus report in 1991, protein requirements have been examined in additional studies, but controversy continues regarding the impact of exercise, especially exercise as intense as that top sport athletes must perform, on protein requirements (Tarnopolsky, 1999; Rennie and Tipton, 2000; Wolfe, 2000). The basis of the argument for increased protein needs by exercising individuals is often an increase in amino acid (usually represented by leucine) oxidation during dynamic exercise. Leucine oxidation was found to be increased during dynamic exercise in recent studies (Tarnopolsky *et al.*, 1992; Phillips *et al.*, 1993; El Khoury *et al.*, 1997; Lemon *et al.*, 1997; Bowtell *et al.*, 1998, 2000; Forslund *et al.*, 1998; Lamont *et al.*, 1999; Millward, 1999). Increased amino acid oxidation during exercise is thought to be due to increased utilization of amino acids as fuel; therefore, regular and repeated exercise would then lead to increased protein requirements.

On the other hand, previous work from our laboratory showed that the fate of leucine during exercise might not reflect that of all amino acids and leucine oxidation is not matched by urea production (Wolfe *et al.*, 1984). Also, lysine oxidation was not increased, suggesting that short-term increases in leucine oxidation do not reflect whole-body protein breakdown. Training does not increase branched-chain amino acids (BCAA) oxidation (Lamont *et al.*, 1999) and, in fact, may attenuate the increase due to exercise (McKenzie *et al.*, 2000). Furthermore, increased amino acid oxidation during exercise must influence 24-h oxidation of amino acids and thus nitrogen balance for protein requirements to be changed. The 24-h leucine oxidation and balance were measured in healthy men performing 180 min of cycling exercise at protein intakes of 1.0 and 2.5 g protein $\cdot$ kg^{-1} BW $\cdot$ day^{-1} (El Khoury *et al.*, 1997; Forslund *et al.*, 1998). Whereas leucine oxidation was increased during exercise and by the higher protein intake, 24-h whole-body leucine remained in equilibrium at both protein intakes. It is thought that the increased leucine oxidation during exercise was compensated for by small and undetectable changes throughout the day. Support for this notion comes from Devlin *et al.* (1990), who showed that during 3 h of cycling at 75% $\dot{V}O_{2max}$, leucine oxidation was less than at rest. These data do not support the contention that dynamic exercise increases protein requirements. The impact of resistance exercise on amino acid oxidation has received far less attention, but there is no indication that resistance exercise increases leucine oxidation either during or after exercise (Tarnopolsky *et al.*,

1991). Thus, it seems that the whole-body amino acid data are somewhat equivocal and it cannot be concluded with certainty that habitual exercise increases protein requirements. Leucine oxidation appears to be increased by endurance exercise, but this increase may not reflect an increased requirement for dietary protein.

Nitrogen balance is the most common method used to determine protein requirements. Using this method, many authors have concluded that both endurance and resistance athletes require more than the 0.8 g protein $\cdot$ kg^{-1} BW $\cdot$ day^{-1} dietary recommendation (Lemon, 1991). The results of more recent studies support this argument (Tarnopolsky et al., 1992; Phillips et al., 1993). Feeding athletes different amounts of protein and measuring nitrogen balance, then extrapolating to the zero line, was the basis for the conclusion that athletes require more dietary protein. In all these studies, zero balance was calculated to be above 0.8 g protein $\cdot$ kg^{-1} BW $\cdot$ day^{-1}; thus, a widely accepted notion that athletes need more protein has been promulgated. It is important to note that nitrogen balance is the method that is commonly used to determine the protein needs of sedentary populations; thus comparing like to like, these studies indicate that active individuals, particularly athletes, require more protein in their diet.

On the other hand, the notion that athletes require more protein than sedentary individuals is not universally accepted. There is ample evidence to suggest that protein needs are not increased by habitual exercise. In fact, the opposite interpretation – that is, exercise training increases the efficiency of protein utilization, thus making increased intake unnecessary – has been argued. In a series of studies from the laboratory of the late Gail Butterfield, it was demonstrated that protein utilization is increased and protein requirements are decreased by endurance exercise (Butterfield and Calloway, 1984; Todd et al., 1984). Similarly, in a classic study, Gontzea et al. (1975) demonstrated that nitrogen balance was initially negative upon initiation of an exercise training programme while maintaining constant protein intake, but returned to equilibrium after a period of accommodation. Following the period of accommodation, no increase in protein intake was necessary to maintain nitrogen equilibrium. These studies suggest that it is not necessary for physically active individuals to increase protein intake to maintain nitrogen equilibrium; in fact, exercise may decrease protein needs due to increased efficiency of protein utilization. Critics of this line of thought suggest that the intensity and volume of training in the aforementioned studies was not equivalent to that of top sport athletes and thus may not represent the circumstances the elite athlete faces (Lemon, 1991; Lemon and Proctor, 1991).

A similar argument can be made for strength athletes. Acute resistance exercise in the fasted state has been shown to improve net muscle protein balance (Biolo et al., 1995b; Phillips et al., 1997). Furthermore, training ameliorates the response of muscle to a bout of resistance exercise in both the fasted (Phillips et al., 1999) and fed (Phillips et al., 2002) states. These data suggest that there is an accommodation of muscle protein metabolism such that protein needs for maintenance of body mass in trained individuals would not be increased. On the other hand, maintenance of lean body mass is not the goal of many athletes, especially those who participate in strength and power sports, and so the protein needed to increase body mass might be greater.

Alternative interpretations of the nitrogen balance data can be used to argue that strength athletes may want to consume large amounts of protein. If an athlete is trying to increase muscle mass, then the goal would not be nitrogen equilibrium, but positive nitrogen balance. Examination of the nitrogen balance data presented by Tarnopolsky *et al.* (1992) for strength-trained athletes could be used to support the contention that increased protein intake will increase nitrogen balance in athletes during intense resistance training. There are data to support the notion that all other things being equal, the more protein ingested, the more lean body mass may be increased. Indeed, Hegsted (1978) summarized a variety of nitrogen balance studies of adults, children and pregnant women. Taken together, these studies indicate that there is a retention of $\sim 20\%$ of the intake above the maintenance need, at least at intakes above maintenance (~ 0.5 g nitrogen $\cdot$ kg^{-1} BW $\cdot$ day^{-1}). Furthermore, this retention appeared to continue for as long as the studies were conducted. Tome and Bos (2000) summarize studies that indicate high protein intakes can result in continuous, positive nitrogen balance from 1 to 3 g nitrogen $\cdot$ day^{-1}. For example, positive nitrogen balance was maintained for up to 50 days on a very high protein diet (~ 3 times the RDA) with no adaptation evident (Oddoye and Margen, 1979). To date, there are no nitrogen balance studies that show anything other than increased positive nitrogen balance when protein intake is increased. Interpreted this way, it could be argued that athletes who desire muscle hypertrophy should eat very high protein diets to maximize their muscle gain. These data illustrate that high, positive nitrogen balance can be maintained for an extended period (Oddoye and Margen, 1979), thus providing the capacity for muscle hypertrophy. Whole-body (Forslund *et al.*, 1998) and muscle (Borsheim *et al.*, 2002; Miller *et al.*, 2003) protein synthesis rates are increased with increasing protein or amino acid intake, supporting the notion that the specific requirement for protein intake may be determined by the desired lean body mass. Furthermore, there is evidence from one study that the increase in lean body mass during resistance exercise training is greater with increased protein intake (Burke *et al.*, 2001). Weightlifters were fed either 1.2 or 2.1 g protein $\cdot$ kg^{-1} BW $\cdot$ day^{-1}. The group that ingested the higher amount of protein had increased lean body mass compared with the group receiving less protein (Fig. 3). Results from a recent bed rest study from our laboratory further support the notion that increased nitrogen intake may increase muscle mass. Two groups of individuals rested in bed for 28 days (Paddon-Jones *et al.*, 2003). Both groups were fed weight maintenance diets, but one was given additional nitrogen in the form of an essential amino acid supplement. Whereas the placebo group lost muscle mass, the supplemented group maintained muscle mass during the bed rest period. Furthermore, although

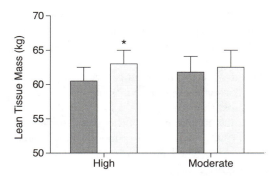

Figure 3. Change in lean body mass in experienced weightlifters consuming either high (2.1 g·kg^{-1}·day^{-1}) or moderate (1.2 g·kg^{-1}·day^{-1}) dietary protein during a 6-week resistance training programme. ■, before training; □, after training. *After training significantly different from before training (adapted from Burke *et al.*, 2001).

both groups lost strength, the loss was significantly ameliorated by the increase in nitrogen.

Not all available evidence supports the notion that ingesting greater amounts of protein leads to greater lean body or muscle mass. The important result of dietary protein intake is maintenance – or increase, in the case of strength and power athletes – of lean body mass. Interestingly, if calculations of body composition are made from the apparent nitrogen retention at high protein intakes, unrealistic estimates of body composition can result (Hegsted, 1976, 1978). Furthermore, studies in which lean body mass was measured during resistance exercise training while consuming different amounts of protein do not offer a clear-cut conclusion that protein needs are greater in the athletic population. That is, nitrogen balance may indicate high nitrogen retention with increased protein intake without any increase in muscle mass (Tarnopolsky *et al.*, 1988, 1992). However, these studies were short (on the order of a few weeks), so it is possible that protein accretion was occurring, but was not sufficient to be measured with existing body composition methods. In a 12-week study, elderly individuals were fed the RDA (0.8 g protein·kg^{-1} BW·day^{-1}) or double the RDA for protein during a resistance-training programme (Campbell *et al.*, 1995). Both nitrogen retention and body composition were similar in the two dietary protein groups. Of course, it is possible that young athletes would have an entirely different response, so the relevance of this study to the athletic population may be questioned. Three groups of rats were fed different amounts of protein during functional overload to stimulate muscle hypertrophy in the overloaded muscle (O'Hagan *et al.*, 1995). Protein intake was 7, 17.5 or 30% of the diet in the three groups. The amount of dietary protein did not affect the experimentally induced muscle growth in either the plantaris or soleus muscles. Thus, it is not clear whether the increased nitrogen retention associated with increased protein intake leads to greater lean body mass or muscle hypertrophy.

If nitrogen retention increases, but does not result in increased lean body mass and muscle mass, then what is the fate of the excess nitrogen? Certainly, whole-body amino acid oxidation increases with increased protein intake (Tarnopolsky *et al.*, 1992; Bowtell *et al.*, 1998; Forslund *et al.*, 1998), but the nitrogen must end up somewhere. It is possible that the amount of protein deposition is too small to be detected by body composition methodology. Alternatively, excretion of nitrogen could be underestimated; thus the apparent nitrogen retention may be due to inherent errors in the calculation of nitrogen balance. Exercise increases urea nitrogen recycling into body proteins (Carraro *et al.*, 1993). Furthermore, increased protein breakdown appears to provide amino acids for plasma proteins (Carraro *et al.*, 1990). However, how this relates to long-term changes in nitrogen balance is unclear. Thus, it is uncertain how these factors would be accounted for in calculations of the fat-free mass from nitrogen retention.

In any discussion of protein requirements, the importance of energy intake must be considered. There is evidence to suggest that energy intake is, in fact, more important for maintenance of nitrogen equilibrium than protein intake. Butterfield and co-workers clearly demonstrated the importance of energy for maintenance of nitrogen balance and lean body mass (Todd *et al.*, 1984; Butterfield, 1987; Butterfield *et al.*, 1997). Almost 100 years ago, it was demonstrated that athletes can gain strength and maintain mass on relatively small protein intakes, as long as sufficient energy is available (Chittenden, 1907). Furthermore, energy intake may be crucial for nitrogen retention and increased lean body mass. In the study of Gater *et al.* (1992), individuals were resistance trained for 10 weeks on one of three dietary regimens. One group performed the training with no additions to their diet, a second was given an amino acid supplement and a third consumed a diet with positive energy balance. Positive energy balance without additional protein engendered the greatest gains in lean body mass during the 10-week training programme. Other investigators also have demonstrated that increases in lean body mass result from increased energy intake in sedentary individuals (Forbes *et al.*, 1986, 1989; Welle *et al.*, 1989; Jebb *et al.*, 1993). So, it would appear that increased energy intake may be crucial to increasing lean body mass during training, possibly more so than protein intake.

Even if we accept that the protein needs of athletes are greater than the RDA, it should not necessarily be a reason for the broad recommendation that athletes increase their protein intake. Most athletes, especially those with training volumes such that energy intake is necessarily high, probably consume sufficient protein in their normal diet (Deuster *et al.*, 1986; Grandjean, 1989), even those from underdeveloped countries (Christensen *et al.*, 2002), to cover even the higher recommendations that have been published (Lemon, 1991; Lemon and Proctor, 1991). Viewed another way, even athletes whose muscle hypertrophy is maximized are probably eating sufficient protein to cover the need for muscle protein accretion (Millward *et al.*, 1994). Millward *et al.* (1994) point out that even the rates of steroid-induced muscle growth are trivial

(~3%) relative to normal dietary intake. Furthermore, the increased energy demands of intense resistance training would increase dietary protein intake such that the diet would supply at least 50% more protein than the maximum rate of accretion that has been reported. Thus, for most athletes, recommendations for increased protein do not seem necessary. Some athletes who need to control their weight may need to increase protein as a proportion of their energy intake. Nitrogen balance is better maintained on a hypoenergetic diet if protein intake is high. Furthermore, as discussed in more detail below, examination of the available data has led to the conclusion that athletes wishing to increase muscle mass may want to consume large amounts of protein. For example, the argument that strength athletes consuming sufficient energy will consume more than enough protein to supply amino acids for protein accretion (Millward *et al.*, 1994) presumes that there is a direct relationship between protein intake and protein accretion. There is ample evidence that amino acids not only function as precursors for protein synthesis, but also act as regulatory molecules to stimulate net muscle protein synthesis (Wolfe and Miller, 1999; Kimball, 2002; Kimball and Jefferson, 2002); thus that there is a direct relationship between protein intake and protein accretion is not necessarily correct.

In addition to limitations of nitrogen balance studies, the discrepancies may be rooted in the inherent limitations of long-term endpoint studies. Whereas longitudinal endpoint studies might best be utilized to answer the question of whether or not increased dietary protein increases muscle mass, these studies are difficult to perform with sufficient control to render readily interpretable results. Strict control of all aspects of an athlete's life (e.g. training, rest, sleep, diet, travel) for a lengthy period is necessary to obtain measurable results. The problem is that these studies may not demonstrate efficacy of increased protein intake even if effective. Assuming that increasing protein intake is effective for increasing muscle mass, the response is likely to be small compared with the normal response to exercise and meal intake, especially for elite athletes. The major stimulus for muscle growth will be the training regimen and normal nutrient intake. Any additional stimulus due to elevated protein intake would be relatively minor. On the other hand, a small response that is difficult to measure may, in fact, be physiologically relevant and, if so, increased protein intake would be important to a nutritional programme. Difficulties with control of variables in longitudinal studies contribute to the uncertainty and it may be virtually impossible to conduct a study with appropriate control that will demonstrate clearly that increased protein results in increased lean body mass.

Thus far, the discussion of protein requirements has strictly been in the context of the amount of protein necessary in the diet. There is abundant evidence to suggest that determination of protein needs is not as simple as merely expressing a quantity to be ingested per day. Evidence from acute metabolic studies, as well as longitudinal studies, indicates that other factors, such as composition of the protein and amino acids, timing of ingestion and other nutrients ingested concurrently, influence the utilization of ingested protein and amino acids.

Thus, for any given protein intake, factors important to an athlete's performance may vary depending on exactly what is ingested and when it is ingested.

Composition of ingested protein and amino acids

Amino acid composition appears to influence the response of muscle protein balance following resistance exercise. Net muscle protein synthesis results from ingestion of essential amino acids only (Tipton *et al.*, 2001, 2003; Borsheim *et al.*, 2002). Thus, it is clear that non-essential amino acids are not necessary for the stimulation of muscle protein synthesis resulting in net muscle protein synthesis. There is evidence that even single amino acids may stimulate protein synthesis and possibly net muscle protein synthesis. Studies in rats demonstrate that leucine ingested after running results in increased muscle protein synthesis by stimulating the protein translation initiation pathways (Gautsch *et al.*, 1998; Anthony *et al.*, 1999). In resting humans, muscle protein synthesis was stimulated by bolus doses of single essential, but not non-essential, amino acids (Smith *et al.*, 1994). Thus, individual amino acids may act as stimuli for muscle protein synthesis and positive net muscle protein balance. These results suggest that essential amino acids may act to stimulate muscle protein synthesis in two ways: (1) by supplying substrate for muscle protein synthesis and (2) acting as a regulatory factor.

The amount of essential amino acids necessary to acutely stimulate muscle protein synthesis and net muscle protein synthesis appears to be relatively small. Ingestion of as little as 6 g of essential amino acids, both with (Tipton *et al.*, 2001) and without carbohydrates (Borsheim *et al.*, 2002), results in dramatic elevations in muscle protein synthesis leading to net muscle protein synthesis. Moreover, some data suggest that there is a dose dependency of the response of muscle protein synthesis to essential amino acid ingestion after exercise. The response of net muscle protein balance to two doses of 6 g each of essential amino acids (Borsheim *et al.*, 2002) was about double that of two doses of 6 g each of mixed amino acids (Miller *et al.*, 2003). The mixed amino acids contained approximately 3 g of essential amino acids in each dose or about half the amount in the two 6-g doses. Thus, there may be a point of essential amino acid availability above which no further stimulation occurs. Support for this concept comes from the fact that net muscle protein synthesis was similar when ~20 g and 40 g of essential amino acids were ingested after resistance exercise (Tipton *et al.*, 1999). Any further stimulation must occur following the next meal. A summary of the response of net muscle protein balance to amino acids, as well as carbohydrates (discussed below), is illustrated in Fig. 4. At this time, the minimum dose of essential amino acids necessary to stimulate net muscle protein synthesis and the amount necessary to stimulate the maximum response remain to be determined. Further studies must be conducted to determine the upper level of this dose dependency of muscle protein balance to essential amino acid intake. The dose–response relationship may help explain

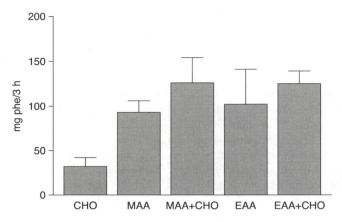

Figure 4. Net phenylalanine uptake over 3 h in response to carbohydrate and amino acid ingestion after resistance exercise in healthy volunteers. CHO = 100 g of sucrose in a single bolus. MAA = 2 × 6 g of mixed – that is, non-essential and essential amino acids (6 g of essential amino acids total) – ingested at 1 and 2 h post-exercise. MAA + CHO = 2 × 6 g of mixed amino acids (6 g of essential amino acids total) + 35 g of sucrose ingested at 1 and 2 h post-exercise. EAA = 2 × 6 g of essential amino acids (12 g of essential amino acids total) only ingested at 1 and 2 h post-exercise. EAA + CHO = 6 g of essential amino acids (6 g of essential amino acids total) + 35 g of sucrose ingested at 1 h post-exercise.

why further increases in protein intake will not result in chronic increases in muscle mass.

The response of muscle protein synthesis and net muscle protein balance to hyperaminoacidaemia may be linked to intracellular amino acid availability (Wolfe and Miller, 1999; Wolfe, 2000). Ingestion of a nutrient that results in hyperaminoacidaemia increases amino acid delivery to the muscle, transport into the muscle cell and intracellular amino acid availability. Increased blood flow due to the exercise bout, as well as elevated rates of protein synthesis due to the exercise, would lead to increased amino acid delivery to the muscle and the potential for increased muscle protein synthesis after exercise. Taken together, these factors may explain the additive effect of exercise and amino acids on net muscle protein balance (Biolo *et al.*, 1997). Alternatively, or in addition to, increased intracellular availability of amino acids, there is evidence linking the stimulation of muscle protein synthesis to the change in arterial amino acid concentrations (Borsheim *et al.*, 2002). Borsheim *et al.* (2002) showed that arterial essential amino acids increased several-fold in response to ingestion of 6 g of essential amino acids after resistance exercise. Net muscle protein balance increased proportionally more than arterial concentrations and declined rapidly when arterial amino acid concentrations began to decline. Interestingly, net muscle protein balance had returned to resting values when arterial amino acid concentrations were still double resting values. Muscle intracellular amino acid concentrations increased, but were not different from resting values by the end of the study (Borsheim *et al.*, 2002). These results are similar to those of a previous study demonstrating rapid changes in net balance without lasting changes in muscle intracellular concentrations (Tipton *et al.*, 2001). Moreover, another study from our laboratory demonstrated that decreased blood amino acid concentrations resulted in decreased muscle protein synthesis and restoration of arterial amino acids resulted in restoration of synthesis (Kobayashi *et al.*, 2003). Much of these changes can be explained by the notion that arterial amino acid concentrations are the key regulating factor. It is possible that muscle protein may be playing a central role in maintenance of blood amino acids. Thus, the changes in muscle protein breakdown and muscle protein synthesis are responsive to the concentration of essential amino acids in the blood and net muscle protein synthesis occurs only when there is an increase in arterial concentrations. In this scenario, the changes in muscle protein synthesis and breakdown may provide amino acids for other tissues (e.g. liver proteins; Wolfe *et al.*, 1984; Carraro *et al.*, 1990).

On the one hand, transiently changing intracellular amino acid concentrations would not appear to support the notion that intracellular amino acid availability regulates muscle protein synthesis and net muscle protein balance (Gibala, 2001). However, the intracellular amino acid pool and rates of metabolic processes are in a constant state of flux. Stimulation of muscle protein synthesis would increase utilization of the amino acids coming into the cell from increased transport, as well as muscle protein breakdown. Any elevation of muscle intracellular amino acid concentrations would thus be transient and may not be measured unless muscle was sampled on a frequent, perhaps even minute-by-minute, basis. It would appear that the two notions of control of muscle protein synthesis are not mutually exclusive. Therefore, the regulation of muscle protein synthesis and net muscle protein balance by amino acids following exercise may respond to either changes in concentrations of arterial amino acids or intracellular amino acid availability, or both.

It is not necessary for hyperaminoacidaemia to result from ingestion of only free amino acids. On a whole-body level, recent studies have demonstrated that a response characterized by a prolonged amino acid appearance of lesser magnitude is superior to a response characterized by a more transient appearance of greater magnitude (Boirie *et al.*, 1997; Dangin *et al.*, 2001). Ingestion of whey proteins resulted in amino acid concentrations in the blood that were higher and less prolonged than those resulting from casein (Boirie *et al.*, 1997). Both resulted in positive whole-body protein balance, but the anabolic response to casein was superior to that of whey proteins. The digestive properties for these proteins are different such that amino acids from casein appear more slowly than those from whey proteins (Dangin *et al.*, 2001). The digestive properties of the proteins appear to play a role in the anabolic response to ingestion on a whole-body level, but it is unclear if the anabolic response of muscle is similar or if exercise influences this response. Thus, whereas it is clear that supply of amino acids is the critical factor for stimulating net muscle protein synthesis following resistance exercise, other factors may also play a role.

Net positive muscle protein synthesis clearly results when amino acids are ingested after resistance exercise, but the response after endurance exercise is not as clear. Blomstrand and Saltin (2001) fed participants a BCAA solution during and after cycling exercise. Ingestion of the solution resulted in slight improvements in net muscle protein balance, but the balance remained negative – that is, net muscle protein synthesis did not result. These results could be interpreted to suggest that the response to endurance exercise combined with amino acid intake is different from that to resistance exercise. Alternatively, they could be interpreted to suggest that feeding BCAA only is not sufficient to stimulate net muscle protein synthesis after exercise. This notion is supported by the fact that net uptake of amino acids resulted when participants were fed a protein–carbohydrate–lipid solution after 60 min of cycling (Levenhagen *et al.*, 2002). Thus, it is more likely that BCAA alone are insufficient to stimulate net muscle protein synthesis and that, given the appropriate nutritional stimulation, net muscle protein synthesis will occur after endurance exercise. However, since the usual response to chronic endurance training is not hypertrophy of muscle, the proteins that respond are probably different from those that respond to nutrient ingestion after resistance exercise. Studies must be conducted to determine the differences between the responses of muscle protein to endurance exercise and those to resistance exercise.

Few studies have examined the impact of carbohydrates and fats on the response of net muscle protein balance after exercise. Any effect of consuming carbohydrates or fats upon net muscle protein balance will probably primarily be due to the resulting elevation of hormones, such as insulin. Carbohydrate ingestion results in stimulation of insulin release. Local insulin infusion, such that arterial amino acid concentrations are maintained, has been demonstrated to stimulate muscle protein synthesis at rest (Biolo *et al.*, 1995a). However, after resistance exercise, additional stimulation of muscle protein synthesis over and above that due to the exercise was limited (Biolo *et al.*, 1999). Whereas ingestion of carbohydrates alone after resistance exercise improves muscle protein balance, without amino acids present the balance does not reach positive levels (Miller *et al.*, 2003). Thus, it would appear that while the response of muscle protein synthesis to exercise and amino acids is additive, the response to exercise and insulin is not additive. The normal post-exercise stimulation of muscle protein breakdown, on the other hand, was ameliorated by local insulin infusion after resistance exercise (Biolo *et al.*, 1999). The amelioration of muscle protein breakdown by insulin infusion resulted in improved net muscle protein balance over the basal, post-exercise value; however, this improvement did not result in positive balance in the absence of amino acid intake. Taken together, the decrease in muscle protein breakdown due to the insulin and the increase in muscle protein synthesis due to increased amino acids suggest that addition of an insulin secretagogue, such as carbohydrate, to an amino acid source may result in an optimal response of muscle protein balance.

No study has compared the anabolic response to the addition of lipids to amino acids to that of amino acids alone but, given the potential importance of digestive properties to the response, it should not be surprising if there was some effect. A recent study provided clear evidence, at least on a whole-body level, that ingesting proteins as part of a meal engendered a different response than when the proteins were ingested alone (Dangin *et al.*, 2003). The rate of appearance of amino acids in the blood suggests that the digestion rate of whey proteins was slower in the presence of carbohydrates and fats than without and the anabolic response was improved. Clearly, this factor could have implications for optimal protein intake for athletes.

Alternatively, the energy provided by these nutrients acutely might act to stimulate net muscle protein balance. It has been suggested that stimulation of muscle protein synthesis and the resultant net muscle protein synthesis due to nutrient ingestion is due to increased energy availability. However, in resting humans, lipid infusion was found not to result in elevated muscle protein synthesis or net balance (Svanberg *et al.*, 1999), suggesting that, at rest, increased energy *per se* is not an effective stimulator of muscle protein synthesis. Energy may be especially important after exercise. Since energy demand is increased after exercise, muscle protein synthesis may be more likely to be limited by energy availability, such that any elevation of muscle protein synthesis resulting in net muscle protein synthesis as a consequence of feeding is due to replenishment of energy rather than hyperaminoacidaemia or hyperinsulinaemia *per se*. Support for this concept comes from *in situ* studies on rat muscle showing that diminished rates of protein synthesis after exercise are linked to reduced concentrations of adenosine triphosphate and phosphocreatine (i.e. a reduced energy state) (Bylund-Fellenius *et al.*, 1984). However, *in vivo* studies do not support this hypothesis. Rats fed a carbohydrate-containing meal post-exercise did not demonstrate elevated rates of muscle protein synthesis; however, muscle protein synthesis was increased in rats fed an isoenergetic meal of protein plus carbohydrates (Gautsch *et al.*, 1998). Recent studies from our laboratory demonstrate that ingestion of additional energy by human volunteers after resistance exercise does not increase *in vivo* net muscle protein synthesis without additional amino acids (Miller *et al.*, 2003). After endurance exercise, ingestion of a carbohydrate–lipid supplement did not result in positive net muscle protein balance, but ingestion of carbohydrates, lipids and proteins did result in net muscle protein synthesis in human volunteers (Levenhagen *et al.*, 2002). These results suggest that acute provision of energy *per se* does not have an influence on muscle protein metabolism after exercise. These results also demonstrate that addition of lipids does not increase muscle protein balance over and above that seen with protein and carbohydrates alone. However, as discussed previously, chronic energy intake has clearly been demonstrated to influence nitrogen balance (Todd *et al.*, 1984; Butterfield, 1987), suggesting that as long as energy balance is sufficient on a chronic basis, other factors are responsible for the response of muscle protein synthesis and muscle protein balance.

Importance of timing of ingestion of nutrients in relation to exercise and other nutrients

The timing of nutrient ingestion also influences the anabolic response after exercise. In a recent study, participants ingested 6 g of essential amino acids plus 35 g of carbohydrates twice in relation to an acute resistance exercise bout (Tipton *et al.*, 2001). The response of net muscle protein balance was considerably greater when the solution was ingested immediately before exercise than immediately after exercise. In a similar study, there was no significant difference in net muscle protein balance between trials with ingestion of the same carbohydrate–amino acid solution at 1 versus 3 h post-exercise (Rasmussen *et al.*, 2000). Further comparison of the two studies indicated that the response of net muscle protein balance was greatest when the carbohydrate–amino acid mixture was consumed immediately before exercise. These results are summarized in Fig. 5. It has also been demonstrated that the anabolic response to resistance exercise is influenced by the timing of ingestion of a mixture of carbohydrate, fat and protein and carbohydrates alone (Roy *et al.*, 1997, 2000). There is also support for this notion from a longitudinal study design. Elderly volunteers were given protein-containing supplements either immediately after resistance exercise or 2 h after exercise (Esmarck *et al.*, 2001) during 12 weeks of resistance training. Those receiving the supplement immediately after exercise experienced greater increases in muscle mass and strength than those receiving the supplement 2 h after exercise.

There is preliminary evidence that the timing of carbohydrate ingestion relative to amino acid ingestion may be important. After resistance exercise, amino acid uptake was greatest in the first hour following amino acid ingestion and declined during the next 2 h (Miller *et al.*, 2003). On the other hand, amino acid uptake was lowest in the first hour after ingestion of carbohydrates, but

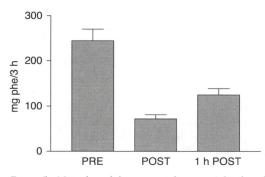

Figure 5. Net phenylalanine uptake over 3 h after the ingestion of a solution containing 6 g of essential amino acids and 35 g of carbohydrates at three times in relation to acute resistance exercise. PRE = solution ingested immediately before exercise; POST = solution ingested immediately after exercise; 1 h POST = solution ingested 1 h after completion of exercise. Data from Tipton *et al.* (2001) and Rasmussen *et al.* (2000).

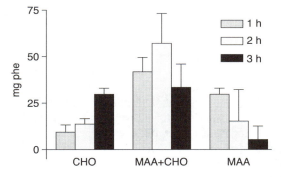

Figure 6. Net phenylalanine uptake after ingestion of amino acids (MAA), carbohydrates (CHO) and the combination of the two (MAA + CHO) at 1, 2 and 3 h after an acute resistance exercise bout.

increased in the next 2 h after ingestion (Fig. 6). These results suggest that the greatest response of muscle protein balance to amino acid and carbohydrate intake may result from staggering the ingestion of carbohydrates and amino acids, such that the responses are superimposed and thus maximized. Studies need to be conducted to test this hypothesis.

After endurance exercise, it would appear that timing of nutrient ingestion also may be important for the response of net muscle protein balance. It has been shown that a protein, carbohydrate and lipid supplement resulted in greater amino acid uptake when ingested immediately after cycling exercise than 3 h after cycling (Levenhagen *et al.*, 2001). In another study, post-exercise macronutrient ingestion resulted in an attenuation of body weight loss and improved nitrogen balance in 10 females during 7 days of endurance training (Roy *et al.*, 2002). Taken together, it seems that timing of nutrient ingestion should be a consideration in designing any post-exercise nutrition regimen. In summary, these studies indicate that, for any given amount of protein ingested, the timing of ingestion, as well as the composition of the protein or amino acids and other nutrients ingested concurrently, will determine the response of the athlete.

Summary and recommendations

There remains much to be elucidated about protein nutrition in athletes. Recent research suggests that quantifying protein to be ingested may be overly simplistic. Certainly, an adequate energy intake appears to be critical for an anabolic response on a chronic basis. If muscle hypertrophy is the primary goal for an athlete, then a hyperenergetic diet may be the most important recommendation. However, a parallel increase in fat mass may be an undesired effect of this approach and should be considered in light of the training and competitive goals of the individual athlete. Furthermore, a specific protein recommendation based solely on the quantity of protein ingested per day is dependent on the assumption that nitrogen retention, and thus muscle hypertrophy, is matched directly with protein intake. Clearly, regulation of the post-exercise response of net muscle protein balance to nutrient ingestion is much more complex than simple quantification of protein ingestion and many other factors (e.g. type and amount of amino acids, protein digestive properties, timing of nutrient intake in relation to exercise and other nutrients, concurrent ingestion of other nutrients and total energy intake) influence muscle and whole-body anabolism. Thus, for any given amount of protein, the response of protein anabolism will vary depending on exactly what is eaten and when.

Perhaps this issue can be examined another way. Since there is evidence that protein intakes above the RDA may be beneficial to athletes, a risk–benefit analysis may be useful. An important consideration is the potential harm that may arise from elevated protein intakes. There is little research into the maximum tolerable protein intake in healthy individuals. It has been suggested that excessive protein intakes may increase calcium loss, thus affecting bone health. However, since a major portion of bone is protein, excessive protein does not appear to influence bone health. High protein intakes have been suggested to pose a risk for the kidneys but, in healthy individuals with no underlying kidney disease (presumably most elite athletes), there is no evidence for harm to kidneys with higher intakes. Certainly, it would be detrimental for an athlete to consume excess protein at the expense of other nutrients required to support the necessary level of training and competition. There is a suggestion that intakes greater than 40% of total energy intake might be the upper limit. Protein intakes greater than 40% may limit intake of fat and/or carbohydrates, thus compromising the benefits of these nutrients. However, given the high energy intakes of most elite athletes, protein intakes higher than 40% are unlikely in most. Even a small female restricting energy intake and consuming only 1500 kcal would need to consume 150 g of protein to reach 40%.

Although there is evidence to the contrary, nitrogen balance methods identical to those used in sedentary individuals indicate that active individuals require more protein. Therefore, it can be argued that athletes may need more protein than sedentary individuals. Recommendations of 1.2–1.7 g protein $\cdot$ kg^{-1} BW $\cdot$ day^{-1} have commonly been made. There is no reason to suspect that intakes in this range would be harmful; however, the vast majority of athletes consume this amount of protein in their habitual diet, so recommending increased protein is unnecessary. It is important to remember that athletes and coaches are not that interested in the scientific arguments on both sides of this issue. Success in competition is what they consider important. It is common practice for athletes involved in strength and power sports to consume amounts of protein well in excess of the amount required to maintain nitrogen balance (Alway et al., 1992). The results of studies of the response of muscle protein metabolism to the intake of protein or amino acids suggest a beneficial effect of high protein intake in conjunction with resistance exercise. On the other hand, there is scant evidence from properly controlled studies of sufficient duration in power athletes to assess quantitatively the value of this practice in terms of gains of muscle mass and strength. Thus, for athletes desiring muscle hypertrophy, there is little reason to limit protein intake and relatively high intakes might be the best recommendation. Of course, muscle anabolism may be enhanced by varying the type and timing of protein and amino acid ingestion. Even if 2.5–3.0 g protein $\cdot$ kg^{-1} BW $\cdot$ day^{-1} is consumed and this amount of protein is more than the synthetic machinery can process, the excess will simply be oxidized. As long as the intake of other nutrients important to the success of an athlete is not compromised, there appears to be little harm in ingesting these high amounts. Furthermore, this amount of protein may be considered to be reasonable given the high energy intakes in these athletes. For example, intakes of ~6400 kcal have been reported in strength athletes (Alway *et al.*, 1992). Protein of only 14% of total kcal would be ~2.5 g protein $\cdot$ kg^{-1} BW $\cdot$ day^{-1} for a large athlete (~90 kg) and 3.2 g protein $\cdot$ kg^{-1} BW $\cdot$ day^{-1} for a smaller athlete (~70 kg).

The protein intake strategy should be tailored to the functional needs of the particular sport and, perhaps even more specifically, to the particular positional requirements within a sport and the individual needs of the athlete. It is unlikely that optimal protein intake for a marathon runner would be the same as for a power lifter. Muscle hypertrophy is rarely a positive factor for success for endurance athletes. Thus, if increased protein intake results in increased muscle mass or if the dietary protein replaces carbohydrates critical to replenishing glycogen stores, then the upper limit may necessarily be lower for endurance athletes. Thus, there appears to be no reason for recommending intakes above 2 g protein $\cdot$ kg^{-1} BW $\cdot$ day^{-1} and there is no evidence that intakes this high confer any advantage to an endurance athlete. In fact, Tarnopolsky *et al.* (1988) have clearly demonstrated that intakes above 1.7 g protein $\cdot$ kg^{-1} BW $\cdot$ day^{-1} simply result in oxidation of the ingested excess. Nevertheless, even 2 g protein $\cdot$ kg^{-1} BW $\cdot$ day^{-1} would only be about 18% of an endurance athlete's diet (based on a 70-kg athlete consuming 3000 kcal $\cdot$ day^{-1}); hardly an excessive amount of protein to be eaten, and most endurance athletes regularly consume this amount of protein in any case. Thus, there is little reason to recommend intakes over and above that which is habitual for most athletes.

Many team sport athletes, such as those who play soccer, basketball, hockey and rugby, may desire both increased mass and endurance. Thus excessive protein intakes, such as those that may be ingested by strength athletes, are unlikely to be advantageous and muscle mass gains may best be sought by attempting to take advantage of timing of ingestion and composition of the proteins or amino acids ingested.

Finally, this review is not meant to advocate very high protein intakes for athletes, but merely to point out that it is possible, if not likely, that many athletes, especially those involved in strength and power sports, may benefit from higher intakes. However, as was concluded in the first consensus paper by Lemon (1991), most athletes habitually ingest sufficient protein, so recommending greater protein intakes does not appear warranted. Perhaps other factors, such as the timing of protein or amino acid intake in relation to exercise and the intake of other nutrients, are more important considerations for those athletes wanting to increase their body mass. Clearly, there is much to be learned about the optimal protein intake for elite athletes. There is a paucity of research examining the impact of various amounts of dietary protein on performance and body composition endpoints in top athletes. Clearly, long-term studies on the impact of different amounts of protein on performance variables, body composition as well as the metabolic and molecular mechanisms responsible for these changes in elite athletes would be valuable; however, proper control of such studies is virtually impossible given the small differences that must be detected. Although extremely difficult to control properly and to carry out, these long-term endpoint studies are necessary to determine definitively the protein needs of athletes and to overcome the controversy surrounding this issue.

References

1 Alway, S.E., Grumbt, W.H., Stray-Gundersen, J. and Gonyea, W.J. (1992). Effects of resistance training on elbow flexors of highly competitive bodybuilders. *Journal of Applied Physiology*, **72**, 1512–1521.

2 Anthony, J.C., Anthony, T.G. and Layman, D.K. (1999). Leucine supplementation enhances skeletal muscle recovery in rats following exercise. *Journal of Nutrition*, **129**, 1102–1106.

3 Balagopal, P., Nair, K.S. and Stirewalt, W.S. (1994). Isolation of myosin heavy chain from small skeletal muscle samples by preparative continuous elution gel electrophoresis: application to measurement of synthesis rate in human and animal tissue. *Analytical Biochemistry*, **221**, 72–77 [published erratum appears in 1994: **222**, 520].

4 Balagopal, P., Ljungqvist, O. and Nair, K.S. (1997a). Skeletal muscle myosin heavy-chain synthesis rate in healthy humans. *American Journal of Physiology*, **272**, E45–E50.

5 Balagopal, P., Rooyackers, O.E., Adey, D.B., Ades, P.A. and Nair, K.S. (1997b). Effects of aging on *in vivo* synthesis of skeletal muscle myosin heavy-chain and sarcoplasmic protein in humans. *American Journal of Physiology*, **273**, E790–E800.

6 Balagopal, P., Schimke, J.C., Ades, P., Adey, D. and Nair, K.S. (2001). Age effect on transcript levels and synthesis rate of muscle MHC and response to resistance exercise. *American Journal of Physiology*, **280**, E203–E208.

7 Biolo, G., Declan Fleming, R.Y. and Wolfe, R.R. (1995a). Physiologic hyperinsulinemia stimulates protein synthesis and enhances transport of selected amino acids in human skeletal muscle. *Journal of Clinical Investigation*, **95**, 811–819.

8 Biolo, G., Maggi, S.P., Williams, B.D., Tipton, K.D. and Wolfe, R.R. (1995b). Increased rates of muscle protein turnover and amino acid transport after resistance exercise in humans. *American Journal of Physiology*, **268**, E514–E520.

9 Biolo, G., Tipton, K.D., Klein, S. and Wolfe, R.R. (1997). An abundant supply of amino acids enhances the metabolic effect of exercise on muscle protein. *American Journal of Physiology*, **273**, E122–E129.

10 Biolo, G., Williams, B.D., Fleming, R.Y. and Wolfe, R.R. (1999). Insulin action on muscle protein kinetics and amino acid transport during recovery after resistance exercise. *Diabetes*, **48**, 949–957.

11 Blomstrand, E. and Saltin, B. (2001). BCAA intake affects protein metabolism in muscle after but not during exercise in humans. *American Journal of Physiology,* **281**, E365–E374.

12 Bohe, J., Low, J.F., Wolfe, R.R. and Rennie, M.J. (2001). Latency and duration of stimulation of human muscle protein synthesis during continuous infusion of amino acids. *Journal of Physiology* **532**, 575–579.

13 Boirie, Y., Dangin, M., Gachon, P., Vasson, M.P., Maubois, J.L. and Beaufrere, B. (1997). Slow and fast dietary proteins differently modulate postprandial protein accretion. *Proceedings of the National Academy of Sciences, USA*, **94**, 14930–14935.

14 Borsheim, E., Tipton, K.D., Wolf, S.E. and Wolfe, R.R. (2002). Essential amino acids and muscle protein recovery from resistance exercise. *American Journal of Physiology*, **283**, E648–E657.

15 Bowtell, J.L., Leese, G.P., Smith, K., Watt, P.W., Nevill, A., Rooyackers, O., Wagenmakers, A.J.M. and Rennie, M.J. (1998). Modulation of whole body protein metabolism, during and after exercise, by variation of dietary protein. *Journal of Applied Physiology*, **85**, 1744–1752.

16 Bowtell, J.L., Leese, G.P., Smith, K., Watt, P.W., Nevill, A., Rooyackers, O., Wagenmakers, A.J. and Rennie, M.J. (2000). Effect of oral glucose on leucine turn-over in human subjects at rest and during exercise at two levels of dietary protein. *Journal of Physiology*, **525**, 271–281.

17 Burke, D.G., Chilibeck, P.D., Davidson, K.S., Candow, D.G., Farthing, J. and Smith-Palmer, T. (2001). The effect of whey protein supplementation with and without creatine monohydrate combined with resistance training on lean tissue mass and muscle strength. *International Journal of Sport Nutrition and Exercise Metabolism*, **11**, 349–364.

18 Butterfield, G.E. (1987). Whole-body protein utilization in humans. *Medicine and Science in Sports and Exercise*, **19**, S157–S165.

19 Butterfield, G.E. and Calloway, D.H. (1984). Physical activity improves protein utilization in young men. *British Journal of Nutrition*, **51**, 171–184.

20 Butterfield, G.E., Thompson, J., Rennie, M.J., Marcus, R., Hintz, R.L. and Hoffman, A.R. (1997). Effect of rhGH and rhIGF-I treatment on protein utilization in elderly women. *American Journal of Physiology*, **272**, E94–E99.

21 Bylund-Fellenius, A.C., Ojamaa, K.M., Flaim, K.E., Li, J.B., Wassner, S.J. and Jefferson, L.S. (1984). Protein synthesis versus energy state in contracting muscles of perfused rat hindlimb. *American Journal of Physiology*, **246**, E297–E305.

22 Campbell, W.W., Crim, M.C., Young, V.R., Joseph, L.J. and Evans, W.J. (1995). Effects of resistance training and dietary protein intake on protein metabolism in older adults. *American Journal of Physiology*, **268**, E1143–E1153.

23 Carraro, F., Hartl, W.H., Stuart, C.A., Layman, D.K., Jahoor, F. and Wolfe, R.R. (1990). Whole body and plasma protein synthesis in exercise and recovery in human subjects. *American Journal of Physiology*, **258**, E821–E831.

24 Carraro, F., Kimbrough, T.D. and Wolfe, R.R. (1993). Urea kinetics in humans at two levels of exercise intensity. *Journal of Applied Physiology*, **75**, 1180–1185.

25 Chittenden, R.H. (1907). *The Nutrition of Man*. London: Heinemann.

26 Christensen, D.L., van Hall, G. and Hambraeus, L. (2002). Food and macronutrient intake of male adolescent Kalenjin runners in Kenya. *British Journal of Nutrition*, **88**, 711–717.

27 Dangin, M., Boirie, Y., Garcia-Rodenas, C., Gachon, P., Fauquant, J., Callier, P., Ballevre, O. and Beaufrere, B. (2001). The digestion rate of protein is an independent regulating factor of postprandial protein retention. *American Journal of Physiology*, **280**, E340–E348.

28 Dangin, M., Guillet, C., Garcia-Rodenas, C., Gachon, P., Bouteloup-Demange, C., Reiffers-Magnani, K., Fauquant, J., Ballevre, O. and Beaufrere, B. (2003). The rate of protein digestion affects protein gain differently during aging in humans. *Journal of Physiology*, **549**, 635–644.

29 Deuster, P.A., Kyle, S.B., Moser, P.B., Vigersky, R.A., Singh, A. and Schoomaker, E.B. (1986). Nutritional survey of highly trained women runners. *American Journal of Clinical Nutrition*, **44**, 954–962.

30 Devlin, J.T., Brodsky, I., Scrimgeour, A., Fuller, S. and Bier, D.M. (1990). Amino acid metabolism after intense exercise. *American Journal of Physiology*, **258**, E249–E255.

31 El Khoury, A.E., Forslund, A., Olsson, R., Branth, S., Sjodin, A., Andersson, A., Atkinson, A., Selvaraj, A., Hambraeus, L. and Young, V.R. (1997). Moderate exercise at energy balance does not affect 24-h leucine oxidation or nitrogen retention in healthy men. *American Journal of Physiology*, **273**, E394–E407.

32 Esmarck, B., Andersen, J.L., Olsen, S., Richter, E.A., Mizuno, M. and Kjaer, M. (2001). Timing of postexercise protein intake is important for muscle hypertrophy with resistance training in elderly humans. *Journal of Physiology*, **535**, 301–311.

33 Forbes, G.B., Brown, M.R., Welle, S.L. and Lipinski, B.A. (1986). Deliberate overfeeding in women and men: energy cost and composition of the weight gain. *British Journal of Nutrition*, **56**, 1–9.

34 Forbes, G.B., Brown, M.R., Welle, S.L. and Underwood, L.E. (1989). Hormonal response to overfeeding. *American Journal of Clinical Nutrition*, **49**, 608–611.

35 Forslund, A.H., Hambraeus, L., Olsson, R.M., El Khoury, A.E., Yu, Y.M. and Young, V.R. (1998). The 24-h whole body leucine and urea kinetics at normal and high protein intakes with exercise in healthy adults. *American Journal of Physiology*, **275**, E310–E320.

36 Gater, D.R., Gater, D.A., Uribe, J.M. and Bunt, J.C. (1992). Impact of nutritional supplements and resistance training on body composition, strength and insulin-like growth factor-1. *Journal of Applied Sport Science Research*, **6**, 66–76.

37 Gautsch, T.A., Anthony, J.C., Kimball, S.R., Paul, G.L., Layman, D.K. and Jefferson, L.S. (1998). Availability of eIF4E regulates skeletal muscle protein synthesis during recovery from exercise. *American Journal of Physiology*, **274**, C406–C414.

38 Gibala, M.J. (2001). Regulation of skeletal muscle amino acid metabolism during exercise. *International Journal of Sport Nutrition and Exercise Metabolism*, **11**, 87–108.

39 Gontzea, I., Suzuki, M. and Dumitrache, S. (1975). The influence of adaptation to physical effort on nitgrogen balance in man. *Nutrition Reports International*, **11**, 231–236.

40 Grandjean, A.C. (1989). Macronutrient intake of US athletes compared with the general population and recommendations made for athletes. *American Journal of Clinical Nutrition*, **49**, 1070–1076.

41 Hasten, D.L., Pak-Loduca, J., Obert, K.A. and Yarasheski, K.E. (2000). Resistance exercise acutely increases MHC and mixed muscle protein synthesis rates in 78–84 and 23–32 yr olds. *American Journal of Physiology*, **278**, E620–E626.

42 Hegsted, D.M. (1976). Balance studies. *Journal of Nutrition*, **106**, 307–311.

43 Hegsted, D.M. (1978). Assessment of nitrogen requirements. *American Journal of Clinical Nutrition*, **31**, 1669–1677.

44 Jebb, S.A., Murgatroyd, P.R., Goldberg, G.R., Prentice, A.M. and Coward, W.A. (1993). *In vivo* measurement of changes in body composition: description of methods and their validation against 12-d continuous whole-body calorimetry. *American Journal of Clinical Nutrition*, **58**, 455–462.

45 Kimball, S.R. (2002). Regulation of global and specific mRNA translation by amino acids. *Journal of Nutrition*, **132**, 883–886.

46 Kimball, S.R. and Jefferson, L.S. (2002). Control of protein synthesis by amino acid availability. *Current Opinion in Clinical Nutrition and Metabolic Care*, **5**, 63–67.

47 Kobayashi, H., Borsheim, E., Anthony, T.G., Traber, D.L., Badalamenti, J., Kimball, S.R., Jefferson, L.S. and Wolfe, R.R. (2003). Reduced amino acid availability inhibits muscle protein synthesis and decreases activity of initiation factor eIF2B. *American Journal of Physiology*, **284**, E488–E498.

48 Lamont, L.S., McCullough, A.J. and Kalhan, S.C. (1999). Comparison of leucine kinetics in endurance-trained and sedentary humans. *Journal of Applied Physiology*, **86**, 320–325.

49 Lemon, P.W. (1991). Effect of exercise on protein requirements. *Journal of Sports Sciences*, **9**(special issue), 53–70.

50 Lemon, P.W. and Proctor, D.N. (1991). Protein intake and athletic performance. *Sports Medicine*, **12**, 313–325.

51 Lemon, P.W., Dolny, D.G. and Yarasheski, K.E. (1997). Moderate physical activity can increase dietary protein needs. *Canadian Journal of Applied Physiology*, **22**, 494–503.

52 Levenhagen, D.K., Gresham, J.D., Carlson, M.G., Maron, D.J., Borel, M.J. and Flakoll, P.J. (2001). Postexercise nutrient intake timing in humans is critical to recovery of leg glucose and protein homeostasis. *American Journal of Physiology*, **280**, E982–E993.

53 Levenhagen, D.K., Carr, C., Carlson, M.G., Maron, D.J., Borel, M.J. and Flakoll, P.J. (2002). Postexercise protein intake enhances whole-body and leg protein accretion in humans. *Medicine and Science in Sports and Exercise*, **34**, 828–837.

54 McKenzie, S., Phillips, S.M., Carter, S.L., Lowther, S., Gibala, M.J. and Tarnopolsky, M.A. (2000). Endurance exercise training attenuates leucine oxidation and BCOAD activation during exercise in humans. *American Journal of Physiology*, **278**, E580–E587.

55 Meredith, C.N., Zackin, M.J., Frontera, W.R. and Evans, W.J. (1989). Dietary protein requirements and body protein metabolism in endurance-trained men. *Journal of Applied Physiology*, **66**, 2850–2856.

56 Miller, S.L., Tipton, K.D., Chinkes, D.L., Wolf, S.E. and Wolfe, R.R. (2003). Independent and combined effects of amino acids and glucose after resistance exercise. *Medicine and Science in Sports and Exercise*, **35**, 449–455.

57 Millward, D.J. (1999). Inherent difficulties in defining amino acid requirements. In *The Role of Protein and Amino Acids in Sustaining and Enhancing Performance* (edited by FaNBIoM Committee on Military Nutrition Research), pp. 169–216. Washington, DC: National Academy Press.

58 Millward, D.J. (2001). Protein and amino acid requirements of adults: current controversies. *Canadian Journal of Applied Physiology*, **26**(suppl.), S130–S140.

59 Millward, D.J., Bowtell, J.L., Pacy, P. and Rennie, M.J. (1994). Physical activity, protein metabolism and protein requirements. *Proceedings of the Nutrition Society*, **53**, 223–240.

60 Neufer, P.D. (1989). The effect of detraining and reduced training on the physiological adaptations to aerobic exercise training. *Sports Medicine*, **8**, 302–320.

61 Oddoye, E.A. and Margen, S. (1979). Nitrogen balance studies in humans: long-term effect of high nitrogen intake on nitrogen accretion. *Journal of Nutrition*, **109**, 363–377.

62 O'Hagan, F.T., Sale, D.G., MacDougall, J.D. and Garner, S.H. (1995). Comparative effectiveness of accommodating and weight resistance training modes. *Medicine and Science in Sports and Exercise*, **27**, 1210–1219.

63 Paddon-Jones, D., Sheffield-Moore, M., Creson, D.L., Sanford, A.P., Wolf, S.E., Wolfe, R.R. and Ferrando, A.A. (2003). Hypercortosolemia alters muscle protein anabolism following ingestion of essential amino acids. *American Journal of Physiology: Endocrinology and Metabolism*, **284**, E946–E953.

64 Phillips, S.M., Atkinson, S.A., Tarnopolsky, M.A. and MacDougall, J.D. (1993). Gender differences in leucine kinetics and nitrogen balance in endurance athletes. *Journal of Applied Physiology*, **75**, 2134–2141.

65 Phillips, S.M., Tipton, K.D., Aarsland, A., Wolf, S.E. and Wolfe, R.R. (1997). Mixed muscle protein synthesis and breakdown after resistance exercise in humans. *American Journal of Physiology*, **273**, E99–E107.

66 Phillips, S.M., Tipton, K.D., Ferrando, A.A. and Wolfe, R.R. (1999). Resistance training reduces the acute exercise-induced increase in muscle protein turnover. *American Journal of Physiology*, **276**, E118–E124.

67 Phillips, S.M., Parise, G., Roy, B.D., Tipton, K.D. and Tarnopolsky, M.A. (2002). Resistance-training-induced adaptations in skeletal muscle protein turnover in the fed state. *Canadian Journal of Physiology and Pharmacology*, **80**, 1045–1053.

68 Rasmussen, B.B., Tipton, K.D., Miller, S.L., Wolf, S.E. and Wolfe, R.R. (2000). An oral essential amino acid–carbohydrate supplement enhances muscle protein anabolism after resistance exercise. *Journal of Applied Physiology*, **88**, 386–392.

69 Rennie, M.J. and Tipton, K.D. (2000). Protein and amino acid metabolism during and after exercise and the effects of nutrition. *Annual Reviews in Nutrition*, **20**, 457–483.

70 Rooyackers, O.E., Balagopal, P. and Nair, K.S. (1997). Measurement of synthesis rates of specific muscle proteins using needle biopsy samples. *Muscle and Nerve*, **5**, S93–S96.

71 Roy, B.D., Tarnopolsky, M.A., MacDougall, J.D., Fowles, J. and Yarasheski, K.E. (1997). Effect of glucose supplement timing on protein metabolism after resistance training. *Journal of Applied Physiology*, **82**, 1882–1888.

72 Roy, B.D., Fowles, J.R., Hill, R. and Tarnopolsky, M.A. (2000). Macronutrient intake and whole body protein metabolism following resistance exercise. *Medicine and Science in Sports and Exercise*, **32**, 1412–1418.

73 Roy, B.D., Luttmer, K., Bosman, M.J. and Tarnopolsky, M.A. (2002). The influence of post-exercise macronutrient intake on energy balance and protein metabolism in active females participating in endurance training. *International Journal of Sport Nutrition and Exercise Metabolism*, **12**, 172–188.

74 Smith, K., Downie, S., Barua, J.M., Watt, P.W., Scrimgeour, C.M. and Rennie, M.J. (1994). Effect of a flooding dose of leucine in stimulating incorporation of constantly infused valine into albumin. *American Journal of Physiology*, **266**, E640–E644.

75 Svanberg, E., Moller-Loswick, A.C., Matthews, D.E., Korner, U., Andersson, M. and Lundholm, K. (1999). The role of glucose, long-chain triglycerides and amino acids for promotion of amino acid balance across peripheral tissues in man. *Clinical Physiology*, **19**, 311–320.

76 Tarnopolsky, M.A. (1999). Protein and physical performance. *Current Opinions in Clinical Nutrition and Metabolic Care*, **2**, 533–537.

77 Tarnopolsky, M.A., MacDougall, J.D. and Atkinson, S.A. (1988). Influence of protein intake and training status on nitrogen balance and lean body mass. *Journal of Applied Physiology*, **64**, 187–193.

78 Tarnopolsky, M.A., Atkinson, S.A., MacDougall, J.D., Senor, B.B., Lemon, P.W. and Schwarcz, H. (1991). Whole body leucine metabolism during and after resistance exercise in fed humans. *Medicine and Science in Sports and Exercise*, **23**, 326–333.

79 Tarnopolsky, M.A., Atkinson, S.A., MacDougall, J.D., Chesley, A., Phillips, S. and Schwarcz, H.P. (1992). Evaluation of protein requirements for trained strength athletes. *Journal of Applied Physiology*, **73**, 1986–1995.

80 Tipton, K.D., Ferrando, A.A., Phillips, S.M., Doyle, D., Jr. and Wolfe, R.R. (1999). Postexercise net protein synthesis in human muscle from orally administered amino acids. *American Journal of Physiology*, **276**, E628–E634.

81 Tipton, K.D., Rasmussen, B.B., Miller, S.L., Wolf, S.E., Owens-Stovall, S.K., Petrini, B.E. and Wolfe, R.R. (2001). Timing of amino acid–carbohydrate ingestion alters anabolic response of muscle to resistance exercise. *American Journal of Physiology*, **281**, E197–E206.

82 Tipton, K.D., Borsheim, E., Wolf, S.E., Sanford, A.P. and Wolfe, R.R. (2003). Acute response of net muscle protein balance reflects 24-h balance after exercise and amino acid ingestion. *American Journal of Physiology*, **284**, E76–E89.

83 Todd, K.S., Butterfield, G.E. and Calloway, D.H. (1984). Nitrogen balance in men with adequate and deficient energy intake at three levels of work. *Journal of Nutrition*, **114**, 2107–2118.

84 Tome, D. and Bos, C. (2000). Dietary protein and nitrogen utilization. *Journal of Nutrition*, **130**, 1868S–1873S.

85 Welle, S., Matthews, D.E., Campbell, R.G. and Nair, K.S. (1989). Stimulation of protein turnover by carbohydrate overfeeding in men. *American Journal of Physiology*, **257**, E413–E417.

86 Welle, S., Thornton, C. and Statt, M. (1995). Myofibrillar protein synthesis in young and old human subjects after three months of resistance training. *American Journal of Physiology*, **268**, E422–E427.

87 Wolfe, R.R. (2000). Protein supplements and exercise. *American Journal of Clinical Nutrition*, **72**, 551S–557S.

88 Wolfe, R.R. and Miller, S.L. (1999). Amino acid availability controls muscle protein metabolism. *Diabetes Nutrition and Metabolism*, **12**, 322–328.

89 Wolfe, R.R., Wolfe, M.H., Nadel, E.R. and Shaw, J.H. (1984). Isotopic determination of amino acid–urea interactions in exercise in humans. *Journal of Applied Physiology*, **56**, 221–229.

90 Young, V.R. (1986). Nutritional balance studies: indicators of human requirements or of adaptive mechanisms? *Journal of Nutrition*, **116**, 700–703.

7 Dietary antioxidants and exercise

SCOTT K. POWERS, KEITH C. DeRUISSEAU, JOHN QUINDRY and KARYN L. HAMILTON

Muscular exercise promotes the production of radicals and other reactive oxygen species in the working muscle. Growing evidence indicates that reactive oxygen species are responsible for exercise-induced protein oxidation and contribute to muscle fatigue. To protect against exercise-induced oxidative injury, muscle cells contain complex endogenous cellular defence mechanisms (enzymatic and non-enzymatic antioxidants) to eliminate reactive oxygen species. Furthermore, exogenous dietary antioxidants interact with endogenous antioxidants to form a cooperative network of cellular antioxidants. Knowledge that exercise-induced oxidant formation can contribute to muscle fatigue has resulted in numerous investigations examining the effects of antioxidant supplementation on human exercise performance. To date, there is limited evidence that dietary supplementation with antioxidants will improve human performance. Furthermore, it is currently unclear whether regular vigorous exercise increases the need for dietary intake of antioxidants. Clearly, additional research that analyses the antioxidant requirements of individual athletes is needed.

Keywords: antioxidants, exercise, oxidative stress, performance, reactive oxygen species.

Introduction

Radicals are molecules or fragments of molecules that possess an unpaired electron in their outer orbital. Because of this molecular instability, radicals are highly reactive and can promote damaging oxidation reactions with cellular proteins, lipids or DNA, leading to oxidative stress and impaired cellular function. Although regular physical exercise has many beneficial effects, it is now clear that muscular exercise results in increased production of radicals and other reactive oxygen species (Davies *et al.*, 1982; Reid *et al.*, 1992b; Borzone *et al.*, 1994; O'Neill *et al.*, 1996; Halliwell and Gutteridge, 1999). Furthermore, strong evidence indicates that reactive oxygen species are the primary cause of exercise-induced disturbances in muscle oxidation–reduction status (i.e. redox balance). Severe disturbances in cellular redox balance have been shown to contribute to oxidative injury and muscle fatigue (Ji *et al.*, 1988; Shindoh *et al.*, 1990; Reid *et al.*, 1992a; Nashawati *et al.*, 1993; O'Neill *et al.*, 1996). Given the potential role of reactive oxygen species in contributing to oxidative stress and muscle fatigue, it is not surprising that skeletal muscle fibres contain defence mechanisms to reduce the risk of oxidative damage. Two major classes of endogenous protective mechanisms, the enzymatic and non-enzymatic antioxidants, work to reduce the harmful effects of reactive oxygen species in cells. Furthermore, dietary antioxidants interact with endogenous antioxidants to form a cooperative antioxidant network.

The aim of this review is to discuss our current understanding of the relationship between dietary antioxidants and muscular exercise. We begin with a short discussion of exercise-induced oxidative stress. We then provide an overview of common dietary antioxidants and address the important questions, 'Do antioxidants improve exercise performance?' and 'Does exercise increase the need for dietary antioxidants?'

Exercise-induced oxidant production

Davies *et al.* (1982) were the first to report that skeletal muscles produce radicals during contractile activity. Since then, many investigations have confirmed these observations and have explored the potential sources of exercise-induced radicals and reactive oxygen species (O'Neill *et al.*, 1996; Jackson, 1998; Reid, 2001; Ji, 2002; Reid and Durham, 2002). Determining the primary sites of reactive oxygen species production in skeletal muscle is a complex undertaking, as many pathways are capable of generating radicals in skeletal muscle. Nonetheless, current evidence indicates that the primary sources of radical production in skeletal muscle are the mitochondria, xanthine oxidase, NAD(P)H oxidase and the production of nitric oxide by nitric oxide synthase (Davies *et al.*, 1982; Jackson *et al.*, 1985; Reid *et al.*, 1992a,b; Borzone *et al.*, 1994; O'Neill *et al.*, 1996; Jackson, 1998). Secondary sources for radical production during exercise include autoxidation of catecholamines, radical generation by phagocytic white cells and radical formation due to the disruption of iron-containing proteins (Jackson, 1998; Halliwell and Gutteridge, 1999). Most investigators have concluded that radical production in the mitochondria is the primary source of radical production in contracting skeletal muscles. Indeed, while 95–98% of the oxygen consumption of skeletal muscle results in the formation of adenosine trisphosphate (ATP) and water, the remaining 2–5% of this oxygen undergoes one electron reduction to produce superoxide radicals (Jackson, 1998; Halliwell and Gutteridge, 1999). It follows that increased muscular activity results in an elevation in oxidative metabolism and a proportional increase in superoxide production. Hence, this increased production of radicals must be balanced by the antioxidant capacity of the muscle to prevent oxidant-mediated damage to proteins, lipids and DNA.

Overview of antioxidants

Oxidative stress occurs due to an imbalance between oxidant production and the antioxidant capacity of the cell (Fig. 1). Cells are protected against oxidant

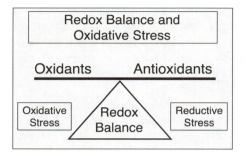

Figure 1. Illustration of the relationship between oxidants and antioxidants in the determination of cellular redox balance. Note that an increase in oxidants or antioxidants results in a disturbance in cellular redox balance. Oxidative stress occurs when oxidants outnumber the available antioxidants. In contrast, reductive stress occurs when antioxidants outnumber the oxidants present in the cell.

injury by a complex network of antioxidants. Specifically, enzymatic and non-enzymatic antioxidants exist in both the intracellular and extracellular environments and work as complex units to remove different reactive oxygen species. To provide maximum intracellular protection, these scavengers are strategically compartmentalized throughout the cell. Figure 2 illustrates the cellular locations of important antioxidants and Tables 1 and 2 provide a brief overview of the antioxidant function of these molecules.

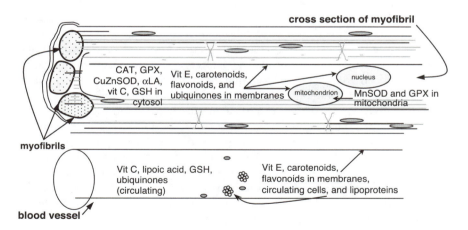

Figure 2. Locations of important intracellular and extracellular antioxidants within the skeletal muscle myocyte. See text and Table 1 for details on antioxidant function. Vit E = vitamin E, Vit C = vitamin C, αLA = α = lipoic acid, GSH = glutathione, CAT = catalase, GPX = glutathione peroxidase.

Table 1. Important enzymatic antioxidants

Enzymatic antioxidants	Properties
Superoxide dismutase	Located in both mitochondria and cytosol; dismutates superoxide radicals
Glutathione peroxidase	Located in both mitochondria and cytosol; removes hydrogen peroxide and organic hydroperoxides
Catalase	Located in cytosol (and in mitochondria of heart); removes hydrogen peroxide

Several strategies are applied by both endogenous and exogenous anti-oxidants to protect against reactive oxygen species-mediated injury. These include conversion of reactive oxygen species into less active molecules (i.e. scavenging) and prevention of the transformation of the least reactive oxygen species into more damaging forms (i.e. conversion of hydrogen peroxide to the hydroxyl radical). In the following sections, we discuss important dietary anti-oxidants and define their role in maintaining muscle redox balance.

Table 2. A list of selected dietary antioxidants

Antioxidant	Properties	DRI[a]	UL[b]
Vitamin E	Lipid-soluble phenolic compound; major chain-breaking antioxidant found in cell membranes	15 mg	1000 mg
Vitamin C	Located in aqueous phase of cell; acts as radical scavenger and recycles vitamin E	90 mg	2000 mg
Glutathione	Non-protein thiol in cells; serves multiple roles in cellular antioxidant defence; can be consumed in diet but is degraded in the gut	NE	NE
α-Lipoic acid	Endogenous thiol; effective as an antioxidant and in recycling vitamin C; may also serve as a glutathione substitute	NE	NE
Carotenoids	Lipid-soluble antioxidants located primarily in membranes of tissues	NE	NE
Flavonoids	Amphipathic antioxidants located throughout cell; able to scavenge radicals in lipid and aqueous environments	NE	NE
Ubiquinones	Lipid-soluble quinone derivatives; reduced forms are efficient antioxidants	NE	NE

[a] Dietary reference intakes (DRI) are the most recent set of dietary recommendations established for Canadians and Americans by the Food and Nutrition Board of the Institute of Medicine, 1997–2001. The values shown are the highest DRI for each nutrient.
[b] The tolerable upper intake level (UL) is the upper level of intake considered to be safe for adults in Canada and the USA. In some cases, lower ULs have been established for children. NE = DRI or UL not established.
Source: Council for Responsible Nutrition, 2001.

Non-enzymatic and dietary antioxidants

Many non-enzymatic antioxidants exist in cells. Important non-enzymatic defences include, but are not limited to, glutathione, vitamin E, vitamin C, lipoic acid, carotenoids, uric acid, bilirubin and ubiquinone.

Glutathione

Glutathione is the most abundant non-protein thiol source in muscle cells (Meister and Anderson, 1983). Glutathione is primarily synthesized in the liver and transported to tissues via the circulation. Because of the peptide structure of glutathione, it is degraded in the small intestine when ingested; hence, cellular concentrations of glutathione are not directly influenced by diet.

Glutathione concentration in the cell is typically in the millimolar range, but there is wide variability in glutathione content across organs depending on their basal levels of radical production. For example, the two highest concentrations of glutathione in the body are found in the lens of the eye ($10 \text{ mmol} \cdot l^{-1}$) and the liver ($5$–$7 \text{ mmol} \cdot l^{-1}$) (Halliwell and Gutteridge, 1999). Other key organs such as the lung, kidney and heart contain about 2–$3 \text{ mmol} \cdot l^{-1}$ of glutathione (Ji, 1995a). Skeletal muscle glutathione concentration varies depending on muscle fibre type and animal species. In rats, (slow) type I fibres contain 600% more glutathione ($\sim 3 \text{ mmol} \cdot l^{-1}$) than (fast) type IIb fibres ($0.5 \text{ mmol} \cdot l^{-1}$) (Ji, 1995a,b; Ji et al., 1992).

Glutathione serves several roles in the cellular antioxidant defence system. First, glutathione directly scavenges a variety of radicals, including hydroxyl and carbon centred radicals, by donating a hydrogen atom (Yu, 1994). A second key antioxidant function of glutathione is to remove both hydrogen and organic peroxides (e.g. lipid peroxide) during a reaction catalysed by the enzyme glutathione peroxidase. During this reaction, glutathione donates a pair of hydrogen atoms and two glutathione are oxidized to form glutathione disulphide. Glutathione has also been shown to be involved in reducing or 'recycling' a variety of antioxidants in the cell. For example, glutathione has been postulated to reduce vitamin E radicals that are formed in the chain-breaking reactions with alkoxyl or lipid peroxyl radicals (Packer, 1991). Furthermore, glutathione can also reduce the semi-dehydroascorbate radical (vitamin C radical) derived in the recycling of vitamin E and to reduce alpha-lipoic acid to dihydrolipoate. This reaction has recently been hypothesized to play an important role in the recycling of ascorbic acid (Packer, 1991). More will be said about these functions of glutathione in later sections.

Vitamin E

The generic term vitamin E refers to at least eight structural isomers of tocopherols or tocotrienols. Among these, α-tocopherol is the best known and possesses the most potent antioxidant activity (Burton and Ingold, 1989; Janero, 1991). From an antioxidant perspective, vitamin E is the primary chain-breaking antioxidant in cell membranes (Burton and Ingold, 1989; Janero, 1991).

Because of its high lipid solubility, vitamin E is associated with lipid-rich structures such as mitochondria, sarcoplasmic reticulum and the plasma membrane. Under most dietary conditions, the concentration of vitamin E in tissues is relatively low. For example, the ratio of vitamin E to lipids in the membrane may range from 1:1000 in red blood cells to 1:3000 in other tissues and organelles (Janero, 1991; Packer, 1991). Note, however, that vitamin E concentrations in tissues and organelles can be elevated with dietary supplementation (Janero, 1991).

As an antioxidant, vitamin E is particularly important because of its ability to convert superoxide, hydroxyl and lipid peroxyl radicals to less reactive forms. Vitamin E can also break lipid peroxidation chain reactions that occur during free radical reactions in biological membranes (Burton and Traber, 1990).

Although vitamin E is an efficient radical scavenger, the interaction of vitamin E with a radical results in a decrease in functional vitamin E and the formation of a vitamin E radical. Indeed, oxidative stress has been shown to significantly decrease tissue vitamin E concentrations (Burton and Traber, 1990; Janero, 1991; Packer, 1991). However, the vitamin E radical can be 'recycled' back to its native state by a variety of other antioxidants (Packer *et al.*, 1979; Burton and Traber, 1990). Therefore, it is postulated that the ability of vitamin E to serve as an antioxidant is synergistically connected to other antioxidants, such as glutathione, vitamin C and α-lipoic acid, which are capable of recycling vitamin E during periods of oxidative stress. This point is discussed in more detail in the next sections on vitamin C and α-lipoic acid.

Vitamin C

In contrast to vitamin E, vitamin C (ascorbic acid) is hydrophilic and functions better in aqueous environments than vitamin E. Because the pKa of ascorbic acid is 4.25, the ascorbate anion is the predominant form that exists at physiological pH (Yu, 1994). Ascorbate is widely distributed in mammalian tissues, but is present in relatively high amounts in the adrenal and pituitary glands (Yu, 1994).

The role of vitamin C as an antioxidant is two-fold. Vitamin C can directly scavenge superoxide, hydroxyl and lipid hydroperoxide radicals. Additionally, vitamin C plays an important role in recycling the vitamin E radical back to its reduced state (Packer *et al.*, 1979). In the process of recycling vitamin E, reduced vitamin C is converted to a vitamin C (semiascorbyl) radical (Packer *et al.*, 1979). Recycling of the vitamin C radical can be achieved by NADH semiascorbyl reductase, or cellular thiols such as glutathione and dihydrolipoic acid (Sevanian *et al.*, 1985).

In light of the role of vitamin C in the recycling of vitamin E, increased cellular concentrations of vitamin C should provide protection against radical-mediated injury (Yu, 1994). However, in high concentrations (i.e. ~1 mmol·l^{-1}) vitamin C can exert pro-oxidant effects in the presence of transition metals such as Fe^{3+} or Cu^{2+}. The pro-oxidant action of vitamin C stems from its ability to reduce ferric iron (Fe^{3+}) to the ferrous (Fe^{2+}) state. Ferrous iron is known to be a potent catalyst in the production of free radicals. Therefore, the wisdom of mega-dose vitamin C supplementation has been questioned by some investigators due to its pro-oxidant potential (Yu, 1994).

α-Lipoic acid

α-Lipoic acid is an endogenous thiol that serves as a co-factor for α-dehydrogenase complexes and participates in S–O transfer reactions (Packer, 1994). Normally, α-lipoic acid is present in very small quantities (5–25 nmol·g^{-1}) in animal tissues and is generally bound to an enzyme complex that renders α-lipoic acid unavailable as an antioxidant (Packer, 1994). However, unbound α-lipoic acid may be effective as an antioxidant and in recycling vitamin C (Kagan et al., 1992; Packer, 1994). α-Lipoic acid can be consumed in the diet and has no known toxic side-effects (Packer, 1994). Following dietary supplementation, α-lipoic acid is reduced to dihydrolipoic acid (DHLA), which is a potent antioxidant against all major oxyradical species (Packer, 1994). Furthermore, DHLA is an important agent in recycling vitamin C during periods of oxidative stress and can be an effective glutathione substitute (Kagan et al., 1992; Packer, 1994).

Figure 3 illustrates the role of vitamin C and DHLA in the recycling of vitamin E during periods of oxidative stress. After the recycling of vitamin E, the vitamin C radical can be reduced back to vitamin C by DHLA. Dihydrolipoic acid is then converted back to α-lipoic acid in this process and can be reconverted to DHLA by cellular enzymatic mechanisms (Packer, 1994).

Carotenoids

Carotenoids (e.g. β-carotene) are lipid-soluble antioxidants located primarily in biological membranes. The antioxidant properties of carotenoids come from their structural arrangement consisting of long chains of conjugated double bonds; this arrangement permits the scavenging of several reactive oxygen species, including superoxide radicals and peroxyl radicals (Yu, 1994). Indeed, carotenoids display an efficient biological antioxidant activity, as evidenced by their ability to reduce the rate of lipid peroxidation induced by radical generating systems (Krinsky and Deneke, 1982).

Similar to vitamin C, β-carotene can function both as an antioxidant and a pro-oxidant. Under physiological oxygen partial pressures (i.e. < 100 mmHg), β-carotene exhibits radical scavenging activity. However, exposure to hyperoxic

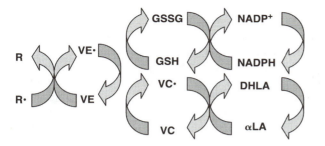

Figure 3. Illustration of the interaction between α-lipoic acid (αLA), glutathione and vitamin C (VC) in the recycling of vitamin E (VE). VC• = ascorbate radical; VE• = vitamin E; DHLA = dihydrolipoic acid; GSSG = oxidized glutathione (adapted from Ji, 1995a).

partial pressures (i.e. >150 mmHg) results in β-carotene exerting pro-oxidant properties with a concomitant loss of its antioxidant capacity (Burton and Ingold, 1989; Palozza *et al.*, 1997).

Ubiquinone

Ubiquinones are lipid-soluble quinone derivatives that contain an isoprene or farnesyl tail. Ubiquinone homologues containing 1–12 isoprene units occur in nature. Reduced forms of ubiquinones are better antioxidants by several orders of magnitude (Mellors and Tappel, 1966).

The predominant form of ubiquinone in humans and many mammals is ubiquinone-10 (often called co-enzyme Q) (Karlsson, 1997). The major sources of ubiquinone-10 in the diet are soybean oil, meats, fish, nuts, wheat germ and vegetables (beans, garlic, spinach, cabbage) (Kamei *et al.*, 1986). The concentration of ubiquinone-10 in human plasma varies between 0.4 and 1.0 $\mu mol \cdot l^{-1}$; approximately 80% is present in the reduced (ubiquinol) state (Stocker *et al.*, 1987; Aberg *et al.*, 1992). In human tissue, ubiquinone-10 is found in relatively high concentrations (60–110 $\mu g \cdot g^{-1}$) in heart, liver and kidney, of which 70–100% is in the reduced state (Aberg *et al.*, 1992). With regard to the intracellular location, approximately 40–50% of the total cellular ubiquinone is located within the mitochondria, 25–30% in the nucleus, 15–20% in the endoplasmic reticulum and the remaining 5–10% in the cytosol (Sustry *et al.*, 1961).

The antioxidant effect of ubiquinone is attributed to its phenol ring structure (Mellors and Tappel, 1966; Karlsson, 1997). Ubiquinones react with reactive oxygen species to prevent lipid peroxidation in membranes and other lipid structures in the cell (Karlsson, 1997). Also, some ubiquinones play an important role in the recycling of vitamin E during periods of oxidative stress via an NADPH-dependent system (Kagan *et al.*, 1990).

Flavonoids

Flavonoids are a large family of diphenylpropanes (over 4000 members have been identified) that are commonly found in plants consumed by humans. Family members include, but are not limited to, flavones, isoflavones, flavanones, anthocyanins and catechins (Das, 1994). Flavonoids have been reported to possess a wide variety of biological activities ranging from inhibition of inflammatory enzymes (e.g. lipoxygenase, cyclooxygenase, xanthine oxidase, NADH-oxidase, phospholipase A_2) to anti-tumoral, anti-viral, anti-mutagen, anti-inflammatory, anti-ischaemic and anti-allergic activities (Cao et al., 1997). Many of these biological effects are thought to be a result of the antioxidant capacity of flavonoids (Bors et al., 1994; Saija et al., 1995; Scalbert et al., 2002). Radical scavenging activities of flavonoids appear to vary greatly among family members, but include quenching of peroxyl, hydroxyl and superoxide radicals, as well as hydrogen peroxide and a variety of chemically generated radicals not naturally found in the body (Cao et al., 1997).

Among the many flavonoids under investigation for their potential role in protecting against radical-mediated disease processes is the polyphenolic flavonoid family, the catechins, which are found in significant concentrations in green and black tea and red wine. Catechins are amphipathic and thus exert their antioxidant activities in both lipid and aqueous environments. They have been shown to be efficient scavengers of superoxide, hydroxyl and peroxyl radicals, to inhibit metal ion-mediated radical formation and to inhibit formation of lipid peroxyl radical species (Sichel et al., 1991; Salah et al., 1995; Lotito et al., 2002). In addition to inhibiting lipid peroxidation, catechins were reported to prevent the radical-mediated depletion of vitamin E and β-carotene in human plasma in a dose-dependent manner (Lotito and Fraga, 1999).

Trace minerals associated with antioxidant defences

Several trace minerals play important but indirect roles in providing antioxidant protection in cells (Table 3). Trace minerals involved in antioxidant-related functions include copper (Cu), zinc (Zn), iron (Fe), selenium (Se) and manganese (Mn). These trace minerals contribute to the body's antioxidant defence system by acting as co-factors for antioxidant enzymes. In the following paragraphs, we provide a brief overview of the antioxidant function of each of these trace minerals. Supplementation of trace minerals is not generally necessary in well-nourished populations, but possible deficiencies of these minerals are addressed in the following discussion.

Copper contributes to cellular antioxidant protection as a co-factor for the antioxidant enzyme, CuZn-superoxide dismutase (CuZnSOD). This enzyme, located in the cytosol of cells, is responsible for eliminating superoxide radicals. Although copper deficiencies are uncommon in Western society, a copper deficiency would result in reduced levels of functioning CuZnSOD and an impaired cellular antioxidant defence system. Signs and symptoms of copper deficiency

Table 3. A list of trace minerals involved in antioxidant protection

Mineral	Function	DRI[a]	UL[b]
Copper	Co-factor for CuZnSOD-catalysed superoxide quenching	0.9 mg	10 mg
Iron	Co-factor for catalase-catalysed hydrogen peroxide decomposition	18 mg	45 mg
Manganese	Co-factor for MnSOD-catalysed superoxide quenching	2.3 mg	11 mg
Selenium	Co-factor for glutathione peroxidase-catalysed hydrogen peroxide decomposition	55 μg	400 μg
Zinc	Co-factor for CuZnSOD-catalysed superoxide quenching	11 mg	40 mg

[a] Dietary reference intakes (DRI) are the most recent set of dietary recommendations established for Canadians and Americans by the Food and Nutrition Board of the Institute of Medicine, 1997–2001. The values shown are the highest DRI for each nutrient.
[b] The tolerable upper intake level (UL) is the upper level of intake considered to be safe for adults in Canada and the USA. In some cases, lower ULs have been established for children.

include anaemia, a reduction in circulating neutrophils, bone loss and heart disease (Wardlaw and Insel, 1996; Halliwell and Gutteridge, 1999).

Zinc has been recognized as an essential nutrient since the early 1900s and is a co-factor for over 300 different enzymes (Wardlaw and Insel, 1996). In terms of the role of zinc as an antioxidant, it is an essential co-factor for CuZnSOD. As mentioned above, this enzyme is responsible for the removal of superoxide radicals from the cytosol of cells. It follows that a zinc deficiency would result in diminished CuZnSOD activity that would contribute to an impaired antioxidant capacity.

Iron is the most abundant transition metal in the body and plays a key role in the function of both haemoglobin and myoglobin (Halliwell and Gutteridge, 1999). Furthermore, iron is an essential co-factor in the antioxidant enzyme catalase. Catalase is located in both the cytosol and the mitochondria and is responsible for removing hydrogen peroxide from cells. An iron deficiency would not only impair oxygen transport in the body, but would also compromise the body's antioxidant capacity by lowering catalase activity in cells (Halliwell and Gutteridge, 1999).

Selenium plays a critical role in antioxidant defence as a co-factor for the antioxidant enzyme glutathione peroxidase. Glutathione peroxidase is located in both the cytosol and mitochondria of cells and is responsible for removing hydrogen peroxide and other organic hydroperoxides from the cell (Halliwell and Gutteridge, 1999). Selenium deficiency in humans has been reported in some areas of Europe and China and is associated with muscle pain, muscle wasting and cardiomyopathy (Wardlaw and Insel, 1996).

Manganese is a co-factor for several enzymes, including the important anti-oxidant enzyme, manganese-superoxide dismutase. This key antioxidant enzyme is located in the mitochondria and is responsible for eliminating superoxide radicals produced by oxidative phosphorylation (Halliwell and Gutteridge, 1999). Manganese deficiency in animals results in impaired brain development and reproduction. Nonetheless, manganese deficiency has not been reported in humans (Wardlaw and Insel, 1996).

Antioxidants and exercise performance

Antioxidant deficiencies and exercise performance

Antioxidant nutrient deficiencies are not widely reported among athletes (Clarkson, 1995). However, it is conceivable that an antioxidant nutrient deficiency could result in an increased susceptibility to exercise-induced damage by reactive oxygen species and thus lead to impaired exercise performance. Indeed, studies utilizing animal models have documented that vitamin E deficiency results in skeletal muscle degeneration and impaired exercise performance in rats (Davies *et al.*, 1982; Gohil *et al.*, 1986; Coombes *et al.*, 2002). Vitamin C deficiency in guinea pigs has also been shown to reduce times to exhaustion during treadmill running (Packer *et al.*, 1986). Failure to reverse the effects of vitamin E deficiency by vitamin C supplementation highlights the synergistic nature of antioxidant action (Gohil *et al.*, 1986).

It is important to emphasize caution when extrapolating results of animal studies to human populations. Although it is well established that a vitamin C deficiency impairs exercise performance in humans, marginally deficient individuals have not demonstrated similar adverse effects (van der Beek *et al.*, 1990). Additionally, in contrast to the findings of animal studies, vitamin E deficiency in humans does not appear to be associated with impaired exercise performance. Males who were made vitamin E deficient over a period of 13 months did not suffer from impaired performance or muscle weakness despite blood concentrations of vitamin E that were indicative of deficiency (Bunnell *et al.*, 1975). While the potential for antioxidant nutrient deficiencies do exist in athletes, the low incidence of vitamin deficiencies among athletes indicates that antioxidant deficiencies are not common (Clarkson, 1995).

Antioxidant effects on muscle contraction and exercise performance

It is well documented that exercise-related oxidant stress is associated with damage to lipids and protein in both muscle and blood cells (Alessio, 1993; Lawler *et al.*, 1993; Jackson, 1998; Mastaloudis *et al.*, 2001). In addition to imposing cellular damage, excessive reactive oxygen species has been shown to have an adverse effect on skeletal muscle contractile function and to exert a negative impact on performance (Reid and Durham, 2002). Pharmacologic antioxidant administration has been reported to decrease fatigue after electrically stimulated contractions of animal skeletal muscle (Barclay and Hansel, 1991; Reid *et al.*, 1992a; Supinski *et al.*, 1997). Additionally, infusion of N-acetylcysteine, a cysteine donor thought to increase the endogenous antioxidant glutathione, has been shown to attenuate muscle fatigue of the tibialis anterior and diaphragm muscles after low-frequency electrical stimulation in humans (Reid *et al.*, 1994; Travaline *et al.*, 1997). Collectively, these findings suggest that antioxidant supplementation may play a role in preserving skeletal muscle contractile function by scavenging exercise-induced reactive oxygen species and reactive nitrogen species.

The most convincing data suggesting ergogenic benefits from dietary antioxidant supplementation come from animal studies. Rodents with adequate nutritional status have demonstrated improved exercise performance after the administration of various forms of antioxidants (Novelli *et al.*, 1990, 1991; Asha Devi *et al.*, 2003). However, not all animal studies have demonstrated enhanced performance following antioxidant administration. For example, rats supplemented with vitamin E failed to improve treadmill endurance time to exhaustion (Mehlhorn *et al.*, 1989; de Oliveira *et al.*, 2003). One of these reports, however, was based on a preliminary experiment involving only one animal (Mehlhorn *et al.*, 1989).

In contrast to studies conducted on animals, studies in humans generally have not demonstrated enhanced exercise performance after antioxidant supplementation. The vast majority of studies investigating vitamin E supplementation have not demonstrated improvements in exercise performance (Shephard *et al.*, 1974; Lawrence *et al.*, 1975; Sumida *et al.*, 1989; Rokitzki *et al.*, 1994a,b). The main exception is a study conducted at high altitude in which the consumption of vitamin E was associated with a preservation of the anaerobic threshold (Simon-Schnass and Pabst, 1988). It was hypothesized that vitamin E supplementation at high altitude reduced red cell fragility and allowed for more efficient oxygen transport (Simon-Schnass and Pabst, 1988). Lack of a whole-body ergogenic effect for other antioxidants has also been reported in humans. In contrast to the findings of Reid *et al.* (1994), who found that administration of N-acetylcysteine resulted in decreased fatigue development in the tibialis anterior, infusion of N-acetylcysteine did not improve high-intensity cycling performance in untrained males (Medved *et al.*, 2003). Furthermore, other studies using antioxidant mixtures (Snider *et al.*, 1992) or selenium (Tessier *et al.*, 1995; Margaritis *et al.*, 1997) have not demonstrated improved exercise performance.

Investigations into the effects of vitamin C supplementation on exercise performance have demonstrated variable results. Vitamin C reportedly did not decrease markers of lipid peroxidation or improve recovery from unaccustomed exercise unless administered for 2 weeks prior to the exercise stress, which then resulted in modest improvements in muscle soreness (Thompson *et al.*, 2001, 2003). Other well-controlled studies with vitamin C have reported no beneficial effects on performance (Clarkson, 1995; Ashton *et al.*, 1999).

Ubiquinone-10 has been touted to possess ergogenic properties by increasing energy production via facilitating electron flux through the mitochondria and by functioning as an antioxidant. Nonetheless, among healthy individuals, only limited data illustrate the potential ergogenic properties of ubiquinone-10. In one study, a positive relationship between exercise capacity and the concentration of ubiquinone-10 in the vastus lateralis was reported in physically active males (Karlsson *et al.*, 1996). However, most studies investigating the effects of ubiquinone-10 supplementation on exercise performance have failed to authenticate these ergogenic claims. For example, supplementation of ubiquinone-10 alone (Braun *et al.*, 1991; Weston *et al.*, 1997; Bonetti *et al.*, 2000) or in combination with other antioxidants (Snider *et al.*, 1992) among groups of male athletes did not enhance performance. Additionally, male triathletes consuming ubiquinone-10 with ascorbic acid and vitamin E did not demonstrate altered energy metabolism or fatigue of the gastrocnemius muscle after plantar flexion exercise (Nielsen *et al.*, 1999). Furthermore, some studies have actually demonstrated impaired performance following high-intensity (Malm *et al.*, 1997) and endurance exercise tests (Laaksonen *et al.*, 1995) among males supplemented with ubiquinone-10. Collectively, these studies do not support the use of ubiquinone-10 as a dietary supplement for the purpose of enhancing exercise performance.

Summary

Many factors may account for the observed discrepancies between studies examining the effects of antioxidant supplementation on exercise performance, including: (1) the antioxidants delivered, (2) the antioxidant dose and (3) the type and intensity of the exercise performed. Furthermore, in many of these studies, it is unlikely that an optimal dosing strategy was identified or utilized. Evidence also suggests that high doses of antioxidants may shift the intracellular redox balance towards a reduced state and impair skeletal muscle contractile function and exercise performance (Coombes *et al.*, 2001; Marshall *et al.*, 2002). Therefore, from an exercise performance standpoint, indiscriminant antioxidant supplementation could be detrimental. Hence, to date, little evidence exists to recommend antioxidant supplementation for the purpose of performance enhancement.

Exercise and antioxidant requirements

As discussed earlier, current opinion holds that exercise-induced oxidative stress may be deleterious to exercise performance. This notion is based on cellular (Alessio, 1993; Lawler *et al.*, 1993) and extracellular (Mastaloudis *et al.*, 2001) indices of oxidant damage to lipids and proteins after exercise. Empirical data usually demonstrate that dietary antioxidant supplementation diminishes blood (Sumida *et al.*, 1989; Ashton *et al.*, 1999) and cellular markers (Goldfarb *et al.*, 1994) of radical-mediated damage during exercise. Excessive exposure to environmental pollutants during training may further support the need for anti-oxidant supplementation (Papas, 1996). However, the current consensus on antioxidant supplementation for athletes remains equivocal because of a paucity of well-designed studies that clearly outline the need for dietary antioxidants in highly trained populations. The remainder of this review will address athletes' risk for exercise-induced oxidative stress, existing evidence for supplementation efficacy and perspectives for future directions in antioxidant supplement research and athletics.

Exercise and oxidative stress: are athletes at increased risk?

Though not fully supported experimentally, a plausible rationale for supple-mentation of antioxidants does exist. The increased oxidant load experienced by competitive athletes during training is thought to necessitate antioxidant supplementation (van der Beek, 1985). Training-related oxidant stress is asso-ciated with adaptations that improve the ability of the muscle cells to quench reactive oxygen species. Well-characterized examples of these adaptations include increases in enzymatic antioxidants within active skeletal muscle (for reviews, see Powers *et al.*, 1999; Powers and Shanely, 2002). Despite these protec-tive adaptations of exercise training against cellular oxidative stress, sustained exercise imposes an acute cellular oxidative stress even in highly adapted skeletal muscle (Higuchi *et al.*, 1985). The greater training loads of competitive athletes, compared with their recreationally fit counterparts, may further compound this oxidative stress (Tiidus, 1998). In support of this notion, the magnitude of blood oxidative stress markers appears to be dose-dependent relative to increased exer-cise duration (Hessel *et al.*, 2000) and intensity (Alessio *et al.*, 2000; Quindry *et al.*, 2003).

If the need for dietary antioxidant supplements exists, however, one would expect a causal relationship between acute physical activity and decreased concentrations of key plasma antioxidants. A recent investigation reported a 75% increase in a plasma marker of lipid peroxidation that corresponded with an increased rate of plasma vitamin E turnover after an ultramarathon run (Mastaloudis *et al.*, 2001). Similarly, Bergholm and colleagues reported that chronic endurance running resulted in decreases of 18, 20 and 15% of plasma concentrations of α-tocopherol, β-carotene and retinal, respectively (Bergholm *et al.*, 1999). Nonetheless, others have found either no change or even an increase in blood concentrations of both vitamin E and ascorbate after an acute bout of endurance exercise (Liu *et al.*, 1999).

Importantly, caution is recommended when interpreting altered plasma anti-oxidant concentrations in response to acute exercise. Indeed, changes in plasma vitamin E and vitamin C during exercise may represent a complex redistribution between tissue and plasma antioxidant stores (Ji, 1995a; Liu *et al.*, 1999). One also cannot assume that plasma redox status is indicative of cellular (e.g. muscle) redox balance (Quindry *et al.*, 2003).

Extended exposure to environmental air pollutants, including ozone, sulphur dioxide and nitrogen dioxide, during endurance training may present an additional oxidant source (van Klaveren and Nemery, 1999). Moreover, high amounts of environmental air pollutants can limit exercise performance (Pierson *et al.*, 1986). Certainly, exposure to these and other environmental factors, including ultraviolet radiation, has led to the suggested need for antioxidant supplementation (Papas, 1996; Packer and Valacchi, 2002). However, logic would suggest that if exercise creates a clear need for dietary antioxidant supplementation, epidemiological and/or empirical data would directly link exercise and oxidative stress to some form of morbidity. On the contrary, epidemiological data generally indicate that fit individuals are healthier than their sedentary counterparts (Blair *et al.*, 2001).

Efficacy of antioxidant supplementation to reduce oxidative stress

Evidence addressing the efficacy of supplementation in athletic populations remains ambiguous. Existing studies generally report decreased oxidative damage after antioxidant supplementation. However, only limited data demonstrate the ability of antioxidant supplementation to prevent the exercise-associated rise in markers of oxidative stress. For example, Sumida *et al.* (1989) demonstrated that 4 weeks of vitamin E supplementation prevented the rise in plasma malondialdehyde and markers of muscle damage observed in non-supplemented controls after maximal-intensity cycle exercise. In contrast to these findings, daily supplementation with an antioxidant mixture (30 mg β-carotene, 592 mg α-tocopherol and 1000 mg ascorbate) did not prevent the exercise-induced rise in plasma malondialdehyde after moderate- to high-intensity treadmill running (Kanter *et al.*, 1993). Additionally, Helgheim *et al.* (1979) reported that vitamin E supplementation was ineffective in preventing a rise in blood markers of muscle damage. Collectively, these studies illustrate the mixed results that have been reported about the effectiveness of antioxidant supplementation in decreasing exercise-induced oxidative stress.

Perspectives and future directions

While a firm case for the necessity of dietary antioxidant supplementation in athletes cannot be made at this time, limited supplementation of antioxidants may not harm the athlete (Tiidus, 1998). Nonetheless, mega-dosing antioxidant supplements can be detrimental to health. For example, augmentation of cellular antioxidant status may attenuate the inflammatory response to muscle-damaging exercise, thereby limiting the rate of muscle regeneration (Tiidus, 1998). Furthermore, some investigators have also reported that antioxidant supplementation appears to allosterically decrease cellular and extracellular antioxidant enzyme activity during exercise (Goldfarb *et al.*, 1994; Reddy *et al.*, 1998). These findings may simply indicate that supplementation altered redox balance such that elevated endogenous antioxidant enzyme activity was unnecessary. Finally, transient pro-oxidant shifts in redox balance, as experienced during exercise, regulate signal transduction for gene transcripts, including heat shock proteins and endogenous antioxidants (Sen, 2001). Thus, high levels of antioxidant supplementation may blunt some cellular adaptations induced by exercise. Clearly, additional research is necessary before it can be stated with certainty that exercise creates a need for dietary antioxidant supplementation in athletes without nutritional deficiency.

Conclusions

Muscular exercise results in an increased production of radicals and other forms of reactive oxygen species. Furthermore, growing evidence implicates cytotoxic reactive oxygen species as an underlying aetiology in exercise-induced disturbances in muscle redox status that could result in muscle fatigue or injury.

Muscle cells contain complex cellular defence mechanisms to minimize the risk of oxidative injury. Two major classes of endogenous protective mechanisms work together to decrease the harmful effects of oxidants in cells: (1) endogenous (enzymatic and non-enzymatic antioxidants) and (2) exogenous (non-enzymatic) antioxidants. Important antioxidant enzymes include superoxide dismutase, glutathione peroxidase and catalase. The trace minerals copper, zinc, manganese, selenium and iron serve as co-factors for these essential antioxidants. Important non-enzymatic antioxidants include vitamins E and C, β-carotene, glutathione and ubiquinone. Collectively, these endogenous and exogenous antioxidants form a network to protect the cell against oxidative stress.

Although many animal experiments have demonstrated that the addition of antioxidants can improve muscular performance, to date there is limited evidence that dietary supplementation with antioxidants will improve human performance. Furthermore, it is not known if vigorous exercise training increases the need for dietary antioxidants. Therefore, dietary supplementation with antioxidants cannot be recommended at the present time.

Acknowledgements

This work was supported, in part, by grants from the American Heart Association-Florida and the National Institutes of Health awarded to S.K.P.

References

1 Aberg, F., Appelkvist, E.L., Dallner, G. and Ernster, L. (1992). Distribution and redox state of ubiquinones in rat and human tissues. *Archives of Biochemistry and Biophysics*, **295**, 230–234.

2 Alessio, H.M. (1993). Exercise-induced oxidative stress. *Medicine and Science in Sports and Exercise*, **25**, 218–224.

3 Alessio, H., Hagerman, A., Fulkerson, B., Ambrose, J., Rice, R. and Wiley, L. (2000). Generation of reactive oxygen species after exhaustive and isometric exercise. *Medicine and Science in Sports and Exercise*, **32**, 1576–1581.

4 Asha Devi, S., Prathima, S. and Subramanyam, M.V. (2003). Dietary vitamin E and physical exercise: I. Altered endurance capacity and plasma lipid profile in ageing rats. *Experimental Gerontology*, **38**, 285–290.

5 Ashton, T., Young, I.S., Peters, J.R., Jones, E., Jackson, S.K., Davies, B. and Rowlands, C.C. (1999). Electron spin resonance spectroscopy, exercise and oxidative stress: an ascorbic acid intervention. *Journal of Applied Physiology*, **87**, 2032–2036.

6 Barclay, J.K. and Hansel, M. (1991). Free radicals may contribute to oxidative skeletal muscle fatigue. *Canadian Journal of Physiology and Pharmacology*, **69**, 279–284.

7 Bergholm, R., Makimattila, S., Valkonen, M., Liu, M.-I., Lahdenpera, S., Taskinen, M.-R., Sovijarvi, A., Malmberg, P. and Yki-Jarvinen, H. (1999). Intense physical training decreases circulating antioxidants and endothelium-dependent vaso-dilation. *Atherosclerosis*, **145**, 341–349.

8 Blair, S.N., Cheng, Y. and Holder, J.S. (2001). Is physical activity or physical fitness more important in defining health benefits? *Medicine and Science in Sports and Exercise*, **33**(suppl. 6), S379–S399 (discussion S419–S420).

9 Bonetti, A., Solito, F., Carmosino, G., Bargossi, A.M. and Fiorella, P.L. (2000). Effect of ubidecarenone oral treatment on aerobic power in middle-aged trained subjects. *Journal of Sports Medicine and Physical Fitness*, **40**, 51–57.

10 Bors, W., Michel, C. and Saran, M. (1994). Flavonoid antioxidants: rate constants for reactions with oxygen radicals. *Methods in Enzymology*, **234**, 420–429.

11 Borzone, G., Zhao, B., Merola, A.J., Berliner, L. and Clanton, T.L. (1994). Detection of free radicals by electron spin resonance in rat diaphragm after resistive loading. *Journal of Applied Physiology*, **77**, 812–818.

12 Braun, B., Clarkson, P.M., Freedson, P.S. and Kohl, R.L. (1991). Effects of co-enzyme Q10 supplementation on exercise performance, $\dot{V}O_{2max}$ and lipid peroxidation in trained cyclists. *International Journal of Sport Nutrition*, **1**, 353–365.

13 Bunnell, R.H., De Ritter, E. and Rubin, S.H. (1975). Effect of feeding polyunsaturated fatty acids with a low vitamin E diet on blood levels of tocopherol in men performing hard physical labor. *American Journal of Clinical Nutrition*, **28**, 706–711.

14 Burton, G.W. and Ingold, K.U. (1989). Vitamin E as an *in vitro* and *in vivo* antioxidant. *Annals of the New York Academy of Sciences*, **570**, 7–22.

15 Burton, G.W. and Traber, M.G. (1990). Vitamin E: antioxidant activity, biokinetics and bioavailability. *Annual Review of Nutrition*, **10**, 357–382.

16 Cao, G., Sofic, E. and Prior, R.L. (1997). Antioxidant and prooxidant behavior of flavonoids: structure–activity relationships. *Free Radical Biology and Medicine*, **22**, 749–760.

17 Clarkson, P.M. (1995). Antioxidants and physical performance. *Critical Reviews in Food Science and Nutrition*, **35**, 131–141.

18 Coombes, J.S., Powers, S.K., Rowell, B., Hamilton, K.L., Dodd, S.L., Shanely, R.A., Sen, C.K. and Packer, L. (2001). Effects of vitamin E and alpha-lipoic acid on skeletal muscle contractile properties. *Journal of Applied Physiology*, **90**, 1424–1430.

19 Coombes, J.S., Rowell, B., Dodd, S.L., Demirel, H.A., Naito, H., Shanely, R.A. and Powers, S.K. (2002). Effects of vitamin E deficiency on fatigue and muscle contractile properties. *European Journal of Applied Physiology*, **87**, 272–277.

20 Das, D.K. (1994). Naturally occurring flavonoids: structure, chemistry and high-performance liquid chromatography methods for separation and characterization. *Methods in Enzymology*, **234**, 410–420.

21 Davies, K.J., Quintanilha, A.T., Brooks, G.A. and Packer, L. (1982). Free radicals and tissue damage produced by exercise. *Biochemical and Biophysical Research Communications*, **107**, 1198–1205.

22 de Oliveira, S.L., Diniz, D.B. and Amaya-Farfan, J. (2003). Carbohydrate-energy restriction may protect the rat brain against oxidative damage and improve physical performance. *British Journal of Nutrition*, **89**, 89–96.

23 Gohil, K., Packer, L., de Lumen, B., Brooks, G.A. and Terblanche, S.E. (1986). Vitamin E deficiency and vitamin C supplements: exercise and mitochondrial oxidation. *Journal of Applied Physiology*, **60**, 1986–1991.

24 Goldfarb, A.H., McIntosh, M.K., Boyer, B.T. and Fatouros, J. (1994). Vitamin E effects on indexes of lipid peroxidation in muscle from DHEA-treated and exercised rats. *Journal of Applied Physiology*, **76**, 1630–1635.

25 Halliwell, B. and Gutteridge, J. (1999). *Free Radicals in Biology and Medicine*. New York: Oxford University Press.

26 Helgheim, I., Hetland, O., Nilsson, S., Ingjer, F. and Stromme, S.B. (1979). The effects of vitamin E on serum enzyme levels following heavy exercise. *European Journal of Applied Physiology and Occupational Physiology*, **40**, 283–289.

27 Hessel, E., Haberland, A., Muller, M., Lerche, D. and Schimke, I. (2000). Oxygen radical generation of neutrophils: a reason for oxidative stress during marathon running? *Clinica Chimica Acta*, **298**, 145–156.

28 Higuchi, M., Cartier, L.-J., Chen, M. and Holloszy, J.O. (1985). Superoxide dismutase and catalase in skeletal muscle: adaptive response to exercise. *Journal of Gerontology*, **40**, 281–286.

29 Jackson, M.J. (1998). Free radical mechanisms in exercise-related muscle damage. In *Oxidative Stress in Skeletal Muscle* (edited by A.Z. Reznick, L. Packer, C.K. Sen, J.O. Holloszy and M.J. Jackson) pp. 75–86. Basel: Birkhauser Verlag.

30 Jackson, M.J., Edwards, R.H. and Symons, M.C. (1985). Electron spin resonance studies of intact mammalian skeletal muscle. *Biochimica et Biophysica Acta*, **847**, 185–190.

31 Janero, D.R. (1991). Therapeutic potential of vitamin E against myocardial ischemic-reperfusion injury. *Free Radical Biology and Medicine*, **10**, 315–324.

32 Ji, L.L. (1995a). Exercise and oxidative stress: role of the cellular antioxidant systems. In *Exercise and Sport Sciences Reviews* (edited by J.O. Holloszy), Vol. 23, pp. 135–166. Baltimore, MD: Williams & Wilkins.

33 Ji, L.L. (1995b). Oxidative stress during exercise: implication of antioxidant nutrients. *Free Radical Biology and Medicine*, **18**, 1079–1086.

34 Ji, L.L. (2002). Exercise-induced modulation of antioxidant defense. *Annals of the New York Academy of Sciences*, **959**, 82–92.

35 Ji, L.L., Stratman, F.W. and Lardy, H.A. (1988). Antioxidant enzyme systems in rat liver and skeletal muscle: influences of selenium deficiency, chronic training and acute exercise. *Archives of Biochemistry and Biophysics*, **263**, 150–160.

36 Ji, L.L., Fu, R. and Mitchell, E.W. (1992). Glutathione and antioxidant enzymes in skeletal muscle: effects of fiber type and exercise intensity. *Journal of Applied Physiology*, **73**, 1854–1859.

37 Kagan, V.E., Bakalova, R.A., Serbinova, E.E. and Stoytchev, T.S. (1990). Fluorescence measurements of incorporation and hydrolysis of tocopherol and tocopheryl esters in biomembranes. *Methods in Enzymology*, **186**, 355–367.

38 Kagan, V.E., Shvedova, A., Serbinova, E., Khan, S., Swanson, C., Powell, R. and Packer, L. (1992). Dihydrolipoic acid – a universal antioxidant both in the membrane and in the aqueous phase. Reduction of peroxyl, ascorbyl and chromanoxyl radicals. *Biochemical Pharmacology*, **44**, 1637–1649.

39 Kamei, M., Fujita, T., Kanbe, T., Sasaki, K., Oshiba, K., Otani, S., Matsui-Yuasa, I. and Morisawa, S. (1986). The distribution and content of ubiquinone in foods. *International Journal for Vitamin and Nutrition Research*, **56**, 57–63.

40 Kanter, M.M., Nolte, L.A. and Holloszy, J.O. (1993). Effects of an antioxidant vitamin mixture on lipid peroxidation at rest and postexercise. *Journal of Applied Physiology*, **74**, 965–969.

41 Karlsson, J. (1997). *Antioxidants and Exercise*. Champaign, IL: Human Kinetics.

42 Karlsson, J., Lin, L., Sylven, C. and Jansson, E. (1996). Muscle ubiquinone in healthy physically active males. *Molecular and Cellular Biochemistry*, **156**, 169–172.

43 Krinsky, N.I. and Deneke, S.M. (1982). Interaction of oxygen and oxy-radicals with carotenoids. *Journal of the National Cancer Institute*, **69**, 205–210.

44 Laaksonen, R., Fogelholm, M., Himberg, J.J., Laakso, J. and Salorinne, Y. (1995). Ubiquinone supplementation and exercise capacity in trained young and older men. *European Journal of Applied Physiology and Occupational Physiology*, **72**, 95–100.

45 Lawler, J.M., Powers, S.K., Visser, T., Van Dijk, H., Kordus, M.J. and Ji, L.L. (1993). Acute exercise and skeletal muscle antioxidant and metabolic enzymes: effects of fiber type and age. *American Journal of Physiology*, **265**, R1344–R1350.

46 Lawrence, J.D., Bower, R.C., Riehl, W.P. and Smith, J.L. (1975). Effects of alpha-tocopherol acetate on the swimming endurance of trained swimmers. *American Journal of Clinical Nutrition*, **28**, 205–208.

47 Liu, M.-L., Bergholm, R., Makitmattila, S., Lahdenpera, S., Valkonen, M., Hilden, H., Yki-Jarvinen, H. and Taskinen, M.-R. (1999). A marathon run increases the susceptibility of LDL to oxidation *in vitro* and modifies plasma antioxidants. *American Journal of Physiology*, **276**, E1083–E1091.

48 Lotito, S.B. and Fraga, C.G. (1999). (+)-Catechin as antioxidant: mechanisms preventing human plasma oxidation and activity in red wines. *Biofactors*, **10**, 125–130.

49 Lotito, S.B., Renart, M.L. and Fraga, C.G. (2002). Assessing the antioxidant capacity in the hydrophilic and lipophilic domains: study of a sample of Argentine wines. *Annals of the New York Academy of Sciences*, **957**, 284–287.

50 Malm, C., Svensson, M., Ekblom, B. and Sjodin, B. (1997). Effects of ubiquinone-10 supplementation and high intensity training on physical performance in humans. *Acta Physiologica Scandinavica*, **161**, 379–384.

51 Margaritis, I., Tessier, F., Prou, E., Marconnet, P. and Marini, J.F. (1997). Effects of endurance training on skeletal muscle oxidative capacities with and without selenium supplementation. *Journal of Trace Elements in Medicine and Biology*, **11**, 37–43.

52 Marshall, R.J., Scott, K.C., Hill, R.C., Lewis, D.D., Sundstrom, D., Jones, G.L. and Harper, J. (2002). Supplemental vitamin C appears to slow racing greyhounds. *Journal of Nutrition*, **132**(suppl. 2), 1616S–1621S.

53 Mastaloudis, A., Leonard, S.W. and Traber, M.G. (2001). Oxidative stress in athletes during extreme endurance exercise. *Free Radical Biology and Medicine*, **31**, 911–922.

54 Medved, I., Brown, M.J., Bjorksten, A.R., Leppik, J.A., Sostaric, S. and McKenna, M.J. (2003). N-acetylcysteine infusion alters blood redox status but not time to fatigue during intense exercise in humans. *Journal of Applied Physiology*, **94**, 1572–1582.

55 Mehlhorn, R.J., Sumida, S. and Packer, L. (1989). Tocopheroxyl radical persistence and tocopherol consumption in liposomes and in vitamin E-enriched rat liver mitochondria and microsomes. *Journal of Biological Chemistry*, **264**, 13448–13452.

56 Meister, A. and Anderson, M.E. (1983). Glutathione. *Annual Review of Biochemistry*, **52**, 711–760.

57 Mellors, A. and Tappel, A.L. (1966). The inhibition of mitochondrial peroxidation by ubiquinone and ubiquinol. *Journal of Biological Chemistry*, **241**, 4353–4356.

58 Nashawati, E., Dimarco, A. and Supinski, G. (1993). Effects produced by infusion of a free radical-generating solution into the diaphragm. *American Review of Respiratory Disease*, **147**, 60–65.

59 Nielsen, A.N., Mizuno, M., Ratkevicius, A., Mohr, T., Rohde, M., Mortensen, S.A. and Quistorff, B. (1999). No effect of antioxidant supplementation in triathletes on maximal oxygen uptake, 31P-NMRS detected muscle energy metabolism and muscle fatigue. *International Journal of Sports Medicine*, **20**, 154–158.

60 Novelli, G.P., Bracciotti, G. and Falsini, S. (1990). Spin-trappers and vitamin E prolong endurance to muscle fatigue in mice. *Free Radical Biology and Medicine*, **8**, 9–13.

61 Novelli, G.P., Falsini, S. and Bracciotti, G. (1991). Exogenous glutathione increases endurance to muscle effort in mice. *Pharmacological Research*, **23**, 149–155.

62 O'Neill, C.A., Stebbins, C.L., Bonigut, S., Halliwell, B. and Longhurst, J.C. (1996). Production of hydroxyl radicals in contracting skeletal muscle of cats. *Journal of Applied Physiology*, **81**, 1197–1206.

63 Packer, J.E., Slater, T.F. and Willson, R.L. (1979). Direct observation of a free radical interaction between vitamin E and vitamin C. *Nature*, **278**, 737–738.

64 Packer, L. (1991). Protective role of vitamin E in biological systems. *American Journal of Clinical Nutrition*, **53**(suppl.), 1050S–1055S.

65 Packer, L. (1994). Antioxidant properties of lipoic acid and its therapeutic effects in prevention of diabetes complications and cataracts. *Annals of the New York Academy of Sciences*, **738**, 257–264.

66 Packer, L. and Valacchi, G. (2002). Antioxidants and the response of skin to oxidative stress: vitamin E as a key indicator. *Skin Pharmacology and Applied Skin Physiology*, **15**, 282–290.

67 Packer, L., Gohil, K., deLumen, B. and Terblanche, S.E. (1986). A comparative study on the effects of ascorbic acid deficiency and supplementation on endurance and mitochondrial oxidative capacities in various tissues of the guinea pig. *Comparative Biochemistry and Physiology. B: Comparative Biochemistry*, **83**, 235–240.

68 Palozza, P., Luberto, C., Calviello, G., Ricci, P. and Bartoli, G.M. (1997). Antioxidant and prooxidant role of beta-carotene in murine normal and tumor thymocytes: effects of oxygen partial pressure. *Free Radical Biology and Medicine*, **22**, 1065–1073.

69 Papas, A.M. (1996). Determinants of antioxidant status in humans. *Lipids*, **31**(suppl.), S77–S82.

70 Pierson, W.E., Covert, D.S., Koenig, J.Q., Namekata, T. and Kim, Y.S. (1986). Implications of air pollution effects on athletic performance. *Medicine and Science in Sports and Exercise*, **18**, 322–327.

71 Powers, S.K. and Shanely, R.A. (2002). Exercise-induced changes in diaphragmatic bioenergetic and antioxidant capacity. *Exercise and Sport Sciences Reviews*, **30**, 69–74.

72 Powers, S.K., Ji, L.L. and Leeuwenburgh, C. (1999). Exercise training-induced alterations in skeletal muscle antioxidant capacity: a brief review. *Medicine and Science in Sports and Exercise*, **31**, 987–997.

73 Quindry, J., Stone, W., King, J. and Broeder, C. (2003). The effects of acute exercise on neutrophils and plasma oxidative stress. *Medicine and Science in Sports and Exercise*, **35**, 1139–1145.

74 Reddy, K.V., Kumar, T.C., Prasad, M. and Reddanna, P. (1998). Pulmonary lipid peroxidation and antioxidant defenses during exhaustive physical exercise: the role of vitamin E and selenium. *Nutrition*, **14**, 448–451.

75 Reid, M.B. (2001). Nitric oxide, reactive oxygen species and skeletal muscle contraction. *Medicine and Science in Sports and Exercise*, **33**, 371–376.

76 Reid, M.B. and Durham, W.J. (2002). Generation of reactive oxygen and nitrogen species in contracting skeletal muscle: potential impact on aging. *Annals of the New York Academy of Sciences*, **959**, 108–116.

77 Reid, M.B., Shoji, T., Moody, M.R. and Entman, M.L. (1992a). Reactive oxygen in skeletal muscle. II. Extracellular release of free radicals. *Journal of Applied Physiology*, **73**, 1805–1809.

78 Reid, M.B., Haack, K.E., Franchek, K.M., Valberg, P.A., Kobzik, L. and West, M.S. (1992b). Reactive oxygen in skeletal muscle. I. Intracellular oxidant kinetics and fatigue *in vitro*. *Journal of Applied Physiology*, **73**, 1797–1804.

79 Reid, M.B., Stokic, D.S., Koch, S.M., Khawli, F.A. and Leis, A.A. (1994). N-acetylcysteine inhibits muscle fatigue in humans. *Journal of Clinical Investigation*, **94**, 2468–2474.

80 Rokitzki, L., Logemann, E., Huber, G., Keck, E. and Keul, J. (1994a). Alpha-tocopherol supplementation in racing cyclists during extreme endurance training. *International Journal of Sport Nutrition*, **4**, 253–264.

81 Rokitzki, L., Logemann, E., Sagredos, A.N., Murphy, M., Wetzel-Roth, W. and Keul, J. (1994b). Lipid peroxidation and antioxidative vitamins under extreme endurance stress. *Acta Physiologica Scandinavica*, **151**, 149–158.

82 Saija, A., Scalese, M., Lanza, M., Marzullo, D., Bonina, F. and Castelli, F. (1995). Flavonoids as antioxidant agents: importance of their interaction with biomembranes. *Free Radical Biology and Medicine*, **19**, 481–486.

83 Salah, N., Miller, N.J., Paganga, G., Tijburg, L., Bolwell, G.P. and Rice-Evans, C. (1995). Polyphenolic flavanols as scavengers of aqueous phase radicals and as chain-breaking antioxidants. *Archives of Biochemistry and Biophysics*, **322**, 339–346.

84 Scalbert, A., Morand, C., Manach, C. and Remesy, C. (2002). Absorption and metabolism of polyphenols in the gut and impact on health. *Biomedicine and Pharmacotherapy*, **56**, 276–282.

85 Sen, C.K. (2001). Antioxidant and redox regulation of cellular signaling: introduction. *Medicine and Science in Sports and Exercise*, **33**, 368–370.

86 Sevanian, A., Davies, K.J. and Hochstein, P. (1985). Conservation of vitamin C by uric acid in blood. *Journal of Free Radicals in Biology and Medicine*, **1**, 117–124.

87 Shephard, R.J., Campbell, R., Pimm, P., Stuart, D. and Wright, G.R. (1974). Vitamin E, exercise and the recovery from physical activity. *European Journal of Applied Physiology and Occupational Physiology*, **33**, 119–126.

88 Shindoh, C., DiMarco, A., Thomas, A., Manubay, P. and Supinski, G. (1990). Effect of N-acetylcysteine on diaphragm fatigue. *Journal of Applied Physiology*, **68**, 2107–2113.

89 Sichel, G., Corsaro, C., Scalia, M., Di Bilio, A.J. and Bonomo, R.P. (1991). In vitro scavenger activity of some flavonoids and melanins against O2-($\cdot$). *Free Radical Biology and Medicine*, **11**, 1–8.

90 Simon-Schnass, I. and Pabst, H. (1988). Influence of vitamin E on physical performance. *International Journal for Vitamin and Nutrition Research*, **58**, 49–54.

91 Snider, I.P., Bazzarre, T.L., Murdoch, S.D. and Goldfarb, A. (1992). Effects of coenzyme athletic performance system as an ergogenic aid on endurance performance to exhaustion. *International Journal of Sport Nutrition*, **2**, 272–286.

92 Stocker, R., Glazer, A.N. and Ames, B.N. (1987). Antioxidant activity of albumin-bound bilirubin. *Proceedings of the National Academy of Sciences of the United States of America*, **84**, 5918–5922.

93 Sumida, S., Tanaka, K., Kitao, H. and Nakadomo, F. (1989). Exercise-induced lipid peroxidation and leakage of enzymes before and after vitamin E supplementation. *International Journal of Biochemistry*, **21**, 835–838.

94 Supinski, G., Nethery, D., Stofan, D. and DiMarco, A. (1997). Effect of free radical scavengers on diaphragmatic fatigue. *American Journal of Respiratory and Critical Care Medicine*, **155**, 622–629.

95 Sustry, P., Jayaraman, J. and Ramasarma, T. (1961). Distribution of coenzyme Q in rat liver cell fractions. *Nature*, **189**, 577.

96 Tessier, F., Margaritis, I., Richard, M.J., Moynot, C. and Marconnet, P. (1995). Selenium and training effects on the glutathione system and aerobic performance. *Medicine and Science in Sports and Exercise*, **27**, 390–396.

97 Thompson, D., Williams, C., McGregor, S.J., Nicholas, C.W., McArdle, F., Jackson, M.J. and Powell, J.R. (2001). Prolonged vitamin C supplementation and recovery from demanding exercise. *International Journal of Sport Nutrition and Exercise Metabolism*, **11**, 466–481.

98 Thompson, D., Williams, C., Garcia-Roves, P., McGregor, S.J., McArdle, F. and Jackson, M.J. (2003). Post-exercise vitamin C supplementation and recovery from demanding exercise. *European Journal of Applied Physiology*, **89**, 393–400.

99 Tiidus, P.M. (1998). Radical species in inflammation and overtraining. *Canadian Journal of Pharmacology*, **76**, 533–538.

100 Travaline, J.M., Sudarshan, S., Roy, B.G., Cordova, F., Leyenson, V. and Criner, G.J. (1997). Effect of N-acetylcysteine on human diaphragm strength and fatigability. *American Journal of Respiratory and Critical Care Medicine*, **156**, 1567–1571.

101 van der Beek, E.J. (1985). Vitamins and endurance training: food for running or faddish claims? *Sports Medicine*, **2**, 175–197.

102 van der Beek, E.J., van Dokkum, W., Schrijver, J., Wesstra, A., Kistemaker, C. and Hermus, R.J. (1990). Controlled vitamin C restriction and physical performance in volunteers. *Journal of the American College of Nutrition*, **9**, 332–339.

103 van Klaveren, R.J. and Nemery, B. (1999). Role of reactive oxygen species in occupational and environmental obstructive pulmonary diseases. *Current Opinion in Pulmonary Medicine*, **5**, 118–123.

104 Wardlaw, G. and Insel, P. (1996). *Perspectives in Nutrition*. St Louis, MO: C.V. Mosby.

105 Weston, S.B., Zhou, S., Weatherby, R.P. and Robson, S.J. (1997). Does exogenous coenzyme Q10 affect aerobic capacity in endurance athletes? *International Journal of Sport Nutrition*, **7**, 197–206.

106 Yu, B.P. (1994). Cellular defenses against damage from reactive oxygen species. *Physiological Reviews*, **74**, 139–162.

8 Dietary supplements

RON J. MAUGHAN, DOUG S. KING and
TREVOR LEA

For the athlete training hard, nutritional supplements are often seen as promoting adaptations to training, allowing more consistent and intensive training by promoting recovery between training sessions, reducing interruptions to training because of illness or injury, and enhancing competitive performance. Surveys show that the prevalence of supplement use is widespread among sportsmen and women, but the use of few of these products is supported by a sound research base and some may even be harmful to the athlete. Special sports foods, including energy bars and sports drinks, have a real role to play, and some protein supplements and meal replacements may also be useful in some circumstances. Where there is a demonstrated deficiency of an essential nutrient, an increased intake from food or from supplementation may help, but many athletes ignore the need for caution in supplement use and take supplements in doses that are not necessary or may even be harmful. Some supplements do offer the prospect of improved performance; these include creatine, caffeine, bicarbonate and, perhaps, a very few others. There is no evidence that prohormones such as androstenedione are effective in enhancing muscle mass or strength, and these prohormones may result in negative health consequences, as well as positive drug tests. Contamination of supplements that may cause an athlete to fail a doping test is widespread.

Keywords: bicarbonate, caffeine, carnitine, creatine, dietary supplements, drugs, nutrition.

Introduction

Talent is undoubtedly the most important attribute of the elite performer, but it is difficult to define. Other factors that characterize the elite athlete include a sustained effective training programme, a range of psychological and cognitive characteristics, resistance to injury and effective nutrition support. At a time when the world standard in sport is moving to ever-higher levels, the athlete who wants to make it to the top and to stay there must explore all possible means of securing an advantage.

As training programmes become ever more demanding, every possible advantage must be seized, and nutrition is an obvious area that can make a difference. The foods that an athlete chooses can make the difference between success and failure. Although wise food choices will not make a champion out of the athlete who does not have the talent or motivation to succeed, an inadequate diet can prevent the talented athlete from making it to the top. A varied diet eaten in an amount sufficient to meet the energy needs of the athlete in training should provide all the essential nutrients in adequate amounts, but not all athletes eat a varied diet and the total food intake may at times be restricted. Because nutritional deficiencies may be difficult to detect in their early stages, athletes are often tempted to take individual nutrients in a concentrated form to guard against the possibility of a deficiency developing. To cater for the demand for specialist nutritional supplements for athletes, an enormous multinational industry has grown up, encouraged by a popular culture of supplement use among the general population in the belief that this can in some way compensate for poor food choices and the increased stresses of modern life. This supplement culture has extended to include an enormous diversity of compounds that extends beyond nutritional components to embrace more exotic edible compounds.

The following sections will review the various categories of nutritional supplements that are used by athletes and will present evidence for or against the use of selected supplements. Some recent comprehensive publications have reviewed a wide range of individual supplements (Antonio and Stout, 2001; Talbott, 2003). In this review article, we do not attempt to review all of the available information on even a few of the hundreds (perhaps thousands) of different supplements in widespread use, but instead focus on some of the general issues associated with supplement use, using examples to highlight specific issues. Further information on some of these supplements will be found in some of the other reviews contained in this issue.

The use of any nutritional supplement that is effective in improving performance inevitably raises ethical issues. Ergogenic aids are banned by the governing bodies of sport for one of two reasons: on the grounds that they pose threat to the health of the individual, or because they confer what is seen to be an 'unfair' advantage. These issues must always be borne in mind when considering the use of any supplement.

The scope of supplement use

Limited information is available on the extent of dietary supplement use among athletes. The global market for supplements in 2001 was estimated at US$46 billion, with the US supplement market in 2000 being estimated at US$16.7 billion (*Financial Times*, 19 April 2002). Athletes account for a significant fraction of the total market and a wide range of products are aimed at both the active population and at those engaged in competitive sport.

Many surveys of supplement use in athletes have been published, with a meta-analysis of 51 published surveys involving 10,274 male and female athletes showing an overall prevalence of use of 46% (Sobal and Marquart, 1994). Prevalence of use, however, varies widely among sports and among athletes of different ages, standards of performance and cultural background. In some sports, especially strength and power sports, supplement use is the norm. A report of supplement use among 100 Norwegian national-level competitors from various sports revealed that 84% surveyed used some form of micronutrient supplement (Ronsen *et al.*, 1999). Most athletes in this survey took multiple supplements, although many had nutritional habits that were described as 'unsatisfactory', implying that these athletes might have benefited more from attention to the foods they ate.

Only a few surveys have attempted to quantify the frequency or amount of supplement use, but it appears to be common for athletes to exceed the recommended doses of supplements. This may be because of a feeling that 'more is better' or because team-mates or opponents are known to use higher doses. In some cases, for example creatine, the dose recommended by some suppliers may be far higher than the maximum effective dose. On the other hand, the amount of supplement in some preparations may be far less than the amount used in laboratory studies of efficacy, especially where expensive ingredients are concerned. Estimates of use by individual athletes suggest that some may ingest very large numbers of different supplements on a regular basis and that the amounts used may be far in excess of those shown to be safe. Most people believe that 'natural' supplements are harmless, but high intakes of many of these supplements on a long-term basis may be harmful. Iron, zinc and other metallic elements are frequently consumed in amounts that are known to be harmful. It would appear that athletes – and often also those who advise them – are usually unaware of the risks.

Most surveys have failed to examine the reasons for supplement use by athletes, information that is fundamental to any effort to change the behaviour of athletes. In one study, attitudes to dietary supplement use were assessed in 1737 young (14–19 years) male and female (58% male, 42% female) high school athletes (Perko, 2000). Coaches, parents, physicians, athletic trainers and peers all influenced the decision to take supplements. There was a good relationship between behaviour and perceived normal behaviour, but knowledge about the effects of supplements was poor. Other surveys have found no association between the prevalence of supplement use and gender, race, marital status, educational background, dietary habits or training status. Commonly cited reasons for supplement use include:

- to compensate for an inadequate diet;
- to meet abnormal demands of hard training or frequent competition;
- to benefit performance;
- to keep up with team-mates or opponents;
- recommended by coach, parent or other influential individual.

However, even when athletes are informed on the basis of biochemical measurement of nutrient status that their diet is adequate or that the status of their body stores is normal (e.g. iron), the use of supplements persists, suggesting that the decision to use supplements is not a rational one.

Improving strength and power: promoting tissue growth and repair

The use of dietary supplements seems to be particularly prevalent among athletes in strength and power sports, with some surveys showing that all athletes from these events were using one or more supplements. A wide range of supplements are sold as 'anabolic' or 'anti-catabolic' agents, with either direct or indirect effects on protein synthetic pathways in muscle. Proposed mechanisms of action include a mass action effect on synthetic pathways by increasing amino acid availability, stimulation of hormone release or potentiation of hormone action, an increase in cell volume, or by acting as an adaptogen (i.e. promoting adaptation to training). Supplements on sale in this broad category include amino acids, boron, chromium, chrysin, colostrum, creatine, hydroxymethylbutyrate (HMB), ornithine alphaketoglutarate, protein, tribulus terrestris, vanadium and zinc.

Although protein products are by far the largest selling products in this group, sales of creatine (a product that is not used except in sports nutrition) and of some other products are also substantial. For most of these supplements, there are few supporting data – indeed, few experimental data at all. In many cases, there are suggestions from *in vitro* studies of effects that may be relevant, but there is no experimental evidence from studies on healthy humans.

Proteins and amino acids

The use of high-protein diets has a long history in sports nutrition and such diets were reportedly popular with athletes in the Olympics of ancient Greece. There is good evidence that protein requirements are increased by hard training and it is often recommended that the protein intake of strength athletes should be 50–100% greater than that of their sedentary counterparts (Tarnopolsky, 2001). Athletes often insist that much higher amounts of protein are necessary to increase muscle mass, but the literature does not support this supposition. This apparent inconsistency may be explained by Millward's adaptive metabolic demand model, which proposes that the body adapts to either high or low intakes, and that this adjustment to changes in intake occurs only very slowly (Millward, 2001). With high protein intakes, there is an up-regulation of protein degradation and amino acid oxidation. The athlete consuming a high protein diet who acutely reduces protein intake will experience a loss of lean tissue until a new equilibrium has been achieved.

Whether protein supplements are necessary is a separate issue, and this is discussed by Tipton and Wolfe (2004). It is clearly possible to achieve very high protein intakes by choosing appropriate foods, but it is also true that many high protein foods have a high fat content. Knowledge about the composition of foods among athletes is not generally good, which means that a restricted choice of foods is almost inevitable. Protein supplements offer athletes the possibility of achieving their desired protein intake without an unacceptable increase in fat intake and without major changes to their eating habits.

In the case of some amino acids, there are data from clinical studies involving severely stressed individuals (by trauma, burn injury or surgery) showing that supplementation may reduce the extent of muscle wasting that occurs, but this catabolic state is hardly relevant to the healthy athlete trying to increase muscle mass. Individual amino acids claimed to promote muscle growth include glutamine, branched-chain amino acids, leucine, lysine, arginine and ornithine. There is little evidence to support the benefit of supplementation of any of these amino acids for athletes eating a normal diet. Although high doses of arginine, ornithine and lysine may result in increased circulating growth hormone and insulin concentrations, these have not been shown to result in changes in lean body mass or in muscle function (Merimee *et al.*, 1969). The changes in growth hormone that result are transient and small relative to the normal fluctuations that occur and are also small relative to the increases that result from even a short period of very high-intensity effort.

β-Hydroxy-β-methylbutyrate

A relatively recent addition to the plethora of nutritional supplements is β-hydroxy-β-methylbutyrate (HMB), a metabolite of leucine. Although the mechanism of action of HMB is unknown, it has been hypothesized that it either acts by decreasing muscle proteolysis or by improving cell integrity by providing substrate for cholesterol synthesis (Nissen and Sharp, 2003). In previously untrained individuals, HMB may increase lean body mass and strength more than resistance training alone (Nissen *et al.*, 1996; Gallagher *et al.*, 2000a; Panton *et al.*, 2000). Direct measures of muscle membrane integrity have not been made, but intake of HMB has been reported to reduce blood concentrations of creatine kinase during resistance training in previously untrained individuals (Nissen *et al.*, 1996; Gallagher *et al.*, 2000a; Panton *et al.*, 2000). In addition, Nissen *et al.* (1996) reported that HMB intake reduced urinary excretion of 3-methylhistidine, a finding that is consistent with a decrease in muscle proteolysis. In trained individuals and elite power athletes, however, HMB intake does not appear to enhance lean body mass or strength (Kreider *et al.*, 1999; Slater *et al.*, 2001; Ransone *et al.*, 2003) or anaerobic exercise capacity (O'Connor and Crowe, 2003). β-Hydroxy-β-methylbutyrate also does not appear to affect markers of catabolic status or muscle membrane integrity in well-trained individuals (Kreider *et al.*, 1999; Paddon-Jones *et al.*, 2001; Slater *et al.*, 2001).

A recent meta-analysis on studies of both trained and untrained individuals (Nissen and Sharp, 2003) reported that HMB intake increases lean body mass by 0.28% per week and strength by 1.40% per week compared with resistance training alone. Effect sizes for these improvements were small (0.15 and 0.19 for lean mass and strength, respectively). Taken together, these findings suggest that HMB may have some value for athletes beginning a resistance training programme. β-Hydroxy-β-methylbutyrate has been reported to reduce the accumulation of creatine kinase in the blood of runners after a 20-km time-trial (Knitter *et al.*, 2000), and may reduce blood lactate accumulation during endurance exercise (Vukovich and Dreifort, 2001). Although HMB appears to be a safe supplement (Gallagher *et al.*, 2000b; Nissen *et al.*, 2000), its relative expense (US\$1.8–2.4 per day) and the limited likelihood of a beneficial effect suggest that it may not have much to offer the athlete.

Trace elements

Several single elements are also promoted as anabolic agents. Chromium plays a role in insulin sensitivity and insulin is a potent anabolic hormone. Exercise may increase urinary chromium excretion, raising concerns among athletes that deficiency may occur. There are limited data on the effects of chromium supplements in athletes, with published studies of chromium supplementation showing an increase, decrease or no change in body mass. The best-controlled studies, however, show no effect on muscle mass or strength (Clarkson and Rawson, 1999; Nissen and Sharp, 2003). In addition, concern has recently been expressed that chromium, if taken as the picolinate salt, may not be entirely safe, with several adverse effects having been reported (Vukovich, 2001).

Vanadium is also advertised as a promoter of the action of insulin, and there are limited animal data to support this. Human data, however, show no effect of supplementation on body composition or strength in resistance-trained athletes (Fawcett *et al.*, 1996). There is some debate as to whether boron is an essential element in human nutrition, but boron supplementation is claimed to increase circulating testosterone, with the prospect for an anabolic action. This result, however, was obtained in post-menopausal women who had been fed a low-boron diet (Nielson *et al.*, 1987), and there are no studies showing that boron feeding results in muscle hypertrophy in normally nourished individuals with normal endocrine function. Administration of boron supplements to a group of male bodybuilders had no effect on circulating free or total testosterone or on muscle size or strength (Ferrando and Green, 1993).

Prohormones and related compounds

A variety of precursors of testosterone and nandrolone (19-nortestosterone) – together referred to as prohormones – are sold as dietary supplements: these include in particular androstenedione ('andro') and 19-norandrostenedione. These are not legal in those countries where they are classified as prescription-only drugs, and are banned in Olympic sports. Nonetheless, their use is permitted in some sports, including baseball, where they have been promoted by successful players, and they are readily available via the Internet or from countries where their sale is not restricted. Recent research in this area has focused on dehydroepiandrosterone (DHEA), androstenedione, androstenediol and 19-norandrostenedione. The rationale for taking these supplements is that these androgens are only one or two chemical reactions away from testosterone.

Dehydroepiandrosterone is formed primarily in the adrenal glands, and is found in high concentrations in the blood, but its physiologic roles(s) are unclear; it can also be converted to androstenedione (Geller, 1985) or androstenediol (Schindler and Aymar, 1975). The intake of DHEA does not increase blood testosterone in men or augment gains in muscle size and strength due to resistance training (Brown *et al.*, 1999; Wallace *et al.*, 1999). While replacement doses of DHEA in ageing women increase both serum testosterone and dihydrotestosterone (DHT) concentrations (Morales *et al.*, 1994), the effect of DHEA intake on serum sex hormones, muscle size and muscle strength in young healthy women is not known.

In men, the intake of 100–200 mg of androstenedione or androstenediol does not affect blood testosterone concentrations (King *et al.*, 1999; Wallace *et al.*, 1999; Ballantyne *et al.*, 2000; Earnest *et al.*, 2000). The effect of higher doses of androstenedione on blood testosterone is not clear (Leder *et al.*, 2000). Chronic intake of 200–300 mg androstenedione or 200 mg androstenediol per day does not result in greater gains in muscle size and strength during resistance training than training alone (King *et al.*, 1999; Broeder *et al.*, 2000). Norandrostenedione and norandrostenediol have also been shown not to raise blood concentrations of nandrolone (19-nortestosterone) or to affect body composition or strength in young healthy men (Dehennin *et al.*, 2002; van Gammeren *et al.*, 2002). In middle-aged (30–60 years) men, 300 mg of either androstenedione or androstenediol per day raises blood free testosterone by approximately 35%. In healthy young women, the effect of androstenedione intake is not clear. One study reported that the intake of 100 mg androstenedione increases blood total testosterone to concentrations typically observed in young healthy men (Kicman *et al.*, 2003). In another study, however, blood testosterone was elevated after the intake of 300 mg of androstenedione, but remained at levels less than one-half of normal values for young men (Brown *et al.*, in press). Although the effect of androstenedione on muscle size and strength in women has not been studied, the likely virilization and other possible side-effects of androstenedione use in women suggest that women should not take this supplement.

Since androstenedione is similar in structure to testosterone, it is reasonable to hypothesize that androstenedione might be an anabolic agent, independent of any effect on testosterone concentrations. However, androstenedione does not increase muscle protein synthesis *in vivo* (Rasmussen *et al.*, 2000) and does not increase satellite cell proliferation or differentiation *in vitro* (Vierck *et al.*, 2003).

The intake of androstenedione and androstenediol decreases blood concentrations of high-density lipoprotein cholesterol in males (Brown *et al.*, 2000a,b, 2001a,b), corresponding to a 10–15% increase in the risk for cardiovascular disease. In all participants, ingested androstenedione and androstenediol appeared to be preferentially converted to oestrogens and DHT, rather than to testosterone. Dihydrotestosterone is associated with male pattern baldness and benign prostate hypertrophy. Elevated concentrations of oestrogens have been linked to pancreatic cancer and gynecomastia (breast growth). Increased blood concentrations of androstenedione may increase the risk of pancreatic and prostate cancer, and may promote behavioural changes.

Because the liver removes a significant amount of androgen that is taken orally, it is possible that an androgen that is taken by allowing a pill to dissolve under the tongue may be more readily converted to testosterone. Androstene-diol taken in this form increases blood total testosterone by 125% (Brown *et al.*, 2002). Whether this product enhances muscle size or strength remains to be determined. Finally, androstenedione and other prohormones undergo extensive metabolism to other steroids. Recent reports suggest that athletes taking these steroids are at risk for positive drug tests (Catlin *et al.*, 2000; Uralets and Gillette, 1999).

In summary, 'testosterone prohormones' taken orally do not significantly raise blood testosterone in young men and do not increase muscle size or strength. These supplements may pose significant health risks and may result in positive drug tests.

Herbal supplements

Many herbal supplements are claimed to increase testosterone concentrations and hence have an anabolic action. These include tribulis terrestris, chrysin, indole-3-carbinol, saw palmetto, gamma-oryzanol, yohimbine, smilax and mummio. All of these claims are based on *in vitro* data. Attempts have been made to formulate combinations of some of these herbal extracts with androstenedione and androstenediol to minimize aromatization to oestrogens and reduction to DHT. Recently, it has been shown that a formulation containing tribulus terrestris, chrysin, indole-3-carbinol and saw palmetto, together with androstenedione or androstenediol and DHEA, does not increase serum testosterone or augment the increases in muscle size and strength achieved through strength training alone (Brown *et al.*, 2000a,b, 2001a,b). These human data suggest that these herbal extracts are of no value.

Weight loss and fat loss

Supplements in this category are used by athletes who need to limit body mass, and especially body fat, in weight category, weight-sensitive or aesthetic sports.

Carnitine

The supply of plasma free fatty acids to the exercising muscle is important for determining the relative contributions of fat and carbohydrate to oxidative metabolism, but a number of other steps are recognized as being involved in fat oxidation. Fatty acid uptake into the cell and translocation across the mitochondrial membrane are also key steps. Carnitine combines with fatty acyl-coenzyme A (acyl-CoA) in the cytoplasm and allows that fatty acid to enter the mitochondrion. The first step is catalysed by carnitine palmitoyl transferase 1 (CPT1) and the trans-membrane transport is facilitated by acylcarnitine transferase. Within the mitochondrion, the action of carnitine palmitoyl transferase 2 (CPT2) regenerates free carnitine and the fatty acyl-CoA is released for entry into the β-oxidation pathway.

Within the mitochondrion, carnitine also functions to regulate the acetyl-CoA concentration and the concentration of free CoA. Free CoA is involved in the pyruvate dehydrogenase reaction as well as in the process of β-oxidation and thus plays a key role in the integration of fat and carbohydrate oxidation. It has been proposed that an increased availability of carnitine within the mitochondrion might allow the cell to maintain a higher free CoA concentration, with a stimulatory effect on oxidative metabolism.

Because of the key role of carnitine in the oxidation of both fat and carbohydrate, it has been proposed that carnitine supplementation may improve exercise performance. On the basis of this logic, carnitine is widely sold in sports shops as a supplement for endurance athletes. It is also sold as a weight loss product with claims of increased fat oxidation. There is, however, no good evidence that carnitine deficiency occurs in the general population or in athletes. Carnitine is present in the diet in red meat and dairy products, so it might be thought that individuals who follow a vegan lifestyle might be at increased risk of deficiency, but carnitine can also be synthesized from lysine and methionine in the liver and kidney. Measurement of the effects of exercise and diet on muscle carnitine concentrations in humans (muscle accounts for about 98% of the total body carnitine content) has only been carried out relatively recently, and there have been few attempts to measure the effects of supplementation on muscle carnitine. Barnett *et al.* (1994) and Vukovich *et al.* (1994) reported that short-term supplementation with carnitine (4–6 $g \cdot day^{-1}$ for 7–14 days) had no effect on muscle carnitine concentrations or on the metabolic response to exercise. Even when fatty acid mobilization was stimulated by high fat meals or heparin, there was no effect of carnitine supplementation on fat oxidation (Vukovich *et al.*, 1994).

In contrast to these negative findings, there are published reports suggesting that carnitine supplementation can increase the contribution of fatty acids to oxidative metabolism and thus promote the use of body fat stores. In a comprehensive review of the literature, Spriet (1997) identified eight studies that examined the effects of supplementation on the metabolic response to endurance exercise, and found that three of those studies reported an increased rate of fat oxidation. There is more recent evidence to support this, with one study showing an increased oxidation of 13C-labelled palmitate after 10 days of carnitine supplementation (Muller *et al.*, 2002). This finding alone is not, however, evidence that weight loss and a reduction in body fat content will result.

Most of the products that have been shown to be effective in promoting weight loss contain ingredients prohibited by doping regulations and also raise questions about safety. Combinations of caffeine (sometimes in the form of guarana), ephedrine (sometimes as herbal ephedra) and aspirin (sometimes as naturally occurring salicylates) have been shown to be more effective than any of these ingredients in isolation, but both caffeine and ephedrine can cause positive doping results and ephedrine has been associated with a significant number of positive doping results. There also appear to be significant health risks associated with the use of ephedrine (Bent *et al.*, 2003) and the use of these products is strongly discouraged.

Promoting energy supply

One view of exercise-induced fatigue is that it occurs when the rate of ATP hydrolysis in the active muscles exceeds the rate at which ATP can be regenerated. It follows that the onset of fatigue can be delayed and exercise performance improved if a higher rate of ATP resynthesis can be maintained. Supplements that are claimed to improve performance by increasing energy supply and delaying fatigue include bicarbonate, caffeine, carnitine, creatine, guarana, hornet juice, iron, magnesium, pyruvate and ribose. It must be emphasized at the outset that not all of these claims are supported by experimental evidence. There is reason to believe that some athletes may benefit in some circumstances from the use of bicarbonate, caffeine, creatine and iron. Caffeine will be discussed later in this review and is also discussed by Spriet and Gibala (2004).

Bicarbonate

For exercise that results in fatigue within a few minutes, anaerobic glycolysis makes a major contribution to energy metabolism. Although glycolysis allows higher rates of ATP resynthesis than can be achieved by aerobic metabolism, the capacity of the system is limited, and fatigue is inevitable when high rates of anaerobic glycolysis occur. The metabolic acidosis that accompanies glycolysis has been implicated in the fatigue process, either by inhibition of key glycolytic enzymes, by interfering with calcium transport and binding, or by a direct effect on the actin–myosin interaction. Therefore, it is intuitively attractive to believe that induction of alkalosis before exercise, an increase in the muscle buffering capacity, and an increased rate of efflux of hydrogen ions from the active muscles all have the potential to delay fatigue and improve exercise performance. Many studies have looked at the effects of metabolic alkalosis (usually induced by ingestion of sodium bicarbonate or sodium citrate) on the performance of high-intensity exercise, but the results are by no means consistent or conclusive (Maughan, 1999; McNaughton, 2000).

In one study designed to simulate athletic competition, trained non-elite (best 800-m time about 2 min 5 s) middle-distance runners performed a simulated 800-m race. In the alkalotic condition, they ran almost 3 s faster than in the placebo or control trials (Wilkes *et al.*, 1983). A more recent report indicated similar improvements (3–4 s) over a distance of 1500 m in runners who completed simulated races in about 4 min 15 s (Bird *et al.*, 1995). Although these effects on performance might appear small, they are of considerable significance to the athlete, for whom an improvement of even a fraction of a second in these events is considered to be a major achievement.

The reasons for the conflicting effects reported in the published literature are not altogether clear, but are at least in part due to variations in the intensity and duration of the exercise tests used, the nature of the exercise task, the dosage of sodium bicarbonate administered and the time delay between bicarbonate administration and the beginning of the exercise test (i.e. the amount of metabolic alkalosis induced). Performance has been monitored over exercise durations ranging from a few seconds to more than 1 h, and during continuous, incremental and intermittent dynamic exercise as well as during sustained isometric contractions.

There is no clear pattern of exercise duration between those studies where a positive effect was observed and those where no effect was seen. In most studies, a dose of 0.3 g of sodium bicarbonate or citrate per kilogram of body weight has been used to induce alkalosis, and this has usually been administered orally in solution or in capsule form. Such a dose has usually resulted in an increase of 4–5 mmol $\cdot$ l^{-1} in the plasma buffer base 2–3 h after administration, although the time-course of changes in acid–base status was not carefully followed in most of these studies. Horswill *et al.* (1988) examined the effects of ingesting 0.1–0.2 g bicarbonate $\cdot$ kg^{-1} BW (where BW = body weight) on cycle ergometer sprint performance over 2 min. They found no improvement in performance even though the blood bicarbonate concentration was elevated; on the basis of these results, they suggested that a dose of less than 0.3 g $\cdot$ kg^{-1} BW might be ineffective in improving exercise performance. McKenzie *et al.* (1986), however, reported that a dose of 0.3 g $\cdot$ kg^{-1} BW was no more effective than one half this dose.

There are potential problems associated with the use of high doses of bicarbonate. Vomiting and diarrhoea are frequently reported as a result of ingestion of even relatively small doses of bicarbonate, thus limiting any improvement in performance among those individuals susceptible to gastrointestinal problems. There are anecdotal reports of athletes using this intervention, which is not prohibited by the rules of sport, being unable to compete because of the severity of these symptoms. Although unpleasant and to some extent debilitating, these effects are not serious and there seem to be no long-term adverse consequences of occasional use. Sodium citrate administration, which also results in an alkaline shift in the extracellular fluid, has also been reported to improve peak power and total work output in a 60-s exercise test, but without any adverse gastrointestinal symptoms (McNaughton, 2000).

When an increase in performance after bicarbonate ingestion has been observed, it has been ascribed to an increased rate of hydrogen ion efflux from the exercising muscles, which reduces both the rate of fall of intracellular pH and the pH-mediated inhibition of phosphofructokinase (Sutton *et al.*, 1981). The higher blood lactate concentrations after exercise associated with metabolic alkalosis, even when the exercise duration is the same, may therefore be indicative not only of a higher rate of lactate efflux, but also of an increased contribution of anaerobic glycolysis to energy production. Associated with the development of fatigue during high-intensity exercise is a decline in the muscle adenine nucleotide content. The extent of the fall in muscle ATP concentration that occurs during maximal exercise in humans has been shown to approach 40% of pre-exercise values: even greater losses of ATP (60%) have been reported upon exhaustion in the horse (Snow *et al.*, 1985). There is evidence to suggest that an increase in hydrogen ion efflux during near maximal intensity exercise after bicarbonate administration may decrease the extent of muscle adenine nucleotide loss during exercise (Greenhaff *et al.*, 1990), but whether this is due to a pH-mediated decrease in the activation of AMP deaminase or an increased rate of ADP rephosphorylation via glycolysis is not clear. Whatever the mechanism, it seems reasonable to suggest that bicarbonate administration before high-intensity exercise will only enhance performance when the intensity and duration of the exercise are sufficient to result in significant muscle acidosis and adenine nucleotide loss.

Creatine

Creatine has been used by many successful athletes, particularly in track and field athletics, but in many other sports as well. Some indication of the extent of its use comes from the fact that the estimated sales of creatine to athletes in the USA alone in 1997 amounted to over 300,000 kg. This represents a remarkable growth, as its use first became popular in sport after the 1992 Olympic Games in Barcelona. What distinguishes creatine from most other purported ergogenic aids is that it seems to be effective in improving performance. More significantly, perhaps, its use is not prohibited by the governing bodies of sport and, although long-term safety studies have not been undertaken, there appear to be no harmful side-effects even when very large doses are taken, at least in the quantities that are necessary to produce an ergogenic effect. There are many excellent reviews of the effects of creatine supplementation, but the picture changes rapidly as new information emerges in this topical area. Greenhaff (2000) and Williams *et al.* (1999) have provided recent overviews.

The highest tissue concentrations of creatine are found in skeletal muscle, and approximately two-thirds of the total is in the form of creatine phosphate. Creatine phosphate is capable of rapid regeneration of ATP within the cell cytoplasm, but a limited amount is available. Increasing muscle creatine phosphate should increase the available energy supply. Creatine occurs naturally in the diet, being present in meat: 1 kg of fresh steak contains about 5 g of creatine. The normal daily intake is less than 1 g, but the estimated daily requirement for the average individual is about 2 g. The body has a limited capacity to synthesize creatine in the liver, kidney and pancreas and in other tissues, but the primary site of synthesis in humans is the kidney. This supplies the amount required in excess of the dietary intake, and is also the only way in which vegetarians can meet their requirement. Synthesis occurs from amino acid precursors (arginine and glycine), but the synthetic pathway is suppressed when dietary creatine intake is high.

The first study to systematically investigate the effects of supplementation of large amounts of creatine was that of Harris *et al.* (1992). In a comprehensive study, they showed that ingestion of small amounts of creatine (1 g or less) had a negligible effect on the circulating creatine concentration, whereas feeding higher doses (5 g) resulted in an approximately 15-fold increase. Repeated feeding of 5-g doses every 2 h maintained the plasma concentration at about 1 mmol·l^{-1} over an 8-h period. Repeated feeding of creatine (5 g four times a day) over 4–5 days resulted in a marked increase in the total creatine content of the quadriceps femoris muscle. An increase in muscle creatine content was apparent within 2 days of starting this regimen, and the increase was greatest in those with a low initial concentration; in some cases, an increase of 50% was observed. Approximately 20% of the increase in total muscle creatine content is accounted for by creatine phosphate. Co-ingestion of creatine and carbohydrate, which results in high circulating insulin, may increase the storage of creatine in muscle (Green *et al.*, 1996a,b).

Most authors who have reviewed the published literature have concluded that the available evidence supports a beneficial effect of creatine on performance in short-term high-intensity exercise (Greenhaff, 2000). Of three recently published meta-analyses, two have concluded that creatine supplementation has positive effects on strength, power and lean body mass (Branch, 2003; Nissen and Sharp, 2003), while the other (Misic and Kelley, 2002) concluded that there was no effect. The reasons for this discrepancy are not entirely clear. Effects are seen in particular in the later stages of multiple short efforts with limited recovery, but improvements are sometimes seen in single sprints lasting less than 30 s. There is little information on the effects of creatine supplementation on the performance of more prolonged exercise, but there is little reason to suspect a positive effect.

The mechanism by which creatine supplementation might improve performance is not entirely clear, although it is clear that this effect is related to increased muscle creatine phosphate. The rate of creatine phosphate resynthesis after intense exercise is enhanced after high-dose creatine supplementation (Greenhaff *et al.*, 1994). This allows faster recovery after sprints as well as allowing more work to be done during each subsequent high-intensity effort. These effects will allow a greater amount of work to be done in training and should therefore result in a greater training response, although it is possible that by maintaining the energy charge better during training, the response will be less. This is especially important in that the muscle creatine content remains high for weeks or even months after only a few days of high-dose dietary creatine supplementation (Hultman *et al.*, 1996).

Many studies and much anecdotal evidence support the suggestion that acute supplementation with creatine is associated with a prompt gain in body mass. This typically amounts to about 1–2 kg over a supplementation period of 4–5 days, but may be more than this. In reviewing those studies where changes in body mass were reported, Branch (2003) reported 43 studies in which body mass increased and 24 where no change was seen; there was a statistically significant effect size for both body mass and lean body mass. Another recent meta-analysis puts the increases in muscle size and strength in perspective. Nissen and Sharp (2003) reported that creatine supplementation increases lean mass and strength by 0.35% and 1.09% per week in excess of the changes observed with resistance training alone, but again effect sizes for the increased lean mass and strength were small (0.26 and 0.36, respectively).

The rapid increases in body mass may be accounted for by water retention. Increasing the creatine content of muscle by 80–100 $mmol \cdot kg^{-1}$ will increase intracellular osmolality, leading to water retention. Hultman *et al.* (1996) found a reduction in urinary output during supplementation, which tends to confirm this. The increased intramuscular osmolality due to creatine itself, however, is not likely to be sufficient to account for all of this water retention. It has been suggested that co-ingestion of creatine and carbohydrate, which results in high circulating insulin (Green *et al.*, 1996a,b), may stimulate glycogen synthesis, which will further increase the water content of muscle. There is some preliminary evidence for a stimulation of protein synthesis in response to creatine supplementation (Ziegenfuss *et al.*, 1997), but further experimentation is required. It is unlikely that major effects on muscle protein content can be achieved within 4–5 days, so the reported gains in muscle strength within the same time-scale are difficult to explain.

The effects of the long-term use of large doses of creatine are unknown and its use may pose a health risk. There is concern about possible adverse effects on renal function, in particular in individuals with impaired renal capacity. Studies on the response to long-term creatine use are in progress but results are not yet available. There have, however, been no reports of adverse effects in any of the studies published in the literature. One study that specifically examined renal function in individuals supplementing with creatine found no reason to believe that renal complications were likely (Poortmans *et al.*, 1997). Anecdotal reports of an increased prevalence of muscle cramps in athletes taking creatine supplements have been circulating for some time, but there is no substance to these stories. It is likely that any injury suffered by an athlete will be ascribed to an easily identifiable change in habit, such as the introduction of a new supplement.

Uninformed comment ascribed the deaths of three American collegiate wrestlers in December 1999 to creatine use, but this was not substantiated at the formal inquiries conducted. Given the increase in body mass that often accompanies supplementation, it is possible that athletes who must reduce body mass acutely to qualify for a particular weight category might face particular problems. It is not unusual in some sports for body mass to be reduced by as much as 10% in the few days before competition: if the mass loss necessary to make the qualifying weight is 1–2 kg more than anticipated, the measures required to achieve the target mass will be unusually severe and may provoke serious and potentially fatal complications related to dehydration and hyperthermia.

It is usually recommended that athletes take 20 g creatine $\cdot$ day^{-1} for 4–5 days (a loading dose) followed by 1–2 g $\cdot$ day^{-1} (maintenance dose). The muscle may be saturated with creatine when a dose as small as 10 g $\cdot$ day^{-1} is consumed for 3–4 days if this is taken together with sufficient carbohydrate to stimulate a marked elevation in circulating insulin. Many athletes, however, work on the principle that more is better and may greatly exceed these amounts. Even with very large doses, however, the possibility of adverse effects is remote. Creatine is a small water-soluble molecule easily cleared by the kidney, and the additional nitrogen load resulting from supplementation is small. The same concerns about renal damage have been raised in the context of protein supplementation among strength athletes and bodybuilders: these athletes may consume up to 3–4 g protein $\cdot$ kg^{-1} BM $\cdot$ day^{-1} over very long periods (Burke and Inge, 1994), but there is no evidence that the theoretical problems of clearance of the extra solute load are real.

Although there is no reason to suppose that there are any risks to health associated with the long-term use of high doses of creatine, the studies quoted above that have used high doses (in the order of 20–30 g $\cdot$ day^{-1}) have been of relatively short duration (5–14 days), and long-term safety studies have not been performed. Studies are currently under way to determine some of the effects of long-term creatine supplementation; their results will become available in due course. This leaves the ethical question of whether the use of creatine should be disallowed on the grounds of its ergogenic effect, as is the case with other normal dietary components such as caffeine. As more information emerges, this issue will be resolved and the governing bodies of sport will make a decision.

Carnitine

Depletion of intramuscular glycogen stores is one of the main factors involved in the fatigue that accompanies prolonged exercise. A recent review of published work in this area is provided by Coyle (1997). The importance of carbohydrate as a fuel for the working muscles is confirmed by the close relationship between the pre-exercise glycogen concentration and the length of time exercise can be sustained. Further evidence comes from studies which showed that increasing the combustion of fat during prolonged exercise, and thus sparing the limited carbohydrate stores, can improve endurance capacity. Increasing fatty acid mobilization by heparin administration after ingestion of a high fat meal or by caffeine ingestion has been shown to be effective in improving performance. The former method, however, is not acceptable in sport.

The possible effects of carnitine supplementation on fatty acid metabolism are described above. In a review of studies that examined the effects of carnitine supplementation on exercise performance, Spriet (1997) concluded that their findings did not generally support an ergogenic effect of carnitine. It must be concluded that, although there is a theoretical basis for an ergogenic effect of carnitine on performance of both high-intensity and prolonged exercise, this is not supported by the experimental evidence. Supplementation of the diet with carnitine is unlikely to be beneficial for athletes. Spriet also cautioned against the use of racemic mixtures of L- and D-carnitine, as these may result in depletion of L-carnitine.

Promoting immune function and resistance to illness and infection

Exercise, nutrition and immune function are covered in detail elsewhere in this issue (Gleeson *et al.*, 2004) and will be discussed only briefly here in relation to supplement use. Modest amounts of regular exercise are generally associated with an increased sensation of physical well-being and a decreased risk of upper respiratory tract infections (URTI) (Nieman *et al.*, 1993, 1998). The consequences of minor URTI symptoms are usually minimal, but any injury or illness that interrupts training or prevents participation in competition can have a devastating effect on an athlete. Several recent epidemiological surveys have suggested that athletes in intensive training or competing in extreme endurance events are more susceptible to minor opportunistic infections than sedentary individuals (Nieman, 1997; Peters-Futre, 1997; Shephard and Shek, 1997). It has been suggested that severe exercise results in a temporary reduction in the body's ability to respond to a challenge to its immune system and that an inflammatory response similar to that which occurs with sepsis and trauma is invoked (Nieman, 1997). On this basis, a wide range of nutritional supplements is promoted for use by athletes (Table 1). For most of these supplements, there is little evidence of efficacy from properly controlled trials in humans. For many, there is some evidence of some anti-bacterial or immune stimulating effect *in vitro*, but this is far removed from evidence to support their use in athletes.

In view of the role of glutamine as a fuel for the cells of the immune system, the fall in circulating glutamine that occurs in response to prolonged exercise has been proposed as a mechanism that compromises the ability to respond to infection (Newsholme, 1994). Other studies have shown that athletes suffering

Table 1. Supplements sold as immune system stimulants

Antioxidants	*Echinacea*	Pycnogenol
Astragalus	Ginseng	Selenium
Bee pollen	Glutamine	*Spirulina*
Chlorella	Hydroxymethylbutyrate	Vitamin C
Co-enzyme Q10	Inosine	Zinc
Cordyceps	Multivitamins	

from chronic fatigue symptoms attributed to overtraining also have low circulating glutamine concentrations (Rowbottom *et al.*, 1995). At present, the limited information on glutamine supplementation provides no clear pattern of results. Studies by Newsholme and colleagues suggest a beneficial effect of glutamine supplementation on resistance to infection after endurance exercise (Castell *et al.*, 1996; Castell and Newsholme, 1997), although a positive effect was not always seen (Castell *et al.*, 1997). In the rat, prolonged treadmill running has been shown to reduce the plasma glutamine concentration after exercise and to reduce the proliferative response of leucocytes to a mitogen challenge (Moriguchi *et al.*, 1995); in contrast, animals fed a glutamine-supplemented diet for 3 weeks before exercise maintained their plasma glutamine concentration and showed a higher response to mitogens than the control group. A similar study carried out with humans found no beneficial effect of acute glutamine supplementation on these same parameters (Rohde *et al.*, 1998). Although this hypothesis is undoubtedly attractive, a clear link between hard exercise, compromised immune function and susceptibility to infection has not been established. Nonetheless, glutamine supplementation for athletes is being promoted and supplements are widely available in sports nutrition outlets.

Zinc is commonly believed to be effective in protecting against the common cold and other infectious illnesses. Since 1984, 11 studies of zinc for treatment of the common cold have been published in reputable medical journals. Of these, five found that zinc had beneficial effects and six did not, so the picture is unclear. The study that has drawn the most attention was a 1996 report from the Cleveland Clinic (Mossad *et al.*, 1996). Participants who started taking zinc lozenges within 24 h of the onset of symptoms were free of cold symptoms on average by about $4\frac{1}{2}$ days. Those who took a placebo had symptoms for $7\frac{1}{2}$ days. Twenty percent of zinc-takers reported nausea, as opposed to only 4% of those taking the placebo. A subsequent study involving children did not confirm these results (Macknin *et al.*, 1998) and a later review by the same authors concluded that further research is necessary before the use of zinc supplements can be recommended (Macknin, 1999). There is no evidence that taking zinc prevents anyone from catching a cold, although there may be benefits by reducing the severity and duration of symptoms. However, it would appear that supplementary zinc must be taken within 24 h of the onset of symptoms to have any benefit. This effectively means continuous supplementation, and side-effects include nausea and bad taste reactions. Long-term high doses of zinc are probably not a good idea, as they lower high-density lipoprotein cholesterol, suppress immune system function and interfere with the absorption of copper, resulting in microcytic anaemia. It has been suggested that when zinc is taken in lozenge form, it may act locally on the upper respiratory tract.

Preparations made from various plants and plant parts of the genus *Echinacea* constituted the top-selling herbal medicine in health food stores in the USA over the last 5 years and it is also popular in Europe. *Echinacea* is promoted for preventing and treating the common cold, flu and upper respiratory tract infections. It is also claimed to increase general immune system function and is used to treat vaginal candidiasis. The clinical literature tends to provide some support for its use in the treatment for symptoms of colds, flu and URTI. Recent studies do not support its use to prevent URTI. Melchart *et al.* (2000) reviewed the available literature and identified 16 trials with a total of 3396 participants that investigated the effects of preparations containing *Echinacea* extracts. The methodological quality of the trials was assessed and deemed insufficient to perform a quantitative meta-analysis. However, the authors concluded that existing controlled clinical trials indicated that preparations containing the juice or extracts of *Echinacea* can have a positive effect. In the most recent literature review of clinical trials conducted on various *Echinacea* preparations for prevention or treatment of URTI, Barrett (2003) concluded that 'while there is a great deal of moderately good-quality scientific data regarding *E. purpurea*, effectiveness in treating illness or in enhancing human health has not yet been proven beyond a reasonable doubt'. In both of these reviews, the authors emphasized that the highest quality trials suggest that early dosing of sufficient doses is important. As with all herbal supplements, there must be concerns about possible adverse effects in some individuals and the use of *Echinacea* is not free from risk.

Antioxidant nutrients

It has long been common practice for athletes to take vitamin supplements, usually without any thought as to the vitamin status of the individual concerned. There has been much interest recently among athletes in vitamins C and E, which have been shown to have antioxidant properties, and which may be involved in protecting cells, especially muscle cells, from the harmful effects of the highly reactive free radicals that are produced when the rate of oxygen consumption is increased during exercise (Kanter, 1995). Many studies have shown that unaccustomed exercise, particularly if it involves eccentric exercise in which the muscle is forcibly lengthened as it is activated, results in damage to the muscle structure and post-exercise soreness. Because it normally peaks 1–3 days after exercise, this is often referred to as delayed-onset muscle soreness. It is believed that free radicals, highly reactive chemical species, may be involved in the damage that occurs to muscle membranes. Alleviating or avoiding these symptoms would allow a greater training load to be sustained. An increased generation of free radicals is also associated with damage to cellular DNA and to a variety of lipids and proteins. If the post-exercise damage can be reduced by an increased intake of antioxidants, then recovery after training and competition may be more rapid and more complete. The evidence for this at present suggests a possible role but is not conclusive. Even the suggestion, however, is enough to convince many athletes to take supplements of these vitamins 'just in case'.

The source of the free radicals generated during exercise seems to be primarily related to the increased oxygen use within the mitochondria (McCord, 1979). This suggests that the extent of free radical generation will be directly proportional to the intensity and duration of exercise. Infiltration of damaged muscle by leucocytes may also account for some of the elevation in free radicals that is observed after exercise as these cells generate free radicals as part of their cytotoxic defence mechanisms (Smith *et al.*, 1989). A variety of other mechanisms that may promote free radical generation has been described (Kanter, 1995).

Free radicals have been implicated in several disease processes, including cardiovascular disease, diabetes and some forms of cancer, as well as in the ageing process. The body has a number of endogenous defence mechanisms that effectively neutralize free radicals before they cause tissue damage: important enzymes are superoxide dismutase, glutathione peroxidase and catalase. Several nutritional antioxidants also play important roles. Nutritional antioxidants include vitamins A, C and E. Other dietary components, including selenium, which has a structural role in glutathione peroxidase, and ubiquinone (or co-enzyme Q10) may also play important roles but are less well researched. Copper, zinc and manganese are structural components of superoxide dismutase and iron is a co-factor for catalase.

Several studies have examined the effects of antioxidant supplementation on indices of free radical-induced muscle damage in exercise, and there is some evidence of a protective effect of supplementation; for reviews of these studies, see Kanter (1995) and Dekkers *et al.* (1996). The evidence appears to suggest that there may be a reduction in the signs of muscle damage after supplementation, but there is no evidence for any beneficial effect on performance. There are concerns about possible adverse effects of supplementation, as several of these nutrients can also function as pro-oxidants. Toxic effects of megadose supplementation are unlikely, but there are concerns about the possible consequences of the long-term use of megadoses of single antioxidants. One study has reported increased exercise muscle damage after supplementation with ubiquinone (Malm *et al.*, 1996), and it is well recognized that many antioxidant nutrients can function as pro-oxidants at high doses.

Regular training increases the effectiveness of the endogenous antioxidant mechanisms so that even extreme exercise (e.g. long-distance triathlon) may not cause any indications of oxidative damage in well-trained athletes (Margaritis *et al.*, 1997). In contrast, short periods of modest exercise (8 weeks of training, 3 sessions of 35 min per week) do not result in any signs of increased capacity to neutralize free radicals (Tiidus *et al.*, 1996). It is not clear from this whether individuals engaged in regular exercise have an increased requirement for exogenous antioxidants.

In conclusion, there is little evidence to support the suggestion that supplementation with antioxidant nutrients can improve exercise performance, but there is a growing body of evidence to suggest that supplementation may reduce the extent of exercise-induced oxidative damage to tissues. If this is indeed the case, it may be that the athlete undertaking a strenuous training programme may benefit in the long term by being able to sustain a higher training load. There is also evidence, however, that prolonged exposure to training increases the effectiveness of the endogenous antioxidant mechanisms, and it may be that supplementation is unnecessary (Margaritis *et al.*, 1997).

Promoting joint health

Many products are sold with the aim of promoting joint health and reducing the wear and tear caused by overuse, ageing and inflammatory conditions, including arthritis. Some of the products sold are listed in Table 2. An extensive range of herbs, botanicals, and so on are also sold, including turmeric, *Boswellia serrata*, cayenne pepper, ashwagandha, autumn crocus, meadowsweet, stinging nettle, willow bark (*Salix*) and devil's claw. Animal extracts, including green-lipped mussel and sea cucumber, are also promoted.

The cartilage in joints is made up of proteoglycans (protein molecules to which are bound various complex sugars) and the protein collagen. Chondroitin, one of the main glycosaminoglycans, is a long-chain molecule consisting of many molecules of two components: galactosamine and glucuronic acid. Commercial preparations are extracted from the cartilaginous tissues of animals. Glucosamine is a carbohydrate–amino compound that is produced from the chitin that forms the main structural element of sea shells. Both compounds are reported to stimulate the formation of components of cartilage when given orally to humans.

There is now a considerable amount of information from clinical trials involving patients with osteoarthritis to show that regular (once or twice per day) long-term (about 2–6 months) treatment with glucosamine and chondroitin sulphate can reduce the severity of subjective symptoms and prevent progression of the disease (Fillmore *et al.*, 1999). A meta-analysis of published studies concluded that 'some degree of efficacy appears probable for these preparations' but did express cautions about the quality of the available data (McAlindon *et al.*, 2000). A recent report (Braham *et al.*, 2003) of the effects of 12 weeks of supplementation in individuals with knee pain showed similar improvements

Table 2. Supplements promoted for joint health and protection against ageing and overuse

---

Antioxidants
Essential fatty acids
Vitamins: niacin (B3), pantothenate (B5), D
Minerals: boron, calcium
Proteolytic enzymes
Glucosamine
Chondroitin
Methylsulphonylmethane (MSM)
S-Adenosyl methionine (SaME)
Type 2 collagen
Hyaluronic acid
Soy isoflavones

---

in clinical and functional tests in the treatment and placebo groups, but 88% of the treatment group reported some improvement in knee pain compared with only 17% in the placebo group. At present, there is no evidence of a benefit for athletes with joint pain, but there seem to have been no properly controlled trials in athletes. One study of US military special operations personnel with knee and back pain showed subjective improvements after treatment but no effect on tests of running performance (Leffler *et al.*, 1999). Nonetheless, subjective relief alone has some value and this possible benefit cannot be ignored. There seems to have been little discussion of possible adverse effects of supplementation, but the widespread use of these products means that any problems should have become apparent.

Central nervous system effects

The list of compounds prohibited for use by athletes includes stimulants, and there is a long history of stimulant use in sport. In some cases, fatalities have resulted from the use of amphetamines, sympathomimetics and other stimulant compounds. Some of these agents (including, for example, cocaine) are more commonly used as social drugs rather than for performance enhancement, while others are commonly found in low doses in cough medicines and herbal tonics.

Caffeine

Caffeine occupies a unique place in that it is consumed in a wide range of foods and beverages and is prohibited in competition above a urinary threshold value but its use is not monitored in out-of-competition testing. Caffeine has effects on the central nervous system and on adipose tissue and skeletal muscle that give reason to believe that it may influence exercise performance. Early studies on the effects of caffeine on endurance performance focused on its role in the mobilization of free fatty acids from adipose tissue to increase fat supply to the muscle, which, in turn, can increase fat oxidation, spare glycogen and thus extend exercise time. Caffeine ingestion before exercise to exhaustion at 80% $\dot{V}O_{2max}$ increased exercise time from 75 min on the placebo trial to 96 min on the caffeine trial (Costill *et al.*, 1978). A positive effect was also observed on the total amount of work achieved in a fixed 2-h exercise test. In this and other studies, caffeine was shown to increase circulating free fatty acids, increase fat oxidation and spare muscle glycogen during prolonged exercise (see Spriet, 1995, for a review of these studies). The consistency and clarity of these findings led to the widespread popularity of caffeine consumption (usually in the form of coffee) before marathon running, although caffeine in much higher doses had long been used, especially in professional cycling. It is also important to note that coffee may not produce an ergogenic effect in circumstances where caffeine is effective, even though the same plasma caffeine concentration results (Graham *et al.*, 1998).

Growing evidence of a positive effect of caffeine on performance in the absence of any glycogen sparing effect, and of effects on high-intensity exercise where glycogen availability is not a limiting factor, has stimulated the search for alternative mechanisms of action. There is evidence for a number of effects of caffeine directly on skeletal muscle. It may affect the activity of Na/K ATPase and the intracellular localization and binding of calcium, it can cause an elevation in intracellular cyclic AMP as a result of inhibition of the action of phosphodiesterase, and it may have direct effects on a number of enzymes, including glycogen phosphorylase (Spriet, 1997; Graham, 2001). Whether all these effects can occur at the tissue concentrations of caffeine that occur after ingestion of moderate doses of caffeine remains unclear. Effects on the central nervous system, either in modifying the perception of effort or affecting the higher motor centres, have been proposed, but in the absence of evidence this remains speculation.

There have been several recent and comprehensive reviews of the effects of caffeine on exercise performance, and a detailed review of the literature will not be attempted here (Spriet, 1997; Graham, 2001). Several studies have reported beneficial effects of caffeine ingestion on a variety of laboratory tests of endurance performance. An increased time to exhaustion has been observed in a number of tests, but performance in simulated race conditions, where a fixed amount of work has to be done in the shortest possible time, is also improved. There appears to be no effect on maximal oxygen uptake. More recent studies have focused on exercise of shorter duration, and a number of studies have shown beneficial effects on performances lasting only a few (about 1–6) minutes; there is less information on performance in sprint tasks or on resistance exercise, but the available evidence does support performance-enhancing effects, although there is no effect on muscle strength (Graham, 2001).

It is clear from the published studies that positive effects of caffeine can be obtained in a variety of exercise conditions with caffeine doses of 3 mg $\cdot$ kg^{-1} or less. The reasons for this variability are not altogether clear, but, perhaps surprisingly, they do not appear to be related to the habitual amount of caffeine consumption.

Caffeine has a number of unwanted side-effects that may limit its use in some sports or by sensitive individuals: these effects include insomnia, headache, gastrointestinal irritation and bleeding, and a stimulation of diuresis. There are also some suggestions that high caffeine intakes may be a risk factor for bladder cancer. This is unlikely to be modified by occasional use of modest doses before competition, but the athlete who may contemplate using high doses of caffeine before training on a daily basis should consider this. With the very high doses sometimes used by athletes, noticeable muscle tremor and impairment of coordination have been noted (Spriet, 1995).

The diuretic action of caffeine is often stressed, especially when dehydration is a major issue. This affects in particular competitions held in hot, humid climates where the risk of dehydration is high, and is more important for endurance athletes for whom dehydration has a greater negative effect on performance. Athletes competing in these conditions are advised to increase their intake of fluid, but are usually also advised to avoid tea and coffee because of their diuretic effect. It would appear, however, that this effect is small for those habituated to caffeine use (Wemple *et al.*, 1997) and the negative effects caused by the symptoms of caffeine withdrawal may be more damaging.

Until January 2004, an athlete found to have a urine caffeine concentration of more than 12 mg·l^{-1} was deemed to be guilty of a doping offence and was liable to suspension from competition. It is clear from this that caffeine is considered by the International Olympic Committee to be a drug, but an outright ban on its use is impractical and manifestly unfair to those who normally drink tea and coffee. It is equally clear, however, that the amount of coffee that must be drunk to exceed the permitted limit (about six cups of strong coffee within about 1 h) is such that it is unlikely that this would normally be achieved. In addition, in endurance events, a urine sample taken after the event would probably not register a positive test, even if large amounts had been consumed before the start.

It is also clear that beneficial effects on performance can be achieved with caffeine doses that are less than those that would result in the old IOC urine threshold concentration of 12 mg·l^{-1} being exceeded, so athletes may feel justified in their view that using these amounts is acceptable. It is difficult, but not impossible, to achieve an effective intake from drinks such as tea or coffee, but there are various products on the market that contain significant amounts of caffeine (Table 3). Caffeine tablets, commonly used by overworked students studying for examinations, are also commonly used, and these can easily lead to an intake that exceeds the permissible limit. These concerns resulted in the decision by the World Anti-Doping Agency to remove caffeine from the list of prohibited substances with effect from January 2004.

Contamination of dietary supplements

The Dietary Supplements Health and Education Act 1994 (DSHEA) passed by US Congress has meant that nutritional supplements that do not claim to

Table 3. Caffeine content of some commonly used beverages when prepared and consumed in standard amounts

Beverage	Caffeine content (mg)
Tea	15–50
Instant coffee	50–70
Filter coffee	60–120
Hot chocolate	8–15
Cola	20–50

Note: Doses of as little as 2–3 mg·kg^{-1} BM can result in performance enhancement.

diagnose, treat, prevent or cure disease are not subject to regulation by the Food and Drug Administration (FDA). From this it follows that there is no requirement to prove claimed benefits, no requirement to show safety with acute or chronic administration, no quality assurance and liberal labelling requirements. Product recalls by the FDA because of inadequate content include a folic acid product with 34% of the stated dose (FDA, 2003). They have also recently recalled products containing excessive doses of vitamins A, D, B6 and selenium because of potentially toxic effects (FDA, 2003). Some products have been shown to contain impurities (lead, broken glass, animal faeces, etc.) because of poor manufacturing practice (FDA, 2003). Some products do not contain the expensive ingredients listed on the label but only inexpensive materials. There is no way for athletes to know what is in any of these products.

A paper from the IOC laboratory in Cologne reported the results of an analysis carried out on legitimate dietary supplements, none of which declared on the label that they contained steroids, none of which would reasonably be expected to contain prohibited compounds, and none of which gave any warning to athletes that problems might result from their use. Nandrolone, testosterone and other steroids were identified in these supplements: when they were fed to healthy volunteers, they resulted in urinary norandrosterone concentrations of up to 360 ng·ml^{-1} (the threshold for a positive test is 2 ng·ml^{-1} for men and 5 ng·ml^{-1} for women). The supplements tested were chrysin, tribulus terrestris and guarana.

The Cologne laboratory followed this up with a much bigger survey. In total, 634 different product samples were purchased from 13 countries and were analysed for the presence of steroid hormones and their precursors. Altogether, 94 supplements (14.8% of the total) were shown definitely to contain prohibited substances, and for another 10% the analysis was not conclusive but steroids may have been present. That is close to a 1 in 4 risk! Substantial numbers of positive tests were obtained from products bought in The Netherlands (26%), the USA (19%), UK (19%) and elsewhere. The names of the prohibited supplements have not been published, but they included vitamins and minerals, protein and amino acid supplements, creatine and many others. Further details of this study can be found on the website of the Cologne laboratory (www.dopinginfo.de).

The IOC-accredited laboratory in Vienna has repeated the Cologne study, although with a smaller number ($n = 57$) of supplements. They found that 12 of these (22%) contained prohibited steroids. Unlike the German results, the identities of the companies and the products have been published on the Internet, and can also be found on the Cologne website at the address above.

The presence of these various anabolic androgenic steroids is commonly assumed to be the result of inadvertent contamination in the manufacturing or distribution process, as the contamination is generally minimal and highly variable between and within batches. Events took a more sinister turn in 2002, however, when the Vienna laboratory found one of the 'hard' anabolic steroids (methanedieneone, commonly known as Dianabol) in three supplements that were bought in England (Gmeiner, 2002). This drug was present in high amounts, enough to have an anabolic effect, but also enough to produce serious side-effects. These results were confirmed by the Cologne laboratory (Geyer *et al.*, 2002) and the presence of this steroid has been described as a 'deliberate and criminal act'.

More recent results come from the analysis of 110 supplements advertised as having tonic or stimulant properties and bought from different international markets: analysis of these samples showed that a significant proportion of products contained either caffeine (14 samples) or ephedrine (2 samples), even though these were not listed on the label (Parr *et al.*, in press). It is not immediately obvious that this contamination can be accidental. Athletes using these products may be liable to sanctions if a positive doping test results.

The picture has not changed greatly as a result of the availability of this information, although proposed changes in legislation might make the supplement industry more accountable than they are at present. The principle of strict liability still applies, so athletes have to be extremely careful.

Costs and benefits of supplement use

Supplements for use in sport with the aim of improving performance should meet certain criteria, although the considerations will not be the same for all athletes. Supplements used by athletes should have demonstrated effectiveness in laboratory and field conditions. They should have a well-identified and plausible mechanism of action based on what is known of metabolism and of the factors that limit performance. They should be free of harmful side-effects and not pose any health risk, and they should be free of any risk of an adverse drug test.

A full analysis of the costs and benefits cannot be completed for most supplements as several parts of the equation are unknown. The risks of falling foul of the drug testing rules cannot be quantified but they are nonetheless very real. The sensible athlete will want to see positive reasons for using any supplement.

Conclusions

Supplement use is widespread in sport, even though most supplements used are probably ineffective. Athletes who take supplements should only do so after carrying out a careful cost–benefit analysis. Although these supplements are mostly benign, this is not always the case. Routine iron supplementation, for example, can do more harm than good, and the risk of iron toxicity is very real. Athletes are therefore cautioned against the indiscriminate use of dietary supplements. Supplement use can have a role when food intake or food choice is restricted, or as a short-term remedy where a deficiency syndrome has been shown to exist. Supplement use does not compensate for poor food choices. For a few supplements, the balance of evidence supports a beneficial effect on some types of performance; these supplements include creatine, caffeine and bicarbonate. There is no evidence that androstenedione and similar pro-hormones are anabolic agents, and these supplements may pose serious health risks. The risk of a positive drugs test resulting from the use of sports supplements contaminated with prohibited compounds is also very real. The evidence for a performance benefit must be very strong to outweigh the well-established risks.

References

1 Antonio, J. and Stout, J.R. (2001). *Sports Supplements*. Philadelphia, PA: Lippincott Williams & Wilkins.

2 Ballantyne, C.S., Phillips, S.M., MacDonald, J.R., Tarnopolsky, M.A. and MacDougall, J.D. (2000). The acute effects of androstenedione supplementation in healthy young males. *Canadian Journal of Applied Physiology*, **25**, 68–78.

3 Barrett, B. (2003). Medicinal properties of *Echinacea*: a critical review. *Phytomedicine* **10**, 66–86.

4 Barnett, C., Costill, D.L., Vukovich, M.D., Cole, K.J., Goodpaster, B.H., Trappe, S.W. and Fink, W.J. (1994). Effect of L-carnitine supplementation on muscle and blood carnitine content and lactate accumulation during high-intensity sprint cycling. *International Journal of Sport Nutrition*, **4**, 280–288.

5 Bent, S., Tiedt, T.N., Odden, M.C. and Shlipak, M.G. (2003). The relative safety of ephedra compared with other herbal products. *Annals of Internal Medicine*, **138**, 468–471.

6 Bird, S.R., Wiles, J. and Robbins, J. (1995). The effect of sodium bicarbonate ingestion on 1500-m racing time. *Journal of Sports Sciences*, **13**, 399–403.

7 Braham, R., Dawson, B. and Goodman, C. (2003). The effect of glucosamine supplementation on people experiencing regular knee pain. *British Journal of Sports Medicine*, **37**, 45–49.

8 Branch, J.D. (2003). Effects of creatine supplementation on body composition and performance: a meta-analysis. *International Journal of Sports Nutrition and Exercise Metabolism*, **13**, 198–226.

9 Broeder, C.E., Quindry, J., Brittingham, K., Panton, L., Thomson, J., Appakondu, S., Breuel, K., Byrd, R., Douglas, J., Earnest, C., Mitchell, C., Olson, M., Roy, T. and Yarlagadda, C. (2000). The Andro Project: physiological and hormonal influences of androstenedione supplementation in men 35 to 65 years old participating in a high-intensity resistance training program. *Archives of Internal Medicine*, **160**, 3093–3104.

10 Brown, G.A., Vukovich, M.D., Sharp, R.L., Reifenrath, T.A., Parsons, K.A. and King, D.S. (1999). Effect of oral dehydroepiandrosterone on serum testosterone and adaptations to resistance training. *Journal of Applied Physiology*, **87**, 2274–2283.

11 Brown, G.A, Vukovich, M.D., Martini, E.R., Kohut, M.L., Franke, W.D., Jackson, D.A. and King, D.S. (2000a). Endocrine responses to chronic androstenedione intake in 30–56 year old men. *Journal of Clinical Endocrinology and Metabolism*, **85**, 4074–4080.

12 Brown, G.A., Vukovich, M.D., Reifenrath, T.A., Uhl, N.L., Parsons, K.A., Sharp, R.L. and King, D.S. (2000b). Effects of anabolic precursors on serum testos-

terone concentrations and adaptations to resistance training in young men. *International Journal of Sport Nutrition and Exercise Metabolism*, **10**, 340–359.

13 Brown, G.A., Vukovich, M.D., Martini, E.R., Kohut, M.L., Franke, W.D., Jackson, D.A. and King, D.S. (2001a). Endocrine and lipid responses to chronic androstenediol-herbal supplementation in 30–58 year old men. *Journal of the American College of Nutrition*, **20**, 520–528.

14 Brown, G.A., Vukovich, M.D., Martini, E.R., Kohut, M.L., Franke, W.D., Jackson, D.A. and King, D.S. (2001b). Effects of androstenedione-herbal supplementation on serum sex hormone concentrations in 30–59 year old men. *International Journal of Vitamin and Nutrition Research*, **71**, 27–31.

15 Brown, G.A., Martini, E.R., Roberts, B.S., Vukovich, M.D. and King, D.S. (2002). Acute hormonal responses to sublingual androstenediol intake in young men. *Journal of Applied Physiology*, **92**, 142–146.

16 Brown, G.A., Dewey, J.C., Brunkhorst, J.A., Vukovich, M.D. and King, D.S. (in press). Changes in serum testosterone and estradiol concentrations following acute androstenedione ingestion in young women. *Hormone and Metabolic Research*.

17 Burke, L.M. and Inge, K. (1994). Protein requirements for training and 'bulking up'. In *Clinical Sports Nutrition* (edited by L.M. Burke and V. Deakin), pp. 124–150. Sydney, NSW: McGraw-Hill.

18 Castell, L.M. and Newsholme, E.A. (1997). The effects of oral glutamine supplementation on athletes after prolonged exhaustive exercise. *Nutrition*, **13**, 738–742.

19 Castell, L.M., Poortmans, J.R. and Newsholme, E.A. (1996). Does glutamine have a role in reducing infections in athletes? *European Journal of Applied Physiology*, **73**, 488–490.

20 Castell, L.M., Poortmans, J.R., Leclerq, R., Brasseur, M., Duchateau, J. and Newsholme, E.A. (1997). Some aspects of the acute phase response after a marathon race, and the effects of glutamine supplementation. *European Journal of Applied Physiology*, **75**, 47–53.

21 Catlin, D.H., Leder, B.Z., Ahrens, B., Starcevic, B., Hatton, C.K., Green, G.A. and Finkelstein, J.S. (2000). Trace contamination of over-the-counter androstenedione and positive urine test results for a nandrolone metabolite. *Journal of the American Medical Association*, **284**, 2618–2621.

22 Clarkson, P.M. and Rawson, E.S. (1999). Nutritional supplements to increase muscle mass. *Critical Reviews in Food Science and Nutrition*, **39**, 317–328.

23 Costill, D.L., Dalsky, G.P. and Fink, W.J. (1978). Effects of caffeine ingestion on metabolism and exercise performance. *Medicine and Science in Sport*, **10**, 155–158.

24 Coyle, E.F. (1997). Fuels for sport performance. In *Perspectives in Exercise Science and Sports Medicine, Vol. 10: Optimizing Sport Performance* (edited by D.R. Lamb and R. Murray), pp. 95–138. Carmel, IN: Benchmark Press.

25 Dehennin, L., Bonnaire, Y. and Plou, P. (2002). Human nutritional supplements in the horse: comparative effects of 19-norandrostenedione and 19-norandrostenediol on the 19-norsteroid profile and consequences for doping control. *Journal of Chromatography B*, **766**, 257–263.

26 Dekkers, J.C., van Doornen, L.J. and Kemper, H.C. (1996). The role of anti-oxidant vitamins and enzymes in the prevention of exercise-induced muscle damage. *Sports Medicine*, **21**, 213–238.

27 Earnest, C.P., Olson, M.A., Broeder, C.E., Breuel, K.F. and Beckham, S.G. (2000). In vivo 4-androstene-3,17-dione and 4-androstene-3 beta,17 beta-diol supplementation in young men. *European Journal of Applied Physiology*, **81**, 229–232.

28 Fawcett, J.P., Farquhar, S.J., Walker, R.J., Thou, T., Lowe, G. and Goulding, A. (1996). The effect or oral vanadyl sulphate on body composition and performance in weight-training athletes. *International Journal of Sport Nutrition*, **6**, 382–390.

29 Ferrando, A.A. and Green, N.R. (1993). The effect of boron supplementation on lean body mass, plasma testosterone levels and strength in male body builders. *International Journal of Sports Medicine*, **3**, 140–149.

30 Fillmore, C.M., Bartoli, L., Bach, R. and Park, Y. (1999). Nutrition and dietary supplements. *Physical and Medical Rehabilitation Clinics of North America*, **10**, 673–703.

31 Food and Drug Administration (2003). Current good manufacturing practice in manufacturing, packing, or holding dietary ingredients and dietary supplements. *Federal Register*, **68**(49), 12157–12263.

32 Gallagher, P.M., Carrithers, J.A., Godard, M.P., Schulze, K.E. and Trappe, S.W. (2000a). Beta-hydroxy-beta-methylbutyrate ingestion. Part I: Effects on strength and fat free mass. *Medicine and Science in Sports and Exercise*, **32**, 2109–2115.

33 Gallagher, P.M., Carrithers, J.A., Godard, M.P., Schulze, K.E. and Trappe, S.W. (2000b). Beta-hydroxy-beta-methylbutyrate ingestion. Part II: Effects on hematology, hepatic and renal function. *Medicine and Science in Sports and Exercise*, **32**, 2116–2119.

34 Geller, J. (1985). Rationale for blockade of adrenal as well as testicular androgens in the treatment of advanced prostate cancer. *Seminars in Oncology*, **12**, 28–35.

35 Geyer, H., Bredehöft, M., Mareck, U., Parr, M. and Schänzer, W. (2002). Hohe Dosen des Anabolikums Metandienon in Nahrungsergänzungsmitteln. *Deutsch Apoth Zeitung*, **142**, 29.

36 Gleeson, M., Nieman, D.C. and Pedersen, B.K. (2004). Exercise, nutrition and immune function. *Journal of Sports Sciences*, **22**, 115–125.

37 Gmeiner, G. (2002). Methandienon in Sportnahrung. *Österreichisches Journal für Sportmedizin*, **2**, 33–34.

38 Graham, T.E. (2001). Caffeine, coffee and ephedrine: impact on exercise performance and metabolism. *Canadian Journal of Applied Physiology*, **26**, S103–S119.

39 Graham, T.E., Hibbert, E. and Sathasivam, P. (1998). The metabolic and exercise endurance effects of coffee and caffeine ingestion. *Journal of Applied Physiology*, **85**, 883–889.

40 Green, A.L., Simpson, E.J., Littlewood, J.J., Macdonald, I.A. and Greenhaff, P.L. (1996a). Carbohydrate ingestion augments creatine retention during creatine feeding in humans. *Acta Physiologica Scandinavica*, **158**, 195–202.

41 Green, A.L., Hultman, E., Macdonald, I.A., Sewell, D.A. and Greenhaff, P.L. (1996b). Carbohydrate ingestion augments skeletal muscle creatine accumulation during creatine supplementation in humans. *American Journal of Physiology*, **271**, E821–E826.

42 Greenhaff, P.L. (2000). Creatine. In *Nutrition in Sport* (edited by R.J. Maughan), pp. 379–392. Oxford: Blackwell.

43 Greenhaff, P.L., Harris, R.C. and Snow, D.H. (1990). The effect of sodium bicarbonate (NaHCO3) administration upon exercise metabolism in the thoroughbred horse. *Journal of Physiology*, **420**, 69P.

44 Greenhaff, P.L., Bodin, K., Soderlund, K. and Hultman, E. (1994). Effect of oral creatine supplementation on skeletal muscle phosphocreatine resynthesis. *American Journal of Physiology*, **266**, E725–E730.

45 Harris, R.C., Soderlund, K. and Hultman, E. (1992). Elevation of creatine in resting and exercised muscle of normal subjects by creatine supplementation. *Clinical Science*, **83**, 367–374.

46 Horswill, C.A., Costill, D.L., Fink, W.J., Flynn, M.G., Kirwan, J.P., Mitchell, J.B. and Houmard, J.A. (1988). Influence of sodium bicarbonate on sprint performance: relationship to dosage. *Medicine and Science in Sports and Exercise*, **20**, 566–569.

47 Hultman, E., Soderlund, K., Timmons, J.A., Cederblad, G. and Greenhaff, P.L. (1996). Muscle creatine loading in men. *Journal of Applied Physiology*, **81**, 232–237.

48 Kanter, M. (1995). Free radicals and exercise: effects of nutritional antioxidant supplementation. *Exercise and Sport Science Reviews*, **23**, 375–397.

49 Kicman, A.T., Bassindale, T., Cowan, D.A., Dale, S., Hutt, A.J. and Leeds, A.R. (2003). Effect of androstenedione ingestion on plasma testosterone in young women: a dietary supplement with potential health risks. *Clinical Chemistry*, **49**, 167–169.

50 King, D.S., Sharp, R.J. and Vukovich, M.D. (1999). Effect of oral androstenedione on serum testosterone and adaptations to resistance training in young men. *Journal of the American Medical Association*, **281**, 2020–2028.

51 Knitter, A.E., Panton, L., Rathmacher, J.A., Petersen, A. and Sharp, R. (2000). Effects of beta-hydroxy-beta-methylbutyrate on muscle damage after a prolonged run. *Journal of Applied Physiology*, **89**, 1340–1344.

52 Kreider, R.B., Ferreira, M., Wilson, M. and Almada, A.L. (1999). Effects of calcium beta-hydroxy-beta-methylbutyrate (HMB) supplementation during resistance-training on markers of catabolism, body composition and strength. *International Journal of Sports Medicine*, **20**, 503–509.

53 Leder, B.Z., Longcope, C., Catlin, D.H., Ahrens, B., Schoenfeld, D.A. and Finkelstein, J.S. (2000). Oral androstenedione administration and serum testosterone concentrations in young men. *Journal of the American Medical Association*, **283**, 79–82.

54 Leffler, C.T., Philippi, A.F., Keffler, S.G., Mosure, J.C. and Kim, P.D. (1999). Glucosamine, chondroitin, and manganese ascorbate for degenerative joint disease of the knee or low back: a randomized, double-blind, placebo-controlled pilot study. *Military Medicine*, **164**, 85–91.

55 Macknin, M.L. (1999). Zinc lozenges for the common cold. *Cleveland Clinic Journal of Medicine*, **66**, 27–32.

56 Macknin, M.L., Piedmonte, M., Calendine, C., Janosky, J. and Wald, E. (1998). Zinc gluconate lozenges for treating the common cold in children: a randomized controlled trial. *Journal of the American Medical Association*, **279**, 1962–1967.

57 Malm, C., Svensson, M., Sjöberg, B., Ekblom, B. and Sjödin, B. (1996). Supplementation with ubiquinone-10 causes cellular damage during intense exercise. *Acta Physiologica Scandinavica*, **157**, 511–512.

58 Maragritis, I., Tessier, F., Richard, M.J. and Marconnet, P. (1997). No evidence of oxidative stress after a triathlon race in highly trained competitors. *International Journal of Sports Medicine*, **18**, 186–190.

59 Maughan, R.J. (1999). Nutritional ergogenic aids and exercise performance. *Nutrition Research Reviews*, **12**, 255–280.

60 McAlindon, T.E., LaValley, M.P., Gulin, J.P. and Felson, D.T. (2000). Glucosamine and chondroitin for treatment of osteoarthritis: a systematic quality assessment and meta-analysis. *Journal of the American Medical Association*, **283**, 1469–1475.

61 McCord, J.M. (1979). Superoxide, superoxide dismutase and oxygen toxicity. *Reviews in Biochemistry and Toxicology*, 1, 109–124.

62 McKenzie, D.C., Coutts, K.D., Stirling, D.R., Hoeben, H.H. and Kuzara, G. (1986). Maximal work production following two levels of artificially induced metabolic alkalosis. *Journal of Sports Sciences*, 4, 35–38.

63 McNaughton, L. (2000). Bicarbonate and citrate. In *Nutrition in Sport* (edited by R.J. Maughan), pp. 393–404. Oxford: Blackwell.

64 Melchart, D., Linde, K., Fischer, P. and Kaesmayr, J. (2000). *Echinacea* for preventing and treating the common cold. *Cochran Database Systematic Reviews*, CD000530.

65 Merimee, T.J., Rabinowitz, D. and Fineberg, S.E. (1969). Arginine-initiated release of human growth hormone: factors modifying the response in normal man. *New England Journal of Medicine*, 280, 1434–1438.

66 Millward, D.J. (2001). Protein and amino acid requirements of adults: current controversies. *Canadian Journal of Applied Physiology*, 26, S130–S140.

67 Misic, M. and Kelley, G.E. (2002). The impact of creatine supplementation on anaerobic performance: a meta-analysis. *American Journal of Medicine and Sports*, 4, 116–124.

68 Morales, A.J., Nolan, J.J., Nelson, J.C. and Yen, S.S. (1994). Effects of replacement dose of dehydroepiandrosterone in men and women of advancing age. *Journal of Clinical Endocrinology and Metabolism*, 78, 1360–1367.

69 Moriguchi, S., Miwa, H. and Kishino, Y. (1995). Glutamine supplementation prevents the decrease of mitogen response after a treadmill exercise in rats. *Journal of the Nutrition and Science of Vitamins*, 41, 115–125.

70 Mossad, S.B., Macknin, M.L., Medendorp, S.V. and Mason, P. (1996). Zinc gluconate lozenges for treating the common cold: a randomized double-blind placebo-controlled study. *Annals of Internal Medicine*, 125, 81–88.

71 Muller, D.M., Seim, H., Kiess, W., Loster, H. and Richter, T. (2002). Effects or oral L-carnitine supplementation on *in vivo* long-chain fatty acid oxidation in healthy adults. *Metabolism*, 51, 1389–1391.

72 Newsholme, E.A. (1994). Biochemical mechanisms to explain immunosuppression in well-trained and overtrained athletes. *International Journal of Sports Medicine*, 15(suppl. 3), S142–S147.

73 Nielson, F.H., Hunt, C.D., Mullen, L.M. and Hunt, J.R. (1987). Effect of dietary boron on mineral, estrogen and testosterone metabolism in post-menopausal women. *Federation of the American Societies for Experimental Biology Journal*, 1, 394–397.

74 Nieman, D.C. (1997). Exercise immunology: practical applications. *International Journal of Sports Medicine*, 18(suppl. 1), S91–S100.

75 Nieman, D.C., Henson, D.S., Gusewitch, G., Warren, B.J., Dotson, R.C., Butterworth, D.E. and Nelson-Cannarella, S.L. (1993). Physical activity and immune function in elderly women. *Medicine and Science in Sports and Exercise*, 25, 823–831.

76 Nieman, D.C., Nelson-Cannarella, S.L., Henson, D.A., Koch, A.J., Butterworth, D.E., Fagaoga, O.R. and Utter, A. (1998). Immune response to exercise training and/or energy restriction in obese women. *Medicine and Science in Sports and Exercise*, 30, 679–686.

77 Nissen, S.L. and Sharp, R.L. (2003). Effect of dietary supplements on lean mass and strength gains with resistance exercise: a meta-analysis. *Journal of Applied Physiology*, **94**, 651–659.

78 Nissen, S., Sharp, R., Ray, M., Rathmacher, J.A., Rice, D., Fuller, J.C., Jr., Connelly, A.S. and Abumrad, N. (1996). Effect of leucine metabolite beta-hydroxy-beta-methylbutyrate on muscle metabolism during resistance-exercise training. *Journal of Applied Physiology*, **81**, 2095–2110.

79 Nissen, S., Sharp, R.L., Panton, L., Vukovich, M., Trappe, S. and Fuller, J.C., Jr. (2000). Beta-hydroxy-beta-methylbutyrate (HMB) supplementation in humans is safe and may decrease cardiovascular risk factors. *Journal of Nutrition*, **130**, 1937–1945.

80 O'Connor, D.M. and Crowe, M.J. (2003). Effects of beta-hydroxy-beta-methylbutyrate and creatine monohydrate supplementation on the aerobic and anaerobic capacity of highly trained athletes. *Journal of Sports Medicine and Physical Fitness*, **43**, 64–68.

81 Paddon-Jones, D., Keech, A. and Jenkins, D. (2001). Short-term beta-hydroxy-beta-methylbutyrate supplementation does not reduce symptoms of eccentric muscle damage. *International Journal of Sport Nutrition and Exercise Metabolism*, **11**, 442–450.

82 Panton, L.B., Rathmacher, J.A., Baier, S. and Nissen, S. (2000). Nutritional supplementation of the leucine metabolite beta-hydroxy-beta-methylbutyrate (hmb) during resistance training. *Nutrition*, **16**, 734–739.

83 Parr, M.K., Geyer, H., Sigmund, G., Köhler, K. and Schänzer, W. (in press). Screening of nutritional supplements for stimulants and other drugs. In *Recent Advances in Doping Analysis*, Vol. II (edited by W. Schänzer, H. Geyer, A. Gotzmann and U. Mareck-Engelke). Köln: Sport und Buch Strauß.

84 Perko, M. (2000). Taking one for the team – coaches, athletes and dietary supplements. *American Journal of Health Studies*, **16**, 99–106.

85 Peters-Futre, E.M. (1997). Vitamin C, neutrophil function, and URTI risk in distance runners: the missing link. *Exercise Immunology Reviews*, **3**, 32–52.

86 Poortmans, J.R., Auquier, H., Renault, V., Durussel, A., Saugy, M. and Brisson, G.R. (1997). Effect of short-term creatine supplementation on renal responses in men. *European Journal of Applied Physiology*, **76**, 566–567.

87 Ransone, J., Neighbors, K., Lefavi, R. and Chromiak, J. (2003). The effect of beta-hydroxy beta-methylbutyrate on muscular strength and body composition in collegiate football players. *Journal of Strength and Conditioning Research*, **17**, 34–39.

88 Rasmussen, B.B., Volpi, E., Gore, D.C. and Wolfe, R.R. (2000). Androstenedione does not stimulate muscle protein anabolism in young healthy men. *Journal of Clinical Endocrinology and Metabolism*, **85**, 55–59.

89 Rohde, T., MacLean, D.A. and Pedersen, B.K. (1998). Effect of glutamine supplementation on changes in the immune system induced by repeated exercise. *Medicine and Science in Sports and Exercise*, **30**, 856–862.

90 Ronsen, O., Sundgot-Borgen, J. and Maehlum, S. (1999). Supplement use and nutritional habits in Norwegian elite athletes. *Scandinavian Journal of Medicine and Science in Sports*, **9**, 28–35.

91 Rowbottom, D.G., Keast, D., Goodman, C. and Morton, A.R. (1995). The haematological, biochemical and immunological profile of athletes suffering from the overtraining syndrome. *European Journal of Applied Physiology*, **70**, 502–509.

92 Schindler, A.E. and Aymar, M. (1975). Metabolism of 14C-dehydroepiandrosterone in female adipose tissue and venous blood. *Endocrinology*, **9**, 215–222.

93 Shephard, R.J. and Shek, P.N. (1997). Heavy exercise, nutrition and immune function: is there a connection? *International Journal of Sports Medicine*, **16**, 491–497.

94 Slater, G., Jenkins, D., Logan, P., Lee, H., Vukovich, M., Rathmacher, J.A. and Hahn, A.G. (2001). Beta-hydroxy-beta-methylbutyrate (HMB) supplementation does not affect changes in strength or body composition during resistance training in trained men. *International Journal of Sport Nutrition and Exercise Metabolism*, **11**, 384–396.

95 Smith, J.K., Grisham, M.B., Granger, D.N. and Korthuis, R.J. (1989). Free radical defense mechanisms and neutrophil infiltration in postischemic skeletal muscle. *American Journal of Physiology*, **256**, H789–H793.

96 Snow, D.H., Harris, R.C. and Gash, S.P. (1985). Metabolic response of equine muscle to intermittent maximal exercise. *Journal of Applied Physiology*, **58**, 1689–1697.

97 Sobal, J. and Marquart, L.F. (1994). Vitamin/mineral supplement use among athletes: a review of the literature. *International Journal of Sport Nutrition*, **4**, 320–324.

98 Spriet, L.L. (1995). Caffeine and performance. *International Journal of Sport Nutrition*, **5**, S84–S99.

99 Spriet, L.L. (1997). Ergogenic aids: recent advances and retreats. In *Optimizing Sports Performance* (edited by D.R. Lamb and D. Murray), pp. 185–238. Carmel, IN: Cooper Publishing.

100 Spriet, L.L. and Gibala, M.J. (2004) Nutritional strategies to influence adaptations to training. *Journal of Sports Sciences*, **22**, 127–141.

101 Sutton, J.R., Jones, N.L. and Toews, C.J. (1981). Effect of pH on muscle glycolysis during exercise. *Clinical Science*, **61**, 331–338.

102 Talbott, S.M. (2003). *A Guide to Understanding Dietary Supplements*. Binghampton, NY: Haworth Press.

103 Tarnopolsky, M. (2001). Protein and amino acid needs for training and bulking up. In *Clinical Sports Nutrition*, 2nd edn (edited by L. Burke and V. Deakin), pp. 90–123. Roseville, Australia: McGraw Hill.

104 Tiidus, P.M., Pushkarenko, J. and Houston, M.E. (1996). Lack of antioxidant adaptation to short-term aerobic training in human muscle. *American Journal of Physiology*, **271**, R832–R836.

105 Tipton, K.D. and Wolfe, R.R. (2004). Protein and amino acids for athletes. *Journal of Sports Scienecs*, **22**, 65–79.

106 Uralets, V.P. and Gillette, P.A. (1999). Over-the-counter anabolic steroids 4-androsten-3,17-dione; 4-androsten-3beta,17beta-diol; and 19-nor-4-androsten-3,17-dione: excretion studies in men. *Journal of Analytical Toxicology*, **23**, 357–366.

107 van Gammeren, D., Falk, D. and Antonio, J. (2002). Effects of norandrostenedione and norandrostenediol in resistance-trained men. *Nutrition*, **18**, 734–737.

108 Vierck, J.L., Icenoggle, D.L., Bucci, L. and Dodson, M.V. (2003). The effects of ergogenic compounds on myogenic satellite cells. *Medicine and Science in Sports and Exercise*, **35**, 769–776.

109 Vukovich, M. (2001). Fat reduction. In *Sports Supplements* (edited by J. Antonio and J.R. Stout), pp. 84–110. Philadelphia, PA: Lippincott Williams & Wilkins.

110 Vukovich, M.D. and Dreifort, G.D. (2001). Effect of beta-hydroxy beta-methylbutyrate on the onset of blood lactate accumulation and $\dot{V}O_2$ peak in endurance-trained cyclists. *Journal of Strength and Conditioning Research*, **15**, 491–497.

111 Vukovich, M.D., Costill, D.L. and Fink, W.J. (1994). Carnitine supplementation: effect on muscle carnitine and glycogen content during exercise. *Medicine and Science in Sports and Exercise*, **26**, 1122–1129.

112 Wallace, M.B., Lim, J., Cutler, A. and Bucci, L. (1999). Effects of dehydro-epiandrosterone *vs* androstenedione supplementation in men. *Medicine and Science in Sports and Exercise*, **31**, 1788–1792.

113 Wemple, R.D., Lamb, D.R. and McKeever, K.H. (1997). Caffeine *vs* caffeine-free sports drinks: effects on urine production at rest and during prolonged exercise. *International Journal of Sports Medicine*, **18**, 40–46.

114 Wilkes, D., Gledhill, N. and Smyth, R. (1983). Effect of acute induced metabolic alkalosis on 800-m racing time. *Medicine and Science in Sports and Exercise*, **15**, 277–280.

115 Williams, M.H., Kreider, R.B. and Branch, J.D. (1999) *Creatine: The Power Supplement*. Champaign, IL: Human Kinetics.

116 Ziegenfuss, T.N., Lemon, P.W.R., Rogers, M.R., Ross, R. and Yarasheski, K.E. (1997). Acute creatine ingestion: effects on muscle volume, anaerobic power, fluid volumes, and protein turnover. *Medicine and Science in Sports and Exercise*, **29**, S127.

9 Exercise, nutrition and immune function

MICHAEL GLEESON, DAVID C. NIEMAN
and BENTE K. PEDERSEN

Strenuous bouts of prolonged exercise and heavy training are associated with depressed immune cell function. Furthermore, inadequate or inappropriate nutrition can compound the negative influence of heavy exertion on immunocompetence. Dietary deficiencies of protein and specific micronutrients have long been associated with immune dysfunction. An adequate intake of iron, zinc and vitamins A, E, B6 and B12 is particularly important for the maintenance of immune function, but excess intakes of some micronutrients can also impair immune function and have other adverse effects on health. Immune system depression has also been associated with an excess intake of fat. To maintain immune function, athletes should eat a well-balanced diet sufficient to meet their energy requirements. An athlete exercising in a carbohydrate-depleted state experiences larger increases in circulating stress hormones and a greater perturbation of several immune function indices. Conversely, consuming 30–60 g carbohydrate $\cdot$ h^{-1} during sustained intensive exercise attenuates rises in stress hormones such as cortisol and appears to limit the degree of exercise-induced immune depression. Convincing evidence that so-called 'immune-boosting' supplements, including high doses of antioxidant vitamins, glutamine, zinc, probiotics and *Echinacea*, prevent exercise-induced immune impairment is currently lacking.

Keywords: exercise, immunity, leucocytes, macronutrients, micronutrients, training.

Immune function and the nutrition of elite athletes

The immune system protects against, recognizes, attacks and destroys elements that are foreign to the body. The immune system can be divided into two broad functions: innate (natural and non-specific) and acquired (adaptive and specific) immunity, which work together synergistically. The attempt of an infectious agent to enter the body immediately activates the innate system. This so-called 'first-line of defence' comprises three general mechanisms with the common goal of restricting the entry of microorganisms into the body: (1) physical/structural barriers (skin, epithelial linings, mucosal secretions); (2) chemical barriers (pH of bodily fluids and soluble factors such as lysozymes and complement proteins); and (3) phagocytic cells (e.g. neutrophils and monocytes/macrophages). Failure of the innate system and the resulting infection activates the acquired system, which aids recovery from infection. Monocytes or macrophages ingest, process and present foreign material (antigens) to lymphocytes. This is followed by clonal proliferation of T- and B-lymphocytes that possess receptors that recognize the antigen, engendering specificity and 'memory' that enable the immune system to mount an augmented cell-mediated and humoral response when the host is reinfected by the same pathogen. Critical to the activation and regulation of immune function is the production of cytokines, including interferons, interleukins and colony-stimulating factors. For further details of the normal immune response, see Gleeson and Bishop (1999). A fundamental characteristic of the immune system is that it involves multiple functionally different cell types, which permits a large variety of defence mechanisms. Assessing immune function status, therefore, requires a thorough methodological approach targeting a large spectrum of immune system parameters. However, currently no instruments are available to predict the cumulative effects of several small changes in immune system parameters on host resistance to infection (Keil *et al.*, 2001).

A heavy schedule of training and competition can lead to immune impairment in athletes, which is associated with an increased susceptibility to infections, particularly upper respiratory tract infections (URTI) (Peters and Bateman, 1983; Nieman *et al.*, 1990). This exercise-induced immune dysfunction seems to be mostly due to the immunosuppressive actions of stress hormones such as adrenaline and cortisol. Nutritional deficiencies can also impair immune function and there is a vast body of evidence that many infections are increased in prevalence or severity by specific nutritional deficiencies (Scrimshaw and SanGiovanni, 1997; Calder and Jackson, 2000). However, it is also true that excessive intakes of individual micronutrients (e.g. *n*-3 polyunsaturated fatty acids, iron, zinc, vitamins A and E) can impair immune function and increase the risk of infection (Chandra, 1997). As most athletes will be aware, even medically harmless infections can result in a decrement in athletic performance.

Avoiding nutrient deficiencies

The key to maintaining an effective immune system is to avoid deficiencies of the nutrients that play an essential role in immune cell triggering, interaction, differentiation or functional expression. Malnutrition decreases immune defences against invading pathogens and makes the individual more susceptible to infection (Calder and Jackson, 2000; Calder *et al.*, 2002). Infections with certain pathogens can also affect nutritional status by causing appetite suppression, malabsorption, increased nutrient requirements and increased losses of endogenous nutrients.

Protein and energy

It is well accepted that an inadequate intake of protein impairs host immunity with particularly detrimental effects on the T-cell system, resulting in an increased incidence of opportunistic infections (Chandra, 1997; Scrimshaw and SanGiovanni, 1997; Calder *et al.*, 2002). It is not surprising that protein deficiency impairs immunity because immune defences are dependent on rapid cell replication and the production of proteins with important biological activities, such as immunoglobulins, acute phase proteins and cytokines. In humans, protein-energy malnutrition has been found to depress the number of mature, fully differentiated T-lymphocytes and the *in vitro* proliferative response to mitogens, although the latter is reversible with nutritional repletion (Daly *et al.*, 1990; Reynolds *et al.*, 1990). Additionally, in protein-energy malnutrition the T-lymphocyte CD4+/CD8+ (helper/suppressor cell) ratio is markedly decreased and phagocytic cell function, cytokine production and complement formation are all impaired. Essentially, all forms of immunity have been shown to be affected by protein-energy malnutrition in humans, depending on the severity of the protein deficiency relative to energy intake. Although it is unlikely that athletes would ever reach a state of such extreme malnutrition unless dieting very severely, some impairment of host defence mechanisms is observed even in moderate protein deficiency (Daly *et al.*, 1990). Among the athletic population, individuals at most risk from protein deficiency are those undertaking a programme of food restriction to lose weight, vegetarians and athletes consuming unbalanced diets (e.g. with an excessive amount of carbohydrate at the expense of protein). Often, deficiencies in protein and energy will be accompanied by deficiencies in micronutrients. Energy-restricted diets are common in sports where leanness or low body mass is thought to confer a performance or aesthetic advantage (e.g. gymnastics, figure skating, endurance running) or is required to meet certain body weight criteria (e.g. boxing, martial arts, weightlifting, rowing). Indeed, this has led to the identification of a new subclinical eating disorder, anorexia athletica, which has been associated with an increased susceptibility to infection (Beals and Manore, 1994). Even short-term dieting can influence immune function in athletes. For example, it has been shown that a loss of 2 kg of body mass over 2 weeks adversely affects macrophage phagocytic function (Kono *et al.*, 1988).

Vitamins and minerals

Several vitamins are essential for normal immune function. Deficiencies of fat-soluble vitamins A and E and water-soluble vitamins folic acid, B6, B12 and C impair immune function and decrease the body's resistance to infection (Scrimshaw and SanGiovanni, 1997; Calder and Jackson, 2000; Calder *et al.*, 2002). Correcting existing deficiencies with specific vitamin supplements can be effective in restoring immune function to normal (Calder and Jackson, 2000).

Several minerals are known to exert modulatory effects on immune function, including zinc, iron, magnesium, manganese, selenium and copper, yet with the exception of zinc and iron, isolated deficiencies are rare. Field studies consistently associate iron deficiency with increased morbidity from infectious disease

(Sherman, 1992). Furthermore, exercise has a pronounced effect on both zinc and iron metabolism (Gleeson, 2000). Requirements for these minerals are certainly higher in athletes than sedentary individuals because of increased losses in sweat and urine. However, excesses of some minerals (particularly iron and zinc) can impair immune function and increase susceptibility to infection (Chandra, 1984; Sherman, 1992; Gleeson, 2000). Hence, supplements should be taken only as required and regular monitoring of iron status (serum ferritin and blood haemoglobin) and zinc status (erythrocyte zinc) is probably a good idea. The efficacy of zinc supplementation as a treatment for the common cold has been investigated in at least 11 studies that have been published since 1984. The findings have been equivocal and recent reviews of this topic have concluded that further research is necessary before the use of zinc supplements to treat the common cold can be recommended (Macknin, 1999; Marshall, 2000). Although there is only limited evidence that taking zinc supplements reduces the incidence of URTI (McElroy and Miller, 2002), in the studies that have reported a beneficial effect of zinc in treating the common cold (i.e. reduction of symptom duration and/or severity) it has been emphasized that zinc must be taken within 24 h of the onset of symptoms to be of any benefit. Potential problems with zinc supplements include nausea, bad taste reactions, lowering of high-density lipoprotein cholesterol, depression of some immune cell functions (e.g. neutrophil oxidative burst) and interference with the absorption of copper (Gleeson, 2000).

Eating the right amount and type of fat

Relatively little is known about the potential contribution of dietary fatty acids to the regulation of exercise-induced modification of immune function. Two groups of polyunsaturated fatty acids (PUFA) are essential to the body: the omega-6 (*n*-6) series, derived from linoleic acid, and the omega-3 (*n*-3) series, derived from linolenic acid. These fatty acids cannot be synthesized in the body and therefore must be derived from the diet. There are reports that diets rich in either of these polyunsaturated fatty acids improve the conditions of patients suffering from diseases characterized by an over-active immune system, such as rheumatoid arthritis; that is, they have anti-inflammatory effects (Calder, 1996; Calder *et al.*, 2002). It has been suggested that high intakes of arachidonic acid relative to intakes of fatty acids of the *n*-3 group may exert an undesirable influence on inflammation and immune function during and after exercise (Konig *et al.*, 1997). However, a recent study showed that *n*-3 PUFA supplementation did not influence the exercise-induced elevation of pro- or anti-inflammatory cytokines (Toft *et al.*, 2000). More research is needed on the effects of altering essential fatty acid intake on immune function after exercise and during periods of heavy training.

A recent study that investigated the effects of endurance training for 7 weeks on a carbohydrate-rich diet (65% of dietary energy from carbohydrate) or a fat-rich diet (62% of dietary energy from fat) concluded that diet composition during training may influence natural immunity since natural killer (NK) cell activity increased on the carbohydrate-rich diet compared with the fat-rich diet in response to training (Pedersen *et al.*, 2000). The results of this study suggest that a fat-rich diet is detrimental to immune function compared with a carbohydrate-rich diet, but do not clarify whether this effect is due to a lack of dietary carbohydrate or an excess of a specific dietary fat component.

Are megadoses of vitamins needed?

Moderately increasing the intake of some vitamins (notably vitamins A and E) above the amounts normally recommended may enhance immune function in the very young (Coutsoudis *et al.*, 1992) and the elderly (Meydani *et al.*, 1990), but is probably not effective in young adults. Consuming megadoses of individual vitamins, which appears to be a common practice in athletes, can impair immune function and have other toxic effects (Calder *et al.*, 2002; Food Standards Agency, 2003). For example, 300 mg of vitamin E given daily to men (the UK reference nutrient intake for men is $4 \text{ mg} \cdot \text{day}^{-1}$; COMA, 1991) for 3 weeks significantly depressed phagocyte function and lymphocyte proliferation (Prasad, 1980). In a recent exercise study, supplementation of athletes with $600 \text{ mg} \cdot \text{day}^{-1}$ vitamin E for 2 months before an Ironman triathlon event resulted in elevated oxidative stress and inflammatory cytokine responses during the triathlon compared with placebo (D.C. Nieman *et al.*, unpublished). In elderly people ($n = 652$), a daily 200-mg vitamin E supplement increased the severity of infections, including total illness duration, duration of fever and restriction of physical activity (Graat *et al.*, 2002). Recently, vitamin E supplementation ($600 \text{ mg} \cdot \text{day}^{-1}$) in patients with ischaemic heart disease has been demonstrated to have either no effect on all-cause mortality (MRC/BHF Heart Protection Study, 2002) or to increase the number of cases who died compared with placebo (Waters *et al.*, 2002). Megadoses of vitamin A may impair the inflammatory response and complement formation as well as having other pathological effects, including causing an increased risk of foetal abnormalities when consumed by pregnant women (Food Standards Agency, 2003).

Vitamins with antioxidant properties including vitamins A, C, E and β-carotene (provitamin A) may be required in increased quantities in athletes to inactivate the products of exercise-induced lipid peroxidation (Packer, 1997). However, there are no convincing data to demonstrate an effect of nutritional antioxidants on muscle damage or delayed-onset muscle soreness. Increased oxygen free-radical formation that accompanies the dramatic rise in oxidative metabolism during exercise could potentially inhibit immune responses (Peters, 1997; Petersen and Pedersen, 2002). Reactive oxygen species inhibit locomotory and bactericidal activity of neutrophils, reduce the proliferation of T- and B-lymphocytes and inhibit natural killer cell cytotoxic activity. Sustained endurance training appears to be associated with an adaptive up-regulation of the antioxidant defence system (Duthie *et al.*, 1996). However, such adaptations may be insufficient to protect athletes who train extensively (Clarkson, 1992; Packer, 1997).

Vitamin C (ascorbic acid) is found in high concentrations in leucocytes and has been implicated in a variety of anti-infective functions, including promotion of T-lymphocyte proliferation, prevention of corticosteroid-induced suppression of neutrophil activity and inhibition of virus replication (Peters, 2000). It is also a major water-soluble antioxidant that is effective as a scavenger of reactive oxygen species in both intracellular and extracellular fluids. Vitamin C is also required for the regeneration of the reduced form of the lipid-soluble antioxidant, vitamin E. The UK reference nutrient intake (RNI) for vitamin C is 40 mg·day^{-1} (COMA, 1991).

In a study by Peters *et al.* (1993), using a double-blind placebo research design, it was determined that daily supplementation of 600 mg (15 times the RNI) of vitamin C for 3 weeks before a 90-km ultramarathon reduced the incidence of symptoms of URTI (68% compared with 33% in age- and sex-matched control runners) in the 2 weeks after the race. In a follow-up study, Peters *et al.* (1996) randomly divided participants in a 90-km ultramarathon ($n = 178$) and their matched controls ($n = 162$) into four treatment groups receiving one of 500 mg vitamin C alone, 500 mg vitamin C plus 400 IU vitamin E (1 IU is equivalent to 0.67 mg), 300 mg vitamin C plus 300 IU vitamin E plus 18 mg β-carotene, or placebo. As runners were requested to continue with their usual habits in terms of dietary intake and the use of nutritional supplements, total vitamin C intake of the four groups was 1004, 893, 665 and 585 mg·day^{-1}, respectively. The study confirmed previous findings of a lower incidence of symptoms of URTI in those runners with the highest mean daily intake of vitamin C and also indicated that the combination of water-soluble and fat-soluble antioxidants was not more successful in attenuating the post-exercise infection risk than vitamin C alone. This study certainly provides some support for the notion that megadoses of vitamin C reduce URTI risk in endurance athletes. However, some similar studies have not been able to replicate these findings: Himmelstein *et al.* (1998), for example, reported no difference in URTI incidence among 44 marathon runners and 48 sedentary individuals randomly assigned to a 2-month regimen of 1000 mg·day^{-1} vitamin C or placebo. Furthermore, a subsequent double-blind, placebo-controlled study found no effect of vitamin C supplementation (1000 mg·day^{-1} for 8 days) on the immune response to 2.5 h running (Nieman *et al.*, 1997a), although a larger dose of vitamin C supplementation (1500 mg·day^{-1} for 7 days before the race and on race day) did reduce the cortisol and cytokine response to a 90-km ultramarathon race (Nieman *et al.*, 2000). However, in the latter study, no difference in URTI incidence was found between participants on vitamin C and placebo treatments; also, the participants consumed carbohydrate during the race *ad libitum* and this was retrospectively estimated.

In a more recent randomized, double-blind, placebo-controlled study, ingestion of 1500 mg vitamin C·day^{-1} for 7 days before an ultramarathon race with consumption of vitamin C in a carbohydrate beverage during the race (participants in the placebo group consumed the same carbohydrate beverage without added vitamin C) did not affect oxidative stress, cytokines or immune function during or after the race (Nieman *et al.*, 2002a). In contrast, it has recently been reported that 7 days supplementation with vitamin C (800 mg·day^{-1}) before a downhill treadmill run reduced the exercise-induced rise in plasma interleukin (IL)-6, monocyte respiratory burst and natural killer cell numbers compared with a placebo treatment (Hurst *et al.*, 2001). Nieman *et al.* (2002a) summarized the available literature on vitamin C supplementation and immune responses to exercise and concluded that vitamin C supplementation before prolonged intensive exercise 'does not have a consistent effect on blood measures of oxidative stress and muscle damage and that any linkage to immune perturbations remains speculative and more than likely improbable'. It should be noted that consumption of doses in excess of 1000 mg can cause abdominal pain and diarrhoea (Food Standards Agency, 2003), although there are insufficient data on adverse effects to set a safe upper level for vitamin C intake.

Nutritional manipulations to decrease exercise-induced immune impairment in athletes

Since exercise-induced immune function impairment appears mainly to be caused by elevated concentrations of stress hormones, nutritional strategies that effectively reduce the stress hormone response to exercise should limit the degree of exercise-induced immune dysfunction (Nieman and Pedersen, 2000). There is certainly considerable experimental evidence to support this notion, although it is not clear if the magnitude of such effects is sufficient to affect infection risk.

Carbohydrate intake before and during exercise

In recent years, several studies have examined the impact of dietary carbohydrate on hormonal and immune responses to exercise. These studies (Gleeson *et al.*, 1998; Mitchell *et al.*, 1998; Bishop *et al.*, 2001b) have found that when individuals perform prolonged exercise after several days on very low carbohydrate diets (typically < 10% of dietary energy intake from carbohydrate), the magnitude of the stress hormone (e.g. adrenaline and cortisol) and cytokine (e.g. IL-6, IL-1ra and IL-10) response is markedly higher than on normal or high carbohydrate diets. It has been speculated that athletes deficient in carbohydrate are placing themselves at risk from the known immunosuppressive effects of cortisol, including the suppression of antibody production, lymphocyte proliferation and natural killer cell cytotoxic activity. Mitchell *et al.* (1998) observed that exercising (1 h at 75% $\dot{V}O_{2max}$) in a glycogen-depleted state (induced by prior exercise and 2 days on a low carbohydrate diet) resulted in a greater fall in circulating lymphocyte numbers 2 h after exercise compared with the same exercise performed after 2 days on a high carbohydrate diet. However, the manipulation of carbohydrate status did not affect the decrease in mitogen-stimulated lymphocyte proliferation that occurred after exercise.

Consumption of carbohydrate during exercise also attenuates rises in plasma catecholamines, adrenocorticotrophic hormone, growth hormone, cortisol and cytokines (Nehlsen-Cannarella *et al.*, 1997; Nieman, 1998). Carbohydrate intake during exercise also attenuates the trafficking of most leucocyte and lymphocyte subsets, including the rise in the neutrophil:lymphocyte ratio (Nieman *et al.*, 1997b; Bishop *et al.*, 1999a), prevents the exercise-induced fall in neutrophil function (Bishop *et al.*, 2000b) and reduces the extent of the diminution of mitogen-stimulated T-lymphocyte proliferation (Henson *et al.*, 1998) following prolonged exercise. Very recently, it was shown that consuming 30–60 g carbohydrate $\cdot$ h^{-1} during 2.5 h of strenuous cycling prevented both the decrease in the number and percentage of interferon (IFN)-γ-positive T-lymphocytes and the suppression of IFN-γ production from stimulated T-lymphocytes observed on the placebo control trial (Lancaster *et al.*, 2003). Interferon-γ production is critical to anti-viral defence and it has been suggested that the suppression of IFN-γ production may be an important mechanism leading to an increased risk of infection after prolonged exercise bouts (Northoff *et al.*, 1998).

Compared with placebo, carbohydrate ingestion during a 3-h treadmill run attenuated plasma concentrations of IL-1ra, IL-6 and IL-10, as well as muscle gene expression for IL-6 and IL-8 (Nieman *et al.*, 2003). The 3-h treadmill run in both the carbohydrate and placebo trials induced gene expression within the muscle for two primary pro-inflammatory cytokines, IL-1β and TNF-α. Interleukin-6 and IL-8, which are often considered to be components of the secondary inflammatory cascade, were also expressed, but to a lesser extent in the carbohydrate trial. Anti-inflammatory indicators, including plasma IL-1ra, IL-10 and cortisol, were also decreased with carbohydrate feeding. These results suggest that carbohydrate ingestion attenuates the secondary but not the primary pro-inflammatory cascade, decreasing the need for immune responses related to anti-inflammation. However, when carbohydrate is ingested during prolonged exercise, the release of IL-6 from working muscles can be totally inhibited (Febbraio *et al.*, 2003) and the exercise-induced expression of several metabolic genes are blunted compared with exercise in the fasted state (Pilegaard *et al.*, 2002). Infusion of IL-6 in humans stimulates cortisol secretion (with plasma cortisol reaching similar values to those observed during exercise and with a similar time-course) and induces lipolysis as well as eliciting a strong anti-inflammatory response (Pedersen *et al.*, 2003; Starkie *et al.*, 2003). Thus, although carbohydrate ingestion during exercise attenuates the IL-6 response and so reduces the magnitude of the cortisol-induced lymphocytopaenia, it will, at the same time, inhibit lipolysis, reduce the anti-inflammatory effects of exercise and attenuate the expression of several metabolic genes in the exercised muscle. In other words, it is possible that carbohydrate ingestion during exercise sessions could limit adaptation to training. However, it can also be argued that carbohydrate intake during training allows the athlete to work harder and for longer and as yet there is no evidence that physiological and performance adaptations are impaired by carbohydrate intake during training sessions. Further research is needed to determine how nutrient intake might affect the transcriptional regulation of metabolic genes in skeletal muscle and what, if any, consequences this has for training adaptation.

While carbohydrate feeding during exercise appears to be effective in minimizing some of the immune perturbations associated with prolonged continuous strenuous exercise, it appears less effective for less demanding exercise of an intermittent nature, for example football (Bishop *et al.*, 1999b) or rowing (Nieman *et al.*, 1999) training. It is also apparent that carbohydrate feeding is not as effective in reducing immune cell trafficking and functional depression when continuous prolonged exercise is performed to the point of fatigue (Bishop *et al.*, 2001a). Pre-exercise feeding of carbohydrate does not seem to be very effective in limiting exercise-induced leucocytosis or depression of neutrophil function (Lancaster *et al.*, 2001). Also, there is no evidence that the beneficial effect of feeding carbohydrate on immune responses to exercise translates into a reduced incidence of URTI after prolonged exercise such as marathon races. Although a trend for a beneficial effect of carbohydrate ingestion on post-race URTI was reported in a study of 98 marathon runners (Nieman *et al.*, 2002b), this did not achieve statistical significance and larger-scale studies are needed to investigate this possibility.

Fluid intake during exercise

The consumption of beverages during exercise not only helps prevent dehydration (which is associated with an increased stress hormone response) but also helps to maintain saliva flow rate during exercise. Saliva contains several proteins with antimicrobial properties, including immunoglobulin-A (IgA), lysozyme and α-amylase. Saliva secretion usually falls during exercise. Regular fluid intake during exercise is reported to prevent this effect and a recent study (Bishop *et al.*, 2000a) has confirmed that regular consumption of lemon-flavoured carbohydrate-containing drinks helps to maintain saliva flow rate and hence saliva IgA secretion rate during prolonged exercise compared with a restricted fluid intake regimen.

Glutamine supplements

Glutamine is the most abundant free amino acid in human muscle and plasma and is utilized at very high rates by leucocytes to provide energy and optimal conditions for nucleotide biosynthesis (Ardawi and Newsholme, 1983, 1994). Indeed, glutamine is considered important, if not essential, to lymphocytes and other rapidly dividing cells, including the gut mucosa and bone marrow stem cells. Prolonged exercise is associated with a fall in the plasma concentration of glutamine and it has been hypothesized that such a decrease could impair immune function (Parry-Billings *et al.*, 1992; Castell, 2003).

It has been suggested that exogenous provision of glutamine supplements may be beneficial by maintaining the plasma glutamine concentration and hence preventing the impairment of immune function after prolonged exercise. Castell *et al.* (1996) have provided the only prophylactic evidence that an oral glutamine supplement (5 g in 330 ml water) consumed immediately after and 2 h after a marathon reduces the incidence of URTI (in the 7 days after the race). However, it is unlikely that this amount of glutamine supplementation could actually have prevented the post-exercise fall in the plasma glutamine concentration. Provision of glutamine has been shown to have a beneficial effect on gut function, morbidity and mortality and on some aspects of immune cell function in clinical studies of diseased or traumatized patients. However, several recent studies that have investigated the effect of large amounts of glutamine supplementation during and after exercise on the exercise-induced fall in lymphokine-activated killer cell activity, neutrophil function and mitogen-stimulated lymphocyte proliferation have failed to find any beneficial effect (Rohde *et al.*, 1998; Walsh *et al.*, 2000). Very recently, Bassit *et al.* (2002) reported that supplementation of branched-chain amino acids (BCAA) (6 g · day^{-1} for 15 days) before a triathlon or 30-km run prevented the approximately 40% decline in mitogen-stimulated lymphocyte proliferation observed in the placebo control group after exercise. Supplementation with BCAA prevented the post-exercise fall in plasma glutamine concentration and was also associated with increased lymphocyte IL-2 and IFN-γ production. More research is needed to resolve these conflicting findings of BCAA and glutamine supplementation on the immune responses to exercise.

Dietary immunostimulants

β-Carotene (pro-vitamin A) acts both as an antioxidant and an immunostimulant, increasing the number of T-helper cells in healthy humans (Alexander *et al.*, 1985) and stimulating natural killer cell activity when added *in vitro* to human lymphatic cultures (Watson *et al.*, 1991). Furthermore, elderly men who had been taking β-carotene supplements (50 mg on alternate days) for 10–12 years were reported to have significantly higher natural killer cell activity than elderly men on placebo (Santos *et al.*, 1996). However, supplementing runners with β-carotene was found to have an insignificant effect on the incidence of URTI after a 90-km ultramarathon (Peters *et al.*, 1992). Furthermore, intakes of supplements in excess of 7 mg · day^{-1} are not advised because of a possible increased risk of lung cancer in smokers (Food Standards Agency, 2003).

Several herbal preparations are reputed to have immunostimulatory effects and consumption of products containing *Echinacea purpurea* is widespread among athletes. However, few controlled studies have examined the effects of dietary immunostimulants on exercise-induced changes in immune function. In one recent double-blind, placebo-controlled study, the effect of a daily oral pre-treatment for 28 days with pressed juice of *E. purpurea* was investigated in

42 triathletes before and after a sprint triathlon (Berg *et al.*, 1998). A sub-group of athletes was also treated with magnesium as a reference for supplementation with a micronutrient important for optimal muscular function. The most important finding was that during the 28-day pre-treatment period, none of the athletes in the *Echinacea* group fell ill, compared with three individuals in the magnesium group and four in the placebo group who became ill. Pre-treatment with *Echinacea* appeared to reduce the release of soluble IL-2 receptor before and after the race and increased the exercise-induced rise in IL-6.

Several experiments have demonstrated that *E. purpurea* extracts do indeed demonstrate significant immunomodulatory activities. Among the many pharmacological properties reported, macrophage activation has been demonstrated most convincingly (Stimpel *et al.*, 1984; Steinmuller *et al.*, 1993). Phagocytotic indices and macrophage-derived cytokine concentrations have been shown to be *Echinacea*-responsive in a variety of assays and activation of polymorpho-nuclear leucocytes and natural killer cells has also been reasonably demonstrated (Barrett, 2003). Changes in the numbers and activities of T- and B-lymphocytes have been reported, but are less certain. Despite this cellular evidence of immunostimulation, the pathways leading to enhanced resistance to infectious disease have not been described adequately. Several dozen human experiments, including a number of blind randomized trials, have reported health benefits. The most robust data come from trials testing *E. purpurea* extracts in the treatment for acute URTI. Although suggestive of modest benefit, these trials are limited both in size and in methodological quality. In a recent randomized, double-blind, placebo-controlled trial, administering unrefined *Echinacea* at the onset of symptoms of URTI in 148 college students did not provide any detectable benefit or harm compared with placebo (Barrett *et al.*, 2002). Hence, while there is a great deal of moderately good-quality scientific data on *Echinacea*, its effectiveness in treating illness or in enhancing human health has not yet been proven beyond a reasonable doubt.

Probiotics are food supplements that contain 'friendly' gut bacteria. There is now a reasonable body of evidence that regular consumption of probiotics can modify the population of the gut microflora and influence immune function (Calder *et al.*, 2002). Some studies have shown that probiotic intake can improve rates of recovery from rotavirus diarrhoea, increase resistance to enteric pathogens and promote anti-tumour activity; there is even some evidence that probiotics may be effective in alleviating some allergic and respiratory disorders in young children (see Kopp-Hoolihan, 2001, for a review). However, to date, there are no published studies of the effectiveness of probiotic use in athletes.

Summary and recommendations

1   Both heavy exercise and nutrition exert separate influences on immune function; these influences appear to be stronger when exercise stress and poor nutrition act synergistically.

2   Dietary deficiencies of energy, protein and specific micronutrients are associated with depressed immune function and increased susceptibility to infection. An adequate intake of iron, zinc and vitamins A, E, B6 and B12 is particularly important for the maintenance of immune function. Athletes need to avoid micronutrient deficiencies.

3   To maintain immune function, athletes should eat a well-balanced diet sufficient to meet their energy requirements. This should ensure an adequate intake of protein and micronutrients.

4   For athletes on energy-restricted diets, vitamin supplements are desirable.

5   An athlete exercising in a carbohydrate-depleted state experiences larger increases in circulating stress hormones and a greater perturbation of several immune function indices.

6   Consumption of carbohydrate (30–$60 \, g \cdot h^{-1}$) in drinks during prolonged exercise is recommended, as this practice appears to attenuate some of the immunosuppressive effects of prolonged exercise. However, the clinical significance of this has to be determined.

7   Consumption of megadoses of vitamins and minerals is not advised. Excess intakes of some micronutrients (e.g. iron, zinc, vitamin E) can impair immune function.

8   High fat diets suppress some aspects of immune cell function.

9   Convincing evidence that so-called 'immune-boosting' supplements, such as high doses of antioxidant vitamins, glutamine, zinc, probiotics and *Echinacea*, prevent exercise-induced immune impairment is currently lacking. Current evidence regarding the efficacy of *Echinacea* extracts, zinc lozenges and probiotics in preventing or treating common infections is limited and there is insufficient evidence to recommend these supplements at this time.

10 It is still debatable as to whether antioxidant supplements are required or are desirable for athletes. There is conflicting evidence of the effects of high-dose vitamin C in reducing the post-exercise incidence of URTI and this practice has not been shown to prevent exercise-induced immune impairment.

11 Glutamine supplementation is beneficial to immune function in the clinical setting but has not proved effective in abolishing the post-exercise impairment of immune cell function.

References

1 Alexander, M., Newmark, H. and Miller, R.G. (1985). Oral beta-carotene can increase the number of CD4+ cells in human blood. *Immunology Letters*, **9**, 221–224.

2 Ardawi, M.S.M. and Newsholme, E.A. (1983). Glutamine metabolism in lymphocytes of the rat. *Biochemical Journal*, **212**, 835–842.

3 Ardawi, M.S.M. and Newsholme, E.A. (1994). Glutamine metabolism in lymphoid tissues. In *Glutamine Metabolism in Mammalian Tissues* (edited by D. Haussinger and H. Sies), pp. 235–246. Berlin: Springer-Verlag.

4 Barrett, B. (2003). Medicinal properties of Echinacea: critical review. *Phytomedicine*, **10**, 66–86.

5 Barrett, B.P., Brown, R.L., Locken, K., Maberry, R., Bobula, J.A. and D'Alessio, D. (2002). Treatment of the common cold with unrefined *Echinacea*: a randomized, double-blind, placebo-controlled trial. *Annals of Internal Medicine*, **137**, 939–946.

6 Bassit, R.A., Sawada, L.A., Bacurau, R.F.P., Navarro, F., Martins, E., Santos, R.V.T., Caperuto, E.C., Rogeri, P. and Costa-Rosa, L.F.B.P. (2002). Branched-chain amino acid supplementation and the immune response of long-distance athletes. *Nutrition*, **18**, 376–379.

7 Beals, K.A. and Manore, M.M. (1994). The prevalence and consequence of eating disorders in female athletes. *International Journal of Sport Nutrition*, **4**, 175–195.

8 Berg, A., Northoff, H. and Konig, D. (1998). Influence of Echinacin (E31) treatment on the exercise-induced immune response in athletes. *Journal of Clinical Research*, **1**, 367–380.

9 Bishop, N.C., Blannin, A.K., Rand, L., Johnson, R. and Gleeson, M. (1999a). Effects of carbohydrate and fluid intake on the blood leucocyte responses to prolonged cycling. *Journal of Sports Sciences*, **17**, 26–27.

10 Bishop, N.C., Blannin, A.K., Robson, P.J., Walsh, N.P. and Gleeson, M. (1999b). The effects of carbohydrate supplementation on neutrophil degranulation responses to a soccer-specific exercise protocol. *Journal of Sports Sciences*, **17**, 787–796.

11 Bishop, N.C., Blannin, A.K., Armstrong, E., Rickman, M. and Gleeson, M. (2000a). Carbohydrate and fluid intake affect the saliva flow rate and IgA response to cycling. *Medicine and Science in Sports and Exercise*, **32**, 2046–2051.

12 Bishop, N.C., Blannin, A.K., Rand, L., Johnson, R. and Gleeson, M. (2000b). The effects of carbohydrate supplementation on neutrophil degranulation responses to prolonged cycling. *International Journal of Sports Medicine*, **21**(suppl. 1), S73.

13 Bishop, N.C., Blannin, A.K., Walsh, N.P. and Gleeson, M. (2001a). Carbohydrate beverage ingestion and neutrophil degranulation responses following cycling to fatigue at 75% $\dot{V}O_{2max}$. *International Journal of Sports Medicine*, **22**, 226–231.

14 Bishop, N.C., Walsh, N.P., Haines, D.L., Richards, E.E. and Gleeson, M. (2001b). Pre-exercise carbohydrate status and immune responses to prolonged cycling: II. Effect on plasma cytokine concentration. *International Journal of Sport Nutrition and Exercise Metabolism*, **11**, 503–512.

15 Calder, P.C. (1996). Fatty acids, dietary lipids and lymphocyte functions. *Biochemical Society Transactions*, **23**, 302–309.

16 Calder, P.C. and Jackson, A.A. (2000). Undernutrition, infection and immune function. *Nutrition Research Reviews*, **13**, 3–29.

17 Calder, P.C., Field, C.J. and Gill, H.S. (2002). *Nutrition and Immune Function*. Oxford: CABI Publishing.

18 Castell, L. (2003). Glutamine supplementation *in vitro* and *in vivo*, in exercise and in immunodepression. *Sports Medicine*, **33**, 323–345.

19 Castell, L.M., Poortmans, J.R. and Newsholme, E.A. (1996). Does glutamine have a role in reducing infections in athletes? *European Journal of Applied Physiology*, **73**, 488–490.

20 Chandra, R.K. (1984). Excessive intake of zinc impairs immune responses. *Journal of the American Medical Association*, **52**, 1443–1446.

21 Chandra, R.K. (1997). Nutrition and the immune system: an introduction. *American Journal of Clinical Nutrition*, **66**, 460S–463S.
22 Clarkson, P.M. (1992). Minerals: exercise performance and supplementation in athletes. In *Foods, Nutrition and Sports Performance* (edited by C. Williams and J. Devlin), pp. 113–146. London: E & FN Spon.
23 COMA (1991). *Dietary Reference Values for Food Energy and Nutrients for the United Kingdom*. Report of the Panel on Dietary Reference Values, Committee on Medical Aspects of Food and Nutrition Policy. London: HMSO.
24 Coutsoudis, A., Kiepiela, P., Coovadia, H.M. and Broughton, M. (1992). Vitamin A supplementation enhances specific IgG antibody levels and total lymphocyte numbers while improving morbidity in measles. *Paediatric Infectious Disease Journal*, **11**, 203–209.
25 Daly, J.M., Reynolds, J., Sigal, R.K., Shou, J. and Liberman, M.D. (1990). Effect of dietary protein and amino acids on immune function. *Critical Care Medicine*, **18**(suppl. 2), S86–S93.
26 Duthie, G.G., Jenkinson, A.McE., Morrice, P.C. and Arthur, J.R. (1996). Antioxidant adaptations to exercise. In *Biochemistry of Exercise IX* (edited by R.J. Maughan and S.M. Shirreffs), pp. 465–470. Champaign, IL: Human Kinetics.
27 Febbraio, M.A., Steensberg, A., Keller, C., Starkie, R.L., Nielsen, H.B., Krustrup, P., Ott, P., Secher, N.H. and Pedersen, B.K. (2003). Glucose ingestion attenuates interleukin-6 release from contracting skeletal muscle in humans. *Journal of Physiology*, **549**, 607–612.
28 Food Standards Agency (2003). Safe upper levels for vitamins and minerals. Report of Expert Group on Vitamins and Minerals (http://www.foodstandards.gov.uk).
29 Gleeson, M. (2000). Minerals and exercise immunology. In *Nutrition and Exercise Immunology* (edited by D.C. Nieman and B.K. Pedersen), pp. 137–154. Boca Raton, FL: CRC Press.
30 Gleeson, M. and Bishop, N.C. (1999). Immunology. In *Basic and Applied Sciences for Sports Medicine* (edited by R.J. Maughan), pp. 199–236. Oxford: Butterworth Heinemann.
31 Gleeson, M., Blannin, A.K., Walsh, N.P., Bishop, N.C. and Clark, A.M. (1998). Effect of low and high carbohydrate diets on the plasma glutamine and circulating leucocyte responses to exercise. *International Journal of Sport Nutrition*, **8**, 49–59.
32 Graat, J.M., Schouten, E.G. and Kok, F.J. (2002). Effect of daily vitamin E and multivitamin–mineral supplementation on acute respiratory tract infections in elderly persons: a randomised control trial. *Journal of the American Medical Association*, **288**, 715–721.
33 Henson, D.A., Nieman, D.C., Parker, J.C.D., Rainwater, M.K., Butterworth, D.E., Warren, B.J., Utter, A., Davis, J.M., Fagoaga, O.R. and Nehlsen-Cannarella, S.L. (1998). Carbohydrate supplementation and the lymphocyte proliferative response to long endurance running. *International Journal of Sports Medicine*, **19**, 574–580.
34 Himmelstein, S.A., Robergs, R.A., Koehler, K.M., Lewis, S.L. and Qualls, C.R. (1998). Vitamin C supplementation and upper respiratory tract infection in marathon runners. *Journal of Exercise Physiology*, **1**, 1–17.
35 Hurst, T.L., Bailey, D.M., Powell, J.R. and Williams, C. (2001). Immune function changes in downhill running subjects following ascorbic acid supplementation. *Medicine and Science in Sports and Exercise*, **33**(suppl. 5), ISEI abstract 2.

36 Keil, D., Luebke, R.W. and Pruett, S.B. (2001). Quantifying the relationship between multiple immunological parameters and host resistance: probing the limits of reductionism. *Journal of Immunology*, **167**, 4543–4552.

37 Konig, D., Berg, A., Weinstock, C., Keul, J. and Northoff, H. (1997). Essential fatty acids, immune function and exercise. *Exercise Immunology Review*, **3**, 1–31.

38 Kono, I., Kitao, H., Matsuda, M., Haga, S., Fukushima, H. and Kashigawa, H. (1988). Weight reduction in athletes may adversely affect the phagocytic function of monocytes. *Physician and Sportsmedicine*, **16**, 56–65.

39 Kopp-Hoolihan, L. (2001). Prophylactic and therapeutic uses of probiotics: a review. *Journal of the American Dietetic Association*, **101**, 229–238.

40 Lancaster, G.I., Jentjens, R.L.P.G., Moseley, L., Jeukendrup, A.E. and Gleeson, M. (2001). Effect of timing and amount of pre-exercise feeding of carbohydrate on blood neutrophil responses to time trial cycling. *Medicine and Science in Sports and Exercise*, **33**(suppl. 5), ISEI abstract 7.

41 Lancaster, G.I., Khan, Q., Drysdale, P.T., Jeukendrup, A.E., Drayson, M.T. and Gleeson, M. (2003). Effect of feeding different amounts of carbohydrate during prolonged exercise on human T-lymphocyte intracellular cytokine production. *Journal of Physiology*, **548P**, 98.

42 Macknin, M.L. (1999). Zinc lozenges for the common cold. *Cleveland Clinical Journal of Medicine*, **66**, 27–32.

43 Marshall, I. (2000). Zinc for the common cold. *Cochrane Database Systematic Reviews*, 2000(2), CD001364.

44 McElroy, B.H. and Miller, S.P. (2002). Effectiveness of zinc gluconate glycine lozenges (Cold-Eeze) against the common cold in school-aged subjects: a retrospective chart review. *American Journal of Therapeutics*, **9**, 472–475.

45 Meydani, S.N., Barklund, P.M. and Liu, S. (1990). Vitamin E supplementation enhances cell mediated immunity in elderly subjects. *American Journal of Clinical Nutrition*, **52**, 557–563.

46 Mitchell, J.B., Pizza, F.X., Paquet, A., Davis, J.B., Forrest, M.B. and Braun, W.A. (1998). Influence of carbohydrate status on immune responses before and after endurance exercise. *Journal of Applied Physiology*, **84**, 1917–1925.

47 MRC/BHF Heart Protection Study (2002). MRC/BHF Heart Protection Study of antioxidant vitamin supplementation in 20,536 high-risk individuals: a randomised placebo-controlled trial. *Lancet*, **360**, 23–33.

48 Nehlsen-Cannarella, S.L., Fagoaga, O.R., Nieman, D.C., Henson, D.A., Butterworth, D.E., Schmitt, R.L., Bailey, E.M., Warren, B.J., Utter, A. and Davis, J.M. (1997). Carbohydrate and the cytokine response to 2.5 h of running. *Journal of Applied Physiology*, **82**, 1662–1667.

49 Nieman, D.C. (1998). Influence of carbohydrate on the immune responses to intensive, prolonged exercise. *Exercise Immunology Review*, **4**, 64–76.

50 Nieman, D.C. and Pedersen, B.K. (2000). *Nutrition and Exercise Immunology*. Boca Raton, FL: CRC Press.

51 Nieman, D.C., Johansen, L.M., Lee, J.W. and Arabatzis, K. (1990). Infectious episodes in runners before and after the Los Angeles Marathon. *Journal of Sports Medicine and Physical Fitness*, **30**, 316–328.

52 Nieman, D.C., Henson, D.A., Butterworth, D.E., Warren, B.J., Davis, J.M., Fagoaga, O.R. and Nehlsen-Cannarella, S.L. (1997a). Vitamin C supplementation does not alter the immune response to 2.5 hours of running. *International Journal of Sport Nutrition*, **7**, 173–184.

53 Nieman, D.C., Henson, D.A., Garner, E.B., Butterworth, D.E., Warren, B.J., Utter, A., Davis, J.M., Fagoaga, O.R. and Nehlsen-Cannarella, S.L. (1997b). Carbohydrate affects natural killer cell redistribution but not function after running. *Medicine and Science in Sports and Exercise*, **20**, 1318–1324.

54 Nieman, D.C., Nehlsen-Cannarella, S.L., Fagoaga, O.R., Henson, D.A., Shannon, M., Davis, J.M., Austin, M.D., Hisey, C.L., Holbeck, J.C., Hjertman, J.M., Bolton, M.R. and Schilling, B.K. (1999). Immune response to two hours of rowing in elite female rowers. *International Journal of Sports Medicine*, **20**, 476–481.

55 Nieman, D.C., Peters, E.M., Henson, D.A., Nevines, E.I. and Thompson, M.M. (2000). Influence of vitamin C supplementation on cytokine changes following an ultramarathon. *Journal of Interferon and Cytokine Research*, **20**, 1029–1035.

56 Nieman, D.C., Henson, D.A., McAnulty, S.R., McAnulty, L., Swick, N.S., Utter, A.C., Vinci, D.M., Opiela, S.J. and Morrow, J.D. (2002a). Influence of vitamin C supplementation on oxidative and immune changes after an ultramarathon. *Journal of Applied Physiology*, **92**, 1970–1977.

57 Nieman, D.C., Henson, D.A., Fagoaga, O.R., Utter, A.C., Vinci, D.M., Davis, J.M. and Nehlsen-Cannarella, S.L. (2002b). Change in salivary IgA following a competitive marathon race. *International Journal of Sports Medicine*, **23**, 69–75.

58 Nieman, D.C., Davis, J.M., Henson, D.A., Walberg-Rankin, J., Shute, M., Dumke, C.L., Utter, A.C., Vinci, D.M., Carson, J.A., Brown, A., Lee, W.J., McAnulty, S.R. and McAnulty, L.S. (2003). Carbohydrate ingestion influences skeletal muscle cytokine mRNA and plasma cytokine levels after a 3-h run. *Journal of Applied Physiology*, **94**, 1917–1925.

59 Nieman, D.C., Henson, D.A., McAnulty, S.R., McAnulty, L.S. and Heward, C. (in press). Influence of vitamin E supplementation on oxidative and immune changes following the Kona Triathlon World Championship. *Medicine and Science in Sports and Exercise*, submitted for publication.

60 Northoff, H., Berg, A. and Weinstock, C. (1998). Similarities and differences of the immune response to exercise and trauma: the IFN-gamma concept. *Canadian Journal of Physiology and Pharmacology*, **76**, 497–504.

61 Packer, L. (1997). Oxidants, antioxidant nutrients and the athlete. *Journal of Sports Sciences*, **15**, 353–363.

62 Parry-Billings, M., Budgett, R., Koutedakis, Y., Blomstrand, E., Brooks, S., Williams, C., Calder, P.C., Pillings, S., Baigre, R. and Newsholme, E.A. (1992). Plasma amino acid concentrations in the overtraining syndrome: possible effects on the immune system. *Medicine and Science in Sports and Exercise*, **24**, 1353–1358.

63 Pedersen, B.K., Helge, J., Richter, E., Rhode, T., Ostrowski, K. and Kiens, B. (2000). Training and natural immunity: effects of diets rich in fat or carbohydrate. *European Journal of Applied Physiology*, **82**, 98–102.

64 Pedersen, B.K., Steensberg, A., Keller, P., Keller, C., Fischer, C., Hiscock, N., van Hall, G., Plomgaard, P. and Febbraio, M.A. (2003). Muscle-derived interleukin-6: lipolytic, anti-inflammatory and immune regulatory effects. *Pflugers Archives*, **446**, 9–16.

65 Peters, E.M. (1997). Exercise, immunology and upper respiratory tract infections. *International Journal of Sports Medicine*, **18** (suppl. 1), S69–S77.

66 Peters, E.M. (2000). Vitamins, immunity and infection risk in athletes. In *Nutrition and Exercise Immunology* (edited by D.C. Nieman and B.K. Pedersen), pp. 109–135. Boca Raton, FL: CRC Press.

67 Peters, E.M. and Bateman, E.D. (1983). Ultramarathon running and URTI: an epidemiological survey. *South African Medical Journal*, **64**, 582–584.

68 Peters, E.M., Campbell, A. and Pawley, L. (1992). Vitamin A fails to increase resistance to upper respiratory infection in distance runners. *South African Journal of Sports Medicine*, **7**, 3–7.

69 Peters, E.M., Goetzsche, J.M., Grobbelaar, B. and Noakes, T.D. (1993). Vitamin C supplementation reduces the incidence of post-race symptoms of upper respiratory tract infection in ultramarathon runners. *American Journal of Clinical Nutrition*, **57**, 170–174.

70 Peters, E.M., Goetzsche, J.M., Joseph, L.E. and Noakes, T.D. (1996). Vitamin C is effective as combinations of anti-oxidant nutrients in reducing symptoms of upper respiratory tract infections in ultramarathon runners. *South African Journal of Sports Medicine*, **11**, 23–27.

71 Petersen, E.W. and Pedersen, B.K. (2002). Exercise and immune function – effect of nutrition. In *Nutrition and Immune Function* (edited by P.C. Calder, C.J. Field and H.S. Gill), pp. 347–355. Oxford: CABI Publishing.

72 Pilegaard, H., Keller, C., Steensberg, A., Helge, J.W., Pedersen, B.K., Saltin, B. and Neufer, P.D. (2002). Influence of pre-exercise muscle glycogen content on exercise-induced transcriptional regulation of metabolic genes. *Journal of Physiology*, **541**, 261–271.

73 Prasad, J.S. (1980). Effect of vitamin E supplementation on leucocyte function. *American Journal of Clinical Nutrition*, **33**, 606–608.

74 Reynolds, J., Shou, J., Sigal, R., Ziegler, M. and Daly, J.M. (1990). The influence of protein malnutrition on T cell, natural killer cell, and lymphokine-activated killer cell function, and on biological responsiveness to high-dose interleukin-2. *Cellular Immunology*, **128**, 569.

75 Rohde, T., Asp, S., Maclean, D. and Pedersen, B.K. (1998). Competitive sustained exercise in humans, and lymphokine activated killer cell activity – an intervention study. *European Journal of Applied Physiology*, **78**, 448–453.

76 Santos, M.S., Meydani, S.N., Leka, L., Wu, D., Fotouhi, N., Meydani, M., Hennekens, C.H. and Gaziano, J.M. (1996). Natural killer cell activity in elderly men is enhanced by beta-carotene supplementation. *American Journal of Clinical Nutrition*, **64**, 772–777.

77 Scrimshaw, N.S. and SanGiovanni, J.P. (1997). Synergism of nutrition, infection and immunity: an overview. *American Journal of Clinical Nutrition*, **66**, 464S–477S.

78 Sherman, A.R. (1992). Zinc, copper and iron nutriture and immunity. *Journal of Nutrition*, **122**, 604–609.

79 Starkie, R., Ostrowski, S.R., Jauffred, S., Febbraio, M. and Pedersen, B.K. (2003). Exercise and IL-6 infusion inhibit endotoxin-induced TNF-alpha production in humans. *FASEB Journal*, **17**, 884–886.

80 Steinmuller, C., Roesler, J., Grottrup, E., Franke, G., Wagner, H. and Lohmann-Matthes, M.L. (1993). Polysaccharides isolated from plant cultures of *Echinacea purpurea* enhance the resistance of immunosuppressed mice against systemic infections with *Candida albicans* and *Listeria monocytogenes*. *International Journal of Immunopharmacology*, **15**, 605–614.

81 Stimpel, M., Proksch, A., Wagner, H. and Lohmann-Matthes, M.L. (1984). Macrophage activation and induction of macrophage cytotoxicity by purified polysaccharide fractions from the plant *Echinacea purpurea*. *Infection and Immunology*, **46**, 845–849.

82 Toft, A.D., Ostrowski, K., Asp, S., Moller, K., Iversen, S., Hermann, C., Sondergaard, S.R. and Pedersen, B.K. (2000). The effects of n-3 PUFA on the cytokine response to strenuous exercise. *Journal of Applied Physiology*, **89**, 2401–2405.

83 Walsh, N.P., Blannin, A.K., Bishop, N.C., Robson, P.J. and Gleeson, M. (2000). Oral glutamine supplementation does not attenuate the fall in human neutrophil lipopolysaccharide-stimulated degranulation following prolonged exercise. *International Journal of Sport Nutrition*, **10**, 39–50.

84 Waters, D.D., Alderman, E.L., Hsia, J., Howard, B.V., Cobb, F.R., Rogers, W.J., Ouyang, P., Thompson, P., Tardif, J.C., Higginson, L., Bittner, V., Steffes, M., Gordon, D.J., Proschan, M., Younes, N. and Verter, J.I. (2002). Effects of hormone replacement therapy and antioxidant vitamin supplements on coronary atherosclerosis in postmenopausal women: a randomized controlled trial. *Journal of the American Medical Association*, **288**, 2432–2440.

85 Watson, R.R., Prabhala, R.H., Plezia, P.M. and Alberts, D.S. (1991). Effect of beta-carotene on lymphocyte subpopulation in elderly humans: evidence for a dose response relationship. *American Journal of Clinical Nutrition*, **53**, 90–94.

10 Nutritional strategies to influence adaptations to training

LAWRENCE L. SPRIET and MARTIN J. GIBALA

This article highlights new nutritional concerns or practices that may influence the adaptation to training. The discussion is based on the assumption that the adaptation to repeated bouts of training occurs during recovery periods and that if one can train harder, the adaptation will be greater. The goal is to maximize with nutrition the recovery/adaptation that occurs in all rest periods, such that recovery before the next training session is complete. Four issues have been identified where recent scientific information will force sports nutritionists to embrace new issues and reassess old issues and, ultimately, alter the nutritional recommendations they give to athletes. These are: (1) caffeine ingestion; (2) creatine ingestion; (3) the use of intramuscular triacylglycerol (IMTG) as a fuel during exercise and the nutritional effects on IMTG repletion following exercise; and (4) the role nutrition may play in regulating the expression of genes during and after exercise training sessions. Recent findings suggest that low doses of caffeine exert significant ergogenic effects by directly affecting the central nervous system during exercise. Caffeine can cross the blood–brain barrier and antagonize the effects of adenosine, resulting in higher concentrations of stimulatory neurotransmitters. These new data strengthen the case for using low doses of caffeine during training. On the other hand, the data on the role that supplemental creatine ingestion plays in augmenting the increase in skeletal muscle mass and strength during resistance training remain equivocal. Some studies are able to demonstrate increases in muscle fibre size with creatine ingestion and some are not. The final two nutritional topics are new and have not progressed to the point that we can specifically identify strategies to enhance the adaptation to training. However, it is likely that nutritional strategies will be needed to replenish the IMTG that is used during endurance exercise. It is not presently clear whether the IMTG store is chronically reduced when engaging in daily sessions of endurance training or if this impacts negatively on the ability to train. It is also likely that the increased interest in gene and protein expression measurements will lead to nutritional strategies to optimize the adaptations that occur in skeletal muscle during and after exercise training sessions. Research in these areas in the coming years will lead to strategies designed to improve the adaptive response to training.

Keywords: caffeine, creatine, gene expression, muscle triacylglycerol, nutrition, training.

Introduction

Here, we highlight new nutritional concerns or practices that may influence the adaptation to training. We have identified four areas where recent scientific information will force sports nutritionists to embrace new issues and reassess old issues and, potentially, alter some nutritional recommendations to athletes. These are: (1) caffeine ingestion; (2) creatine ingestion; (3) the use of intramuscular triacylglycerol (IMTG) as a fuel during exercise and the nutritional effects on IMTG repletion following exercise; and (4) the role that nutrition may play in determining the expression of genes during and after exercise training sessions. Recent experiments examining the effects of caffeine on the central nervous system during exercise strengthen the case for using low doses of caffeine during training. On the other hand, equivocal data on the role that creatine plays in augmenting the increase in skeletal muscle mass and strength during resistance training may do the opposite. Will the recent surge in information examining IMTG use during exercise and recovery after exercise alter our post-exercise nutritional advice to include a greater emphasis on fat? Lastly, based on recent measurements of gene expression, are there nutritional strategies that we should adopt to maximize the adaptation that occurs in skeletal muscle following training sessions?

This article works on the assumption that the adaptation to repeated bouts of training occurs during the recovery periods and that if one can train harder, the adaptation will be greater. This can only be achieved if recovery before the next training session is complete. The goal is to use nutrition to maximize the recovery/adaptation that occurs in the rest periods between training sessions. It is also clear that characteristics of each training session (e.g. duration, intensity and nutritional intake) will also influence the rest period recovery/adaptation processes.

Caffeine and the central nervous system

Traditionally, it was believed that the ergogenic effect of caffeine during endurance exercise was due to a peripheral mechanism. The finding that caffeine in high doses of 5–9 mg·kg^{-1} BM (where BM = body mass) spared the use of muscle glycogen early in exercise supported this contention (Essig *et al.*, 1980; Spriet *et al.*, 1992). However, recent studies using 9 mg·kg^{-1} BM reported a variable glycogen sparing response (Chesley *et al.*, 1998) and other studies have reported no effect on glycogen use when consuming 6 mg·kg^{-1} BM (Graham *et al.*, 2000; Laurent *et al.*, 2000). Of course, there was always the realization that caffeine may also have a central effect during endurance exercise, but separating the peripheral and central effects of caffeine in studies with humans is difficult, as caffeine has the potential to affect many tissues at once. In addition, the recent finding that caffeine is also ergogenic during exercise of varying duration and intensities at doses as low as 3 mg·kg^{-1} BM (Graham and Spriet, 1995; Pasman *et al.*, 1995) suggests that its main effect is on the central nervous system (CNS). At these low doses, the risk of adverse side-effects is greatly diminished. Additional peripheral effects of caffeine acting directly on skeletal muscle (inhibition of enzymes or alterations of ion handling) also appear unlikely given the low plasma caffeine concentrations reported at these low doses. This suggests that the CNS is sensitive to lower caffeine doses and responsible for improved performance during endurance exercise and exercise of shorter duration.

Caffeine is known to be a CNS stimulant, causing increased arousal, wakefulness, alertness and vigilance as well as elevations of mood (Nehlig et al., 1992; Daly, 1993). Caffeine increases brain neurotransmitter concentrations, leading to increased locomotor activity and neuronal firing in animals (Nehlig et al., 1992). It is generally believed that the effects of caffeine are exerted via adenosine receptor antagonism. The brain has high levels of adenosine receptors (Fernstrom and Fernstrom, 1984; Daly, 1993; Fredholm, 1995) and adenosine generally decreases the concentration of the major neurotransmitters, including serotonin, dopamine, acetylcholine, norepinephrine and glutamate. This leads to lower motor activity, wakefulness and vigilance. Caffeine is an adenosine receptor antagonist and increases the concentration of these major neurotransmitters. However, the exact consequences of these changes for exercise performance are currently unclear.

Two recent studies have re-examined the role the CNS may play in the ability of caffeine to enhance exercise performance. Davis et al. (2003) examined the effects of direct intracerebroventricular injections of caffeine on the ability of rats to run to exhaustion on a treadmill. Rats were injected 30 min before running with either vehicle (placebo), caffeine, an adenosine receptor agonist (5-N-ethylcarboxamidoadenosine, NECA), or caffeine and NECA together. Rats were able to run ~80 min in the placebo trial, 120 min after caffeine injection and only 25 min with NECA (Fig. 1). When caffeine and NECA were given together, run time was not different from placebo. Rats were encouraged to run when needed by gentle hand prodding and mild electric shock. Fatigue was defined as the time when the rats would no longer run and chose to rest on the electric wires despite continual hand prodding and mild electric shocks for 30 s. When the study was repeated with peripheral intraperitoneal injections instead of brain injections, there was no effect on run performance. The authors concluded that caffeine delayed fatigue through CNS effects in part by blocking adenosine receptors (Davis et al., 2003).

A second study examined the effects of ingesting flat cola late in a simulated cycle race. This practice is common among endurance cyclists and was undertaken to determine if either the ingestion of extra carbohydrate and/or caffeine late in exercise could increase performance. Eight well-trained cyclists ($\dot{V}O_{2max}$, ~71 ml·kg^{-1}·min^{-1}) rode for 2 h at 70% maximal oxygen uptake ($\dot{V}O_{2max}$) and then completed a time-trial in which each cyclist was asked to complete 7 kJ of work per kilogram of body mass as quickly as possible (~30 min) on four separate occasions (Cox et al., 2002). They consumed 5 ml of a 6% sports drink every 20 min for the first hour and then switched to the same volume of flat cola at 80 and 100 min (and 120 min if desired). The cola beverage was varied in the four conditions to include: (a) no caffeine and 6% carbohydrate (Control); (b) caffeine (90 mg+) and 11% carbohydrate (Cola); (c) no caffeine

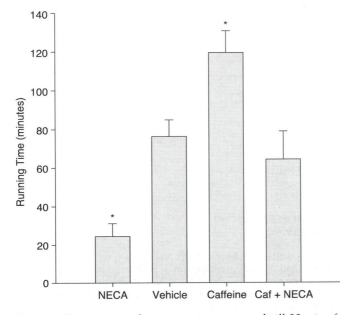

Figure 1. Running time for rats running on a treadmill 30 min after direct intracerebroventricular injections of (1) vehicle (placebo), (2) caffeine, (3) an adenosine receptor agonist (5-N-ethylcarboxamidoadenosine, NECA) or (4) caffeine and NECA together. *Significantly different than vehicle. Adapted from Davis *et al.* (2003).

and 11% carbohydrate (Extra carbohydrate); and (d) caffeine (90 mg+) and 6% carbohydrate (Caffeine). Performance times (min: s) to complete the time-trials were 27:05 ± 0:42 (Control), 26:15 ± 0:43 (Cola), 26:55 ± 0:43 (Extra Cola) and 26:36 ± 0:42 (Caffeine) (Fig. 2). The flat cola, with the extra carbo-hydrate and caffeine, significantly improved performance time by 50 s. Caffeine appeared to be the most important ingredient, as caffeine alone improved performance by 29 s (significant effect for caffeine compared with no caffeine), whereas the extra carbohydrate alone improved performance by a non-significant 10 s. In the trials with caffeine ingestion, plasma caffeine increased to low levels, suggesting that the performance-enhancing effects were unlikely to be peripheral and more likely to be centrally mediated. It appeared that caffeine reduced the normal progression of fatigue late in endurance exercise.

These recent studies add strong support to the body of evidence suggesting that caffeine can improve performance by directly affecting the CNS. Clearly, this implies that caffeine in low doses should enhance the ability to perform in both training and competition. During training, the ability to train harder should lead to greater training adaptations.

CONTROL	CAFFEINE
27:05 ± 0:42 min	26:36 ± 0:42 min
	1.9% [−0.6 − 4.41%]
ExtraCHO	**COKE**
26:55 ± 0:43 min	26:15* ± 0:43 min
0.6% [−1.8 − 3.1%]	3.3*% [0.8 − 5.9%]

Effect of caffeine:
2.2%* [0.5 − 3.8%]

Effect of additional CHO:
1.0% [−0.7 − 2.7%]

Figure 2. Time taken for eight well-trained cyclists to complete a time-trial. Each cyclist was asked to complete 7 kJ of work per kilogram of body mass as quickly as possible (∼30 min) after cycling for 2 h at 70% $\dot{V}O_{2max}$. The participants completed the protocol on four separate occasions and consumed 5 ml of a 6% sports drink every 20 min for the first hour and then switched to the same volume of flat cola at 80 and 100 min (and 120 min if desired). The cola beverage was varied in the four conditions to include: (1) no caffeine and 6% carbohydrate (Control); (2) caffeine (90 mg+) and 11% carbohydrate (Cola); (3) no caffeine and 11% carbohydrate (Extra CHO); or (4) caffeine (90 mg+) and 6% carbohydrate (Caffeine). There was a significant main effect for caffeine compared with no caffeine. Adapted from Cox *et al.* (2002).

Does creatine supplementation enhance gains in muscle size in response to resistance training?

Over the past decade, no other nutritional supplement has received as much attention from athletes and coaches as creatine, an amino acid derivative formed naturally in the body but also present in relatively small quantities in the diet. The topic of creatine supplementation and high-intensity exercise performance is reviewed by Maughan *et al.* (2004) and will not be reviewed again here. Rather, our purpose is to review evidence for and against a potential role for creatine in enhancing resistance training-induced gains in skeletal muscle size. It has been consistently reported that creatine ingestion during heavy resistance training augments gains in body mass, fat-free mass and muscular strength (e.g. Earnest *et al.*, 1995; Vandenberghe *et al.*, 1997; for a recent review, see Krieder, 2003). These adaptations have often been attributed to an accelerated rate of muscle protein accretion, but only recently have investigators tested this hypothesis directly by examining changes within skeletal muscle.

The first study to directly examine creatine supplementation in conjunction with heavy resistance training on skeletal muscle hypertrophy in humans was published by Volek and colleagues in 1999. Nineteen resistance-trained men were randomly assigned in a double-blind fashion to either a creatine or placebo (cellulose) group, and then performed whole-body, periodized heavy resistance training for 12 weeks. The supplementation consisted of 25 g·day^{-1} of creatine/placebo for the first 7 days after baseline testing, followed by 5 g·day^{-1} until the end of the study. After training, the creatine-supplemented group displayed significantly greater gains in bench press and squat strength, as well as large increases in body mass and fat-free mass. The most notable finding, however, was a significantly greater increase in Type I, IIa and IIb muscle fibre cross-sectional area (CSA) in the creatine-supplemented group compared with placebo. When expressed as a relative change, the mean increase in CSA for the fibre types examined was ~34% in the creatine group versus ~10% in the placebo group. A potential limitation to the study, however, was the unexpected finding that the participants assigned to the creatine group had ~20% smaller muscle fibre areas at baseline. Thus, while the relative increase in CSA was larger in the creatine group, there were no differences between conditions in absolute CSA for any fibre type after training (Fig. 3).

Since the first report by Volek *et al.* (1999), four other studies have described the effects of creatine supplementation on resistive-training-induced changes in skeletal muscle (Hespel *et al.*, 2001; Stevenson and Dudley, 2001; Tarnopolsky *et al.*, 2001; Willoughby and Rosene, 2001). These latter investigations have produced equivocal findings, with two studies supporting the initial work of Volek *et al.* (1999) (Hespel *et al.*, 2001; Willoughby and Rosene, 2001) and two studies concluding that creatine supplementation does not augment training-induced gains in muscle size (Stevenson and Dudley, 2001; Tarnopolsky *et al.*, 2001). The lack of congruent results may be related in part to differences

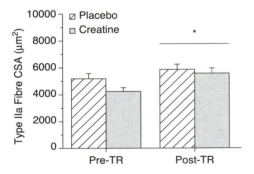

Figure 3. Cross-sectional area (CSA) of type IIa muscle fibres in the vastus lateralis of resistance-trained volunteers before (Pre-TR) and after (Post-TR) a 12-week periodized leg resistance training programme, during which the participants were supplemented with either creatine or placebo (cellulose). The relative increases in CSA for Type I, IIa, IIab and IIb fibres were higher for the creatine-supplemented group than the placebo group (mean change of 36 and 10%, respectively). However, the absolute muscle fibre CSAs were not different between groups after training, due to the unexpected finding that the creatine group had 20% smaller muscle CSA than the placebo group before training. Adapted from Volek *et al.* (1999).

in study methodology, including: the study population (i.e. resistance-trained or untrained); mode, frequency and duration of the training intervention; technique used to assess muscle adaptation; and, possibly, the type of 'placebo' intervention employed.

Hespel and colleagues (2001) examined the effect of creatine ingestion on the contractile, biochemical and histochemical properties of human skeletal muscle during immobilization and rehabilitation. Participants had their right leg immobilized with a polyester cast for 2 weeks before participating in a 10-week rehabilitation programme that consisted of 4–6 sets of unilateral knee extension exercises, with 12 repetitions per set at an intensity of 60% one-repetition maximum (1-RM), three times a week. The participants were divided into two groups and throughout the entire period of immobilization and rehabilitation received either creatine monohydrate (initial loading dose of $20 \text{ g} \cdot \text{day}^{-1}$, followed by $5 \text{ g} \cdot \text{day}^{-1}$) or a placebo (not stated). After immobilization, quadriceps muscle CSA and isometric knee extension torque were decreased to the same extent in both conditions when compared with baseline. However, muscle CSA and peak torque recovered faster in the creatine-supplemented group than the placebo group, when assessed after 3 and 10 weeks of the rehabilitation period. Biopsies obtained from the vastus lateralis revealed that type I, IIa and IIb muscle fibre cross-sectional areas after 10 weeks of rehabilitation when compared with baseline were only elevated in the creatine-supplemented group. A unique aspect of that study was that biopsy samples were also examined to assess, for the first time in humans, the expression of the myogenic transcription factors MyoD, myogenin, Myf5 and MRF4. There is substantial evidence from experiments with rats to suggest that these factors are involved in regulating processes intrinsic to muscle cell catabolism and anabolism (e.g. Marsh *et al.*, 1997; Adams *et al.*, 1999). After 10 weeks of rehabilitation, MRF4 protein content was higher in the creatine-supplemented group than in the placebo group, whereas myogenin protein showed the opposite effect, and protein expression of Myf5 and MyoD remained unchanged. The authors suggested that changes in specific myogenic transcription factors induced by oral creatine supplementation might influence the muscle hypertrophy response during rehabilitative strength training.

In support of the findings of Volek *et al.* (1999) and Hespel *et al.* (2001), Willoughby and Rosene (2001) concluded that creatine supplementation during chronic resistance training increased muscle strength and size, possibly as a result of increased myosin heavy chain (MHC) synthesis. Untrained young men were randomly assigned to a control, placebo ($6 \text{ g} \cdot \text{dextrose day}^{-1}$) or creatine-supplemented group ($6 \text{ g} \cdot \text{day}^{-1}$) in a double-blind fashion. They then performed 12 weeks of lower-body heavy resistance training (leg press, leg extension, leg curl; three sets of 6–8 repetitions at 85–90% 1-RM, 3 times per week). Needle biopsy samples from the vastus lateralis revealed that, following training, myofibrillar protein increased by 58% in the creatine-supplemented group, and this was significantly greater compared with the relative increases in the placebo and controls groups (12% and 3%, respectively). The relative changes in MHC isoform mRNA for Type I, IIa and IIx were also higher in the creatine-supplemented condition than in the placebo and control conditions. A subsequent report by the same authors (Willoughby and Rosene, 2003), based on additional analyses of muscle samples collected during their original study, concluded that creatine supplementation combined with heavy resistance training increased the mRNA and protein expression of MRF4 and myogenin. This latter finding differs from the results of Hespel *et al.* (2001), although direct comparisons between studies are hampered by differences in study design.

In contrast to the studies described above, which concluded creatine supplementation augments muscle protein accretion during resistance training in humans, two well-controlled studies from separate laboratories have failed to support this hypothesis (Stevenson and Dudley, 2001; Tarnopolsky *et al.*, 2001). Stevenson and Dudley (2001) studied 18 resistance-trained individuals who ingested either creatine or table sugar (initial loading dose of 20 $g \cdot day^{-1}$ for 7 days followed by 5 $g \cdot day^{-1}$ thereafter) and then performed an 8-week electrostimulation resistive-training programme. The authors' laboratory previously showed that electrostimulation can induce marked hypertrophy in a few months without requiring voluntary effort or the participants to alter their resistance training (Ruther *et al.*, 1995). The specific electrostimulation protocol consisted of 3–5 sets of coupled concentric and eccentric actions that were applied to the left quadriceps femoris twice weekly while the participants continued voluntary resistance training on both lower limbs unsupervised. Quadriceps femoris CSA, assessed using magnetic resonance imaging, increased after electrostimulation by 10% and 12% in the placebo and creatine-supplemented groups, respectively, with no significant differences between conditions. A notable observation was that the CSA of the right quadriceps, which did not receive electrostimulation but continued to experience a chronic, unsupervised training stimulus, increased by 5% in the creatine-supplemented group, whereas the placebo group showed no change. Although speculative, one potential explanation for this finding was that the participants in the creatine-supplemented group may have performed a larger overall volume of unsupervised leg training and this provided a greater cumulative stimulus to the right (non-electrostimulated) leg compared with the placebo condition.

Finally, Tarnopolsky and colleagues (2001) provided a unique perspective on this issue by highlighting that virtually all studies have compared a creatine-supplemented group with a group who received either a non-isoenergetic or non-isonitrogenous placebo (e.g. cellulose or dextrose). In addition, these authors noted that few creatine supplementation studies controlled the timing of supplement ingestion after exercise. This is an important consideration, given that the composition and timing of nutrient delivery can profoundly alter post-exercise protein metabolism and thus potentially impact gains in mass, strength and muscle protein balance (Tipton and Wolfe, 2004). Tarnopolsky *et al.* (2001) specifically tested the hypothesis that a post-exercise creatine–carbohydrate supplement would result in similar gains in strength and muscle fibre area as an isoenergetic and isonitrogenous protein–carbohydrate supplement. In a double-blind fashion, young male participants were randomized to receive either 10 g of creatine + 75 g glucose or 10 g of casein + 75 g glucose, immediately after each exercise bout during an 8-week whole-body progressive resistance training programme. Training increased Type I and II muscle fibre CSA by ∼20 and ∼25%, respectively, but there was no significant difference between groups, and gains in 1-RM strength for each of 16 tested exercises were similar (Fig. 4). The only difference between conditions was that the body mass gains were higher in the creatine-supplemented group. From a practical standpoint, therefore, the authors concluded that athletes who are engaged in sports where a high strength:lean mass ratio is important may wish to consider a protein–carbohydrate supplement, whereas athletes who desire a high absolute mass might consider a creatine–carbohydrate supplement.

In summary, there are equivocal data to suggest that creatine supplementation may enhance resistance training-induced gains in muscle size, but the potential mechanisms involved and the potential confounding influence of nutrient composition/timing remain unclear. From a theoretical standpoint, the increase in body water retention that typically accompanies creatine supplementation could alter protein turnover through changes in cellular hydration status (Haussinger *et al.*, 1993), but there is no direct evidence for this in human muscle following either acute or chronic creatine ingestion. There are *in vitro* data which suggest that creatine administration may stimulate muscle protein synthesis (Ingwall *et al.*, 1972, 1974), although this is not a universal finding (Fry and Morales, 1980). Vierck *et al.* (2003) recently reported that

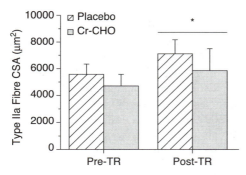

Figure 4. Cross-sectional area (CSA) of type II muscle fibres in the vastus lateralis of untrained volunteers before (Pre-TR) and after (Post-TR) an 8-week progressive leg resistance training programme, during which the participants were provided with a creatine–carbohydrate supplement (Cr-CHO) or isonitrogenous and isoenergetic protein (casein)–carbohydrate supplement (PRO-CHO). The relative increases in CSA for Type I and II fibres were not different between groups after training. Adapted from Tarnopolsky *et al.* (2001).

treatment with creatine induced modest differentiation of myogenic satellite cells. This is a noteworthy observation given that adult myofibres are terminally differentiated and muscle regeneration after injury (e.g. myotrauma induced by resistance exercise training) appears to be dependent upon satellite cell activation and proliferation (Hawke and Garry, 2001). Nonetheless, the human studies that have been conducted to date have largely failed to detect any specific effect of creatine ingestion on skeletal muscle protein turnover. Parise *et al.* (2001) reported no effect of short-term creatine loading (20 g · day^{-1} for 7 days) on whole-body or mixed-muscle protein fractional synthetic rate in humans, although the breakdown and oxidation of some proteins were lower in men, suggesting a possible anticatabolic effect of creatine. However, a recent comprehensive study by Louis *et al.* (2003) concluded that creatine supplementation (21 g · day^{-1} for 5 days) had no effect on human muscle protein turnover (synthesis or degradation) at rest in both the post-absorptive and fed states. Similarly, Phillips *et al.* (2002) examined the combined effects of creatine supplementation and chronic resistance training on skeletal muscle protein turnover in men, and reported no significant difference compared with a group that received an isoenergetic and isonitrogenous placebo. Given that creatine supplementation facilitates muscle recovery during repeated bouts of high-intensity exercise, it has been suggested that strength athletes who supplement with creatine may be able to tolerate higher training volumes and chronically this leads to greater cumulative overload on the muscles (Krieder, 2003). While this theory appears plausible, at present there is insufficient evidence to directly evaluate it. Moreover, one of the few relevant studies that accurately quantified training volumes (Volek *et al.*, 1999) reported greater gains in leg muscle hypertrophy in a creatine-supplemented group, even though the volume of leg training performed was not different from that performed by the placebo group. Clearly, additional work is warranted to clarify our understanding of the potential interactive effect of creatine supplementation and chronic resistance exercise training on skeletal muscle hypertrophy and the potential regulatory mechanisms involved.

Post-exercise nutrition: is fat intake a concern?

The importance of ingesting carbohydrates in the minutes and hours after a training bout to maximize the resynthesis of muscle glycogen is examined by Burke *et al.* (2004). Essentially, as soon as one exercise training session ends, the athlete is in recovery mode and preparing for the next training session. It seems fair to conclude that carbohydrate repletion is of paramount importance, as most training sessions for most sports will require muscle glycogen as a fuel for exercise.

Of late, concern has been raised about post-exercise nutrition by a series of experiments examining the use and replenishment of intramuscular triacylglycerol (IMTG) during and after exercise. It is interesting to note that skeletal muscle stores a significant amount of IMTG, enough that the energy equivalent represents 67–100% of the energy stored as muscle glycogen in both untrained and trained individuals. Until recently, there had been considerable controversy about whether IMTG contributes a significant amount of fuel during exercise where fat makes a major contribution. However, recent studies using new techniques for measuring IMTG and examining the variability of direct assessments of IMTG have largely resolved this controversy. In short, there appears to be general consensus that IMTG is an important fuel during prolonged moderate-intensity exercise (and up to $\sim$85% $\dot{V}O_{2max}$ in well-trained athletes) and that the fat content of the post-exercise diet (and, therefore, carbohydrate) influences the rate that IMTG recovers (Watt et al., 2002b; van Loon et al., 2003).

Many laboratories have measured net IMTG use with direct biochemical analysis of needle biopsy samples taken from the vastus lateralis muscles of men and reported that IMTG was not an important fuel during exercise lasting 90–120 min at a power output of 50–65% $\dot{V}O_{2max}$. Others have reported net IMTG use during exercise in men and women (see Watt et al., 2002b, for a review). A major criticism of this work was that the needle muscle biopsy samples were contaminated by the presence of adipose tissue triacylglycerol, making any estimation of IMTG inaccurate. The fact that the *between-biopsy* (3 biopsies) variability of this measurement was about $\sim$20–26% in a group of untrained and active individuals supported this contention (Wendling et al., 1996). Interestingly, the *within-biopsy* variability was low ($\sim$6%) and in the same range reported for other fuels and metabolites measured in human muscle biopsies. At the same time, almost all of the studies that have estimated the use of IMTG during exercise by measuring whole-body respiratory exchange ratio (RER) and exogenous free fatty acids reported a significant use of IMTG during prolonged exercise. In addition, many studies employing histochemical IMTG staining techniques reported that IMTG was reduced after endurance exercise (Watt et al., 2002b).

Recently, a new technique that uses 1H-magnetic resonance spectroscopy (MRS) to distinguish between intra- and extramuscular triacylglycerol has been used to examine this issue (Szczepaniak et al., 1999). Again, the studies using this technique have for the most part reported a net IMTG use during endurance exercise in a variety of upper and lower leg muscles (see Watt et al., 2002b). In addition, Watt et al. (2002a) re-investigated the issue of IMTG use during exercise when measured biochemically by taking double biopsy samples throughout exercise in a group of well-trained cyclists. They reported that the between-biopsy variability was lower in trained ($\sim$12%) than untrained ($\sim$24%) cyclists and that this allowed for the detection of significant decreases in IMTG content during 2 h of cycling at 57% $\dot{V}O_{2max}$. Therefore, the authors argued in a recent review (Watt et al., 2002b) that much of the controversy regarding IMTG use during exercise in the studies employing biochemical analyses of muscle biopsy samples is a function of two things: (1) there is significant variability between muscle biopsy samples in human skeletal muscle, although this is less in trained individuals; (2) because of the high energy density of fat, the amount of IMTG used during 90–120 min of cycling at 50–65% $\dot{V}O_{2max}$ is not large and can be less than the between-biopsy variability in untrained/active individuals. Another point that is apparent from these recent studies is that adipose tissue contamination of the biochemical estimates of IMTG is not present or is minimal, as the measured values are in the same range as or lower than the IMTG values reported using the 1H-MRS technique. A final point is that the few studies that have examined this issue in well-trained females all suggest that IMTG is a significant fuel source during endurance exercise. Interestingly, this includes one study that used muscle biopsies and biochemical IMTG determination (Steffensen *et al.*, 2002), one that deduced IMTG use from RER and plasma free fatty acid oxidation estimates (Romijn *et al.*, 2000) and one that used the 1H-MRS technique (Larson-Meyer *et al.*, 2002). In summary, it would appear that there is general consensus that IMTG is a significant source of fuel during moderate aerobic exercise in active and trained individuals. This may extend to intense aerobic power outputs ($\sim$85% $\dot{V}O_{2max}$) in well-trained individuals. However, there still exists controversy over the accuracy of the various methods used to estimate IMTG use during exercise and, therefore, the magnitude of the IMTG contribution to total fuel use.

The practical reality of using IMTG during exercise training sessions is that it will need to be replenished during the recovery period between workouts. Although it is unclear at present whether beginning an exercise session with an IMTG store that is less than normal will actually limit the ability to exercise or train, it is clear that an inability to replenish this store over repeated training sessions could lead to such a situation. The remainder of this section will highlight the recent work that has examined the issue of IMTG repletion after exercise.

Starling *et al.* (1997) reported that the vastus lateralis IMTG content (biochemical measurement) was higher 1 day after exercise when participants ingested a high fat diet (68% of energy) rather than a very low fat diet (5%). The participants first completed 120 min of exercise at 65% $\dot{V}O_{2max}$, then consumed one of the diets for 12 h and fasted another 12 h. The IMTG concentration increased in the 24 h after exercise on the high fat diet (from 32.8 to 44.7 mmol·kg^{-1} dry mass) but did not recover when on the low fat diet (from 30.9 to 27.5 mmol·kg^{-1} dry mass). However, the high fat diet was also a low carbohydrate diet and the repletion of glycogen was impaired and performance during a subsequent self-paced cycling time-trial decreased (time to complete 1600 kJ; high fat = 139 min, low fat = 117 min). Two other studies measured recovery IMTG after exhaustive cycling using muscle biopsies and biochemical techniques. In both cases, the well-trained athletes consumed a diet high in carbohydrate (65–70% carbohydrate, 20% fat, 10–15% protein) in the first 18–30 h after a prolonged and exhaustive exercise bout. Neither study found evidence of an increase in IMTG after exercise. Kiens and Richter (1998) reported significantly lower IMTG concentrations at 3, 6, 18 and 30 h with a low point of 20% below the immediate post-exercise value 18 h after exercise. On the other hand, Kimber *et al.* (2003) reported no significant change in IMTG after 3, 6 and 18 h of recovery compared with the immediate post-exercise value. Additional studies have specifically examined the effects of two or more diets on IMTG use and recovery.

Coyle *et al.* (2001) examined the effect of 7-day diets that contained 32, 22 or 2% of energy intake from fat on IMTG and glycogen stores and subsequent fuel utilization during 2 h of exercise at 67% $\dot{V}O_{2max}$ in well-trained cyclists. The changes in carbohydrate consumption were reciprocal with fat and energy intake from protein constant at 10%, such that all diets were eucaloric. Participants exercised for 2 h at 67% $\dot{V}O_{2max}$ in the morning on all days of the 7-day diets except the first day. The pre-exercise IMTG store was unaffected by a reduction in fat intake from 32 to 22%, but was decreased by $\sim 20\%$ following the 2% fat diet. Muscle glycogen increased from a low of ~ 530 mmol $\cdot$ kg^{-1} dry mass after consuming 32% fat to ~ 700 and 825 mmol $\cdot$ kg^{-1} dry mass after the 22 and 2% fat diets, respectively. During exercise, there were no differences in estimated fuel use between the 32 and 22% fat diets, but the 2% fat diet decreased fat and increased carbohydrate oxidation rates compared with the 22% fat diet (RER, 0.908 *vs* 0.876). The amount of plasma free fatty acid oxidation was not decreased in the 2% fat condition, implying that the reduction in whole-body fat oxidation was solely due to a reduction in free fatty acid oxidation from IMTG. The finding that IMTG was well maintained even during the very low fat intake diet led the authors to suggest that fat may be synthesized from carbohydrate in such a low fat/high carbohydrate condition.

Surprisingly, the small decrement in IMTG and increase in muscle glycogen contents following the low fat diet led to increased glycogen oxidation and reduced IMTG oxidation while not affecting the amount of extramuscular fuel that was oxidized. It is not known how the changes in initial fuel stores predisposed the muscle to these changes in fuel use. It could be argued that, at an intensity of 67% $\dot{V}O_{2max}$, it doesn't matter whether the athlete consumes a diet of 2–22% fat, 10% protein and the balance carbohydrate, as fuel reliance simply follows dietary intake. However, what happens to the IMTG store over time with repeated bouts of training and a low fat diet?

Subsequent studies have specifically examined the time-course of IMTG repletion after a single bout of prolonged exercise. Decombaz *et al.* (2001) examined the effect of post-exercise diets containing either 14.5 or 55.5% of the total energy intake from fat on IMTG and glycogen repletion in the tibialis anterior of six untrained men and six trained male runners at 9 and 30 h post-exercise. The protein contribution was constant at 14% and carbohydrate was reciprocal with fat such that diets were eucaloric. The exercise consisted of 2 h of running or walking uphill on a treadmill at $\sim 50\%$ $\dot{V}O_{2max}$. The resting IMTG and glycogen contents were higher in the muscles of trained participants. The IMTG content decreased by about 22–26% in both groups but the absolute decrease was almost double in the trained group (Fig. 5). Whole-body RER averaged ~ 0.89 and ~ 0.93 in the trained and untrained groups, respectively, and IMTG was estimated to contribute $\sim 15\%$ and $\sim 17\%$ of whole-body fat metabolism, respectively. Repletion of IMTG on the high fat diet was apparent at 9 h of recovery and reached values $\sim 30\%$ higher than pre-exercise at 30 h of recovery in both groups. Recovery on the low fat diet produced no recovery in IMTG during the initial 9 h, with values reaching $\sim 80\%$ and $\sim 95\%$ of that pre-exercise at 30 h in the trained and untrained groups (Fig. 5). Glycogen use during exercise was 35–43% of the resting store in both groups. Glycogen repletion was faster on the low fat (high carbohydrate, $\sim 70\%$) diet, reaching pre-exercise values by 9 h. No further changes occurred in the trained group but the untrained participants supercompensated glycogen stores to 155% of pre-exercise by 30 h. In contrast, on the high fat (low carbohydrate, $\sim 30\%$) diet, muscle glycogen was not replenished to pre-exercise values until 30 h. The authors concluded that, given the dynamic nature of the IMTG store and the potential for it to spare muscle glycogen, 'it would be wise to try and optimize [IMTG] storage before competition, at the same time ensuring that glycogen storage is not compromised' (Decombaz *et al.*, 2001). However, this statement seems premature given that there is no evidence to demonstrate that IMTG is ever limiting for an athlete during training or competition. Also, there is no information determining the importance of IMTG during the higher exercise intensities that are employed during training and competitions. Exercise at power outputs of $\sim 50\%$ would have little relevance to a population of trained athletes.

Larson-Meyer *et al.* (2002) also examined this issue by measuring the influence of recovery diet on soleus muscle IMTG repletion after a 2-h treadmill run at $\sim 67\%$ $\dot{V}O_{2max}$ in seven well-trained recreational female runners. Post-exercise diets contained either 10 or 35% of the total energy intake from fat, 15% from protein and, therefore, 75 or 50% from carbohydrate. Soleus IMTG was measured before, immediately after and 22 h (~ 1 day) and 70 h (~ 3 days) after the exercise bout. Participants were allowed to run for 45 min after the

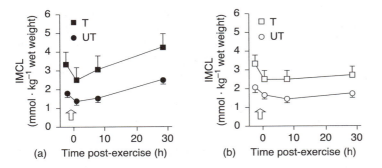

Figure 5. Effects of recovery diet on intramuscular triacylglycerol (IMCL) content in the tibialis anterior of six trained male runners (T) and six untrained men (UT). Arrows indicate exercise that consisted of 2 h of running/walking uphill on a treadmill at $\sim 50\%$ $\dot{V}O_{2max}$. The participants then consumed eucaloric diets containing either 55.5% (a) or 14.5% (b) of the total caloric intake from fat (14% protein, balance carbohydrate) for the next 30 h.

IMTG measurement on the first recovery day and again on the second recovery day. Exercise decreased IMTG content by ∼25%, and the higher fat diet repleted IMTG by 22 h and to a value ∼22% higher than pre-exercise by 70 h. In contrast, the low fat diet did not allow complete repletion of IMTG, reaching ∼88% of pre-exercise levels, even after 70 h. Absolute IMTG numbers were not reported, only changes relative to the bone marrow peak 1H-MRS signal. The authors noted that the consequences of compromised IMTG stores on the low fat recovery diet need to be investigated during heavy training and performance (Larson-Meyer et al., 2002). They also stated that, 'the current study provides evidence that diets too low in fat are probably not ideal for endurance athletes'.

Johnson et al. (2003) recently examined the effects of a strenuous exercise bout, followed by a recovery diet with varying fat contents for 2 days, on vastus lateralis IMTG concentrations and the ability to complete a subsequent cycling time-trial (∼3 h) in six highly trained male cyclists. The high fat/low carbohydrate diet contained 56% fat, 6% carbohydrate and 37% of total energy from protein; the low fat/high carbohydrate diet contained 19% fat, 63% carbohydrate and 17% protein. Unfortunately, the diets were not iso-energetic and the participants consumed ∼33% more energy on the low fat/high carbohydrate diet. Calculated IMTG was ∼10.7 and 7.0 $mmol \cdot kg^{-1}$ after the high and low fat recovery diets, respectively. Muscle glycogen was very low after the high fat/low carbohydrate diet and high after the low fat/high carbohydrate diet. During the subsequent time-trial rides, performance time was worse (∼200 vs 178 min), exercise intensity was lower (66 vs 71% $\dot{V}O_{2max}$) and RER was lower (∼0.80 vs 0.90) after the high fat compared with the low fat diet. Plasma free fatty acids were higher throughout exercise after the high fat diet and the participants received a carbohydrate drink at timed intervals during exercise in both trials. The IMTG concentration decreased by about 55–65% in both time-trial rides, but the absolute amount of IMTG used was much higher in the high than in the low fat trial (6.63 vs 3.63 $mmol \cdot kg^{-1}$ wet weight). The authors concluded that near-depletion of IMTG was evident in some of the athletes during prolonged strenuous cycling, regardless of the pre-diet. If the depletion of IMTG was prevalent in the Type I fibres, it remains to be seen whether this could have a negative effect on training or competition performance.

Lastly, van Loon et al. (2003) had nine endurance-trained athletes cycle for 3 h at 55% $\dot{V}O_{2max}$ on two occasions followed by either a diet high in fat (39% fat, 49% carbohydrate, 14% protein) or low in fat (24% fat, 62% carbohydrate and 14% protein) for 3 days. Vastus lateralis IMTG decreased by ∼21% after the 3-h cycle and had repleted towards normal in the high fat diet at 24 h and reached pre-exercise values at 48 h. In the low fat trial, IMTG was not significantly repleted even after 48 h. In addition, quantitative fluorescence microscopy of the muscle following 48 h of recovery and ingestion of the high fat diet revealed higher IMTG content in Type 1 muscle fibres than with the low fat diet (2.1 vs 1.4% area staining). These results are surprising given that the so-called 'low fat diet' contained 24% of the total energy intake as fat.

In summary, it is clear that high fat intakes (35–57% of energy) in the recovery periods following a prolonged exercise bout will replete IMTG stores quicker than low fat intakes (10–24%). The amount of ingested fat required for IMTG repletion has been estimated to be $\sim$2 g$\cdot$kg^{-1} BM$\cdot$day^{-1} (Decombaz, 2003). However, a high fat intake may compromise the ability to replete muscle glycogen and impair performance. One might expect that diets with moderate fat intake (about 20–30% fat) would be adequate for IMTG replenishment, but the findings with intakes of 19 and 24% do not support this contention. However, the 19% fat diet in the study of Johnson *et al.* (2003) was confounded by a low energy intake and although van Loon *et al.* (2003) reported no repletion in 48 h with a 24% fat recovery diet, the exercise-induced decrease in IMTG was only of the order of $\sim$20%. It must be borne in mind that there is considerable discussion in these papers regarding the best way to express the IMTG data – against a muscle water or creatine reference or a bone marrow reference (for discussion, see Larson-Meyer *et al.*, 2002). Given the possibility for water shifts during exercise and the variability in the creatine measurement in some studies (Johnson *et al.*, 2003), it is possible that 20% changes in IMTG content are near the detectable limit of the 1H-MRS technique. However, van Loon *et al.* (2003) reported IMTG repeatability of the order of 5%. Recovery of IMTG was complete after only 22 h when a 35% fat diet was consumed after exercise. Additional studies examining fat intake after exercise in the range of 20–30% are needed to clarify this issue. It may be that when 2 days are available for recovery, a diet that provides sufficient energy and includes about 2 g fat$\cdot$kg^{-1} and 6–10 g carbohydrate$\cdot$kg^{-1} will be optimal. If prolonged exercise occurs nearly every day, is a chronically low IMTG content simply a reality? This would leave the endurance athlete in a carbohydrate dependent state where their post-exercise diet would concentrate on adequate carbohydrate and protein intake. Decombaz (2003) has suggested that carbohydrate content should be high and fat content low in the initial 6–8 h of recovery and then fat can be added in the form of regular meals.

Nutrient–gene interactions

Exercise physiologists have been interested in the ability of skeletal muscle to adapt to repeated bouts of exercise since this field of study began. Understanding of the basic mechanisms that regulate these changes has progressed tremendously in the last 10 years with the increasing use of powerful molecular and cellular tools (Booth, 1998; Hargreaves and Cameron-Smith, 2002). Numerous investigations have now reported that exercise upregulates the expression of several genes that encode for skeletal muscle proteins that play a role in meeting the demands of exercise (Kraniou *et al.*, 2000; Pilegaard *et al.*, 2000; Tunstall *et al.*, 2002; Nordsborg *et al.*, 2003; see Hargreaves and Cameron-Smith, 2002, for a review). It has been suggested that the cellular adaptations to exercise training may be due to the cumulative effects of the transient increases in gene transcription that occur during and after repeated exercise bouts (Williams and Neufer, 1996; Hargreaves and Cameron-Smith, 2002). In this section, we are interested in particular in the recent work that has been done that links nutrition to the adaptations that occur in human skeletal muscle during training. Selected examples of the consequences of short-term dietary manipulations on gene expression in human skeletal muscle are discussed below.

Peters *et al.* (2001) examined the effects of consuming an isoenergetic high fat diet (73% fat, 5% carbohydrate, 22% protein) following a standardized pre-diet (30% fat, 50% carbohydrate, 21% protein) on pyruvate dehydrogenase kinase (PDK) isoform mRNA and protein content and PDK activity in human skeletal muscle. Six active males had muscle biopsies taken from the vastus lateralis before the high fat diet (day 0) and in the morning 1, 2 and 3 days after being on the high fat diet. One confounding factor in this study was that the participants were not allowed to exercise as they normally would have during the 3 days of the high fat diet. The resting RER decreased progressively from ~0.8 on day 0 to ~0.7 on day 3. Ketone body and free fatty acid (0.38–0.83 mmol·l^{-1}) concentrations increased progressively during the high fat diet while fasting insulin decreased by 50%. The PDK activity increased after only 1 day on the high fat diet and continued to increase in a linear fashion while on this diet (Fig. 6). Concentrations of both mRNA and protein PDK 4 isoform increased dramatically after 1 day on the high fat diet and remained high with no further increases on days 2 or 3, while PDK 2 concentrations were unchanged (Fig. 7). The linear increase in PDK activity in the face of a

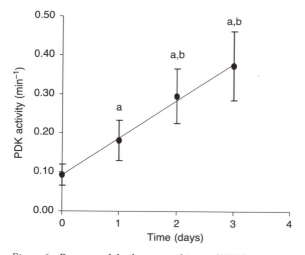

Figure 6. Pyruvate dehydrogenase kinase (PDK) activity in the vastus lateralis of men following a normal diet (time 0) and following 1, 2 and 3 days on a high fat/low carbohydrate diet (73% fat, 5% carbohydrate, 22% protein). [a] Significantly different from time 0. [b] Significantly different from 'a' alone.

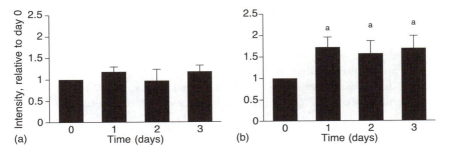

Figure 7. Pyruvate dehydrogenase kinase 2 (a) and 4 (b) isoform protein content in the vastus lateralis of men following a normal diet (time 0) and following 1, 2 and 3 days on a high fat/low carbohydrate diet (73% fat, 5% carbohydrate, 22% protein). [a] Significantly different from time 0.

constant PDK 4 protein concentration during high fat ingestion, suggested that either another PDK isoform (i.e. PDK 1 or 3 – there are only four) contributed to the increase in PDK activity or there was an increase in PDK-specific activity. Given that it has been shown that the abundance of PDK 1 and 3 are very low in human skeletal muscle and do not respond to 40 h of fasting (Spriet *et al.*, 2002), it is likely that the latter explanation is correct. There are existing data for rodent skeletal muscle that demonstrate the ability of the PDH complex to increase the binding of newly formed PDK 4 protein or existing PDK 2 protein, thereby accounting for the increased PDK-specific activity. This is an impressive adaptive quality for an enzyme that plays such an important role in the oxidation of carbohydrate both at rest and during exercise.

The PDH complex quickly responds to a lack of carbohydrate availability and/or increased fat oxidation by upregulating PDK activity, which drives more of the PDH enzyme into the inactive form and ultimately decreases skeletal muscle carbohydrate oxidation and spares the small store of carbohydrate in the body. Experiments that have artificially elevated plasma free fatty acid for 4–5 h have reported very large increases in PDK 4 mRNA levels, underscoring how rapidly fuel availability can upregulate PDK gene expression and decrease carbohydrate oxidation in skeletal muscle (R. J. Tunstall, unpublished observations). We also recently examined the response of 4 h of exercise at ~55% $\dot{V}O_{2max}$ on PDK activity, as it has been shown that carbohydrate oxidation and PDH activity decrease as exercise is prolonged beyond 2–3 h (Watt *et al.*, 2002a). Muscle biopsies were taken at rest, and at 10 min and 4 h of exercise. Carbohydrate oxidation and PDH activity (at 4 h) decreased and plasma free fatty acid concentration and fat oxidation increased during exercise as expected. The PDK activity was unchanged at 10 min but doubled at 4 h with no changes in PDK 2 and 4 protein levels (Peters *et al.*, 2003). Again, but this time in an exercise context, PDK increased and appeared to account for the decreasing PDH activity without an increase in total PDK protein. The participants consumed only water during this trial, so it is not known whether supplemental carbohydrate ingestion could reverse these changes both at the gene expression and enzyme activity levels.

Cameron-Smith *et al.* (2003) examined the effects of either a high carbohydrate diet (70–75% carbohydrate, <15% fat) or an isoenergetic high fat diet (>65% fat, <29% carbohydrate) for 5 days on the expression of genes encoding proteins for fatty acid transport and beta-oxidation in human skeletal muscle. The participants were 14 well-trained cyclists and triathletes ($\dot{V}O_{2max}$ = 67 ml·kg^{-1}·min^{-1}) who continued to train daily during the 5-day diet interventions. Plasma free fatty acids were significantly higher after 5 days on the high fat diet compared with baseline and after the high carbohydrate diet (~0.85 *vs* 0.39–0.41 mmol·l^{-1}). Carbohydrate oxidation was reduced and fat oxidation was increased during 20 min of cycling at ~70% $\dot{V}O_{2max}$ following the high fat diet compared with the high carbohydrate diet. The mRNA concentrations of carnitine palmitoyltransferase I, uncoupling protein 3 and the plasma membrane fatty acid binding protein (FABPpm) measured in the muscles of six of the participants were unaffected by either diet, although there was large variability in the data. However, there were significant increases in the fatty acid transporter (FAT/CD36) and beta-hydroxyacyl-CoA dehydrogenase mRNA values following the high fat diet compared with the high carbohydrate diet and baseline values. FAT/CD36 protein content was also increased in the muscles of eight participants following the high fat diet, although FABPpm was unchanged. These data provide strong support for the idea that increased dietary fat intake can increase the mRNA content of genes that are necessary for the uptake and oxidation of free fatty acids. This muscle adaptation seems entirely appropriate in the face of reduced availability of carbohydrate and increased availability of plasma free fatty acids. It is also noteworthy that these changes occurred in very well-trained athletes, who presumably have maximized the ability of their muscles to oxidize fat through years of endurance training. It is also important to again stress that increases in mRNA are not always predictive of increases in protein or measures of functional activity (as discussed above). There are many additional steps and points of regulation between increased mRNA contents and increased protein synthesis rates. This fact points to the need for simultaneous measurements of mRNA and proteins and functional measures including substrate transport and enzyme activities.

The mechanisms by which the adaptations to a high fat/low carbohydrate diet are mediated appear to be related to free fatty acid activation of the family of peroxisome proliferator activator receptors (PPARs) (Jump and Clarke, 1999; Duplus *et al.*, 2000) and/or an insulin effect consequent to the decreased carbohydrate availability. However, it has been pointed out that it is unlikely that PPAR-mediated processes are the only mechanism by which free fatty acids can induce gene expression (Duplus and Forest, 2002). Pilegaard *et al.* (2002) have also recently suggested that low concentrations of muscle glycogen may enhance the mRNA content of some genes involved in exercise metabolism. They manipulated pre-exercise muscle glycogen with a combination of exercise and diet and found that the PDK 4 and UCP 3 genes were upregulated to a greater extent in response to exercise. It is not known whether these exaggerated responses translate into greater protein contents or higher functional activities. One would predict that signals responsive both to increased fat availability and decreased carbohydrate availability would work in concert to determine the exact responses in gene expression in skeletal muscle.

In summary, it is clear that nutrition can alter gene expression both at rest and in combination with exercise. However, it is important to note that the dietary manipulations discussed above were for the most part drastic and unlikely to be used by athletes actively engaging in training and competition. It remains to be seen whether smaller changes in dietary carbohydrate and fat content will have effects on gene expression independent of, or in combination with, the training-induced changes.

Summary

In this review, we have attempted to highlight four areas where recent scientific information has forced us to reassess old issues and embrace new ones that may lead to altered nutritional recommendations for athletes. We revisited the issues of supplementing with caffeine and creatine, supplements that are already commonly used by athletes. Recent findings suggest that low doses of caffeine exert a major ergogenic effect on the central nervous system during exercise and strengthen the case for using low doses of caffeine during training. On the other hand, the data on the role that creatine plays in augmenting the increase in skeletal muscle mass and strength during resistance training remain equivocal and further study is required. The final two topics were nutritional issues that are new and have not progressed to the point that we can specifically identify strategies to enhance the adaptation to training. However, it is likely that nutritional strategies will be needed to replenish intramuscular fat stores in individuals engaging in chronic endurance training. It is also likely that the increased interest in gene and protein expression measurements will lead to nutritional strategies that will optimize the adaptations that occur in skeletal muscle during and after exercise training sessions.

References

1 Adams, G.R., Haddad, F. and Baldwin, K.M. (1999). Time course of changes in markers of myogenesis in overloaded rat skeletal muscles. *Journal of Applied Physiology*, **87**, 1705–1712.

2 Booth, F.W. (1988). Perspectives on molecular and cellular exercise physiology. *Journal of Applied Physiology*, **65**, 1461–1471.

3 Burke, L.M., Kiens, B. and Ivy, J.L. (2004). Carbohydrates and fat for training and recovery. *Journal of Sports Sciences*, **22**, 15–30.

4 Cameron-Smith, D., Burke, L.M., Angus, D.J., Tunstall, R.J., Cox, G.C., Bonen, A., Hawley, J.A. and Hargreaves, M. (2003). A short-term, high-fat diet up-regulates lipid metabolism and gene expression in human skeletal muscle. *American Journal of Clinical Nutrition*, **77**, 313–318.

5 Chesley, A., Howlett, R.A., Heigenhauser, G.J.F., Hultman, E. and Spriet, L.L. (1998). Regulation of muscle glycogenolytic flux during intense aerobic exercise following caffeine ingestion. *American Journal of Physiology: Regulatory, Integrative and Comparative Physiology*, **275**, R596–R603.

6 Coyle, E.F., Jeukendrup, A.E., Oseto, M.C., Hodgkinson, B.J. and Zderic, T.W. (2001). Low-fat diet alters intramuscular substrates and reduces lipolysis and fat oxidation during exercise. *American Journal of Physiology: Endocrinology and Metabolism*, **280**, E391–E398.

7 Cox, G.R., Desbrow, B., Montgomery, P.G., Anderson, M.E., Bruce, C.R., Macrides, T.A., Martin, D.T., Moquin, A., Roberts, A., Hawley, J.A. and Burke, L. (2002). Effect of different protocols of caffeine intake on metabolism and endurance performance. *Journal of Applied Physiology*, **93**, 990–999.

8 Daly, J.W. (1993). Mechanism of action of caffeine. In *Caffeine, Coffee, and Health* (edited by S. Garattini), pp. 97–150. New York: Raven Press.

9 Davis, J.M., Zhao, Z., Stock, H.S., Mehl, K.A., Buggy, J. and Hand, G.A. (2003). Central nervous system effects of caffeine and adenosine on fatigue. *American Journal of Physiology: Regulatory, Integrative, and Comparative Physiology*, **284**, R399–R404.

10 Decombaz, J. (2003). Nutrition and recovery of muscle energy stores after exercise. *Sportmedizin und Sporttraumatologie*, **51**, 31–38.

11 Decombaz, J., Schmitt, B., Ith, M., Decarli, B., Diem, P., Kreis, R., Hoppeler, H. and Boesch, C. (2001). Postexercise fat intake repletes intramyocellular lipids but no faster in trained than in sedentary subjects. *American Journal of Physiology: Regulatory, Integrative, and Comparative Physiology*, **281**, R760–R769.

12 Duplus, E. and Forest, C. (2002). Is there a single mechanism for fatty acid regulation of gene transcription? *Biochemical Pharmacology*, **64**, 893–901.

13 Duplus, E., Glorian, M.M. and Forest, C. (2000). Fatty acid regulation of gene transciption. *Journal of Biological Chemistry*, **275**, 30749–30752.

14 Earnest, C.P., Snell, P.G., Rodriguez, R., Almada, A.L. and Mitchell, T.L. (1995). The effect of creatine monohydrate ingestion on anaerobic power indices, muscular strength and body composition. *Acta Physiologica Scandinavica*, **153**, 207–209.

15 Essig, D., Costill, D.L. and vanHandel, P.J. (1980). Effects of caffeine ingestion on utilization of muscle glycogen and lipid during leg ergometer cycling. *International Journal of Sports Medicine*, **1**, 86–90.

16 Fernstrom, J.D. and Fernstrom, M.H. (1984). Effects of caffeine on monamine neurotransmitters in the central and peripheral nervous system. In *Caffeine* (edited by P.B. Dews), pp. 107–118. Berlin: Springer-Verlag.

17 Fredholm, B.B. (1995). Adenosine, adenosine receptors and the actions of caffeine. *Pharmacology and Toxicology*, **76**, 93–101.

18 Fry, D.M. and Morales, M.F. (1980). A reexamination of the effects of creatine on muscle protein in tissue culture. *Journal of Cell Biology*, **84**, 294–297.

19 Graham, T.E. and Spriet, L.L. (1995). Metabolic, catecholamine and exercise performance responses to varying doses of caffeine. *Journal of Applied Physiology*, **78**, 867–874.

20 Graham, T.E., Helge, J.W., MacLean, D.A., Kiens, B. and Richter, E.A. (2000). Caffeine ingestion does not alter carbohydrate or fat metabolism in skeletal muscle during exercise. *Journal of Physiology*, **529**, 837–847.

21 Hargreaves, M. and Cameron-Smith, D. (2002). Exercise, diet, and skeletal muscle gene expression. *Medicine and Science in Sports and Exercise*, **34**, 1505–1508.

22 Haussinger, D., Roth, E., Lang, F. and Gerok, W. (1993). Cellular hydration state: an important determinant of protein catabolism and disease. *Lancet*, **341**, 1330–1332.

23 Hawke, T.J. and Garry, D.J. (2001). Myogenic satellite cells: physiology to molecular biology. *Journal of Applied Physiology*, **91**, 534–551.

24 Hespel, P., Op't Eijnde, B., Van Leemputte, M., Ursø, B., Greenhaff, P.L., Labarque, V., Dynarkowski, S., Van Hecke, P. and Richter, E.A. (2001). Oral creatine supplementation facilitates the rehabilitation of disuse atrophy and alters the expression of muscle myogenic factors in humans. *Journal of Physiology*, **536**, 625–633.

25 Ingwall, J.S., Morales, M.F. and Stockdale, F.E. (1972). Creatine and the control of myosin synthesis in differentiating skeletal muscle. *Proceedings of the National Academy of Sciences USA*, **69**, 2250–2253.

26 Ingwall, J., Weiner, C., Morales, M., Davis, E. and Stockdale, F. (1974). Specificity of creatine in the control of muscle protein synthesis. *Journal of Cell Biology*, **63**, 145–151.

27 Johnson, N.A., Stannard, S.R., Mehalski, K., Trenell, M.I., Sachinwalla, T., Thompson, C.H. and Thompson, M.W. (2003). Intramyocellular triacylglycerol in prolonged cycling with high- and low-carbohydrate availability. *Journal of Applied Physiology*, **94**, 1365–1372.

28 Jump, D.B. and Clarke, S.D. (1999). Regulation of gene expression by dietary fat. *Annual Review of Nutrition*, **19**, 63–90.

29 Kiens, B. and Richter, E.A. (1998). Utilization of skeletal muscle triacylglycerol during postexercise recovery in humans. *American Journal of Physiology: Endocrinology and Metabolism*, **275**, E332–E337.

30 Kimber, N.E., Heigenhauser, G.J.F., Spriet, L.L. and Dyck, D.J. (2003). Skeletal muscle fat and carbohydrate metabolism during recovery from glycogen depleting exercise in humans. *Journal of Physiology*, **548**, 919–928.

31 Kraniou, Y., Cameron-Smith, D., Misso, M., Collier, G. and Hargreaves, M. (2000). Effects of exercise on GLUT-4 and glycogenin gene expression in human skeletal muscle. *Journal of Applied Physiology*, **88**, 794–796.

32 Krieder, R.B. (2003). Effects of creatine supplementation on performance and training adaptations. *Molecular and Cellular Biochemistry*, **244**, 89–94.

33 Larson-Meyer, D.E., Newcomer, B.R. and Hunter, G.R. (2002). Influence of endurance running and recovery diet on intramyocellular lipid content in women: a 1H NMR study. *American Journal of Physiology: Endocrinology and Metabolism*, **282**, E95–E106.

34 Laurent, D., Schneider, K.E., Prusaczyk, W.P., Franklin, C., Vogel, S.M., Krssak, M., Petersen, K.F., Goforth, H.G. and Shulman, G.I. (2000). Effects of caffeine on muscle glycogen utilization and the neuroendocrine axis during exercise. *Journal of Clinical Endocrinology and Metabolism*, **85**, 2170–2175.

35 Louis, M., Poortmans, J.R., Francaux, M., Hultman, E., Berr, J., Boisseau, N., Young, V.R., Smith, K., Meier-Augenstein, W., Babraj, J.A., Waddell, T. and Rennie, M.J. (2003). Creatine supplementation has no effect on human muscle

protein turnover at rest in the postabsorptive or fed states. *American Journal of Physiology: Endocrinology and Metabolism,* **284,** E764–E770.

36 Marsh, D.R., Criswell, D.S., Carson, J.A. and Booth, F.W. (1997). Myogenic regulatory factors during regeneration of skeletal muscle in young, adult and old rats. *Journal of Applied Physiology,* **83,** 1270–1275.

37 Maughan, R.J., King, D.S. and Lea, T. (2004). Dietary supplements. *Journal of Sports Sciences,* **22,** 95–113.

38 Nehlig, A., Daval, J.-L. and Debry, G. (1992). Caffeine and the central nervous system: mechanisms of action, biochemical, metabolic, and psychostimulant effects. *Brain Research Reviews,* **17,** 139–170.

39 Nordsborg, N., Bangsbo, J. and Pilegaard, H. (2003). Effect of high-intensity training on exercise-induced expression of genes involved in ion-homeostasis and metabolism. *Journal of Applied Physiology,* **95,** 1201–1206.

40 Parise, G., Mihic, S., MacLennan, D., Yarasheski, K.E. and Tarnopolsky, M.A. (2001). Effects of acute creatine monohydrate supplementation on leucine kinetics and mixed-muscle protein synthesis. *Journal of Applied Physiology,* **91,** 1041–1047.

41 Pasman, W.J., vanBaak, M.A., Jeukendrup, A.E. and DeHaan, A. (1995). The effect of different dosages of caffeine on endurance performance time. *International Journal of Sports Medicine,* **16,** 225–230.

42 Peters, S.J., Harris, R.A., Wu, P., Pehleman, T.L., Heigenhauser, G.J.F. and Spriet, L.L. (2001). Human skeletal muscle PDH kinase activity and isoform expression during three days of a high fat/low carbohydrate diet. *American Journal of Physiology: Endocrinology and Metabolism,* **281,** E1151–E1158.

43 Peters, S.J., Heigenhauser, G.J.F., Inglis, J.G., Spriet, L.L. and Watt, M.J. (2003). Human skeletal muscle PDH kinase activity increases during prolonged exercise. *Medicine and Science in Sports and Exercise,* **35**(suppl.), S147.

44 Phillips, S.M., Parise, G., Roy, B.D., Tipton, K.D., Wolfe, R.R. and Tarnopolsky, M.A. (2002). Resistance training-induced adaptations in skeletal muscle protein turnover in the fed state. *Canadian Journal of Physiology and Pharmacology,* **80,** 1045–1053.

45 Pilegaard, H., Ordway, G.O., Saltin, B. and Neufer, P.D. (2000). Transcriptional regulation of gene expression in human skeletal muscle during recovery from exercise. *American Journal of Physiology: Endocrinology and Metabolism,* **279,** E806–E814.

46 Pilegaard, H., Keller, C., Steensberg, A., Helge, J.W., Pedersen, B.K., Saltin, B. and Neufer, P.D. (2002). Influence of pre-exercise muscle glycogen content on exercise-induced transcriptional regulation of metabolic genes. *Journal of Physiology,* **541,** 261–271.

47 Romijn, J.A., Coyle, E.F., Sidossis, L.S., Rosenblatt, J. and Wolfe, R.R. (2000). Substrate metabolism during different exercise intensities in endurance-trained women. *Journal of Applied Physiology,* **88,** 1707–1714.

48 Ruther, C.L., Golden, C.L., Harris, R.T. and Dudley, G.A. (1995). Hypertrophy, resistance training, and the nature of skeletal muscle activation. *Journal of Strength and Conditioning Research,* **9,** 155–159.

49 Spriet, L.L., MacLean, D.A., Dyck, D.J., Hultman, E., Cederblad, G. and Graham, T.E. (1992). Caffeine ingestion and muscle metabolism during prolonged exercise in humans. *American Journal of Physiology: Endocrinology and Metabolism,* **262,** E891–E898.

50 Spriet, L.L., Tunstall, R.J., Watt, M.J., Cameron-Smith, D. and Hargreaves, M. (2002). Time course of a 40 hour fast on pyruvate dehydrogenase activation and

kinase expression in human skeletal muscle. *Medicine and Science in Sports and Exercise*, **33**(suppl.), S98.

51 Starling, R.D., Trappe, T.A., Parcell, A.C., Kerr, C.G., Fink, W.J. and Costill, D.L. (1997). Effects of diet on muscle triglyceride and endurance performance. *Journal of Applied Physiology*, **82**, 1185–1189.

52 Steffensen, C.H., Roepstorff, C., Madsen, M. and Kiens, B. (2002). Myocellular triacylglycerol breakdown in females but not in males during exercise. *American Journal of Physiology: Endocrinology and Metabolism*, **282**, E634–E642.

53 Stevenson, S.W. and Dudley, G.A. (2001). Dietary creatine supplementation and muscular adaptation to resistive overload. *Medicine and Science in Sports and Exercise*, **33**, 1304–1310.

54 Szczepaniak, L.S., Babcock, E.E., Schick, F., Dobbins, R.L., Garg, A., Burns, D.K., McGarry, J.D. and Stein, D.T. (1999). Measurement of intracellular triglyceride stores by 1H spectroscopy: validation *in vivo*. *American Journal of Physiology: Endocrinology and Metabolism*, **276**, E977–E989.

55 Tarnopolsky, M.A., Parise, G., Yardley, N.J., Ballantyne, C.S., Olatunji, S. and Phillips, S.M. (2001). Creatine-dextrose and protein-dextrose induce similar strength gains during training. *Medicine and Science in Sports and Exercise*, **33**, 2044–2052.

56 Tipton, K.D. and Wolfe, R.R. (2004) Protein and amino acids for athletes. *Journal of Sports Sciences*, **22**, 65–79.

57 Tunstall, R.J., Mehan, K.A., Wadley, G.D., Collier, G.R., Bonen, A., Hargreaves, M. and Cameron-Smith, D. (2002). Exercise training increases lipid metabolism gene expression in human skeletal muscle. *American Journal of Physiology: Endocrinology and Metabolism*, **283**, E66–E72.

58 Vandenberghe, K., Goris, M., van Hecke, P., van Leemputte, M., Vangerven, L. and Hespel, P. (1997). Long-term creatine intake is beneficial to muscle performance during resistance training. *Journal of Applied Physiology*, **83**, 2055–2063.

59 van Loon, L.J.C., Schrauwen-Hinderling, V.B., Koopman, R., Wagenmakers, A.J.M., Hesselink, M.K.C., Schaart, G., Kooi, M.E. and Saris, W.H.M. (2003). Influence of prolonged endurance cycling and recovery diet on intramuscular triglyceride content in trained males. *American Journal of Physiology: Endocrinology and Metabolism*, **285**, E804–E811.

60 Vierck, J.L., Icenoggle, D.L., Bucci, L. and Dodson, M.V. (2003). The effects of ergogenic compounds on myogenic satellite cells. *Medicine and Science in Sports and Exercise*, **35**, 769–776.

61 Volek, J.S., Duncan, N.D., Mazzetti, S.A., Staron, R.S., Putakian, M., Gomez, A.L., Pearson, D.R., Fink, W.J. and Kraemer, W.J. (1999). Performance and muscle fiber adaptations to creatine supplementation and heavy resistance training. *Medicine and Science in Sports and Exercise*, **31**, 1147–1156.

62 Watt, M.J., Heigenhauser, G.J.F., Dyck, D.J. and Spriet, L.L. (2002a). Intramuscular triacylglycerol, glycogen and acetyl group metabolism during 4 hours of moderate exercise. *Journal of Physiology*, **541**, 969–978.

63 Watt, M.J., Heigenhauser, G.J.F. and Spriet, L.L. (2002b). Intramuscular triacylglycerol utilization in human skeletal muscle during exercise: is there a controversy? *Journal of Applied Physiology*, **93**, 1185–1195.

64 Wendling, P.S., Peters, S.J., Heigenhauser, G.J.F. and Spriet, L.L. (1996). Variability of triacylglycerol content in human skeletal muscle biopsy samples. *Journal of Applied Physiology*, **81**, 1150–1155.

65 Williams, R.S. and Neufer, P.D. (1996). Regulation of gene expression in skeletal muscle by contractile activity. In *Handbook of Physiology, Section 12: Exercise: Regulation and Integration of Multiple Systems* (edited by L.B. Rowell and J.T. Shepherd), pp. 1124–1150. New York: Oxford University Press.

66 Willoughby, D.S. and Rosene, J. (2001). Effects of oral creatine and resistance training on myosin heavy chain expression. *Medicine and Science in Sports and Exercise*, **33**, 1674–1681.

67 Willoughby, D.S. and Rosene, J.M. (2003). Effects of oral creatine and resistance training on myogenic regulatory factor expression. *Medicine and Science in Sports and Exercise*, **35**, 923–929.

COMMENTARIES

Protein and amino acid requirements of athletes

D. JOE MILLWARD

Protein supplements are the most widely used ergogenic aid. The need for, and safety of, additional protein for athletes are important issues, and although controversial more often reflect prejudice rather than evidence (Millward *et al.*, 1994; Rennie and Tipton, 2000). In fact, a nutritionally complete mixed diet (e.g. 14% protein calories) fed to physically active individuals at energy balance (e.g. twice the basal metabolic rate) will require about 1.7 g protein $\cdot$ kg^{-1}, much more than estimates of the minimum requirements for nitrogen balance – that is, 0.8 g $\cdot$ kg^{-1} (Institute of Medicine, 2002), or lower than this on the basis of an adaptive metabolic demands model of protein requirements (Millward, 2003). Furthermore, it has long been known that marked strength gains with appropriate resistance exercise can occur on very modest protein intakes of about 0.8 g $\cdot$ kg^{-1} (Chittenden, 1907), as recently confirmed in elderly individuals (Campbell *et al.*, 2002). This is consistent with the trivial amounts of extra dietary protein required for protein accretion at the highest rates of muscle hypertrophy, the increased efficiency of protein utilization associated with exercise (Millward *et al.*, 1994), and the regulatory anabolic drive of protein on muscle growth (Millward and Rivers, 1989) being delivered by protein intakes of normal food consumed to energy needs. Arguments for additional protein needs within the expected intake range often derive from the positive nitrogen balance associated with high protein intakes, but this is a technical artefact (Millward, 2001). While there are no reported controlled dietary trials of protein intake and performance *per se*, a recent meta-analysis of dietary-supplements and lean mass/strength gains with resistance exercise (Nissen and Sharp, 2003) confirmed that protein did not have a significant effect on lean gain or strength (evidence was found only for creatine and β-hydroxy-β-methylbutyrate). The most important practical issue is probably that of ensuring food protein intake immediately after resistance exercise to optimize recovery/anabolism at a time when muscle protein synthesis is increased (Rennie and Tipton, 2000). As for safety, although this is a complicated and as yet unresolved issue, very high protein diets are a cause for concern. Protein is a major source of net endogenous acid production (through sulphate excretion), which can adversely influence bone mineral density unless balanced by dietary base (e.g. potassium salts of weak organic acids abundant in fruit and vegetables; see New and Millward, 2003). Protein, especially a 'fast' protein such as whey, is the most satiating macronutrient (see Hall *et al.*, 2003), and protein supplements may lead to suboptimal intakes of those starchy foods essential for both performance and long-term health. High protein diets can both increase exercise-induced amino acid oxidation, especially in the untrained and individuals with an inadequate energy intake, and increase risk of negative nitrogen balance and loss of lean body mass between training periods when high intakes are reduced (Millward *et al.*, 1994). With protein, as with most nutrients, the optimum diet for athletes can almost certainly be achieved with a food-based approach focusing on a diet of starchy foods and cereals, moderate amounts of fat and protein-rich foods, and abundant fruit and vegetables.

References

1 Campbell, W.W., Trappe, T.A., Jozsi, A.C., Kruskall, L.J., Wolfe, R.R. and Evans, W.J. (2002). Dietary protein adequacy and lower body versus whole body resistive training in older humans. *Journal of Physiology*, **542**, 631–642.

2 Chittenden, R.H. (1907). *The Nutrition of Man*. London: Heinemann.

3 Hall, W.L., Long, S.J., Morgan, L.M. and Millward, D.J. (2003). Casein and whey exert different effects on appetite, plasma amino acid profiles and gastrointestinal hormone secretion. *British Journal of Nutrition*, **89**, 239–248.

4 Institute of Medicine (2002). *Dietary Reference Intakes for Energy, Carbohydrate, Fiber, Fat, Fatty Acids, Cholesterol, Protein, and Amino Acids*. Washington, DC: National Academies Press.

5 Millward, D.J. (2001). Protein and amino acid requirements: methodological considerations. *Proceedings of the Nutrition Society*, **60**, 3–5.

6 Millward, D.J. (2003). An adaptive metabolic demand model for protein and amino acid requirements. *British Journal of Nutrition*, **90**, 1–13.

7 Millward, D.J. and Rivers, J.P. (1989). The need for indispensable amino acids: the concept of the anabolic drive. *Diabetes-Metabolism Reviews*, **5**, 191–211.

8 Millward, D.J., Bowtell, J.L., Pacy, P. and Rennie, M.J. (1994). Physical activity, protein metabolism and protein requirements. *Proceedings of the Nutrition Society*, **53**, 223–240.

9 New, S.A. and Millward, D.J. (2003). Calcium, protein, and fruit and vegetables as dietary determinants of bone health. *American Journal of Clinical Nutrition*, **77**, 1340–1341.

10 Nissen, S.L. and Sharp, R.L. (2003). Effect of dietary supplements on lean mass and strength gains with resistance exercise: a meta-analysis. *Journal of Applied Physiology*, **94**, 651–659.

11 Rennie, M.J. and Tipton, K.D. (2000). Protein and amino acid metabolism during and after exercise and the effects of nutrition. *Annual Reviews of Nutrition*, **20**, 457–483.

Exertional hyponatraemia

LAWRENCE E. ARMSTRONG

Although dehydration affects performance negatively in most Olympic events, athletes should realize that drinking too much water can be harmful. Fluid consumption during exercise, in excess of sweat losses, may dilute body fluids to the point that physiological function is impaired and clinical symptoms appear. Known as exertional hyponatraemia, this fluid–electrolyte imbalance has been reported during endurance running events (i.e. ≥ 42 km) and triathlons in New Zealand, South Africa, Australia, France, Switzerland and the USA (Noakes *et al.*, 1990; Speedy *et al.*, 1999; Armstrong, 2003).

Exertional hyponatraemia involves a reduction of plasma sodium (Na^+) to less than 130 mEq $\cdot$ l^{-1} during endurance exercise and may develop into a medical emergency. In severe cases (approximately 120 mEq $Na^+ \cdot$ l^{-1} or less), the signs and symptoms of exertional hyponatraemia include nausea, vomiting, dizziness, coma, seizures, respiratory arrest and even death if left untreated. The incidence of symptomatic exertional hyponatraemia usually ranges from 0 to 2 per 1000 ultramarathon competitors (Noakes *et al.*, 1990; Speedy *et al.*, 1999; Armstrong, 2003) and 23% of those runners who sought medical care (Speedy *et al.*, 1999).

Although the aetiology of symptomatic exertional hyponatraemia varies (Armstrong, 2003), virtually all athletic cases involve gross fluid overload and a gain of body mass (Speedy *et al.*, 1999) in individuals who replace sweat losses with hypotonic fluid or pure water (Noakes *et al.*, 1990; Armstrong *et al.*, 1993). Exertional hyponatraemia cases differ only in the amount of sodium lost in sweat and the amount of excess fluid consumed.

The ultraendurance athletes who experience symptomatic exertional hyponatraemia consume fluids at a rate greater than 0.7 l $\cdot$ h^{-1}. Interestingly, the rate of maximal renal diuresis during exercise has been calculated to be 0.7–0.9 l $\cdot$ h^{-1}, in response to higher rates of oral intake (Noakes *et al.*, 1990; Speedy *et al.*, 2001). This rate of fluid intake (0.7–0.9 l $\cdot$ h^{-1}) provides a useful upper limit for athletes and coaches who wish to avoid exertional hyponatraemia. Interestingly, sweat rates reportedly range from 0.8 to 1.0 l $\cdot$ h^{-1} in a variety of ultraendurance events (Armstrong, 2003). In terms of total volume, smaller runners who have a high sweat sodium concentration need to consume only 2.2–3.0 litres of excess water (i.e. volume of fluid consumed minus sweat/urine volume) to dilute plasma sodium to 120 mEq $\cdot$ l^{-1}.

The scientific-clinical literature contains no symptomatic reports of exertional hyponatraemia before 1985. This may be due to four factors. First, because of increased emphasis on drinking during exercise, some race competitors may attempt to 'drink as much as possible', thereby increasing their risk of exertional hyponatraemia (Noakes *et al.*, 1990). Second, directors of ultraendurance events may have become more aware of the need for aid stations and water is more readily available on race courses than it was previously. Third, a slower running pace is acknowledged (Speedy *et al.*, 1999) as an important predisposing factor for exertional hyponatraemia because triathletes and runners are on the course for many hours. Fourth, non-steroidal anti-inflammatory drugs are known to potentiate the effect of AVP on the kidney (i.e. the collecting ducts) and reportedly have been associated with hyponatraemia because they impair water diuresis. A recent study (Davis *et al.*, 2001) reported that three hyponatraemic runners used non-steroidal anti-inflammatory drugs during a 42-km marathon.

Athletes may not recognize the subtle difference between *optimizing* and *maximizing* fluid intake during exercise. Therefore, coaches, educators, clinicians, dietitians and race directors have a responsibility to teach athletes to consume *adequate* fluids, but not to consume an *excessive* volume. For example, the American College of Sports Medicine suggests that fluid be consumed during exercise at a rate that matches sweat losses (Convertino *et al.*, 1996).

Even low concentrations of sodium in a beverage can have a measurable effect on plasma sodium concentration, when consumed in amounts that replace large exercise-induced sweat losses (Vrijens and Rehrer, 1999). In 2 h, 10 test participants consumed 2.4 litres of a beverage containing only 18 mmol $Na \cdot l^{-1}$. This beverage resulted in a 4 $mEq \cdot l^{-1}$ increase of plasma sodium, suggesting that ultraendurance competitors may find it beneficial to take brief rest periods, and to consume sodium-containing beverages and foods, in an attempt to maintain normal plasma sodium. Soups and other processed foods typically are better sources of sodium than fluid-electrolyte replacement beverages.

References

1 Armstrong, L.E. (2003). Exertional hyponatremia. In *Exertional Heat Illnesses* (edited by L.E. Armstrong), pp. 103–136. Champaign, IL: Human Kinetics.

2 Armstrong, L.E., Curtis, W.C., Hubbard, R.W., Francesconi, R.P., Moore, R. and Askew, E.W. (1993). Symptomatic hyponatremia during prolonged exercise in heat. *Medicine and Science in Sports and Exercise*, **25**, 543–549.

3 Convertino, V.A., Armstrong, L.E., Coyle, E.F., Mack, G.W., Sawka, M.N., Senay, L.C. and Sherman, W.M. (1996). Exercise and fluid replacement. American College of Sports Medicine Position Stand. *Medicine and Science in Sports and Exercise*, **28**, i–vii.

4 Davis, D.P., Videen, J.S., Marino, A., Vilke, G.M., Dunford, J.V., Van Camp, S.P. and Maharam, L.G. (2001). Exercise-associated hyponatremia in marathon runners: a two-year experience. *Journal of Emergency Medicine*, **21**, 47–57.

5 Noakes, T.D., Norman, R.J., Buck, R.H., Godlonton, J., Stevenson, K. and Pittaway, D. (1990). The incidence of hyponatremia during prolonged ultraendurance exercise. *Medicine and Science in Sports and Exercise*, **22**, 165–170.

6 Speedy, D.B., Noakes, T.D., Rogers, I.R., Thompson, J.M.D., Campbell, R.G.D., Kuttner, J.A., Boswell, D.R., Wright, S. and Hamlin, M. (1999). Hyponatremia in ultraendurance triathletes. *Medicine and Science in Sports and Exercise*, 31, 809–815.

7 Speedy, D.B., Noakes, T.D. and Schneider, C. (2001). Exercise-associated hyponatremia: a review. *Emergency Medicine*, 13, 17–27.

8 Vrijens, D.M.J. and Rehrer, N.J. (1999). Sodium-free fluid ingestion decreases plasma sodium during exercise in the heat. *Journal of Applied Physiology*, 86, 1847–1851.

Index